Hijacked

How Neoliberalism Turned the Work Ethic against Workers and How Workers Can Take It Back

What is the work ethic? Does it justify policies that promote the wealth and power of the One Percent at workers' expense? Or does it advance policies that promote workers' dignity and standing? *Hijacked* explores how the history of political economy has been a contest between these two ideas about whom the work ethic is supposed to serve. Today's neoliberal ideology deploys the work ethic on behalf of the One Percent. However, workers and their advocates have long used the work ethic on behalf of ordinary people. By exposing the ideological roots of contemporary neoliberalism as a perversion of the seventeenth-century Protestant work ethic, Elizabeth Anderson shows how we can reclaim the original goals of the work ethic, and uplift ourselves again. *Hijacked* persuasively and powerfully demonstrates how ideas inspired by the work ethic informed debates among leading political economists of the past, and how these ideas can help us today.

Elizabeth Anderson is the Max Mendel Shaye Professor of Public Philosophy, Politics, and Economics at University of Michigan. She is the author of *Value in Ethics and Economics* (1995), *The Imperative of Integration* (2010), and *Private Government: How Employers Rule Our Lives (and Why We Don't Talk about It)* (2017). She is a MacArthur Fellow and Fellow of the American Academy of Arts and Sciences. In 2019, *The New Yorker* described her as "a champion of the view that equality and freedom are mutually dependent [...] Anderson may be the philosopher best suited to this awkward moment in American life."

Hijacked

How Neoliberalism Turned the Work
Ethic against Workers and How
Workers Can Take It Back

Elizabeth Anderson

CAMBRIDGE
UNIVERSITY PRESS

Shaftesbury Road, Cambridge CB2 8EA, United Kingdom

One Liberty Plaza, 20th Floor, New York, NY 10006, USA

477 Williamstown Road, Port Melbourne, VIC 3207, Australia

314–321, 3rd Floor, Plot 3, Splendor Forum, Jasola District Centre,
New Delhi – 110025, India

103 Penang Road, #05–06/07, Visioncrest Commercial, Singapore 238467

Cambridge University Press is part of Cambridge University Press & Assessment,
a department of the University of Cambridge.

We share the University's mission to contribute to society through the pursuit of
education, learning and research at the highest international levels of excellence.

www.cambridge.org
Information on this title: www.cambridge.org/9781009275439

DOI: 10.1017/9781009275422

First published 2023

Printed in the United Kingdom by TJ Books Limited, Padstow Cornwall

A catalogue record for this publication is available from the British Library.

A Cataloging-in-Publication data record for this book is available from the Library of
Congress.

ISBN 978-1-009-27543-9 Hardback

CONTENTS

Preface   *page* ix

1   The Dual Nature of the Protestant Work Ethic
    and the Birth of Utilitarianism   1
    The Protestant Work Ethic as a Revaluation of Values   1
    The Work Ethic: A Calvinist Solution to a Lutheran Problem   3
    Two Sides of the Puritan Work Ethic   8
    Christian Charity, Effective Altruism, and the Birth of Utilitarianism   16

2   Locke and the Progressive Work Ethic   20
    Locke as Libertarian Capitalist, or as Advocate of a (Mostly)
    Progressive Work Ethic?   20
    The Work Ethic, Natural Law Theory, and Natural Property Rights   25
    The Work Ethic, State Power, and Positive Rights   34
    A Constitution for Workers   38
    Locke's Work Ethic (1): Against the Idle Rich and Slavery   44
    Locke's Work Ethic (2): Distinguishing Industrious Workers
    from the Idle Poor   52

3   How Conservatives Hijacked the Work Ethic and Turned
    It against Workers   63
    Developments in the Work Ethic in the Late Eighteenth Century   63
    Priestley: The Cult of Independence   68
    Bentham: The Dictatorship of the Bourgeoisie   73
    Malthus: Chastity and Personal Responsibility Will Set the Poor
    Free   81
    Paley: The Virtue of Contentment   87
    Burke and Whately: Aristocratic Paternalism   91

4   Welfare Reform, Famine, and the Ideology of the Conservative
    Work Ethic   100
    Applications of the Conservative Work Ethic (1): English Welfare
    Reform   100
    Applications of the Conservative Work Ethic (2): The Irish Poor
    Law   108
    Applications of the Conservative Work Ethic (3): Irish Famine
    Policy   112
    The Conservative Work Ethic as Ideology   119

5 The Progressive Work Ethic (1): Smith, Ricardo, and Ricardian Socialists   127
The Progressive Work Ethic in Classical Political Economy   127
Adam Smith: Sympathy for Workers   130
Free Markets for Workers   135
Pragmatism vs. Dogmatism   148
Ricardo, Rent, and the Stationary State   155
Ricardian Socialists   161

6 The Progressive Work Ethic (2): J. S. Mill   168
John Stuart Mill, Civilization, and the End of Economic Growth   168
Mill's Lockean Theory of Property, with Applications to Corn Laws, Inheritance, and Land Tenure in England and Ireland   173
Promoting Workers' Agency: Division of Labor, Hours, Unions, and Cooperatives   181
Mill's Darker Side (1): Domestic Imperialism   187
Mill's Darker Side (2): Foreign Imperialism   192

7 The Progressive Work Ethic (3): Marx   203
Marx's Ideal of Unalienated Labor as an Expression of the Progressive Work Ethic   203
Alienated Labor and the Critique of Capitalism   206
Communism: Babeuf vs. Marx   213

8 Social Democracy as the Culmination of the Progressive Work Ethic   225
Social Democracy as a Marxist Development of the Progressive Work Ethic   225
The Origins of Social Insurance: Condorcet and Paine   227
Eduard Bernstein and the Path to Social Democracy   234
Social Democracy as a Culmination and Transcendence of the Progressive Work Ethic   242

9 Hijacked Again: Neoliberalism as the Return of the Conservative Work Ethic   254
The Rise of Neoliberalism and the Legacy of the Conservative Work Ethic   254
Neoliberal Welfare Policy: The Return of Whately, Malthus, and the New Poor Law   259
Government Outsourcing and the Carceral State: The Return of Bentham   264
Shareholder Capitalism: Neoliberal Business Ethics vs. Baxter and Locke   272

10   Conclusion: What Should the Work Ethic Mean for Us Today? 284
What Should Economists Make of the Work Ethic Today?   284
What Should We Make of the Work Ethic Today?   290

Acknowledgments 299
Major Works Cited 301
Notes 305
Index 352

Preface

I wrote much of this book during the pandemic of 2020–21. In March 2020, the governors of most of the states of the United States issued stay-at-home orders for all but "essential workers" – people whose services involved in-person interactions necessary to support basic human needs. Health care, agricultural, food production, grocery store, and transportation workers, among others, were rightly designated essential. Many of these workers, including nursing-home health aides and bus drivers, were heavily exposed to the novel coronavirus and suffered high rates of disease and death. Early in the pandemic, public opinion hailed them as heroes and called for hazard pay. Many employers acceded to this demand.

Shortly thereafter, however, employers rolled back hazard pay. Harsh treatment of essential workers became the order of the day. Health-care workers were fired for complaining about the lack of personal protective equipment. Slaughterhouse workers, who must work long hours in close proximity, suffered particularly high rates of severe illness and death. Owners successfully lobbied President Donald Trump to use his authority to keep their plants open, even when they were sites of mass Covid-19 outbreaks. His administration authorized dozens of poultry plants to increase already crushing line speeds by 25 percent. This forced workers to crowd more closely to manage the work and led to much higher rates of infection than in plants with slower line speeds.[1]

This conflict over the proper treatment of workers during the pandemic is but one illustrative episode in a struggle of three centuries over the moral implications of the work ethic. Does the fact that workers are engaged in socially necessary labor, however menial it may be, entitle them to respect, decent pay, and safe working conditions? Or does it mean that they have a duty to work relentlessly, without complaint, under whatever awful conditions and low pay their employer can impose in pursuit of maximum profit? Should workers be treated as truly essential, or as disposable? The first view I call the "progressive" or pro-worker interpretation of the work ethic; the second, the "conservative" work ethic. This book tells the history of this long argument, conducted through the writings of leading theologians, philosophers, economists, and political actors. At various periods in Western European and North American history, one side or the other has held sway over moral thought and economic policy.

The three decades following the end of the Second World War marked the high point of social democracy, which I shall argue is the descendant of the progressive work ethic. These decades were distinguished by the confluence of several developments in the rich democracies of Europe and North America: high rates of economic growth widely shared across economic classes; unprecedented levels of economic equality; strong labor unions and state protections of workers' interests; a growing and robust welfare state centered on universal social insurance; high state investment in education, health care, science, and technology; greater openness to immigration and ethnoracial-religious diversity; the strengthening of liberal democratic institutions; and a general sense of optimism. Four decades since the end of this era, the denizens of Europe and North America are suffering reversals of all these developments. Workers, the welfare state, openness to immigration, and – most ominously – liberal democratic institutions are in retreat or under grave threat, while uncertainty and anxiety about our economic, political, and environmental futures loom large.

Things weren't supposed to turn out this way. Three decades ago, the fall of communist regimes across Eastern Europe, the end of the Cold War, and the global replacement of dictatorships with democratic regimes were widely held to vindicate free markets and liberal democracy as the key institutions of free and flourishing societies. We were supposed to be entering a glorious new era of economic growth, ever-more open to an increasingly diverse and cooperative world, in which these institutions would spread across the globe. What happened?

The *economic* dimensions of the current crisis are not mysterious. Since the mid-1970s, neoliberal economic policies have increasingly prevailed in the rich democracies. A list of such policies would include the following: enacting international trade agreements that strongly favor capital interests and constrain democratic policy making; deregulating markets (especially in the financial sector); tightening bankruptcy regulations and imposing harsher policies toward individual and state debtors; enhancing intellectual property protections; cutting taxes (especially on top incomes, capital income, and inheritance); retrenching the welfare state (especially replacing cash benefits with benefits conditioned on work); weakening antitrust enforcement; assaulting labor unions and laws protecting workers; reducing workers' pensions; delegating labor and trade disputes to private arbitrators; outsourcing public functions to private enterprise; and replacing Keynesian economic policies oriented to full employment with fiscal austerity. Taken together, these policies have had three principal effects. First, they have increased economic inequality and shifted the distribution of income from labor to capital, leading to stagnant wages for lower-tier workers, even as productivity has grown.

Second, these policies have also constrained and undermined democracy, reducing its ability to respond to the needs and interests of ordinary people. Outsourcing reduces state capacities and often leaves citizens with little practical recourse if resulting private providers of public services abuse their effective monopoly power. Tax cuts reduce the resources available to democratic states, and may subject them to harsh discipline by creditors when states borrow to meet their needs for revenue. Trade agreements and fiscal austerity sharply limit the ability of democratic states to provide public goods, protect workers and the environment, and respond to economic crises.

Third, neoliberal policies have shifted economic and political power to private businesses, executives, and the very rich. More and more, these organizations and individuals govern everyone else. Employees are governed by their bosses, not only at work but often off-duty.[2] Even many so-called "independent contractors," purportedly in business for themselves, are minutely governed by the firms that pay them.[3] Businesses that operate prisons, immigrant detention centers, mental hospitals, nursing homes, halfway houses, and residential addiction-treatment facilities govern millions of inmates. The very rich also increasingly influence state decision making.[4]

My objective in this book is not to document these trends or to demonstrate the causal consequences of these policies for inequality and democracy. Others have already done so.[5] Rather, I aim to argue that these trends reflect the ascendance of the conservative work ethic. This ethic tells workers that they owe their employers relentless toil and unquestioning obedience under whatever harsh conditions their employer chooses to impose on them. It tells employers that they have exclusive rights to govern their employees and organize work with the overriding goal of maximizing profit. And it tells the state to recognize and entrench the authority of executives to govern their employees and their business more generally by laws that treat labor as nothing more than a commodity to be deployed as the buyer sees fit. To reinforce the commodification of labor, the state should minimize workers' access to alternative ways of gaining access to subsistence other than wage labor. Hence, the conservative work ethic is hostile to the public provision of goods, regulations of labor contracts that favor workers (such as limits on the length of the working day or mandatory paid vacations), laws that empower labor unions or other modes of worker authority within the firm, and generous social insurance and other forms of welfare benefits for the able-bodied that are not conditioned on work.

What we call neoliberalism is the descendant of this harsh version of the work ethic. This might not be obvious at first sight. Neoliberals define their own position in terms of a systematic preference for market orderings over state action in economic life.[6] They represent the market society they favor as composed of individuals freely choosing to transact with other individuals through markets and contracts. This representation obscures the central fact about the global capitalist economy: it is dominated by hierarchically organized firms in which owners or shareholder representatives govern the firm's workers. Labor markets are simply the conduits by which most workers fall under the government of their particular employer. The neoliberal preference for market orderings over state regulation and provision does not liberate ordinary people from government. It entrenches the commodification of labor, under which most people have no alternative but to submit to the arbitrary government of employers to survive. So-called deregulation of labor and other markets does not create markets without regulations. It transfers regulatory authority from the state to the most powerful private actors in any given market – typically, the dominant firms in that market.[7] This forces even many of the self-employed to submit to the authority of big businesses. The regulations Amazon sets for access by third-party sellers to its massive online market are no less elaborate than state regulations. Not just Amazon workers, but third-party online sellers thereby fall under Amazon's government.

Neoliberalism is thus not properly characterized in terms of individual market freedom. It is government by capital interests – by business and wealthy property owners. It descends from the institutional embodiment of the conservative work ethic in early nineteenth-century England: government by capitalists and landlords over their workers, and over everyone else as well, given the monopoly of the propertied over the franchise and political offices. Neoliberals advocate policies that secure comparable governing power for businesses and the rich despite a vastly expanded franchise. Note that, by this definition, most self-styled conservatives in the US and UK, and indeed most of Europe, are neoliberals.[8]

Neoliberals and libertarians (their fellow travelers) claim a different provenance, in so-called "classical liberalism," a political philosophy originating in the seventeenth and eighteenth centuries, especially in England and Scotland. Everyone agrees that the leading figures of classical liberalism are John Locke, Adam Smith, and John Stuart Mill. Classical liberals argued in favor of individual rights, limits on state power, free trade on a global scale, and private property. They argued that decentralized markets, in which individuals are free to open businesses in competition with others, promote economic growth, personal independence, and broadly shared prosperity. They criticized many state regulations of the economy as unjustly rigged in favor of cronies, and liable to impose costs that exceed their benefits.

You won't find me quarrelling with any of that! – either as an interpretation of what these classical liberals said, or of the normative merits of their arguments *at this level of generality*. The old socialist ideal of comprehensive state ownership of the means of production and centralized planning failed disastrously. A free and prosperous society requires a robust system of private property rights, market competition, freedom to start one's own business, and openness to international trade. I also agree that numerous state regulations are both counterproductive and unfairly rigged in favor of those who have captured the regulatory agencies. Such generalities, however, are hardly sufficient to support neoliberal policies. Any good social democrat from mid-twentieth-century Scandinavia would gladly accept them.

The key disagreements in political economy today arise in the *specification* of these ideas. Neoliberalism promotes particular specifications of private property rights, freedom of contract, free enterprise, and free markets that in effect and often deliberately aim to limit the scope of democratic state action so as to accord power and channel wealth to capital owners over workers, creditors over individual and state debtors, the rich over the poor, and firms that generate profits through predatory or extractive business models over society in general. In the extreme, we find doctrines such as those claiming that redistributive taxation is akin to forced labor, that regulations of private property are "takings" that entitle owners to compensation, that most regulations of enterprise freedom should be treated as presumptively unconstitutional, and that social democracy and labor unions put us on a slippery slope to totalitarianism.[9]

In this book, I argue that the origins of neoliberalism can be traced back somewhat earlier than classical liberalism, to the Protestant work ethic. This ideology was originally developed by seventeenth-century Puritan ministers. At the level of individual morality, the Puritan work ethic comprises a suite of virtues: industry, frugality, temperance, chastity, and prudence. Puritans argued that *everyone* must exercise these virtues in service to our fellow human beings as well as ourselves. At the level of political economy, the work ethic concerns the economic and political institutions that best promote, reward, and express these virtues. This book traces the history of arguments over the latter, focusing on the history of classical political economy. These arguments were fueled by the fact that the Puritan work ethic embodied contradictory attitudes toward work and workers that were ultimately developed into the progressive and conservative work ethics. Classical liberals Locke, Smith, and Mill developed the progressive or pro-worker work ethic. Antislavery and radical labor activists, Ricardian socialists, Karl Marx, Friedrich Engels, Thomas Paine, Eduard Bernstein, and later social democrats further advanced this tradition. Neoliberalism arises from the conservative work ethic, developed by thinkers such as Joseph Priestley, Jeremy Bentham, Thomas Malthus, and Edmund Burke. Capital interests and opponents of the labor movement and the welfare state promoted it.

These two versions of the work ethic developed in parallel. I shall argue that they are not equally valid developments of the Puritans' underlying normative vision of our duties to our fellow human beings. The progressive work ethic embodies a logical development of that vision. The conservative work ethic emerged from the ways the *original targets of Puritan critique* – the idle and predatory rich – *hijacked* the work ethic and turned it against workers, while letting themselves off the hook of its requirements.

My usage of the terms "progressive" and "conservative" is twenty-first-century American. It does not conform to historical or current European usage, which classifies market advocates as uniformly "liberal." From a work-ethic perspective, any classification that lumps the likes of Burke, Bentham, and Malthus with Locke, Smith, and Mill is normatively superficial. While all of these thinkers support markets, they are divided over their aspirations with regard to the empowerment of workers. Should labor itself be reduced to a commodity, so that workers are forced by precarity and poverty to fall under the arbitrary government of their employers? Or should ordinary workers be empowered politically and economically to run their own lives, both at work and off-duty? Every advanced economy needs to grant a weighty role for competitive markets. Every market system is a product of laws that prescribe the constitutive rules of the market game. Different systems of rules – including laws of property, firm governance, and the employment contract – have profoundly different consequences for workers' agency and the distribution of income, wealth, and power. Historically and today, these laws have been designed in view of those consequences. I aim to challenge the idea that there is some *essence* to "free markets" which conservatives then and conservatives and neoliberals today have uniquely captured, which *just so happens* to deliver deeply inegalitarian results. The constitutive rules of the market game have always been contested. The terms of that contestation have always ultimately been over their expected consequences for equality and social hierarchy. Historically and today, assumptions tied to rival conceptions of the work ethic have deeply informed those debates.

For my purposes, then, the fundamental stakes dividing what I call "progressive" from "conservative" theorists of the work ethic lie more in class-based power relations than in arguments over the desirability of competitive markets. Conservatives, in my usage, favor government by and for property owners, at the level of the state and the firm. They assign different fundamental duties to employers and workers, rich and poor. They expect workers to submit to despotic employer authority. They tend to regard poverty as a sign of bad character and hence regard poor workers as morally inferior. Progressives favor democracy and worker self-government. They oppose class-based duties and rights, and reject the stigmatization of poverty.

Much of the history of classical political economy, and of ideological conflict between left and right, workers and capitalists, business and government – over distributive justice, economic regulation; the organization and conditions of work, and the welfare state – can be told through the conflict of these rival conceptions of the work ethic. When neoliberals champion purportedly generic ideals of private property, free trade, and free enterprise, they are masking a commitment to *specifications* of these ideals that express the core attitudes of those who deployed the conservative work ethic to push millions of ordinary workers into precarity, poverty, and subjection to their employers and creditors.

Why should we care about ideological origins? In revealing neoliberalism as the ideological descendant of the conservative work ethic, I aim to unpack its inherent contradictions. It isn't so easy to do this just by considering its surface claims, for ideologies work at multiple levels. At the level of express content, people use them to justify particular policies. They also serve epistemic functions. Ideologies map our social world in ways that promote particular paths around it, and discourage or blind us to others. They mark people occupying different social positions as more or less credible, trustworthy, or suspect. They inform our emotions, habits, social norms, and practices, often in ways that cannot be fully rationalized by the beliefs and values we consciously endorse. We can better grasp the contradictions between these levels at which ideology works, and between ideology and reality, by investigating the historical origins of ideologies, originally designed for a different social world, with different ends in view.

A quarter of a millennium after the Puritans, we are still in the grip of ideas and attitudes they originated. The study of history may thus reveal how we are unwitting prisoners of the past. William Faulkner famously wrote, "[t]he past is never dead. It's not even past."[10] It is rooted in our habits, feelings, and expectations, and adapted to conditions and beliefs that prevailed long ago, which have been passed down by our ancestors. What persists from the past also reflects prior and continuing social conflict. Policy and ideology in the past several decades reflects the triumph of the conservative work ethic over the progressive one, much to the detriment of workers themselves.

In telling the story of the progressive work ethic, I also hope to show how history can be liberating. The study of history may also reveal how differently people thought and acted in the past, and thereby demonstrate the profound contingency of how we think and act today. It may refute the assumption that current ways are necessary or inevitable and spark our imaginations for change. I use history both to reveal the ways we are mired in the past, and how we can mine a forgotten or misremembered past for resources in reconstructing current practices. In particular, I hope economists may draw inspiration from my interpretation of the history of classical economics to enlarge their normative vision, both in terms of the richness of normative standards they use to evaluate institutions, and to imagine bolder remedies for our economic ills, much as their classical predecessors did.

I highlight the neglected role of the Protestant work ethic in the history of political economy, and reassess that ethic. A century ago, Max Weber offered his own gloomy assessment at the conclusion of his pioneering examination of the work ethic: in promoting a disciplined labor regime founded on religious asceticism, the work ethic ultimately gave rise to a secular capitalist system that trapped people in an "iron cage" of meaningless drudgery for the sake of interminable wealth accumulation, irrationally detached from any connection to human welfare or happiness.[11] Weber was only half right. He skips over the ways the progressive work ethic offered a promising vision for workers to enjoy a free, proud, and decent life by vindicating the claims of workers against the idle and predatory rich who tyrannized over them. However, reactionaries ultimately turned the work ethic against the supposedly idle poor, in defense of policies designed to subordinate an ever-expanding group of workers to government by and for capital interests. This goal, detached from any duty of the rich or recipients of capital income to promote the welfare of others, licensed the adoption of predatory and extractive business models. This is why I say that conservatives then and neoliberals today hijacked the work ethic.

My history traces the work ethic from the Puritans through the classical political economists in Britain and, to a lesser extent, Germany. I discuss the influence of this line of thinking on British economic and social welfare policy, the rise of social democracy in Europe, and twenty-first-century US neoliberal practice. My narrative tracks some but not all of the key threads in the complex tapestry of the work ethic. I largely set aside the rise of neoclassical economics and its influence on the neoliberal work ethic. I omit the rich developments of socialist thought in the late nineteenth and twentieth centuries beyond the thread that led to social democracy. I also pass over the historical development of the work ethic in the US, which was profoundly shaped by settler colonialism, slavery, and struggles over the meaning of free labor after emancipation. Without that history, it is impossible to understand the centrality of self-employment in the American work-ethic ideal,[12] the continuing influence of racism on neoliberal welfare and labor policies in the US, and its lack of a large-scale socialist movement. Other aspects of the work ethic are beyond the scope of this study. I set aside the rich Catholic tradition of thinking about work and welfare policy. And of course many countries outside Euro-America have their own work-ethic ideologies, most famously in East Asia. The study of these non-Western work ethics lies beyond my expertise.

I must admit a deep irony in this book. I am thoroughly steeped in the work ethic: dedicated to conscientious, disciplined work and disciplined saving, consuming well below what my family's income could support, disdainful of conspicuous consumption, reluctant to rest until work duties are complete, impatient about wasting time, restless in leisure, eager to get back to work. Work is central to my identity. I do not work only to live, but live to work. I confess that these dispositions impel me to a poor work/life balance. But they have also rewarded me with meaningful, interesting work, immense autonomy, and honored achievements as well as financial security. Yet I aim to criticize the work ethic, for what it has become: an ideological rationalization for the stigmatization and deprivation of the poor, the precarity of the working classes, and the dominion of capital interests over all other interests of humanity, including the future habitability of the planet. What I criticize is a perversion of the work ethic, indeed a reversal of its aspirations under classical liberalism and successor traditions on the left. Yet from the start it contained the seeds of its own corruption, in its epistemology of suspicion toward the poor and excessive credit toward anyone who is busy accumulating wealth, on the mistaken presumption that their business is adding to rather than merely extracting wealth by manipulating the rules of the system, exploiting others, and plundering the environment. Any version of the work ethic worth following today must repudiate these prejudices and reconstruct itself to promote cooperation on terms of equality, in ways that promote the welfare of every member of global society.

1 THE DUAL NATURE OF THE PROTESTANT WORK ETHIC AND THE BIRTH OF UTILITARIANISM

The Protestant Work Ethic as a Revaluation of Values

Would you quit working if you won a lottery big enough to enable you to live comfortably off the annual payout? Numerous surveys of Americans since 1980 find that a majority say they would keep working. Of those Americans who have won huge lotteries, 85–90 percent do continue working.[1] While the numbers are lower for people in low-paying unskilled jobs, these results reflect the continuing power of the Protestant work ethic in American life. Most Americans view work as something more than just a meal ticket. They view it as fulfilling a duty to contribute to society, as a source of pride, and as a locus of meaning.

From a historical point of view, these attitudes toward work are recent. For the vast majority of history, people have regarded work as a curse. The Bible says so (Gen. 3:19). Work was what people were forced to do. Those with means chose leisure. The Catholic Church in the Middle Ages did not particularly extol the value of work. It proclaimed numerous holidays. It praised giving alms to beggars. It created several orders of mendicant friars, who survived on begging. The republican tradition inherited from ancient Greece and Rome also valued leisure over work. Leisure was the domain of free citizens. Labor was what slaves and menial servants did. These attitudes persisted among the traditional English landlords during the Industrial Revolution.[2]

By contrast, in the US today, people with high earnings are more likely to work overtime than low-paid workers.[3] Many of the highest earners work more than 60 hours per week.[4] This confirms the standard assumption of economists, that the supply curve of labor slopes forward – that is, that higher wages lead to people to work more. Far from being a law of human nature, this tendency is a legacy of the work ethic. US policy also discourages begging and imposes work requirements on poor people as a condition of access to numerous benefits.

These attitudes toward work reflect a dramatic revaluation of values that took place during the Reformation. Many Protestant denominations arising at that time reversed the values of work and leisure. Puritan poet John Milton captures this reversal in the voice of Adam upon the expulsion from Eden: "[W]ith labor I must earn my bread; what harm? Idleness had been worse."[5] Puritans put work at the center of life, and attacked most leisure as sinful idleness. Although few workers today toil in response to the theological anxieties that motivated early Protestants to adopt the work ethic, we have inherited their habits and attitudes toward work.

While the work ethic still holds sway in the US, it is a contested ideal. Sociologist Max Weber argued that it had replaced a "leisurely and comfortable attitude toward life" with a "hard frugality" that "legalized the exploitation of ... [the] willingness to work" in the service of unlimited wealth accumulation. What began as an ascetic doctrine of self-denial in the quest for assurance of salvation had ironically generated a capitalist system in which "material goods have gained an increasing and finally an inexorable power over the lives of men as at no previous period in history."[6] Economist John Maynard Keynes looked forward to the day – which he predicted would have arrived by now – when productivity improvements would make a comfortable life available to all, and thereby move us to cast off the love of money as a "somewhat disgusting morbidity." He hoped we would replace a culture of ceaseless toil in service to future material gain with a leisure society devoted to the present enjoyment of intrinsic goods.[7] Recently, anarchist anthropologist David Graeber criticized the soul-killing work ethic that imagines that pointless labor builds character, and urged a radical reduction in the length of the workweek through the abolition of millions of "bullshit jobs" that inflict "spiritual violence" on those consigned to them.[8]

So we should ask hard questions about the work ethic. Does it rationalize the exploitation of workers by subjecting them to relentless, stultifying toil for little reward? Or is it a worthy ideal that gives meaning and purpose to workers' lives? We should also investigate how the work ethic has shaped the ways we organize work, regulate economic institutions, and distribute income and wealth. Has it served to enhance the wealth and power of the One Percent? Or has it supported policies and movements that promote workers' dignity and standing?

I shall argue that the answer to all of these questions is "yes." From the start, the work ethic has contained contradictory ideas, and been put to opposing purposes – some in favor of workers, and some against. Both sides have had profound effects on the history of political economy and public policy in Europe and North America since the seventeenth century. Much of this history can be narrated as a contest between progressive and conservative versions of the work ethic. Today the conservative version dominates in the US and has been advancing even in social democratic Europe.[9] But conservative dominance was not always so. It need not be so in the future. To understand where we stand today with the work ethic, however, we must go back to its origins in the Protestant Reformation.

The Work Ethic: A Calvinist Solution to a Lutheran Problem

In his classic examination of the Protestant work ethic, Weber rightly criticized the assumption of "naive historical materialism" that ideas about how to live are a mere reflection of "economic situations." The Puritan theologians who invented the work ethic were not trying to promote capitalism. Modern capitalism, founded on disciplined wage labor, was not yet on the scene, nor even anticipated. The Puritans' concerns were fundamentally religious, not economic.[10] Nevertheless, Puritans were also notably practical people, obsessed with the consequences of conduct, dismissive of feelings and intentions that bear no fruit. Their contempt for emotional professions of faith and styles of worship,[11] and insistence that faith can be proved only by its fruits, also reflects a revulsion against social disorders that they thought were threatened by the Reformation doctrine of justification by faith alone. Their sacralization of *work* enabled them to solve what they saw as a practical problem generated by the radical devaluation of *works* in Reformation theology.

Let's begin with Martin Luther's revolutionary doctrine of justification by faith alone. On Luther's view, due to our fallen state, all humans are mired in sin. We are utterly helpless to redeem ourselves through our own efforts. Hence, everyone deserves eternal damnation.[12] Our only salvation lies in the fact that Jesus atoned for humanity's sins in dying on the cross. God, in his mercy, has granted a pardon or justification to anyone who has faith in Jesus as their savior. This pardon is an entirely unmerited gift of God, as is faith itself, which we cannot will. Good works do nothing to save us.

To the extent that his followers' motives to avoid wrongdoing depended on belief in divine punishment, Luther's doctrine threatened to unleash social disorder. Luther's habit of expressing his theological claims in hyperbolic language magnified the problem. In the Heidelberg Disputation, Luther insisted that "the works of men" are "likely to be mortal sins."[13] He meant only that those who do good works in the belief that this *earns* them salvation are arrogant in stealing glory from God, and in supposing that God owes humans anything as a matter of just deserts. Yet Luther's characteristic response to criticism of his polemical statements was to double down on them, rather than to temper his claims in view of their likely consequences. A few years later, in *The Bondage of the Will*, Luther insisted that, without faith, the most exalted works are not merely useless for salvation; they are *evil*.[14] Some of his followers naturally concluded that as long as they had faith, they didn't have to avoid sin. And how could they, anyway, given that Luther insisted that the fall of man had made them slaves to sin, and that they lacked free will to resist it?

Luther was enraged by his followers' tendency to draw practical conclusions for this life from theological doctrines oriented to the next. Most notoriously, German peasants took Luther's doctrines of the priesthood of all believers – their right to interpret the Bible for themselves – and the freedom of laypeople to reject laws to which they have not consented as a license to revolt against their oppressive lords in the Peasants' War of 1524–25. Shocked by the conclusions his followers inferred from his premises, Luther urged the rulers to slaughter them mercilessly – and got a bloodbath.[15] Even after that catastrophe, Luther found that he could not control his Wittenberg congregation's disorderliness. Many of his followers, confident that their faith alone secured them salvation without need for ministers – as Luther himself had taught them! – stopped attending church and refused to contribute to it. They became dissolute, even while Luther devoted his sermons to hectoring his congregation for a multitude of sins, including drunkenness, cursing, sexual licentiousness, cheating, and failure to give alms to the poor.[16]

Luther attempted to stem the tide of debauchery by arguing that good works necessarily followed from faith. "The law says, 'Do this', and it is never done. Grace says, 'believe in this', and everything is already done."[17] Faith enables escape from the spiritual coercion of God's law implied by the threat of damnation. Liberated from the threat of damnation, the truly faithful serve others freely. Love of God for his grace leads to brotherly love for humanity, and hence a wholehearted willingness to help one's fellow human beings by working in one's calling.[18]

With his conception of loving obedience to God through work in a calling, Luther thus supplied a seed of the worth ethic. However, Weber argues that Luther never developed the idea of a calling into a positive vision of the institutions needed to promote a systematic ethics of work. His economic thinking was "traditionalistic" in accepting economic arrangements as they were and discouraging people from acquiring more than their station in life requires.[19] Luther also doesn't ask them to reflect on how they should develop and direct their talents to most effectively help their fellow human beings. Hence, individuals don't find inspiration in *seeking* and *choosing* their calling. They simply find themselves in some occupation by custom, law, or necessity, and perform the duties assigned to them.[20] The motive of brotherly love as the spontaneous outgrowth of faith is not subject to disciplined direction in a rationalized economic system oriented to efficiency, technological improvement, or economic growth.[21]

Luther's followers were sure they had faith. But brotherly love did not necessarily follow from this. So they were not fully persuaded by his argument that good works follow from faith. If one knew in one's heart that one has faith, and works really are worthless – even sinful if done without fear of God – then why should one put great effort into them? After all, Luther also said, "[h]e is not righteous who does much, but he who, without work, believes much in Christ."[22]

John Calvin and his successors – including, in England and Scotland, Anglicans and Presbyterians – devised a solution to Luther's

problem. Without dissenting from Luther's theological pronounce-
ments on the value of *works*,[23] they dramatically changed believers'
practical orientation to *work*. It rested on three ideas: (1) a more stringent doctrine of predestination; (2) a shift from an introspective to
a behavioral basis for knowledge of one's faith; and (3) a radical upgrad-
ing of the spiritual meaning of work. In the Lutheran view, God decided
ahead of everyone's birth who would be saved. But anyone could attain
assurance through their faith that they are among the saved. Faith is the
sign of God's grace. Calvin advanced the doctrine of "double predestination," according to which God not only decided ahead of everyone's
birth who would be saved, but also who would be damned.[24] Only
a small elect would be saved.

   The point of this terrifying doctrine was to deny people assurance that they are saved, and thereby to induce in everyone a permanent
anxiety about their state of grace. For, on the Calvinistic view, one could
never know simply from introspection that one has faith. Calvin thereby
swiped away the relief from terror of damnation that Luther hoped to
obtain from the doctrine of justification by faith.

   Turn now to Puritan priest Richard Baxter, the consummate
theologian of the Protestant work ethic, to complete the argument. Like
other Reformed ministers, he holds that salvation cannot be earned by
good works, but arrives unmerited through faith by the grace of God
alone.[25] Yet one cannot know one's faith by mere introspection or
feeling. Given our desperate desire to assure ourselves of salvation, we
are too ready to deceive ourselves on this point. Rather, "[g]race is never
apparent and sensible to the soul but while it is in action; therefore want
of action must cause want of assurance."[26] Faith is manifest only in
action. Moreover, the actions that count as evidence of faith are not
ritualistic. Prayer, sacraments, and following monkish rules count for
naught. The only actions that count as evidence of faith are ones that
have independent consequences in the world – not *works* in the ritualistic sense, but *work*, in the productive sense. One gains assurance of one's
faith only in ceaseless, disciplined work. Work that springs from faith
gains exalted significance, in being done for the greater glory of God.
Hence, "[g]ive diligence to make your calling and election sure."[27]
Although salvation cannot be earned, God will not grant it "without
our earnest seeking and labor."[28] Any relaxation from constant work,
along with any indulgence in spontaneous pleasures, is a sign of lagging
faith. So time must never be wasted on idle pleasures. It must be spent

"wholly in the way of duty" in the service of God.[29] Worldly goods also must never be wasted, since God gave them to us to use in his service. "We must see that nothing of any use, be lost through satiety, negligence or contempt; for the smallest part is of God's gifts and talents, given us, not to cast away, but to use as he would have us."[30] Here we see the core virtues of the work ethic: industry, frugality, ascetic self-control.

The practical results of Baxter's preaching were impressive. "Baxter's activity in Kidderminster, a community absolutely debauched when he arrived ... was almost unique in the history of the ministry for its success."[31] Where Luther complained of empty pews, Baxter converted Kidderminster from a town that had only one or two observant families per street to one in which nearly all turned out for his Sunday sermons.[32] During his ministry, Kidderminster also enjoyed success in the weaving industry. Weber credits this success to his congregation's internalization of the work ethic. Baxter was just one of many Calvinist preachers promoting the work ethic across England. Hence it is not surprising that some economic historians have detected an "industrious revolution" starting in the mid-seventeenth century prior to the Industrial Revolution, in which workers increased the intensity and duration of their labor.[33]

Weber claims that the work ethic was stronger among Calvinists than Lutherans. He credits this difference to their distinctive views of how to attain self-knowledge. Do they know their state of grace by inner feeling, or external behavior?[34] The latter was key to solving the problem Calvinists saw in Luther's view, that introspective knowledge of grace undermines social order.

Yet a morality that rests solely on spiritual coercion – in this case, on exploitation of anxiety over the certainty of salvation – can never be a creative force. It must also appeal to higher ideals of a worthy life. The work ethic sanctified work, turning it into a vehicle for higher purposes than bare survival. This idea could be taken in profoundly egalitarian directions.[35] It uplifted even the lowliest worker by sacralizing ordinary work and repudiating the idea that any particular calling – even the priesthood – is superior. The work ethic also changed the focus of morality from purely expressive acts of piety and self-denial to acts with positive worldly consequences. We shall see that this change, with its stress on practical, empirically observable results, led ultimately to an ultra-secular utilitarian moral theory. These facts are of immense importance for understanding the prospects for a progressive, pro-worker work ethic.

Two Sides of the Puritan Work Ethic

The central ideal of the work ethic is to engage in disciplined labor in a calling – a specialized occupation. Puritan minister William Perkins elaborates an early version of this ideal.[36] Robert Sanderson concisely summarizes it in a widely reprinted sermon. God has given "gifts" or abilities to each individual. Everyone has a duty to cultivate and use their abilities in some "settled course of life, with reference to business, office, or employment" for the glory of God and "for his own and the common good."[37] God would not have given us these gifts if he had not intended that we use them. So it is wrong to waste our time and talents in idleness. There is too much to do: "Life must be preserved, families maintained, the poor relieved."[38]

God has called each person to service in a particular calling. How can you discover what that is? Don't expect any special revelation to determine your calling. Explore your options, and choose the one that best fits your education, talents, and inclination.[39] In other words, find a way to systematically help others that also fulfills yourself by enabling you to exercise your talents in ways that sustain your interest and commitment. Sanderson thus develops the core ideas behind modern career counseling.

Steady work is needed not only to do good, but to avoid sin. Idleness leads people into temptation. Work in a calling amounts to effective ascetic discipline by keeping people too busy for them to succumb.[40] A generation later, Baxter adds a tone of moral panic to Sanderson's genial career counseling. Because idleness and laxity at work are signs of flagging faith, wasting time should trigger spiritual alarm. "We can never do too much .... Much precious time is already misspent."[41] He devotes an entire chapter of his five-volume *Christian Directory*, a comprehensive guide to Christian ethics, to effective time-management.[42] We need to rest, but only to the extent needed to restore our capacity to labor. So "rest must always *follow* labor," as its earned reward.[43] All that busyness takes a toll, but in the service of assurance of salvation. And the reward of salvation is *everlasting* rest, filled with "perfect endless enjoyment of God" in heaven.[44]

We must not waste our time and talents because "we are [God's] workmanship" sent to execute his purposes on Earth.[45] The same logic enjoins us from wasting any of the natural resources God provided us to carry out this task, for "there is nothing that is good so small, but some one hath need of it."[46] "They are our Master's stock," "the tools by which we must do much of our Master's work."[47] Luxury consumption and vain entertainments are wasteful. The resources devoted to them would be better used promoting the public good and helping the needy. "[If] you let the poor lie languishing in necessities, whilst you are at great charges to entertain the rich without a necessity or greater good, you must answer it as an unfaithful servant."[48] All must practice frugality, and avoid self-indulgence and "covetousness," which Baxter defines as desiring more than what one needs to do one's duty.[49]

Weber interprets the work ethic as inherently antagonistic to the interests of workers. Although the Puritans' motives for promoting the work ethic were religious, in effect they advanced the spirit of capitalism, getting the masses to labor and sacrifice in ways that maximized capitalists' profits. Many passages in Baxter's work support this interpretation. Baxter's stress on work as a form of ascetic discipline rationalizes the consignment of workers to tedious drudgery: "Diligent labour mortifieth the flesh."[50] He tells workers who take breaks from their toil that they are robbing their masters: "[U]se every minute ... spend it wholly in the way of duty."[51] Weber claims that the Puritans bequeathed to us "an amazingly good, we may even say a pharisaically good, conscience in the acquisition of money, so long as it took place legally."[52] Indeed, Baxter insists that "he is commendable who ... frugally getteth and saveth as much as he can."[53] Given a choice among lawful callings, one has a duty to choose the highest-paying one.[54] Material inequality is justified: "God giveth not to all alike." It is no sin to earn more than others through honest labor and saving.[55] Puritans frequently quote 2 Thess. 3:10: "[I]f any would not work, neither should he eat."[56] They repeatedly berate able-bodied beggars as parasites. Beggars should not be relieved, as this robs the deserving poor of alms. Rather, they should be whipped and sent to a house of correction, where they will be forced to labor.[57] Baxter even allows the legitimacy of contracts into slavery, driven by the desperation of the poor.[58] Such readiness to resort to harsh and coercive treatment of the poor, and to praise the income and wealth maximization of the rich, expresses key attitudes of the conservative work ethic.

Yet Weber's reading of the work ethic is blinkered. On the Puritans' view, law is not the only thing that properly constrains material acquisition. Cambridge theologian William Perkins insisted that

[t]hey profane their lives and callings that imploy them to get honours, pleasures, profits, worldly commodities, &c. for thus we live to another ende than God hath appointed, and thus we serve ourselves, and consequently neither God nor man.[59]

One must seek worldly goods in the right spirit, only for the sake of serving God and other people, never simply in a self-serving way. Hence we may not in good conscience pursue methods of money making that undermine others' well-being, even if these methods are legal.

Puritans tempered even their harshest claims on workers – sometimes, to the point of contradiction. Consider slavery. Baxter insists that slavery can never make anyone wholly at the disposal of a master. Masters who treat their plantation slaves like beasts are more cruel and odious than cannibals.[60] Although Baxter does not explicitly call for the abolition of chattel slavery, it is impossible to reconcile the moral limits he places on slavery with the law, practice, and ideology of chattel slavery in the colonies. He argues that the laws should abolish the slave trade, require the emancipation of any infidel slave who converts to Christianity, and require slaveholders to teach Christianity to their slaves.[61] Any regime that enforced these laws in the colonies would rapidly put chattel slavery out of existence.

Baxter allows slavery in four cases: (1) by contract in desperation; (2) as punishment for crime; (3) as restitution for theft, when the thief cannot otherwise pay compensation; and (4) of enemy soldiers captured in a just war. None of these cases permit hereditary slavery. In the first case, where innocents are enslaved, they are so only to a "degree." Masters may not reduce such slaves to "misery," must provide them whatever "comforts of life, which nature giveth to man as man," and recognize a duty of charity to their slaves.[62] This isn't chattel slavery, in which the worker is reduced to property and denied all rights. It's more like permanent indentured servitude. Even in the other cases, masters must recognize that "they are reasonable creatures as well as you, and born to as much natural liberty. If their sin have enslaved them to you, yet nature made them your equals."[63] They are equally eligible for salvation as free persons, and are entitled to the same religious services. Masters even owe *more* to their slaves than to their free servants. As political philosophy, such pleas are wholly inadequate. One can hardly place people in subjection and then rely on moral exhortation to motivate their masters to treat them justly or charitably.

But as ethics, Baxter's pleas reflect a foundational moral egalitarianism that informs Puritan thinking about the work ethic.

Puritans did not merely lay moral constraints on how the lowest workers may be treated. More fundamentally, they promoted principles that uplifted the status of ordinary workers. This follows from their sanctification of work. Everyone must "spiritualize their callings and earthly businesses, by going about them in the strength and wisdom of the spirit of God."[64] The spiritualization of callings uplifts the dignity of the lowest worker. *Everyone* who engages in honest labor, however menial, is doing God's work. *All* productive labor promotes the glory of God in realizing God's purpose for humans on earth – that we contribute to preserving human life and helping people. God has instituted the different callings in society because all are needed to work together in their distinct offices to promote his purposes, like the different parts of a clock. Sanderson preaches that "[T]here is no member in the body so mean or small, but hath its proper faculty, function, and use, whereby it becometh useful to the whole body, and helpful to its fellow-members."[65] Everyone needs everyone else to do their part for their own work to fully realize God's purposes. The clock analogy implies a kind of egalitarianism in the value of work from God's point of view.[66] For virtually all of history, servants have been despised and mistreated, their labor held in contempt even though it is socially necessary. The Puritan work ethic exalts them. Puritans endowed work with profound meaning, thereby giving workers a reason to dedicate themselves to it beyond the desire to gain assurance of salvation.

Puritans drew conclusions for how workers should be treated from the equality and dignity of all labor. Baxter sternly warns masters that they must not rule their servants "tyrannically." Workers are entitled to safe, healthful conditions. They must be paid fair and living wages. Wage theft is an "odious oppression."[67] The deserving poor – not idlers, but the disabled and infirm unable to work, as well as poor able-bodied workers – are entitled to charity.

The doctrine of the calling beautifully illustrates how the Puritans turned a sacred duty into a liberty right. If everyone has a duty to work in their God-given calling, and each has the right to determine their calling for themselves in light of their personal talent, temperament, and tastes, it follows that each has the right to free choice of occupation. England in the seventeenth century had an increasingly dynamic economy that led to the rise of "masterless men" who had no identifiable superior with the power to force them to work at any job in particular.[68] While insisting that the masterless choose some calling or other if they could find steady work, Puritans raised the freedom of the masterless to choose their calling from a contingent fact to a universal right.

Regarding the necessity of working in a calling, God is no respecter of persons.[69] So Puritans condemned the idle rich as well as the idle poor. This was a stunning moral innovation. (Moralists and policy makers had long only complained that the poor don't work hard enough.) "Gallants" – "those who think they need not labor due to birth, breeding, or estate," who waste their time on gambling, drinking, sports, and sleeping – are as sinful as monks and beggars, the other two classes of worthless idlers. "[T]he lowest worker deserves more than they."[70] The rich "are no more excused from service and work of one kind or another, than the poorest man."[71] From those to whom God has given much, much more labor is due. For God told *everyone*, "[i]n the sweat of thy face shalt thou eat bread, till thou return unto the ground."[72] The gentry sin in failing to educate their children in a calling. They especially fail their daughters, by letting them waste their time playing cards, adorning themselves, idly chatting, and leaving the rearing of their children to others. Most women would best spend their time as teachers, educating their children.[73]

Not every means of making money, even if positive laws allow it, counts as legitimate work in the eyes of God. Only work that promotes human well-being and advances the good of the commonwealth counts. Business models that merely extract value from others, or that oppress the disadvantaged, are sinful. Sanderson attacks monopolists, usurers, hucksters, engrossers (those who enclose land), and forestallers (those who buy up goods trying to corner the market). He denounces traders who export food from regions experiencing a famine.[74] Baxter castigates the slave trade. "To go as pirates and catch up poor negroes or people of another land, that never forfeited life or liberty, and to make them slaves, and sell them, is one of the worst kinds of thievery in the world." Slave traders are "incarnate devils" and "the common enemies of mankind."[75] Baxter also rejects sharp trading practices that take advantage of the ignorant, gullible, desperate, and poor, even if they are not strictly illegal or fraudulent. While market prices offer a benchmark for a just price, traders also must consider the interests of counterparties. Although they may ask for more than the market price from the rich, if the latter are knowing and willing to pay it, they must ensure that both parties gain from any exchange between equals, and that the poor get an even better bargain than that.[76] Both justice and charity limit the interest one may charge on loans. Extracting interest is wrong "when you allow him not such a proportion of the gain as his labour, hazard, or poverty doth require; but because the money is yours, you will live at ease upon his labours."[77]

Baxter condemns the exploitation of the poor by taking advantage of their weak bargaining position. Such behavior is "oppression," which he defines as "the injuring of inferiors, who are unable to resist, or to right themselves; when men use their power to bear down right."[78] Landlords are especially prone to oppress their tenants. "The voluptuous great ones of the world, do use their tenants and servants, but as their beasts, as if they had been made only to labour and toil for them." Such oppressors are "antichrists," who "make crosses for other men to bear," and "tread on their brethren as stepping stones of their own advancement."[79] Instead of charging what the market may bear, to maximize their profits, landlords and masters should renounce the covetousness that drives them to exploit their inferiors. "Mortify your own lusts ... which maketh you think that you need so much, as tempteth you to get it by oppressing others. Know well how little is truly necessary!"[80] Poor, hardworking tenants may be entitled to pay less than market rents. If they have enjoyed below-market rents by custom for a long time, they acquire a conditional title to them. They may also hold other customary rights that preclude their eviction by enclosure.[81] Ordinary tenants should enjoy such below-market rents as to have a comfortable life, be cheerful at work, and not suffer from "such toil, and care, and pinching want, as shall make them more like slaves than freemen."[82]

Here we see the basis of a pro-worker work ethic, in which honest laborers are entitled to dignity, meaningful work, decent material conditions, comfort, rest, freedom from oppression, and charity. Again, in relying on moral exhortation to secure such outcomes for workers, Baxter fell well short, especially in the face of a rising market society that pressed in opposite directions. Later advocates of the progressive work ethic understood that major political and legal reforms would be needed to vindicate workers' entitlements.

Baxter didn't stop with earthly rewards for hard workers. According to official Calvinist doctrine, steady disciplined work serves only an epistemic function, as a *sign* of faith, and hence of grace. Yet Baxter, in exhorting all to labor diligently in their calling, could hardly avoid supposing than that his flock would heed his message. "Doubt not but the recompense will be according to your labor . . . . Work out your own salvation."[83] He thereby slides into Arminianism, the heresy (from a Calvinistic point of view) that we have the free will to choose our salvation by accepting God's grace, which is extended to all. For Baxter, we accept God's grace in diligently manifesting our faith in work.

Arminianism is a natural response to a shift in perspective on sin. If the model for sin is lust – that is, any kind of sexual arousal outside marriage – it is obvious that we are helpless to avoid it through voluntary acts. The work ethic shifts the model for sin to sloth, which can be avoided by voluntary behavior in compliance with the work ethic. It is but a short step from there to conditional universalism, the view that, as Baxter put it, "God hath Enacted and Given a full Pardon of all Sin to all Mankind, with . . . Right to . . . Heaven, on condition of their acceptance of it."[84] He had to contort himself to fit this Arminian doctrine with Calvin's view of a tiny, predestined elect.

Thus, we see that the Puritan work ethic included both conservative and pro-worker ideals. The dual nature of the work ethic follows in part from the dual nature of work from the Puritans' perspective. Work was both an ascetic discipline and a sanctified activity that glorifies God in promoting human welfare. When work is seen as an ascetic practice, it rationalizes the consignment of workers to stultifying toil. When it is seen as a sanctified activity glorifying God, it raises workers to the same level of awe formerly held by monkish occupants of holy office, while reducing the latter to the status of idle drones to be cast out of the hive.

More fundamentally, the dual nature of the work ethic reflects the duality at the heart of Christianity, its tension between egalitarianism and social hierarchy. Christianity emerged from Jesus's apocalyptic prophecy, that God would – within the lifetimes of some who heard Jesus preach (Mark 9:1, 13:30) – overthrow the present oppressive rulers and bring his kingdom of justice to earth.[85] The Kingdom of God will reverse the fortunes of the high and the low: "[M]any that are first shall be last; and the last first" (Mark 10:31; cf. Luke 13:29–30). Servants – those who help others, who love their neighbors as themselves and thereby enact egalitarian justice – will inherit the earth under God's rule: "The servant of all" will be first (Mark 9:35).

As Christianity spread to the Gentiles, eventually to became the established religion of the Roman Empire, the meaning of Jesus's prophecy required revision. This wasn't just to save it from the embarrassment that the timing of Jesus's prophecy for the arrival of God's direct rule of earth was off. The Roman Empire could hardly embrace a religion that called for God to overthrow it and send its rulers and masters to Hell! Yet the Church could hardly repudiate the foundational egalitarianism of souls: Christ died for everyone, so everyone is equally eligible for salvation, regardless of their station in life. Nor could it repudiate Jesus's egalitarian commandment, derived from the Old Testament (Lev. 19:18) to love one's neighbor as oneself (Mark 12:31). The solution to these difficulties was to remove egalitarian justice in time and place: it will be realized in the *next* life, not this one, and in heaven, not on earth. Social hierarchy, with all its oppression and injustice – including the institution of slavery – could thereby be preserved along with Jesus's teachings.

The Reformation threatened the stability of this solution. Luther's doctrine of the priesthood of all believers, along with the rise of literacy, printing, and translations of the Bible in the vernacular, freed ordinary people to interpret the Bible for themselves. Many Protestants read Jesus's apocalyptic prophecy as imminent, his egalitarian kingdom about to be established on earth. In seventeenth-century England, millennial sects proliferated. Their radical politics added to the agitation during the Civil War of 1642–51.[86] The Puritans preached against the radical sects. Yet they had their own brand of radicalism. Baxter ministered to the Parliamentary Army, which captured King Charles I and backed Cromwell's republic. Although he wished to restrain the radicalism of the Army, Baxter later refused to submit to the Restoration regime. His opposition to the prescribed rites of the Church of England under the 1662 Act of Uniformity led to his ejection from the ministry. He was prosecuted several times for holding nonconforming services. Overall, his politics and his theology tried to steer a middle course between radicalism and reaction.

Hence it is not surprising that Baxter's work ethic does not preach sacrifice alone in this world, with compensation entirely postponed to the next. A purely ascetic, conservative work ethic fit neither the times nor his temperament. Some goods had to be promised to workers in *this* life for the work ethic to inspire them as it did.

From the point of view of philosophical ethics, the dual character of the work ethic points to something more profound than a practical compromise. The concept of a calling – that God calls each person to a specialized occupation – presupposes a division of labor into which workers are sorted. It thereby mostly accepts the existing set of occupations, with its hierarchy of offices. Yet a foundational moral egalitarianism underwrites this hierarchy. The *moral* status of the lowest worker is equal to that of the highest. *All* are called to labor; the idle rich are not excused. Nor does much of the busyness of the rich, based on oppressing the downtrodden, count as work in the ethical sense, since it fails to benefit humanity. The leveling tendencies of Baxter's ethical egalitarianism are so plain that Baxter feels forced to disavow them. He does this twice when railing against pomp and conspicuous consumption, allowing that what counts as excessive may vary by occupation.[87] Illustrating the universal duty of charity with the example of members of the early church, who held everything in common, Baxter insists that he isn't teaching leveling, but only showing that all should "relieve their brethren as themselves."[88]

Baxter needed an ethical theory to reconcile the tensions in the dual character of the work ethic. And he devised one. Here lies the most astonishing fact of all: Puritan theologians invented what was to become the most influential, and the most secular, foundational moral theory of modern times. This is utilitarianism, the doctrine that everyone's fundamental moral duty is to maximize human welfare.

Christian Charity, Effective Altruism, and the Birth of Utilitarianism

Let's briefly skip ahead to the twenty-first century, and consider the ethical advice of Peter Singer, today's most influential utilitarian moral philosopher. Singer tells us that "we should do the most good we can."[89] This is the foundation of his doctrine of effective altruism. One might think that a natural way to follow this doctrine would be to work at a charity that does a lot of good. Singer counsels against this strategy for those with significant earning power. Instead, such people should make as much money as they can, and then give away as much as they can to effective charities. He reasons that, given the high number of talented applicants for jobs at effective charities, those with high earning power can't do that much more good working at the charity than the person who would replace them. If they make a lot of money at a lucrative job and give most of it away to effective charities, they will do much more good than if they worked at a charity, and much more good also than the person who would replace them in the lucrative job, who is likely to spend most of their money on luxuries, or leave it to their privileged children. This is the logic of "earning to give."[90]

Singer cites John Wesley, the eighteenth-century minister who founded Methodism, as the earliest source for this argument. He is on the right track. Wesley launched the last revival of Puritanism, mixed with a heavy dose of Arminianism. Here he followed in Baxter's footsteps. Methodism was devoted to preaching the work ethic to poor and middle-class workers.[91] Wesley told his congregation to "[g]ain all you can by honest industry." "Do not waste" talent or money on "gratifying the desires of the flesh" or mere vanity. Then "give all you can" to help others.[92]

To modern eyes, the idea that utilitarianism could be derived from an ascetic theology is paradoxical. By the late eighteenth century, utilitarians had adopted a hedonistic conception of human well-being. How could a duty to mortify the flesh turn into a duty to impartially maximize pleasure? And how could a wholly secular, this-worldly morality arise from a stern Calvinist theology, overwhelmingly oriented to salvation?

Let's follow the logic that moves from a duty to mortify the flesh through ceaseless work to a duty of universal benevolence. According to Baxter, each individual must

> frugally getteth and saveth as much as he can .... [I]t is no sin, but a duty, to labour ... for that honest increase and provision, which is the end of our labour; and therefore to choose a gainful calling rather than another.[93]

This leads to a tension with the requirements to mortify the flesh and waste nothing. All that wealth accumulation must be used, lest it go to waste.[94] But to spend it on oneself would lead to indulgence in sinful luxury, conspicuous consumption, and worldly pleasure. Baxter offers two solutions to this problem. One is to give some leeway to loving worldly goods for the instrumental good they do. We may eat nourishing food, engage in recreation, and so forth to maintain our health and restore our capacity to work, so that we may labor further in God's service. However, one commits the sin of covetousness in "desiring more than is needful or useful to further us in our duty."[95]

Yet the rich accumulate far more worldly goods than they could spend on themselves simply out of duty. Baxter tries to ward off the leveling implications of this thought by allowing that the rich may have greater needs for worldly goods than the poor. Wealthy officials may need to entertain others in the course of public service or business. "[L]et others pity the poor: I will pity the rich, who seem to be pinched with harder necessities than the poor," because they have to waste time with such frivolity for the sake of the public interest. "The happy poor," by contrast, get to spend their time "in the honest labours of their callings." So they are far safer from the threats to their souls entailed by consorting with worldly pleasures.[96] This rationale for accumulation cannot go very far, however. One might allow that an ambassador must dress finely to display the dignity of the state he represents, and throw parties in a fancy house for foreign officials in the course of diplomacy for the public interest.[97] Yet Baxter concedes that successful private business-men have less justification for such indulgence, and accumulate vastly more wealth than they could legitimately consume, even granting some leeway to the rich.[98]

Hence arises Baxter's second and more fundamental solution to the problem of accumulating wealth beyond personal needs, an inevit-able consequence for the successful businessman. The rich must do good by paying taxes for the public good, giving to their church (thereby helping to save souls), and giving to the poor. The duty of charity to the poor is very demanding. Everyone has a duty to labor to increase his wealth, so "that he may have the more to give to pious and charitable uses."[99] Baxter expresses a thought later echoed by Singer:

> [T]he portions or comeliest clothing of your children must rather be neglected, than the poor be suffered to perish. How else do I love my neighbour as myself, if I make so great a difference between myself and him?[100]

Singer, similarly, praises Alex Foster, who has committed to donating all the income from his business beyond $15,000 per year, and Ian Ross, who has dedicated more than 95 percent of his income to charity, and limits himself to $9,000 annually.[101] Baxter would heartily approve.

Thus Baxter backs his way into a strict utilitarian duty of universal benevolence as a way to reconcile the demands to ceaselessly engage in productive labor, to waste nothing and put everything to use, and to refrain from indulging in worldly pleasures beyond what is necessary to restore our capacity to labor.

Here is Baxter's clearest statement of utilitarianism. What must we do to serve God? Baxter answers:

> It is action that God is most served and honoured by .... The public welfare, or the good of many, is to be valued above our own. Every man therefore is bound to do all the good he can to others, especially for the church and commonwealth. And this is not done by idleness, but by labour![102]
>
> The good of many is to be preferred before the good of a few, and public good to be valued above private .... A continued good is greater than a short and transitory good.[103]

This is the Puritan root of utilitarianism.[104] All of us must practice "universal charity."[105] It is a strict duty to choose the greater good. Anything less is a sin – a waste of God-given resources of the earth and of one's personal energy and time, which God commands us to use for his glory.[106] In a life entirely devoted to duty, no supererogation is possible.[107] Secular utilitarianism simply discards the theological derivation of utilitarianism from the premise that we are God's workmanship and property, the instruments of his will on earth, obliged to pursue his purposes.

2 LOCKE AND THE PROGRESSIVE WORK ETHIC

Locke as Libertarian Capitalist, or as Advocate of a (Mostly) Progressive Work Ethic?

Let us now begin to trace the influence of the Protestant work ethic on the history of political economy and public policy in Britain. This influence is largely unacknowledged, although it continues into the present. As a result, we don't fully understand what we are doing, or why, in disputes about property rights, economic regulation, taxation, labor law, and welfare policy. Making the assumptions underlying our practices explicit affords opportunities to subject them to critical examination. In addition, excavating the history of the long-lost *progressive* work ethic will help us to consider whether the resources there are worth reviving and adapting to current conditions.

All sides recognize John Locke as a seminal figure in the history of political economy. He continues to inspire libertarians and neoliberals today. At least since C. B. Macpherson's *The Political Theory of Possessive Individualism*, libertarians, neoliberals, and leftists alike have projected onto Locke the preoccupations of a rising capitalist class worried that popular government might threaten the unlimited accumulation of wealth.[1] Locke is therefore read as advocating the two central types of constraint that can prevent such threats: constitutional limits to state regulation and redistribution; and property qualifications on the right to vote.

The Lockean case for neoliberal constitutional limits on state regulation and redistribution goes as follows.[2] Before the rise of states, everyone lives in the state of nature, which is depicted as an anarchist libertarian society. In the state of nature, individuals are constrained only by natural law, which limits individual liberty only to the extent required to respect the equal negative liberties of others. They have no duties to help others. They only have duties to not interfere with others. In the original state of nature, the earth and all its resources are an open-access commons. Each individual is free to unilaterally appropriate as much of it as they please, provided they observe three conditions. First, they may only appropriate land and natural resources by mixing their labor with it. Second, they must observe a spoilage proviso, that they don't let anything they appropriate go to waste. Third, they must satisfy a sufficiency proviso, to leave "enough and as good" resources for others to appropriate. Before the invention of money, these conditions limit individuals to appropriating only so much land as they and their families could personally farm, with produce they could personally consume. Hence, all families had small and roughly equal holdings. The introduction of money by consent in the state of nature lifts these practical limits on accumulation. Money enables individuals to acquire others' labor through the wage contract, and thereby acquire as much land as can be farmed by their employees. It enables people to acquire without waste, since any produce not personally consumed can be sold for money, which doesn't spoil. Finally, the chance to accumulate money without limit gives property owners incentives to invest. Investment raises productivity, the demand for labor, and wages. Workers thereby attain a higher standard of living than what they could enjoy in the pre-monetary state of nature. This satisfies the sufficiency proviso. Thus, individuals in the state of nature legitimately accumulate indefinitely large and unequal holdings without violating anyone else's natural rights.

One flaw undermines this anarcho-capitalist utopia: people are on their own in enforcing their natural rights. Individuals are biased in favor of their own interests, so they disagree about the application of natural law in their own cases. They also tend to go overboard when inflicting punishment on violators. These biases render everyone's property insecure. To remedy this defect, individuals agree to form a state to protect their property rights, and turn over their right to enforce the law of nature to it. The resulting state has only two functions: it must serve as a neutral umpire for adjudicating disputes over violations of people's natural rights to negative liberty and property; and it must provide for collective defense against external aggressors. Individuals give up only those liberties necessary to support this minimal state. To ensure that the state respects individual property rights as they existed in the state of nature, propertyless workers must be excluded from the franchise. They become subject to the law without a voice in making it through either of two arguments: According to the doctrine of tacit consent, anyone residing under the jurisdiction of the state becomes a subject without thereby becoming an enfranchised member. Alternatively, propertyless wage laborers along with women are first subordinated to patriarchal household heads, who acquire each subordinate member's natural liberties and dispose of them in the social contract, without returning political rights to other family members.

The resulting neoliberal constitution thus includes the following constraints. (1) Positive laws exclusively protect individual rights to negative liberty and property against external interference. (2) The property rights that individuals are entitled to enjoy under the state are just the ones they had in the state of nature immediately before the creation of the state, as modified by any transfers subsequently effected by voluntary contracts, gifts, and bequests. Justice is based on purely procedural historical entitlements and is not results-oriented. Property holdings are rightful just in case they arose from legitimate original appropriations and consensual transfers. Hence (3) individuals have such absolute natural property rights that the state may not infringe, regulate, or modify them for the public good. (4) Nor may the state interfere with individuals' freedom of contract, or (5) impose taxes on individuals, except the minimum necessary to support the legal enforcement of individual natural rights, and collective defense against external enemies. Finally, (6) no one is entitled to be provided the means of subsistence from others' private property, since all rights are negative. Redistribution of income and wealth is prohibited. Hence, each individual is on their own in providing for themselves and their families. (7) Whether by strict constitutional limits or a restricted franchise or both, the resulting minimal state leaves individuals free to pursue their self-interest in accumulating unequal property without limit, and in operating their businesses without state regulations beyond the minimum implied by respect for others' property rights.

I shall argue that this libertarian reading of Locke is profoundly mistaken on every count. (1) It is wrong about Locke's moral foundations. Far from taking everyone's equal natural rights to negative liberties as a starting point, Locke derives such rights from a more fundamental universal affirmative duty to protect and support other human beings. Locke's foundational moral theory is the Protestant work ethic, not libertarianism. (2) It is wrong about the relationship between natural and positive rights. Far from claiming that the state exists only to enforce preexisting natural rights to property, and that laws may not infringe individual rights for the sake of the public good, Locke claims that individuals' positive (legal) rights are distinct from and narrower than their rights in the state of nature. The ultimate standard of right for positive laws, derived from the work ethic, is that they promote the public good by promoting the survival and flourishing of each individual in society. The laws that do so are the ones that reward "honest industry" – those who adhere to the work ethic – not, for example, profligate aristocrats, their idle heirs, useless gamblers, predatory financiers, or tyrannical kings. (3) The libertarian reading omits some critical normative implications of the rise of large and unequal estates, once enough land is appropriated to generate scarcity and crowding. On Locke's account, scarcity and crowding alter the configuration of property rights and economic regulations needed to ensure the survival and flourishing of everyone in society. They also make it rational for the people to change their constitution from monarchy to parliamentary supremacy, because an assembly of elected representatives is the most trustworthy agent for deciding how to alter property rights and economic regulations when scarcity and crowding prevail. (4) While Locke nowhere takes an explicit stand on who the electors should be, his theory is inconsistent with the patriarchal and tacit-consent accounts of how the franchise can be legitimately restricted to propertied men. As others have argued,[3] Locke's Leveller and radical Whig political affiliations and rhetoric, and the historical context in which he wrote the *Two Treatises*, support an interpretation of Locke as underwriting a broad franchise, along with most of the rest of the Leveller constitutional agenda, and generally pro-worker economic policies. (5) Locke's policies toward the poor demonstrate the legitimacy of state redistribution in terms of his work-ethic principles. However, they also reflect a darker turn of thought, in which the duty to work becomes detached from its underlying rationale – to promote human flourishing – and gets turned against the most vulnerable poor in an authoritarian direction. It is this detached and authoritarian version of the work ethic that later reactionary and neoliberal thinkers pick up, without acknowledging that it contradicts their purported commitments to human flourishing and freedom, respectively.

I propose to replace the standard reading of Locke as a proto-libertarian capitalist with a reading that foregrounds Locke's commitment to the Protestant work ethic.[4] In Locke's day, the work ethic was embraced by the principal supporters of the Whig faction. Its leader, Anthony Ashley Cooper, the first Earl of Shaftesbury, was Locke's mentor and employer. Locke was one of his closest political counselors. Shaftesbury belonged to a small group of "improving landlords" who aimed to increase the productivity of their estates, in contrast to the majority of large landowners of his day. The Whigs competed for the votes of energetic small gentry dedicated to agricultural improvements, along with the industrious artisans, tradesmen, manufacturers, merchants, and other workers. The latter tended to live in urban areas grossly underrepresented in Parliament, and to belong to Dissenting churches persecuted by the Crown.

Relying on this coalition to win office was a viable political strategy due to a dramatic expansion of the franchise during the seventeenth century. Inflation and urban economic growth enabled numerous artisans, tradesmen, and yeomen to meet the 40-shilling threshold for the franchise. By 1641, 41 percent of men could vote – in some boroughs including copyholders and wage laborers, in others all freemen, even including some recipients of alms. After the 1660 Restoration, Parliament exercised its power to extend the franchise even further, to evade Charles II's attempts to control it with bribery.[5]

The opposing Tory faction was dominated by large aristocratic landowners, mostly Anglican and allied with high-church clerics. These groups despised work as fit only for contemptible underlings. Most large landlords spent their fortunes on luxuries rather than productive investment, and preferred to spend their time on leisurely pursuits such as gambling, hunting, dueling, drinking, dining, and dancing.[6] Hence, when Locke appeals to the work ethic, he is not arguing from anodyne assumptions. He is entering highly politically charged claims into debate, attacking the moral authority of the top ranks of English society.

The Protestant work ethic helps to explain several aspects of Locke's views. It explains his readiness to endorse numerous regulations of property and contract, along with redistributive policies, that cannot be rationalized within a libertarian ethic. It explains Locke's attacks on aristocratic and corrupt mercantile property regimes, which promote the material interests of the idle rich, to no public good. It explains Locke's pro-worker political and economic agenda. Finally, although he mostly deployed the work ethic in favor of workers, the dual character of the work ethic appears in his harsh policies toward those he regarded as the idle poor. This final aspect of Locke's view contains the seeds of the ultimate hijacking of the work ethic by capital owners, who turn it against workers. Ironically, the conservative version of the work ethic became dedicated to the enrichment of those whose income accrued from mere ownership of assets, without having to engage in productive work themselves.

The Work Ethic, Natural Law Theory, and Natural Property Rights

The foundations of Locke's moral theory begin with an act of workmanship:

> [M]en being all the workmanship of one omnipotent and infinitely wise Maker ... they are his property ... made to last during his, not another's pleasure: and being furnished with like faculties, sharing all in one community of nature, there cannot be supposed any such subordination among us, that may authorize us to destroy another, as if we were made for one another's uses ....[7]

Libertarians such as Nozick start from a moral premise of self-ownership to justify a right to ignore others' needs when they require the positive assistance of others. Locke starts from a moral premise of God-ownership of people to ground an affirmative duty to come to their assistance. While our being God's property renders us immune from *arbitrary* use by others, and thereby entitles us to rights against such treatment, it also generates the fundamental duty of the law of nature: "[T]o preserve the rest of mankind."[8] Even the right of self-preservation is derived from the duty to preserve all of humanity,[9] the self being merely an instance of God's property that must be protected along with everyone else. This is why suicide is prohibited. As God's property, individuals are not entitled to use themselves arbitrarily either, but must follow God's commands.[10] The executive power of the law of nature – the right to enforce natural law with punishment for violations of it – also derives from the duty to protect all humanity. For crime being "a trespass against the whole species," the right to punish follows from the right "to preserve mankind in general," which follows from the duty to do so.[11] Locke cites Anglican priest Richard Hooker to support his claim that the moral equality of individuals – which also follows from God's workmanship[12] – entails positive duties of assistance: the "equality of men by nature" is "the foundation of that *obligation to mutual love* amongst men ... from whence he derives the great maxims of justice *and charity*."[13]

Locke's premises – that we are God's workmanship and property, all natural equals, set on earth to fulfill his purposes, to protect and promote human life – are, we have seen, the foundational assumptions of the work ethic.[14] Locke derives the work ethic from the fundamental moral duty to preserve the human species. In furtherance of this duty, God commands people to "[b]e fruitful, and multiply, and replenish the earth," a commandment that includes "the improvement too of arts and sciences, and the conveniencies of life."[15] This requires that *everyone* work. "God sets him [Adam and his posterity] to work for his living."[16] In the same passage, Locke, echoing Baxter's reasoning, considers and rejects the possibility that an individual might discharge his duty to work by commanding others to work for him: "[N]o, says God, not only whilst thou art without other help ... but as long as thou livest shalt thou live by thy labour." It follows that the idle rich, living off the labor of others, are neglecting their duties to humanity.

In *The Reasonableness of Christianity*, Locke carries Baxter's suggestion that individuals can attain their salvation through good works to its logical extreme. "To him that worketh is the reward not reckoned of grace, but of debt."[17] In other words, God grants salvation to "him that worketh" as his "title" or "claim of right," not as a gift. Even those who lack faith are saved through work. Locke thinks salvation through work alone is possible because he rejects the doctrine of original sin, according to which our utter depravity makes us unable to save ourselves.[18] Granted, in this text, Locke defines work in terms of obedience to divine law. But the only law that must be obeyed for salvation is "the law of nature, knowable by reason."[19] In the *Second Treatise*, Locke claims that the fundamental law of nature is to promote and protect human life.[20] The duties of the work ethic follow from this law. For Locke, good works consist mainly in working for the benefit of human life.[21]

Situating Locke's moral theory in the work ethic makes sense of Locke's three conditions on just appropriation in the state of nature. These are mysterious on the standard libertarian reading. Nozick wonders how the labor-mixing condition is supposed to generate property: "If I own a can of tomato juice and spill it into the sea ... do I thereby come to own the sea?" More generally, he wonders whether labor that makes things less valuable can establish property.[22] Locke answers: "God, when he gave the world in common to all mankind, commanded man also to labour ... to subdue the earth, i.e., improve it for the benefit of life." Property is justified if and only if it enables people to advance this end. "As much land as a man tills, plants, *improves*, cultivates, and can use the product of, so much is his property."[23] Locke stresses that appropriation from the commons is justified to promote life.[24] Unproductive or destructive activity does not help anyone, so it cannot establish a property claim. (Consider this a warning to polluters.)

From a libertarian point of view, the spoilage proviso is also mysterious. If I have liberty over my conduct and property, why may I not be idle? Why may I not waste or destroy my property? From the point of view of the work ethic, the answer is obvious: the same law of nature that justifies property also limits it to what promotes life. "Nothing was made by God for man to spoil or destroy,"[25] since he provided natural resources for humans to use in fulfilling *his* purpose for us, to preserve and promote human life. God gave the earth "to the use of the industrious and rational, (and labour was to be his title to it) not to the fancy or covetousness of the quarrelsome and contentious."[26] Property is not meant for leisured aristocrats simply to show off the majesty of their useless lawns because it piques their fancy. Nor are those lawns meant for dueling. It is for those who will increase its productivity. The state of nature is no libertarian playground. It is a place for serious industry for the benefit of humanity.

Proponents of the standard libertarian reading of Locke also fail to explain the sufficiency proviso, that just appropriation in the state of nature leave "enough and as good" to others.[27] The sufficiency proviso removes a possible objection to unilateral appropriation in the state of nature. If there is still plenty for others to take after one's appropriation, then doing so does no one else any injury. So no one has grounds to object. Before the invention of money, this proviso is easily satisfied, since no one can appropriate more land than their family can farm, or which produces more than their family can consume. Holdings are small and roughly equal. The population is too small to take all the available land, so no appropriation impoverishes anyone else.[28] Indeed, industrious cultivation increases productivity so much that landowners can make do with one-tenth or one-hundredth of the land they needed to sustain themselves under a hunter-gatherer subsistence strategy. The individual who encloses 10 acres thus effectively gives back to everyone else 90 acres over which they formerly ranged.[29]

However, the introduction of money enables the appropriation of larger plots. Surplus produce can now be traded without waste, as money doesn't spoil.[30] Money and the subsequent rise in trade leads to the complete appropriation of arable land, leaving nothing left in the open-access commons to appropriate.[31] This creates an impoverished class of landless people. The resulting challenge for Locke's property theory calls for close reading:

> [T]he same rule of propriety, (viz.) that every man should have as much as he could make use of, would hold still in the world, without straitening any body; since there is land enough in the world to suffice double the inhabitants, had not the invention of money, and the tacit agreement of men to put a value on it, introduced (by consent) larger possessions, and a right to them.[32]

In the same paragraph, Locke toys with the thought that there are "vacant places of America" where land is still available for appropriation. Locke does *not* claim that this answers the complaint of the landless poor, that enough and as good has not been left for them in the countries where all the land has been appropriated. He is not telling them to shut up and go to America. He raises the point only to suggest that there are still places where the "same rule of propriety" holds – where individuals can still unilaterally appropriate as much land as they can use "without straitening any body." But the invention of money creates conditions in which that rule *no longer holds*. (It *would* still hold *had not money been invented*.)

Advocates of the libertarian reading make much of the fact that Locke goes on to argue that the rise of commerce through the introduction of money produces so much wealth that "a king of a large and fruitful territory there [in America] feeds, lodges, and is clad worse than a day-labourer in England."[33] On the libertarian reading, this amounts to arguing that the sufficiency proviso is met after all, since even the worst-off landless person in commercial society is better off than the best-off person in a purportedly hunter-gatherer society, or in a noncommercial peasant society where land is still available for appropriation. Hence, unequal appropriation in commercial society, even to the point that no land is left in the commons, has injured no one.

Locke certainly allows *unequal* appropriation. But the question at issue is whether he justifies a violation of the sufficiency proviso. Locke never says that the greater prosperity of commercial society shows that the sufficiency proviso is met there. If he had meant to imply this, that would make a mystery of his claim in the *Second Treatise*, §36, that the rule permitting unilateral appropriation of as much as one can use no longer holds after money is invented.

Reading Locke's argument from the perspective of his work ethic, we see that he is sending a quite different message. His comparison of the condition of a day laborer in England with a "king" in America arises in the context of his defense of a 99 percent labor theory of value.[34] In these passages, he is not addressing the sufficiency proviso at all. He is justifying the labor-mixing condition. He advances his labor theory of value to answer the challenge of the *Second Treatise*, §39: in the original state of nature, where the earth was given in common to all, how could labor establish "distinct titles to several parcels of it"? The worry is that although each person owns their own labor, and the products of it, they didn't make the land. How can "the property of labour … be able to over-balance the community of land"?[35] Locke's answer is that "[i]t is labour then which puts the greatest part of the value upon land, without which it would scarcely be worth any thing."[36] Moreover, with the invention of money and consequent rise of commercial society, it isn't just the labor of the farmer that accounts for its value:

> [I]t is not barely the ploughman's pains, the reaper's and thresher's toil, and the baker's sweat is to be counted into the bread we eat; the labour of those who broke the oxen, who digged and wrought the iron and stones, who felled and framed the timber employed about the plough, mill, oven, or any other utensils, which are a vast number requisite to this corn, from its

being seed to be sown, to its being made bread, must all be charged on the account of labour, and received as an effect of that: nature and the earth furnished only the almost worthless materials, as in themselves. It would be a strange "catalogue of things, that industry provided and made use of, about every loaf of bread," before it came to our use, if we could trace them; iron, wood, leather, bark, timber, stone, bricks, coals, lime, cloth, dyeing, drugs, pitch, tar, masts, ropes, and all the materials made use of in the ship, that brought any of the commodities used by any of the workmen, to any part of the work ....[37]

Locke is telling the landowners that they owe their wealth not just to "the ploughman's pains, the reaper's and thresher's toil, and the baker's sweat" but to the labor of *all* the artisans, masons, carpenters, miners, weavers, sailors, and other laborers who participate in commercial society. Their land would be practically worthless without commerce, and hence without the labor of those who make commerce possible. These laborers *don't* own land, and are not directly employed by the landowners.

Granted, after the introduction of money, the activities of improving landlords and yeomen complement the labor of commercial workers. The improving landowners generate a surplus of food that feeds the commercial workers, who in turn manufacture, transport, and sell the durable goods that these landowners demand. As long as landless workers can find employment in the commercial trades that pays enough to support their families, the sufficiency proviso is not violated.

However, some landless workers are impoverished due to the complete enclosure of land. Locke's argument in §§40–44 implies that the vast wealth of the great landowners is due to their appropriation of a considerable portion of the fruits of the labor of others. If the workers themselves are not enjoying all of the value added by their labor (which should be, by Locke's calculation, 90–99 percent of GDP), they should hardly be satisfied by the mere fact that they are better off than a king in America, where land is nearly worthless due to the *lack* of labor engaged in commerce and agricultural improvements. It is difficult to avoid drawing the conclusion that some of these great landowners, at least, do not hold their wealth legitimately. Indeed, Locke implies as much in §38:

[W]hatsoever he tilled and reaped, laid up and made use of, before it spoiled, that was his peculiar right .... But if either the grass of his inclosure rotted on the ground, or the fruit of his planting perished without gathering and laying up; this part of the earth, notwithstanding his inclosure, was still to be looked on as waste, and might be the possession of any other.

To be sure, Locke is speaking here of the no-spoilage rather than the labor-mixing condition for legitimate unilateral appropriation in the state of nature. Nevertheless his comments undermine the legitimacy of the titles of the lazy aristocrats in their vast estates in political society. Their ungrazed lawns leave the grass to waste. Meanwhile, the landless laborers are impoverished by the facts that they are excluded from owning land, no longer enjoy a commons on which they could put a cow, and find that the bulk of the value added by their labor has been appropriated by the rich. Because these landlords are not improving, they fail to produce a surplus that can support all the workers they displace by enlarging and enclosing their estates. Yet the value of their land nevertheless appreciates due to the complementary activities of the improving landlords and commercial workers.

Richard Ashcraft has suggested that this passage is a subtle endorsement of the Diggers' claim that landless laborers are entitled to seize the wastes of the great estates for themselves, even if they have been enclosed.[38] Perhaps. Another possibility, which I shall pursue, is that Locke is building the case for a popular representative government that is empowered to alter existing property relations, precisely because there is no justification for features of the status quo.

Note also that §38 implies that Locke rejects the libertarian historical entitlement theory, which holds that current titles are justified because they descended from prior legitimate appropriations, consensual exchanges, and bequests. From the perspective of Locke's work ethic, *current* uses of property matter for justice. The lazy heir of a vast estate who fails to put it to productive use does not get off the hook simply because his ancestors legitimately acquired it by industriously mixing their labor with it. To anticipate my argument, Locke does *not* say that the "great art of government" is to protect status quo property relations, or to enforce purely procedural rules of property acquisition that obtained in the state of nature. He rather says that it is "by established laws of liberty to secure protection and encouragement to the honest industry of mankind, against the oppression of power and narrowness of party."[39] It was the artisans, merchants, yeoman farmers, and energetic gentry – the Whig party's constituents – *not* the lazy aristocrats or the sycophantic high-church clergy, who engaged in "honest industry." It was the king, his court, his Anglican (and prospectively Catholic) clergy, and his aristocratic Tory supporters who were engaged in "the oppression of power and narrowness of party" that threatened workers' property.[40]

Against these suggestions, Waldron argues that Locke offers a different answer to the §36 objection that the sufficiency proviso is no longer satisfied once enclosure impoverishes the landless laborer. On his reading, Locke claims that once the sufficiency proviso is no longer satisfied, legitimate appropriation requires the consent of others. However, that consent can be obtained very cheaply, by appeal to tacit consent to the use of money.[41] In §36, Locke claims that "the invention of money, and the tacit agreement of men to put a value on it, introduced (by consent) larger possessions, and a right to them." On Waldron's reading of this passage, *the very same fact* – consent to the use of money – has two normative consequences. First, it invalidates the original rule of the state of nature, that individuals may acquire as much land as they can use *without* getting others' consent, because such acts now violate the sufficiency proviso. Second, it enables enclosures to satisfy an *alternative* rule for legitimate appropriation in the state of nature – namely, that individuals may enclose as much land as they can use *with* others' *tacit* consent, *even if doing so violates the sufficiency proviso*. Here is the key passage supporting this interpretation:

> [S]ince gold and silver, being little useful to the life of man in proportion to food, raiment, and carriage, has its value only from the consent of men ... it is plain, that men have agreed to a disproportionate and unequal possession of the earth, they having, by a tacit and voluntary consent, found out a way how a man may fairly possess more land than he himself can use the product of, by receiving in exchange for the overplus, gold and silver, which may be hoarded up without injury to any one; these metals not spoiling .... This partage of things in an inequality of private possessions, men have made practicable ... without compact; only by ... tacitly agreeing in the use of money: for in governments, the laws regulate the right of property, and the possession of land is determined by positive constitutions.[42]

Waldron laments that Locke's argument here "is one of the worst arguments in the *Second Treatise*," since those impoverished by unequal possessions are "least likely to be involved as tacit consenters in assigning conventional value to gold and silver."[43] I would add that it is doubtful that consent to a convention implies consent to every unanticipated disastrous consequence that flows from it, much less a right of the beneficiaries of disaster to maintain the property arrangements that caused it. Indeed, Locke denies that claim: he argues that "when a kind of monopoly, by consent, has put this general commodity [money] into a few hands, it may need regulation."[44] We should be cautious about attributing such a bad argument to Locke, if an alternative interpretation is available.

Here is mine: in this passage, and in all other passages where Locke allows the introduction of money to justify unequal possession, he focuses *only* on how the monetary convention enables large and unequal accumulation without violating the *spoilage* proviso.[45] All by itself, accumulating a lot of *gold* does no injury to anyone else, since such accumulation implies that useful things such as "food, raiment, and carriage" are not rotting away but going to people who need them. But accumulating so much *land* that it leaves workers without any, and impoverished by low wages, *does* injure them. Locke notes that the introduction of money makes people want to enlarge their possessions.[46] From the poor landless laborer's perspective, that adds to the problematic nature of the monetary convention. Locke never suggests that this convention addresses the failure to satisfy the sufficiency proviso, or that anyone either tacitly or explicitly consents to their own impoverishment.

So what is Locke's solution to the failure of the sufficiency proviso, once all the land is appropriated? Waldron, like everyone else bewitched by the libertarian reading of Locke, assumes Locke must have one. That is, Waldron assumes that he must have an argument to rationalize the impoverishment of landless workers in the state of nature, so that unequal holdings can remain legitimate under scarcity. I think this can't be right, because such a state violates the fundamental law of nature: that people secure the survival and flourishing of each individual. By contrast, viewing his thought through the lens of the work ethic, I read Locke as claiming that *there is no general solution to the failure of the sufficiency proviso in the state of nature*. It is a problem we need *the state* to solve.

To be sure, Locke, echoing Baxter, accepts *inequality* of possession, provided this inequality is due to unequal levels of hard work
and continuous investment of productive technology in the land,
through all the generations that inherit it. That is, he accepts unequal
property that is due to assiduous adherence of the owners to the work
ethic. That is the only kind of inequality that he justifies in his chapter on
property. But when inequality leads to *scarcity* of land – when all the
commons is appropriated due to the growth of the great estates – some
workers end up landless, and thereby impoverished. This is a plain
violation of the sufficiency proviso. It also violates the only consideration that Locke thinks can justify inequality – namely, unequal work
and investment. Landless laborers are working hard, but the idle owners
of the great estates are getting nearly all the benefits of their labor. Far
from justifying this state of affairs, Locke claims in §36 that once
workers become straitened due to the scarcity of land, the rule that
had prevailed up to that point – "that every man should have as much as
he could make use of" – *no longer holds*. The mere fact that one is
satisfying the spoilage proviso is not enough to justify one's holdings.
For now, for the first time, the sufficiency proviso has been violated.
There is no evident solution to this problem in the state of nature. Who
is responsible for ensuring that no one is impoverished by the rise of
scarcity, when this cannot be traced to any specific appropriation, but
rather is an effect of all of them together? And what is the remedy?[47]
At this point people need to resort to government to find a solution. No
wonder, then, that the concluding sentence of §50 contrasts the natural
law rules that lead to inequality in the state of nature to the laws that
"regulate the right of property" under governments, where "the possession of land is determined by positive constitutions." I read this as an
indication that Locke thinks the state may legitimately regulate property
to remedy the failure of the sufficiency proviso. So let us turn to Locke's
theory of state creation by compact.

The Work Ethic, State Power, and Positive Rights

Locke argues that people need a state because they lack certain
institutions in the state of nature that are needed to manage conflicts
over property fairly. These institutions include a known, external standard of right and wrong,[48] agreed-upon unbiased judges,[49] and effective
power to administer just punishments for wrongdoing and exact

reparations for damages.[50] But what leads people to conflict in the first place? Locke's answer is *scarcity*. Until the commons is entirely appropriated, people have no reason to quarrel over property. As long as there is enough and as good for others to appropriate, no one could think himself injured by another's enclosure.[51] As long as "there was as good left," it would be covetous to "meddle with what was already improved by another's labour," since this would involve taking "the benefit of another's pains, which he had no right to." (Note Locke's condemnation of covetousness, a major sin within the Puritan work ethic.) Since God commanded everyone to labor, people should instead obtain their subsistence by staking out part of the commons to farm.[52] As long as commons still existed, people typically did stake their own claims there, rather than pick fights with people who already had some. When families grew too large to fit in their accustomed territory, some members would amicably agree to split off and stake claims in new territory.[53] Locke repeatedly stresses that as long as the sufficiency proviso is met, people have "little room for quarrels or contentions about property."[54] Why risk violence by disputing someone else's property claim, when there is plenty of common land that can be taken without conflict?

Domestic conflict over property becomes unmanageable only after the introduction of money. Money supports a burgeoning trade, increased wealth, and hence population growth, all furthering God's command, embodied in the fundamental law of nature, to "be fruitful, and multiply." It also gives people a reason to enlarge their estates beyond what they can personally use. Enlargement of estates, combined with population growth, leads to the complete appropriation of the commons. The loss of the commons has three effects. First, different families' properties now abut each other's, and disputes arise about where one property ends and another begins. Second, one person's use of their property may negatively affect another's, and disputes arise as to whose use should prevail. Third, some workers are impoverished in being deprived of access to the land, and disputes arise about how to remedy this failure of the sufficiency proviso. The laws of nature – that is, what can be discovered by ordinary moral reasoning – cannot definitively settle any of these disputes. There are too many possible ways of settling them, with different distributive consequences. The laws of nature aren't specific enough to guide under these new conditions of crowding, land use conflicts, and scarcity. This is why people need "an established, settled, known law, received and allowed by common consent to be the standard of right and wrong."[55]

On the standard libertarian reading of Locke, the disposition of property – both its distribution, and its rules – is fixed in the state of nature. People consent to create a state for the purpose of protecting their property *as fixed in that state*. Hence, governments are constitutionally forbidden from redistributing or regulating property, and may only tax it to the extent needed to support the legal apparatus for its protection (police and courts), plus a military for collective defense. Yet this view makes no sense of the reasons why people need a state, which involve the indeterminacy of the laws of nature once scarcity enters the scene. Before the creation of a state, the boundaries between properties were not even determinate! People typically had no "fixed property in the ground . . . till they incorporated" and settled ownership by law:[56]

> [Once] the increase of people and stock, with the use of money, had made land scarce and so of some value – the several communities settled the bounds of their distinct territories, and by laws within themselves regulated the properties of the private men of their society, and so, by compact and agreement, settled the property which labour and industry began.[57]

In Nozick's version of the social contract that creates the state – admittedly only Lockean in spirit, rather than a literal interpretation of Locke's text – individuals retain all of the liberties they enjoyed in the state of nature except the right to personally enforce their natural rights, which they give up to the state, along with the taxes needed to support its minimal functions. By contrast, Locke's version of the social contract involves substantial modifications of individuals' natural liberties beyond their rights of enforcement. Everyone gives up their natural liberties to decide how to promote their own and others' survival "to be regulated by laws made by the society, so far forth as the preservation of himself and the rest of that society shall require; *which laws of the society in many things confine the liberty* " they enjoyed "by the law of nature."[58] Under the state, individuals receive from others not only respect for their negative rights against interference, but *positive rights* to "the labour, assistance, and society of others in the same community." In return, each gives up "as much of his natural liberty, in providing for himself, as the good, prosperity, and safety of the society shall require."[59] Political society, even more than the state of nature, is a place for hard work in fulfillment of the positive duties to promote human flourishing prescribed by the fundamental law of nature.

Locke repeatedly stresses that the liberties and constraints of political society, including the rules of property, are *different* from those in the state of nature. Anyone who joins a body politic thereby "authorizes the society, or, which is all one, the legislative thereof, to make laws for him, as the public good of the society shall require."[60] This is *not* to say that society may only make laws for him that replicate the rules as they existed in the state of nature, or to enforce property entitlements as they existed there. Rather, when people enter political society, they consent to be governed "by such rules as the community, or those authorized by them to that purpose, shall agree on."[61]

Following the broadly utilitarian logic of the work ethic, the standard of legitimate legislation is what "the good of the society shall require."[62] The obligations of the fundamental law of nature, to protect and promote human life, still hold under government, but "in many cases are drawn closer."[63] It was always the case that this natural law serves more as a guide than a constraint, supplying the goal of "the general good of those under that law" rather than a fixed list of prohibitions.[64] This doesn't imply that Locke's ethics are strictly utilitarian, ready to sacrifice individuals for the sake of maximizing some aggregate good. His standard incorporates a distributive constraint: he identifies "the public good" with "the good of every particular member of that society, as far as by common rules it can be provided for."[65] "Every particular member" certainly includes the landless laborers impoverished by the scarcity of land.

Of course, no legitimate state could abolish property, since the purpose of entering political society is the protection of property. Communism is ruled out. "The people shall have property," Locke says. But the property they have is "such right to the goods, which *by the law of the community* are theirs." This is *not* to say they have a right to the goods, which by the rules of the state of nature are theirs.[66] Everyone who enters political society "submits to the community, those possessions which he has, or shall acquire ... to be regulated by the laws of the society,"[67] *not* by the rules that held in the state of nature.

I conclude that nothing in Locke's theory of the social contract prevents the legislature from regulating property and contracts, or taxing the rich, or redistributing its revenues to remedy the failure of

the sufficiency proviso that leaves so many landless laborers impoverished. Moreover, the wise state's role in encouraging "honest industry"
should, by Locke's argument, inform laws that enable these workers to
reap the fruits of their labor. For they, not the idle aristocrats who have
appropriated those fruits, are the true followers of the work ethic. To
test this interpretation, let us turn to constitutional disputes in
Locke's day, and his proposed resolution of those disputes.

A Constitution for Workers

In October 1647, Agitators – elected representatives of soldiers
of the New Model Army, which was fighting for Parliamentarians in the
English Civil War – met at the town of Putney with several Grandees or
officers of the Army, including Oliver Cromwell and his son-in-law
Henry Ireton. They discussed constitutional reforms. The Army had
captured Charles I, affording an opportunity for major constitutional
changes. The Grandees seemed ready to cut a deal with the king and
House of Lords that would preserve the latter's veto powers over laws
passed by the House of Commons, and that could expose the soldiers to
punishment for rebellion. The Agitators sought radical reforms, in line
with the demands of the Levellers, a movement whose political program
was summarized in a document known as "The Agreement of the
People."[68] They called for a nearly universal male franchise, apportionment of Ministers of Parliament (MPs) in proportion to district population, biennial Parliaments, legislative supremacy in a unicameral
Parliament (i.e., abolition of the House of Lords), equality under the
law, and free exercise of religion. They based these demands on the
doctrine of popular sovereignty, or the right of the people to decide
the constitution. Three days of debates were recorded verbatim.[69] They
are among the most riveting debates in the history of political thought.
The debates ended inconclusively. In the field, Cromwell managed to
outmaneuver the radical regiments of his Army, defeating their hopes
for immediate egalitarian constitutional reform. Charles I was executed
in 1649, leading to a brief period of republican rule.

The monarchy was restored in 1660 with the accession of
Charles II. The constitutional defects against which the Levellers railed
remained. Parliament was deeply unrepresentative of the people, not
only because of limitations on the franchise, but because districts were
not redrawn to reflect population shifts. Rotten boroughs, which had

almost no population, were represented in Parliament, effectively giving individual landowners handpicked representatives for themselves. Burgeoning cities filled with artisans, tradesmen, merchants, and manufacturers – core Whig constituencies – got little or no representation. Elections were irregular. The Long Parliament managed to avoid facing the voters from 1640 to 1660. And the king could rule without Parliament. Charles I had done so from 1629 to 1640. This problem returned during the Exclusion Crisis of 1679–81, when Charles II dissolved Parliament three times to prevent it from excluding his Catholic brother James from succeeding him. Locke was a Whig partisan in favor of exclusion. This is the background against which we should read Locke's constitutional theory. Chapter 19 of the *Second Treatise*, "Of the Dissolution of Government," contains Locke's list of just causes of rebellion due to a monarch's unconstitutional altering of the legislature. Most of these were charges that the Whig faction was lodging against Charles II during the Exclusion Crisis.

Locke concedes that the earliest constitutions established by popular consent were typically monarchies. His account of why the people originally chose monarchy, and why they later found compelling reasons to insist on vesting legislative authority in a body of elected representatives, supports the work-ethic-based class analysis of Locke's political philosophy.

Locke offers two explanations of the origins of monarchy. In the first account, early states arose from the growth of a single large extended family. The members appointed the father as their leader for three reasons: they had grown up accustomed to his leadership; they trusted him more than anyone else to impartially resolve disputes among siblings; and they trusted him to refrain from excessive punishment, due to his love for family members.[70] In the second account, multiple families agree to form a state for collective defense against external enemies. The single ruler is little more than the head of an army, and starts off with only military authority.[71] In both accounts, these early states had primitive economies with little commerce. Hence everyone was poor, no one had an interest in accumulating more than they could use, and domestic disputes were therefore rare. Out of naivety, the people didn't think to insist on express limits on their ruler's power, because in both cases the people and their ruler had common interests.[72]

The rise of commercial society, inequality, and scarcity exposes the defects of monarchy. Ambition, greed, and a taste for luxury lead monarchs to abuse their prerogative to acquire more by oppressing the people. Flatterers surround monarchs and teach them "to have distinct and separate interests from their people." The people's original naive failure to establish constitutional limits on the monarch's power now renders their property insecure from arbitrary appropriation by the king, his court, and his allies, who try to justify this abuse by appeal to the supposedly divine institution of absolute monarchy – an invention of the clergy.[73] This threat forces them to reflect on the foundations of legitimate government, and to insist on constitutional reforms to protect their property.[74]

Locke's argument clearly specifies the class basis of threats to the people's property. In contrast to libertarian interpretations, these threats come not from the poor, but from the privileged. They don't come from the state as such, but from absolute monarchy – from constitutionally unconstrained, arbitrary government. In Locke's day, ordinary people did not suffer so much from a lack of a common impartial judge to settle disputes among themselves. Common law courts already existed for that purpose. But commoners *did* suffer from the lack of a common impartial judge to settle disputes between themselves and the king, his court, and the lords. They couldn't sue royals or peers in court. The latter enjoyed immunity from arrest for most infractions and didn't have to appear in court in most cases. They were literally above the law with respect to commoners, and exercised their privileges by abusing the latter with impunity. No wonder, then, that when Locke deplores the lack of a common judge in his own day, his main target is the king, who he complains exists in a state of nature relative to the people.[75]

Locke's constitutional remedies reinforce his class analysis. The problem is that legislative power is vested in people – king and lords – who are above the law, and see themselves as having distinct interests from the people. The House of Commons was disempowered and corrupted, because the king abused his prerogative by dissolving Parliament whenever he didn't like its legislation, refusing to call it into session for long periods, or keeping it in session for too long (thereby delaying elections whereby the people could select preferred representatives), and bribing members to vote his way.[76]

Given this list of complaints, it is no surprise that Locke's constitutional agenda corresponds to the Levellers' demands from the Civil War 30 years earlier. (The only clear omission from Locke's agenda is replacing the military draft with a volunteer army and navy.) Let's compare the proposed reforms of the 1647 *Agreement of the People* (italicized) with Locke's corresponding claims:

1. *Apportionment of MPs in proportion to district population.* Locke calls for apportionment to each district in proportion to the "assistance which it affords to the public,"[77] and complains about rotten boroughs.[78] While Locke does not define "assistance," certainly providing men to fill the ranks of the navy and army would count. This would yield apportionment roughly in proportion to population. Everyone paid regressive excise taxes, while rotten boroughs paid almost nothing. Hence, apportionment in proportion to tax revenues would still dramatically shift representation from the large landowners sitting in their rotten boroughs to the populous districts where workers were concentrated.[79]

2. *Parliamentary elections every two years.* Locke does not specify a particular period for elections of legislators in the *Two Treatises*. However, his critique of the dangers of untrammeled monarchy (in which the entire legislative and executive powers of the community are permanently united in a single person) supports his preference for a multimember legislature, distinct from the executive, that is periodically reconstituted in fresh elections. This is the best insurance against a legislative power that "come[s] to have a distinct interest from the rest of the community, contrary to the end of society and government." Legislators who face the prospect of quickly returning to society, where they will be subject to the very laws they passed, are more likely to see their interest as aligned with the interest of the people.[80] Locke's argument is thus in spirit with the Levellers' proposal, even while he allows variation in the constitutional rule specifying by whom and how frequently elections are called.[81] Moreover, when he had power under King William as head of the Board of Trade, which regulated the colonies, Locke recommended annual elections for Virginia's legislature.[82]

3. *Supremacy of the legislative power over all other powers of government (including, by implication, the king).* The "legislative is the supreme power: for what can give laws to another, must needs be superior to him."[83]

4. *Subordination of the legislative power to the will of the people.* The doctrine of popular sovereignty – that the people have the right to design their own constitution, including the most important power

within it, of making laws – was both the basis of the *Agreement*'s claim to authority and the foundation of social contract theory, of which Locke was a leading theorist. His defense of the right to rebellion when the people judge that the legislative or executive have turned their powers against the people,[84] hardly 40 years since the Army rebelled against the king, also ties him to the Levellers' cause.

5. *Supremacy of the elected representatives of the legislature over laws, offices, appointments of officers, treaties, war and peace, without a voice or veto of anyone else.* Unlike the Levellers, Locke did not explicitly call for the abolition of the king's veto or the House of Lords. However, his doctrine of popular sovereignty clearly vests in the majority of the people the power to abolish both.[85] Moreover, Locke's insistence on equality under the law (see 7 below) makes it difficult to see any justification for raising a particular class of people to the privileged position of having a distinct body representing their interests and having a separate voice in legislation, out of all proportion to population.

6. *Free exercise of religion, allowing for noncompulsory religious instruction by the state.* Locke vigorously defends the basis of the *Agreement*'s free-exercise claim, that "matters of religion ... are not at all entrusted by us to any human power." He argues that "the care of souls is not committed to the civil magistrate .... Nor can any such power be vested in the magistrate by the consent of the people; because no man can so far abandon the care of his own salvation, as blindly to leave it to the choice of any other." Yet noncoercive public instruction in religion is permitted.[86]

7. *Equality under the law, with all subject to the same laws and no one entitled to exemption "from the ordinary course of legal proceedings" on account of birth, estate, or any other status.* Like the Levellers, Locke makes clear that his constitutional reforms aim to vindicate the interests of ordinary workers against the unjust powers and privileges of the king, court, and lords. The legislature must "govern by promulgated established laws, not to be varied in particular cases, but to have one rule for rich and poor, for the favourite at court, and the countryman at plough."[87] This is no mere generic statement of abstract principle. It strikes a specific blow against the class privilege of the idle rich against the workers – particularly poor, landless workers. Once the people recognize the dangers of monarchy and aristocratic privilege, they

could never be safe nor at rest, nor think themselves in civil society, till the legislature was placed in collective bodies of men .... By which means *every single person became subject, equally with other the meanest men,* to those laws, which he himself, as part of the legislative, had established; nor could any one, by his own authority, avoid the force of the law, when once made; *nor by any pretence of superiority plead exemption, thereby to license his own, or the miscarriages of any of his dependents.*[88]

The congruence of Locke's arguments and rhetoric with the Levellers' hardly ends here. Locke even devotes chapter 16 of the *Second Treatise* to the illegitimacy of the Norman yoke (see especially §177). This echoes radical Leveller and Digger objections to the unjust seizure of the people's property, and imposition of feudal rule, in the Norman Conquest.

Despite these deep connections between Locke and the Levellers, many scholars insist on the standard reading of Locke as antidemocratic. On this reading, Locke thinks that the poor must be denied the vote, lest they attempt to elect legislators who will redistribute property.[89] Yet Locke claims that the prospect that the legislature might "dispose of the estates of the subject arbitrarily, or take any part of them at pleasure" is

> *not much to be feared* in governments where the legislative consists, wholly or in part, in assemblies which are variable, whose members, upon the dissolution of the assembly, are subjects under the common laws of their country, *equally with the rest.*[90]

The danger of expropriation only comes with monarchy, or "governments, where the legislative is in one lasting assembly always in being,"[91] or legislative bodies, such as the House of Lords, that are not subject to the same laws as everyone else. Furthermore, Locke's expansive definition of "property" to include "lives, liberties, and estates"[92] certainly includes the poor as among those with a vital interest in not having their property arbitrarily seized by the state – for example, by conscription – and hence in having their interests represented there.[93]

To be sure, Locke, unlike the Agitators in the Putney debates, never discussed the proper scope of the franchise. Yet it is not so easy to see how his theory could deny *any* adult, including propertyless men and women, a voice in the exercise of popular sovereignty, when a constitution is adopted. The social contract that constitutes political society consists of an agreement in which *everyone* turns over their executive power of the law of nature, along with other natural liberties needed to create a state, and receives legal rights in return.[94] Locke insists that workers never cede these rights to their employers in the wage contract, nor do women cede them to their husbands in the marriage contract.[95] Nor are these claims optional for him. Locke needs his pro-worker and feminist premises to refute the patriarchalist defense of absolute monarchy.[96] Hence, employers and husbands cannot make their employees or wives subject to the state by disposing of their natural liberties in the social contract. By the lights of his own theory, propertyless workers and women retain all the natural freedom and equality they need to participate as equals in the formation of political society. Once individuals are joined in political society, Locke insists that the consent of a simple unqualified majority is necessary and sufficient to adopt a constitution.[97] It is difficult to avoid the conclusion that women as well as poor male workers are entitled to participate as equals in choosing a constitution.[98] Nor does Locke supply any reason to think that they would adopt a constitution that disenfranchises them. No wonder Tories accused radical Whigs of implying that women and propertyless men should have the vote.[99] Locke never answered this charge.

Locke's Work Ethic (1): Against the Idle Rich and Slavery

We have seen that Locke's commitment to the work ethic underwrites his theory of property and pro-worker orientation. No wonder, then, that "the great art of government" is "to secure protection and encouragement to the honest industry of mankind."[100] "All encouragement should be given to artificers"; "manufacturing deserves to be encouraged"; and merchants should be "cherished and esteemed as the most industrious and beneficial of any of its [England's] subjects" because the prosperity of England depends on "general industry and frugality, joined to a well-ordered trade."[101]

In contrast to his praise of the industrious, Locke disparages the idle landlords. They neglect their business, waste money on luxuries, and spend more than they have, leading farms and thereby the whole country to ruin.[102] Outside the manufacturing areas, where those engaged in industry invest in agriculture, "men live lazily upon the product of the land."[103] Locke blames England's trade deficit on "landed gentlemen" who waste their money on foreign luxuries and fashions, instead of investing in improvements.[104] What of those land-owners who complain that they can't pay their taxes due to high interest rates on mortgages they took out to pay for their profligacy? Locke replies that this is of no concern to "the frugal and thrifty."[105] He attacks the court and "inferior grandees" for "idle and useless employ-ments" that serve their vanity, and for making "honest labor" disgrace-ful. The government should suppress their vain activities and make honest labor "fashionable."[106] The work ethic pervades all of these judgments.

If good government is supposed to encourage the industrious rather than those living slothfully off mere ownership of property, we should expect that Locke's policy prescriptions would reflect that prin-ciple. Instead of a laissez-faire regime, Locke advocates regulations of contracts and property that promote industry over idleness. Such regu-lations favor productive uses of capital and discourage the acquisition of income through merely passive ownership, manipulation of privilege, and exploitation of others. Locke's policy arguments consistently attack corrupt financial, mercantile, and aristocratic practices that reward idle and exploitative modes of income extraction: usury, monopoly, gam-bling, artificial state support of high land prices, excessive copyright protections, feudal property rights, primogeniture, slavery. His argu-ments amount to an attack on the idle and exploitative rich.

Consider Locke's little-known essay, "Venditio."[107] Locke opens with a seemingly libertarian claim: "[T]he measure that ought to regulate the price for which anyone sells so as to keep it within the bounds of equity and justice" is "the market price . . . . Whosoever keeps to that . . . is free from cheat, extortion and oppression," provided they commit no fraud. Yet, by this he means not that one may charge whatever one's counterparty is willing to pay, but rather that all buyers are entitled to the same price. Price discrimination is forbidden. "He that makes use of another's ignorance, fancy, or necessity to sell ribbon or cloth, etc. dearer to him than to another man at the same time, cheats him." This condemnation extends beyond taking advantage of buyer desperation, including even marketing practices that artificially induce demand for a good. Moreover, considerations of charity, beyond what "equity and justice" demand, limit how much one may charge a desperate buyer. While it is not unjust to charge the market price for food in an area struck by famine, it may offend against charity to do so. And if people die because one is not willing to sell at a price they can afford, one is guilty of murder.[108] These qualifications to the liberty to charge whatever the market will bear are somewhat less demanding than Baxter's. Yet they follow from the same work ethic, in paying special attention to ensuring that the needs of the poor and desperate are met, and that profits not be made from stirring up covetousness in others.

Locke's longest work dedicated to pure economic policy, "Some Considerations of the Consequences of the Lowering of Interest," follows a similar pattern. This tract criticizes a proposed law to lower the interest rate to 4 percent, when the market rate in England at the time was 6 percent. Locke objects that such an interest-rate cap will only reduce the availability of credit, rather than make it available to producers on cheaper terms.[109] Yet Locke is no absolutist about freedom of contract, or about letting creditors charge whatever interest rate they can get away with, as Bentham was.[110] He argues, in line with Baxter, that usury laws are needed to protect the desperate and naive from "extortion and oppression." His critique of "money-jobbers" who "prey upon the ignorance and necessity of borrowers" indicates that he thinks such people are merely extracting wealth from others, rather than contributing to the wealth of society.[111] They can do this, he argues, in virtue of a *de facto* monopoly of a few London bankers that has arisen "by consent," because people with spare cash have deposited it with them. Such concentration of money in London has deprived the rest of the country of access to credit, where it is needed to support trade. Even though this monopoly has arisen by consent, the resulting maldistribution of credit calls for regulation to better distribute it.[112] Where the laissez-faire theorist is happy to let the market chips fall where they may, Locke qualifies this principle of distributive indifference. It is "no matter to the kingdom, who amongst ourselves gets or loses: only common charity teaches, that those should be most taken care of by the law, who are least capable of taking care for themselves."[113] The laissez-faire theorist claims that individual natural rights to economic liberty may not be infringed for the greater good.[114] Locke claims that "[p]rivate men's interests ought not thus to be neglected, nor sacrificed to anything, but the manifest advantage of the public," which implies that the public interest is a good reason to sacrifice private interests.[115]

Locke also claims that, because the incidence of taxation falls on the landholder, the laws should give the "greatest care" of him, and he should "enjoy as many privileges, and as much wealth, as the favour of the law can (with regard to the public-weal) confer upon him."[116] Locke makes this claim in a context that clearly distinguishes between improving landlords and those who merely passively realize capital gains due to state policy. Some advocated a reduction in the interest rate, expecting that this would raise the price of land and thereby benefit landowners. Locke replies that raising the price of land in this way would only benefit the person who *sells* his land. England has no interest in favoring the seller over the buyer of land. The laws should rather favor the landowner by promoting foreign trade, which will increase demand for agricultural products. This policy will increase the profits of the *industrious* landowners, not those who "live lazily on the product of the land" and hence have little surplus to sell. Moreover, Locke insists that landowners are entitled to favor *only* to the extent that this advances "the public-weal."

Locke is skeptical of property claims that have no or an attenuated connection to productive work. The monopolistic money-jobber may be very *busy*, but he is not doing anything productive if he is only taking advantage of the desperate, or loaning money to gamblers and profligates. Better to get that money out of London, where it is wasted on luxury, and into the manufacturing centers and surrounding land, where it will advance England's prosperity. Those shopkeepers who keep money tied up in their operations are "lazy and unworking." Gamblers "deserve to be restrained" because they keep piles of money around to play with instead of circulating it in promotion of trade.[117] The idle debauched heir of the industrious landowner who neglects his estate[118] may lose his claim to his unproductive property, which should go to the industrious.[119]

Intellectual property should last only for a limited term. The original authors have a claim to copyright, and also their immediate heirs, as any parent needs to provide for their children upon their own deaths. Yet such rights, although founded in labor, should expire not long after the death of the author. The notion of permanent copyright is "absurd"; there is no "reason in nature" why anyone may not reprint older works.[120] The purpose of grounding property rights in labor is not to reward idle heirs with property their hardworking ancestors acquired long ago, but to encourage "honest industry" in the present day.

Locke's critique of copyright in older works occurs in the context of a broader critique of the state's grant of monopoly printing rights to the Company of Stationers. This policy aimed to enforce state censorship of heretical and seditious works. Besides attacking censorship on free-speech grounds, Locke points to the bad effects of monopoly. The monopoly only helps "a lazy, ignorant Company of Stationers," who can fix the price of books even though their quality of printing is low. This monopoly privilege comes at the expense of scholars who need high-quality printed books, and of the nation, which can't compete with the Low Countries in the international book market with such shoddy and expensive books.[121] The limit on the number of master printers is also inequitable in depriving industrious journeyman printers from establishing their own printing shops.[122]

Locke, like the Levellers, abhorred feudal property rights. Locke's *First Treatise* rejects Filmer's feudalist claim that a monarch's absolute rule could be derived from his title to the land. God commanded people to "increase and multiply." They can hardly do so if they depend for subsistence on the arbitrary will of a landowner, who would rather "tie them to hard service, than by liberal allowance of the conveniencies of life to promote the great design of God."[123] Moreover,

> a man can no more justly make use of another's necessity to force him to become his vassal, by with-holding that relief God requires him to afford to the wants of his brother, than he that has more strength can seize upon a weaker, master him to his obedience, and with a dagger at his throat offer him death or slavery.[124]

Here again, Locke rejects the legitimacy of acquiring the right to dominate others by any contracts that take advantage of another's desperation. If such contracts were valid, then one could become sovereign over a drowning person by rescuing him at sea.[125]

Locke's argument against feudal property rights should be read in the context of seventeenth-century struggles against royal absolutism during the Civil War and after. Charles I ruled without Parliament from 1629 to 1640. Without access to tax revenues authorized by Parliament, he extracted revenues from the people by vigorously enforcing the feudal incidents of property – knight-service, wardship (appropriation of the income of underage heirs, on the pretense that the king was caring for them), and arranged marriages for wards. Heirs would avoid personal military service to the king, and the king's choice of whom they should marry, by paying him a hefty fee.[126] Locke argues that the right to inherit is exclusively based on a private right to support from one's parents. The right to rule – which is asserted in the right to extract military service, or tell people whom they must marry – is exclusively founded on the public duty to advance "the good of every particular member of that society."[127] Hence, even if the king rightly inherited property from his father,[128] he could not claim to inherit a right to rule simply in virtue of inheriting the land.[129] "[G]overnment being for the benefit of the governed ... cannot be inherited by the same title that children have to the goods of their father."[130] This argument supports the 1660 Tenures Abolition Act, which abolished the feudal incidents attached to land and thereby limited an important tool by which the Crown threatened the people's property.[131]

Locke also questions primogeniture, a key institution under-writing the monarchy and aristocracy. By the law of nature, parents owe support to all their children, giving all a right to inheritance.[132] Moreover, they have "a right not only to a bare subsistence, but to the conveniencies and comforts of life, as far as the conditions of their parents can afford it."[133] The younger children have "an equal title" with the first-born to inherit.[134] Locke allows that the positive laws of society may alter the property rights people enjoyed in the state of nature. Nevertheless, the positive laws must respect the fundamental law of nature. While the positive law could give some scope to parents to divide their estates unequally among their children, it is hard to see how primogeniture, which gives everything to the first-born and leaves the rest to shift for themselves, is consistent with the law of nature.

Locke opposed feudal land rights in the colonies. King William appointed Locke to head the Board of Trade, which regulated the colonies, in 1696. In this office, Locke implemented his pro-worker principles in his recommendations for reforming colonial Virginia's laws. Under Charles I and II, colonists acquired land by claiming "head-rights" to 50 acres for every "servant" (Black or white) they imported. Headrights encouraged the formation of vast estates held by landowners whose servants and slaves did all the work. Locke condemned the headright system as "perverted" for leaving "hardly any left for the poor People to take upp" – that is, for violating the sufficiency proviso. He recommended abolishing the headright system, confiscating unculti-vated land held by the large landholders, and redistributing it to immigrants. Virginia should be populated by independent farmers, not servants and slaves ruled by lazy and tyrannical feudal lords. Each new immigrant should be awarded 50 acres in his own name. Locke applauded Francis Nicholson, Governor and Chief Justice of Virginia, for implementing his recommendations.[135] It was those who mixed their labor with the land, not those who gained title by grants from an absolute monarch and left the tilling to others, who should own land.

Locke opposes slavery in all cases but one. There are no natural slaves, since nature "has made no such distinction between one man and another."[136] There are no valid contracts into slavery.[137] Slavery by conquest is also wrong. The sole exception concerns unjust combatants who deserve the death penalty. In that case, slavery amounts to a commutation of sentence.[138] It follows that intergenerational chattel slavery is categorically wrong. The wives and children of unjust combatants captured in war retain all of their rights to their own persons and liberties, and even their rights to their husbands' and fathers' property.[139]

Many critics deny that Locke opposed slavery. They highlight two facts. Locke held shares in the Royal African Company (RAC), which engaged in the slave trade. He also helped to draft *The Fundamental Constitutions of Carolina*,[140] which recognized slavery there. These facts show that Locke was complicit in slavery. However, they should be read in the context of Locke's relations to Shaftesbury and Charles II. Locke was a dependent member of Shaftesbury's household, serving as his physician. Shaftesbury, as head of Charles II's Council of Trade and Foreign Plantations from 1672 to 1674, appointed Locke secretary to the Council. Locke did not invest in the RAC on his own initiative. The RAC was a closely held corporation run by Charles II, who controlled who could hold shares. Charles co-opted members of his administration, including Shaftesbury, into it. Because Charles had run out of money, he paid for Locke's service to the Council in RAC shares. In 1675, Locke and Shaftesbury sold their shares for the same fixed price at which they had received them. That year Shaftesbury denounced Charles II's growing absolutism, while Locke prudently fled to France, where he stayed until 1679, when Shaftesbury (briefly) returned to the king's good graces.[141]

What about Locke's role in creating *The Fundamental Constitutions of Carolina*? Holly Brewer argues that its basic principles had already been drafted. Locke revised it in his capacity as a lawyer for the eight clients – including Shaftesbury – who, as the Lords Proprietors of the colony, commissioned this document. Locke's writing reflected their wishes "as a lawyer writes a will."[142] David Armitage argues that Locke exercised independent authority in drafting the third version of *The Fundamental Constitutions* in 1682. This version retained its provision that slaveholders had "absolute authority" over their slaves.[143] Brewer scoffs at the notion that Locke could have abolished slavery against the wishes of the proprietors and the king. Neither Locke nor Shaftesbury had power to alter such a fundamental feature of the colony. Shaftesbury had mortgaged his shares in Carolina in 1682. Both were "politically and legally almost impotent,"[144] due to their conflicts with the king. Both had been deeply involved in the Exclusion Crisis. Charles had imprisoned Shaftesbury in the Tower on treason charges in 1681. In 1682, Shaftesbury promoted an uprising against the king, and fled to Holland when this failed. Locke followed him shortly thereafter. Locke's complicity with slavery reflects the moral and political dangers of entanglement with an absolutist king, due to his dependence on one of the king's occasional councillors. It does not reflect his personal initiative.

When Locke did have real power as head of William's Board of Trade, he dealt slavery a significant blow by promoting recommendations that ended the headright system – the key institution supporting the creation of large slave plantations – and proposing legal devices to break them up. (These changes did not survive William's death.) He also recommended that "people of all Nations" enjoy equal rights in Virginia, and that the slaves be converted to Christianity. This was a key step toward their emancipation and naturalization as equal subjects, given that the rationale for their enslavement rested on their status as heathens. (This strategy implements Baxter's constraints on slavery.) Finally, Locke recommended the abolition of indentured servitude for all but convicts guilty of capital crimes. Indenturing secured the credit needed by workers too poor to pay for their transport to America. Instead of making them mortgage their labor, Locke argued that the king should pay for their passage, and award them land when they arrived.[145]

Thus we see that Locke consistently attacked systems of property and contract that reward the idle rich, as well as those engaged in unproductive extractive and predatory activity. Locke held that it is perfectly legitimate to accumulate wealth on the basis of industrious improvement of one's business. But hucksters, usurers, gamblers, mon-opolists, slaveholders, idle heirs, lazy landowners, the "unworking" shopkeepers who cater to their debauched tastes, and most of all, the king, who exploited feudal property claims to obtain revenue, merely extract wealth from others without contributing to society. Locke attacked their property claims and methods of acquiring income, and the laws that enabled them to accumulate wealth. He defended the rights of ordinary people who engaged in productive labor, and advocated policies that would enable them to live freely, escape onerous debts, and acquire property.

Locke's Work Ethic (2): Distinguishing Industrious Workers from the Idle Poor

Viewing Locke from the perspective of the work ethic, we can see that he is not fundamentally oriented to the division between rich and poor, but rather to the division between the industrious and the idle. He seeks a social order that rewards the "honest industry" of rich and poor alike, and that restrains the idle and exploitative rich as well as the idle poor. This order is neither a libertarian playground, as on Nozick's reading, nor a "dictatorship of the bourgeoisie,"[146] as Macpherson and later scholars argue.[147] It is a society in which "each of whose parts and members are taken care of, and directed in its peculiar functions for the good of the whole, by the laws of society."[148] Sanderson said as much.[149]

The work-ethic reading claims that Locke supports the interests of ordinary workers, even if they are poor, and focuses his ire only on the idle, whether they be rich or poor. I have already argued that Locke's constitutional principles are Leveller principles, which were clearly pro-worker.[150] So were his arguments concerning property and contracts. Obviously, principles and policies incompatible with slavery and indentured servitude are pro-worker. Locke's opposition to monopoly, like the Levellers' opposition, aims to increase opportunities for workers to establish their own businesses. Anti-usury laws would help workers avoid the debtors' prison. Policies favoring trade would increase opportunities for artisans and workers involved in shipping. Ending primogeniture would lead to the division of the great estates, ultimately making them small enough for purchase by yeoman farmers. Giving away small parcels of land to settlers in the colonies, and not those who hired or enslaved them, would also help to establish an independent yeoman class – although at grave cost to Native Americans, whom Locke mistakenly believed did not practice agriculture. Locke even argues that manual workers should only have to work six hours a day rather than nine, so they may devote three hours per day to study. The slack should be taken up by gentlemen and scholars.[151]

Some scholars insist that Locke was an advocate of capitalist exploitation. Their readings turn on Locke's views about wage labor and enclosures. Macpherson pioneered the argument that Locke defended the subjection of workers to exploitative wage labor. He stresses Locke's claim that, in a commons held by compact, "the Turfs my Servant has cut" become my property, since, by dint of the wage contract, the labor mixed with the turfs is mine.[152] Macpherson infers that Locke allowed great estates to be justly accumulated by means of wage labor, once the invention of money and thereby the power to purchase another's labor eliminated any practical limit imposed by the labor-mixing constraint. Thus, workers were already legitimately thrown into subjection in the state of nature. Because civil society must enforce property rights acquired in the state of nature, it is powerless to elevate wage workers to any higher status.[153]

Macpherson elevates wage labor to a centrality in Locke's theory that would have made little sense in the seventeenth century. Although wage labor was common, it played a considerably less central role in Locke's day than today. Many workers used other means of making a living. Yeoman farmers, master craftsmen, itinerant peddlers and entertainers, and many others were self-employed. Cottagers who participated in putting-out manufacturing supervised themselves as independent contractors. Landless cottagers often had customary rights to glean from farmers' fields, and to gather fuel and graze a cow or sheep in common waste, or in arable fields after the harvest. Merchant seamen were entitled to a share of the profits on any voyage. Even "servants," although paid a wage, were hardly proletarians. Locke defines them as members of the family of their master.[154] In the seventeenth century, the term "servant" referred to workers who lived and worked in the same home as their employer. Work as a servant was typically only a temporary stage of life for adolescents and young adults before marriage.

Macpherson's wage-labor model of original accumulation in the state of nature does not fit Locke's. Locke imagined that enlarged estates were acquired through the growth of families, who accumulate additional land by mixing their labor with it. Wage labor plays no role. Locke shows economic insight here. As long as there is still land to be appropriated and workers are free, large estates cannot be created other than by the growth of families. No one would offer their labor for wages when there is still land available for them to appropriate. Those who wanted estates larger than their families could farm had to resort to unfree labor to establish and maintain them. It was precisely this fact that led to slavery in the New World.[155] Locke, who helped to draft the Carolina constitutions, was vividly aware of the fact that forced labor was needed to secure large estates in America. That's how he knew how to undermine slavery and indentured servitude by the different system of land laws that he recommended for Virginia.

So Locke's state of nature cannot generate, much less justify, the mass proletarianization of the labor force. Wage labor can emerge among free workers only after all land is appropriated and concentrated in large estates. At that point, the sufficiency proviso is violated. Locke's proposed solution to this problem in Virginia was not to rationalize workers' subjection to wage labor. It was to undermine slavery, abolish feudalism, break up the great estates, and distribute free land to workers rather than their masters.

Christopher Hill offers a different objection to the pro-worker reading of Locke. Locke favored the enclosure of the commons. This policy ended the customary rights of copyholders on the estates of the lords and gentry. Copyholders were tenants with proprietary interests in the land they occupied, written in the lease, which offered security of tenure for life and the right of succession to heirs upon payment of a fine to the landowner.[156] Locke's rhetoric of improvement, and claims that enclosure of the commons enables investment that increases agricultural productivity,[157] echoes that of enclosure advocates in the seventeenth century.[158] Hill argues that enclosures devastated hardworking copyholders, and that only the Diggers, who advocated holding land in common, offered a viable solution to their plight. He criticizes the "constitutional" Levellers – whose positions were revived by Locke – for advocating the end of copyhold in order to promote a class of independent yeoman freehold farmers.[159]

Locke, however, like the Levellers, insists on conditions on enclosure that protect copyholders. He distinguishes the open-access commons of the state of nature from land "left common by compact, i.e., by the law of the land" in political society.[160] It would be illegal to unilaterally enclose any part of a commons-by-compact. Moreover, because land is scarce in political society, any further enclosure of a commons by compact would violate the sufficiency proviso: "[T]he remainder, after such enclosure, would not be as good to the rest of the commoners, as the whole was when they could all make use of the whole." Hence, "no one can enclose or appropriate any part, without the consent of all his fellow-commoners." A unanimous consent rule would give each commoner sufficient bargaining power to insist that they be compensated for the loss of their customary rights.

Unanimous consent was the prevailing rule of enclosure in the seventeenth century. In the sixteenth century, English courts had greatly strengthened the security of copyholders' and beneficial lessees' property rights. This regime persisted through most of the seventeenth century, including when Locke was writing the *Second Treatise*. Hence, enclosure by eviction was rare. Robert Allen claims that the seventeenth century was the "golden age" of the English yeoman (peasant freeholder or copyholder) because of the strength of yeomen's property protections at that time.[161]

Ellen Wood concedes that Locke allowed that the legal rights of copyholders must be respected. Yet she claims that in practice, this meant little because so much land was already enclosed,[162] and it was easy for lords to coerce commoners to "consent" to enclosure due to the legal weakness of customary rights.[163] However, the Tenures Abolition Act of 1660 extended explicit protection to copyholders' rights. It is possible that copyhold rights were somewhat eroded due to the abolition in 1641 of the Crown's prerogative courts, which were the traditional venues where copyholders' rights were most vigorously upheld.[164] Nevertheless, other courts continued to uphold copyholders' rights even into the early nineteenth century.[165]

Enclosures in the seventeenth century were not as detrimental to copyholders as Wood supposes. Enclosures from the early seventeenth century to the Glorious Revolution differed both economically and legally from typical enclosures before and after that era. In the first wave of enclosures from 1450 to 1524, landowners frequently enclosed cropland and evicted the peasants so they could convert it to pasture and raise sheep. Peasants suffered hardship because they would lose both their customary rights and opportunities to lease farmland or obtain employment as a hired hand. That was why the Crown, courts, and

Parliament acted to strengthen copyholders' property rights. After 1688 and especially in the eighteenth century, enclosures typically took place by act of Parliament.[166] Such Parliamentary enclosures were coercive, because they could take place without the consent of a majority of property holders, as long as the holders of 75–80 percent of the acres in a parish consented. Due to the great inequality of landholdings, this empowered a very few large owners to force enclosures on everyone else.[167]

Neither type of enclosure was common in the seventeenth century. More typically, copyholders would enter into a collusive agreement with landowners to evade the protections of anti-enclosure laws by showing proof to a judge that they had agreed to cede their rights in exchange for consideration, and allege that their landlord was obstructing the execution of the agreement. The landlord would then accept the agreement before the judge, who would ratify it.[168] Such a procedure, dependent on the legal initiative of copyholders, satisfies Locke's condition on legitimate enclosure. This supports the view that such enclosures were in the copyholders' as well as the landlords' interests.

Enclosures were often in the interest of copyholders in Locke's day because the economics of enclosure had changed from the sixteenth century. Much enclosure in the seventeenth century focused on improving arable lands. Yeoman farmers undertook agricultural innovations that dramatically raised productivity on croplands. More food was produced, a boon to workers everywhere. To fully capture the gains from their investments, some yeoman preferred the conversion of their copyholds to freeholds via enclosure. Landlords, wishing to raise money, accepted payment from yeomen in return for this conversion. At the time of enclosure, they gained the consent of landless agricultural workers with residual rights to the land by reserving common land for them in return for giving up their rights to graze animals on arable land after the harvest. Other copyholders were converted to long-term leaseholders working with superior technology.[169] Advocates of agricultural improvement such as Locke could therefore plausibly argue that the gains from enclosure in his era included most agricultural workers. Further evidence that enclosure's benefits were widespread when Locke was politically active is the fact that controversy over enclosure died down after 1660. Opposition did not pick up again until the mid-eighteenth century, when Parliament aggressively advanced a coercive enclosure regime.[170]

A more challenging objection to my argument that Locke's political philosophy was pro-worker focuses on his harsh attitudes and policy prescriptions toward the poor. I shall argue that much of what he proposes about the poor is consistent with the work ethic. However, some of his proposals, especially regarding poor children, reflect a darker cast of mind that is impossible to reconcile with his foundational moral principles. They express a stinting and severe orientation to the poor that was to have enormous impact on liberalism from the Industrial Revolution forward, ultimately turning the work ethic against workers themselves.

Locke's fundamental law of nature tells everyone to protect and promote all human life.[171] A positive right to subsistence follows from this law. "[M]en, being once born, have a right to their preservation."[172]

> God ... has given no one of his children such a property in his peculiar portion of the things of this world, but that he has given his needy brother a right to the surplusage of his goods; so that it cannot justly be denied him, when his pressing wants call for it ... As justice gives every man a title to the product of his honest industry, and the fair acquisitions of his ancestors descended to him; so charity gives every man a title to so much out of another's plenty as will keep him from extreme want, where he has no means to subsist otherwise.[173]

In Locke's moral system, the right to charity generates a *title*, a property right or entitlement, on a par with the right to property due to labor.

Samuel Fleischacker argues that this passage does not support an institutionalized entitlement to relief. He argues that Locke is merely following the natural law tradition from Aquinas through Grotius and Pufendorf. In that tradition, the duty of charity was purely individual and could not be exacted as a matter of law. The poor also had a "right of necessity" to take another's property in emergencies, when life would otherwise be lost. But this right by definition was extraordinary and extralegal, not something that could justify a regular order of state taxation for poverty relief.[174]

Locke goes considerably further than this, however. In his proposed poor-law reform, he insists that "Every one must have meat, drink, clothing, and firing."[175] Notably, his proposal has little to say about those who are unable to work due to disability or illness. He takes it for granted – as did the Poor Law – that those with means must be taxed to support everyone who is impoverished due to their inability to work. The duty to provide charity is a responsibility of the parish, which should be fined if any member dies from lack of relief.[176]

Locke's proposal focuses on the able-bodied poor. In keeping with the work ethic that lay at the core of the Poor Law, the right to charity arises only when a person "has no means to subsist otherwise."[177] "The true and proper relief of the poor ... consists in finding work for them, and taking care they do not live like drones upon the labour of others."[178] If people are able to work but are unemployed, the first solution should therefore be to put them to work so they can produce or earn enough to survive.

Locke's proposal should be put in the context of seventeenth-century poor-law thinking. Tudor-era poor laws had assumed that the poor could be divided into the deserving "incompetent" poor – those *unable* to work – and the undeserving able-bodied idlers – those *unwilling* to work. The first would receive aid, the second, punishment in a house of correction. Starting in the late sixteenth century, the government directed parishes to undertake surveys of their poor. The surveys discovered a third group of impoverished people, who came to be known as the "laboring poor." These were involuntarily under- and unemployed able-bodied workers who earned less than subsistence. Policy makers were shocked to discover this group. At the turn of the seventeenth century, they reformed the Poor Laws to prioritize finding work for the laboring poor, and training their children for work.[179]

Locke's idea that the desperate poverty of able-bodied workers arises from a violation of the sufficiency proviso is an attempt to theorize why this group exists. His poor-law proposal explains what he thinks should be done about the laboring poor. Recall that the state of nature offers no general solution to the violation of the sufficiency proviso. This violation generates a class of laboring poor for whom society is not fulfilling the fundamental law of nature, and who lack the means to fulfill that law with respect to others. The state is needed to coordinate a response to these facts, for political society is one in which "each of whose ... members are taken care of, and directed in its peculiar functions for the good of the whole, by the laws of society."[180]

Locke's position thus goes well beyond the natural law tradition that merely recognized an extralegal right of necessity. His account of the right to poverty relief offers a distinct natural law justification, based on the need for government to modify property rights so they satisfy the sufficiency proviso and thereby ensure that every member of society is taken care of. The result is a rationale for a type of government-administered relief of the same kind as, although harsher than, the English Poor Law of Locke's day.

Regarding the able-bodied poor, however, Locke's proposal is marked most strongly by suspicion: are they truly involuntarily unemployed, or are they just faking it to get relief? He worries that others' fulfillment of the duty of charity may undermine recipients' willingness to fulfill their duty to work. Although he theorizes involuntary under- and unemployment in the *Second Treatise*, and admits that such people exist in his classification of the poor,[181] Locke wrestles with this reality. The able-bodied are poor due to "vice and idleness," "the relaxation of discipline and corruption of manners," rather than a lack of jobs.[182] Locke's ambivalence was shared by contemporary poor-law policy makers and administrators. Despite their discovery of the laboring poor and attempts to provide work as a solution, in practice they kept trying to fit applicants for relief into the traditional dichotomies of impotent/able-bodied, deserving/undeserving. Like Locke, they had great difficulty distinguishing cases given the diverse circumstances and complex survival strategies of the poor.[183]

Locke allows that poor adults are entitled to a test of their claim that no jobs are available for them. Each parish must appoint a guardian of the poor who will ask employers if they have any jobs for the unemployed. Such jobs will be paid at less than the going wage, to make up for the suspicion that the unemployed are less diligent or skilled than those with a job. If no employer volunteers, the guardian may force them to provide work at a minimum wage.[184] Employers can also be required to accept poor children as apprentices, bound to work for them for longer than normal, to make up for the fact that their parents cannot afford to pay the employer tuition.[185] Adults lacking skills may go to "working schools" where they will learn on the job.[186] Thus, Locke proposes a job and education guarantee to those deemed willing to work. These proposals are in line with the Poor Law reforms enacted at the turn of the seventeenth century. However, he neglects a century of failure in the attempts of parishes to find work for the unemployed poor.[187]

Matters take a harsh turn with respect to those Locke regards as willfully idle, whom he identifies as those caught begging without a pass. Consistent with laws passed in the Tudor era and later, Locke regards begging as a criminal offense. Such intransigence, he claims, is justly punished with hard labor at a house of correction at bare subsistence wage – or, for prime working-age males begging in maritime counties, naval impressment. Those caught with a counterfeit pass may get their ears lopped off, or, if they repeat the offense, be "transported to the plantations" – a fate reserved for unjust combatants deserving death in the *Second Treatise*. Children caught begging without a pass may be whipped and put to a short term of hard labor before being sent home.[188]

So far, his poor-law proposal, while punitive and stigmatizing, is consistent with the view that the work ethic, bound up in the dual claims that able-bodied people have both a right and a duty to work, should be enforced by law. "Honest industry" deserves its just reward: this is the principle underlying his pro-worker agenda. But those who are not honest and industrious, while they still must be provided for, should be forced to work under confinement for bare subsistence, both as punishment and as training for the correction of vice, until they show "manifest proof of amendment."[189]

Work, however, to what end? Officially, Locke's answer is to advance "the good of every particular member" of society, a good that includes not just bare survival, but enjoyment of the "comfort" and "conveniences of life." Yet Locke insists that the *children* of the almstaking poor, starting at three years of age, should be removed from their homes and sent to "working schools," which are little more than putting-out factories.[190] There they will be fed bread, along with "watergruel" in the winter, and "from infancy be inured to work." They should be put to hard-enough labor that the net cost to the parish of maintaining them in such schools will be "nothing," and probably even return a profit.[191] Meanwhile, their mothers will thereby be freed from child care so they can work – as if child care were not itself a form of work. Baxter did not make that error.

Locke's proposal is more severe than contemporary poor-law practice. As a condition of receiving relief, impoverished parents often had to accept that the children they could not support would be bound out to apprenticeship. But most were apprenticed at the age of nine or ten. None were bound out before the age of seven, the typical age at which most English children were expected to contribute to their family's maintenance. Moreover, apprentices would live with the employer's family, not in a workhouse. Parents complained bitterly of suffering separation from their children, reluctant employers were often cruel, and pauper apprentices often ran away.[192] Nevertheless, forced apprenticeship was not as bad as the horrors of workhouses (see Chapter 4), not least because it rarely lasted long. No wonder, then, that Locke's contemporaries rejected his proposal for pauper children as too cruel.[193]

Here we encounter a contradiction in Locke's thinking. It is absurd to suppose that toddlers are willful idlers deserving punishment. Nor was this consistent with Locke's views of children. In his *Some Thoughts Concerning Education*, he insists that "children generally hate to be idle."[194] For all his stern and rigorous work ethic, so relentlessly emphasized throughout his writings, the one place where Locke makes room for fun and spontaneity is childhood education. Locke's revolutionary contribution to pedagogy was his stress on the importance of free play. At a time when the rod was at least as important an instructional tool as the book, Locke condemned the practice of beating lessons into children's bodies. He repeatedly cautions against compulsion in educating children, arguing that children learn far better through play and games.[195]

> Recreation is as necessary as labour or food: but because there can be no recreation without delight, which depends not always on reason, but oftener on fancy, it must be permitted children not only to divert themselves, but to do it after their own fashion.[196]

To tear impoverished toddlers away from their parents and force them into a childhood of drudgery so they can turn a profit for the parish is patently inconsistent with Locke's views about the requirements for proper child development. Here is one place where work does *not* promote human flourishing.

To be sure, Locke describes his "working schools" as good for children. They will be better fed there, whereas cash relief will be squandered by their fathers on drink. He never considered paying cash relief to mothers. They will receive instruction in religion and morality – as if their parents would not do so with proper support. They will learn a trade – as if they had to start doing so as toddlers.[197] My objection is not that Locke explicitly depicts his proposal as punishment for poor children. I am troubled rather by the hard cast of mind that leads him to propose such draconian measures.

In his poor-law proposal, Locke anticipates the harsher turn against the poor that was to gather strength in the course of the eighteenth century. Although workhouses existed in Locke's day, they were rare. The Societies for the Reformation of Manners promoted workhouses for the urban poor in the 1690s. The Society for the Promotion of Christian Knowledge launched a campaign to spread rural workhouses as the standard form of poor relief in the 1710s. Knatchbull's Act, otherwise known as the Workhouse Test Act, authorized parishes to establish workhouses in 1723.[198] Workhouses differed from the houses of correction of the sixteenth and seventeenth centuries. Houses of correction were part of the criminal justice system. People who had broken laws against begging, vagrancy, prostitution, petty theft, and other minor offenses were sentenced to hard labor at a house of correction for terms of days to weeks. Workhouses were part of Poor Law administration. They were places to which the destitute who had broken no laws but who had applied for poor relief could be sent for as long as they remained dependent on relief. They were to become the places where the authors of nineteenth-century poor-law reform ultimately hoped to send all applicants for relief.

Locke's readiness to think the worst of the unemployed poor, to close his mind and heart to more generous treatment, to prescribe punitive treatment to correct their presumed vices, to pretend that this benefits them, to exploit their labor for others' profit, to stunt their development so that they are fit only for a life of drudgery, to subject them to a harsh authoritarian regime: here are the seeds of the dictatorship of the bourgeoisie. Locke, the egalitarian thinker who brilliantly deployed his work ethic to advance a radical pro-worker agenda for most of his life, ultimately turned the work ethic against the most vulnerable workers near the end of his life. The trajectory of Locke's mature thought, starting with such bright promise and ending in moral disaster, would turn out to be the trajectory of conservative thinking about the work ethic. As we shall see in the next two chapters, its advocates were to prove themselves ready to use brutal methods to impart virtue to others, all the while profiting mightily from the arrangement.

3 HOW CONSERVATIVES HIJACKED THE WORK ETHIC AND TURNED IT AGAINST WORKERS

Developments in the Work Ethic in the Late Eighteenth Century

A century after Locke's mature political writings, controversy over policy toward the working classes came roaring back. This was the occasion for thinkers to develop both sides of the work ethic in light of changing economic and cultural conditions. One side, represented by Adam Smith and more radical thinkers including assorted Ricardian socialists, Marquis de Condorcet, Thomas Paine, John Stuart Mill, and Marx, advanced the progressive, pro-worker dimensions of the work ethic that Locke had so skillfully promoted in most of his mature writing. The other side, led by Joseph Priestley, Jeremy Bentham, Thomas Malthus, Edmund Burke, William Paley, Richard Whately, and Nassau Senior, followed the spirit of Locke's suspicious and stinting poor-law reform proposal. This split reflected two large changes in British society near the turn of the nineteenth century: a much sharper division between workers and capitalists caused by the Industrial Revolution, and increasing secularization.

The Industrial Revolution dramatically increased the prevalence of wage labor among workers. In classical economics, wage laborers are a class of workers who satisfy four conditions. (1) They don't own or have rights of access to capital (land, natural resources, tools, machinery, etc.), and don't have rights to capital income. Their only productive asset is their own labor. (2) To make a living, they depend on selling their labor power to an employer in return for a wage. (3) They are formally free to change employers and reject any employment contract offered to them. (4) They live in households distinct from their employer. In the nineteenth century, wage workers became the "standard" workers in the models of political economists. This was not so in seventeenth-century England (see Chapter 2). For the Puritans, as for Locke, model workers were crafts manufacturers, yeoman farmers, and those engaged in merchant trades. Many such workers either owned at least some of their own capital, had rights of access to it, or had rights to capital income in lieu of wages. "Servants," who were overwhelmingly unmarried workers from their teens to their mid-twenties, typically lacked certain freedoms wage workers took for granted: most lived in their employer's household, under their domestic authority, or were indentured. During the eighteenth century, Parliamentary enclosures wiped out most remaining copyholders. The Industrial Revolution brought about dramatic change in productive organization. The factory system replaced master craftsmen, journeymen, and cottage industry workers with wage workers. It also gave rise to a class of managerial capitalists who focused on disciplining workers to maximize their work effort per unit of wages,[1] and a class of rentier capitalists who joined the large landowners in living off their capital income.

This widening of class divisions led to a division in perspectives over the work ethic. The master craftsmen and yeoman farmers of the seventeenth century functioned both as manual workers and as industrious capital owners. The Puritans' and Locke's work ethic exalted them in both these capacities, relative to idle landlords, scheming financial speculators, and other predatory capitalists. Their work ethic entitled them to a decent standard of living, pride in their work, and autonomy over how they conducted themselves at work, and over its pace and timing. Hence, in satisfying the duties of the work ethic, they also counted on reaping its rewards. As the Industrial Revolution proceeded, wage workers and their advocates developed the work ethic to support institutional innovations – notably including social insurance, workers' cooperatives, and labor unions – to enable wage workers to enjoy comparable rewards in the industrial system that the work ethic promised their preindustrial predecessors.

Capitalists, whether managerial or rentier, developed the work ethic in the harsh, suspicious, and stinting direction presaged by Locke's version of poor-law reform. They stressed discipline, frugality, and asceticism for workers, while reaping the lion's share of productivity gains for themselves in their capacity as capital owners. In a period known as "Engels's Pause," real wages stagnated from 1770 to 1840, even as GDP per worker grew and capitalists enjoyed increasing luxury and leisure.[2]

One might think this is not consistent with the fundamental aspirations of the work ethic. Managers and entrepreneurs could lay a legitimate claim to exemplifying the work ethic. But how could lazy landlords, speculators, and predatory capitalists do so? And how could increasingly disciplined and productive wage workers be denied its benefits? In its Puritan origins, the work ethic was class neutral. Rich and poor alike were held accountable to its demands, deemed capable of fulfilling them, and to be honored for doing so, whatever their station in life. Locke followed this universal logic.[3] He condemned the idle and predatory rich as well as able-bodied beggars. He praised improving landlords as well as industrious workers. I shall argue that, during the Industrial Revolution, the upper-class targets of Puritan critique *hijacked* the work ethic and turned it into an instrument of class warfare against workers. Now only workers were held to its demands. Not just the idle rentiers but the busy schemers who profited from business plans that extract value from others cast themselves as heroes of the work ethic, and the poor as the only scoundrels.

To understand how this hijacking happened, we must also take account of the secularization of the work ethic. Already by the time of the *Second Treatise*, appeals to the Bible in English political thought were waning.[4] Although theological premises are foundational to Locke's system, the ratio of secular moral reasoning to scriptural reasoning in the *Second Treatise* is very high compared to that of Baxter's *Christian Directory*, written just 25 years earlier. A half-century after the *Second Treatise*, Benjamin Franklin presented a virtually complete secularized version of the work ethic. Weber took Franklin to be a paragon of this ideology. In Franklin's thinking, the rationale for the work ethic is not theological but utilitarian. The individual's motive to practice it is entirely prudential and focused on this-worldly goods.[5]

While the motive of accumulation came to dominate capitalist societies by the time Weber wrote *The Protestant Ethic*, we should not suppose that secular motives had already decisively taken over religious ones among practitioners of the work ethic in Franklin's day.

Methodism, a popular eighteenth-century evangelical movement within the Church of England that became its own denomination, preached the work ethic to its followers along with the Social Gospel. It is a late version of Puritanism that spread in the US during the First and Second Great Awakenings. It simultaneously inspired the pious practice of the work ethic and powerful progressive movements, including abolitionism.

Although Franklin was an early secularizer, we also should not suppose that the subsequent development of the work ethic lay entirely in the hands of secular thinkers. This was especially true for those who developed the conservative work ethic. Priestley, besides being a famous chemist and political economist, was a Dissenting minister. Malthus was a curate in the Church of England. Paley held various distinguished offices in the Church of England. Whately was Church of Ireland Archbishop of Dublin. Their natural theologies deeply influenced their utilitarian conclusions. I shall argue below that even Bentham, an atheist, expressed fundamentally Puritan attitudes in his judgments of utility.[6]

Secularization entailed a commitment to calculate the utilities realized by the work ethic and public policies designed to promote it in terms of goods and bads experienced on earth, rather than in the next life. The quest for leisure and luxury was no longer considered sinful. Whether it was bad depended entirely on the earthly consequences. Secularized conservative work-ethic theorists promoted the quest for luxury and conspicuous consumption as motives for workers to practice the work ethic. Progressive work-ethic theorists argued that, once society reaches a level of productivity sufficient to end poverty, policy should favor workers' leisure over relentless toil, freeing workers to spend their time as they please and participate in the national culture. Yet, while the surface logic of the secularized work ethic was this-worldly, background theological assumptions and attitudes often continued to influence how thinkers calculated the utilities.

In the hands of advocates of the conservative work ethic, secularization also shifted the locus of individualism from the next world to this world. Now, each individual was personally responsible not just for their own salvation, but for their fate on earth. Conservatives imagined that the laws of the unregulated market were God's natural laws, meting out to each individual their just earthly rewards in accordance with their virtue in fulfilling the demands of the work ethic. Hence, any collective "interference" with those laws was unjust and would lead to earthly punishment. One could infer someone's virtue from their wealth prior to any state redistribution. Thus, the rich are presumptively carrying out the demands of the work ethic; the poor are viciously violating them. To justify this in utilitarian terms, conservatives supposed that any redistribution of income and wealth would lead to bad overall consequences, primarily by corrupting the poor.

This way of thinking made a radical break from Baxter and Locke. Baxter argued that salvation was open to anyone who manifested their faith in God by assiduously following the work ethic. Everyone was equally subject to the demands of the work ethic, and equally eligible to fulfill its demands, *regardless of their station in life.* The logic of this position, which Baxter approached and Locke embraced, is that each individual is therefore personally responsible for their own salvation. In this life, however, a logic of collective responsibility for everyone's well-being reigns. The idea of a calling reflects God's benevolence in establishing a division of labor whereby everyone promotes the welfare of the entire community in performing the specialized role to which God has called them. Sanderson argued that just as each part of a clock's mechanism, however small, plays an essential role in keeping time, each worker, however lowly, fulfills an essential function in the flourishing of the community. In recognizing this fact, we recognize that we all must take care of one another, since the whole point of the division of labor is to enable us to do so effectively. Hence, as Baxter insisted, all workers are entitled to fair and living wages, and the rich must provide for the poor. Locke retains this communitarian perspective in insisting that society's laws and policies provide for "the good of every particular member of that society."[7] The duty of charity is strict, and poor workers are entitled to demand it. From this perspective, it is absurd to suppose that one's station in life reflects one's virtue or commitment to the work ethic. It merely reflects the social structural necessity of a division of labor. Here on earth everyone is their brother's keeper.

From the conservative perspective, however, poverty reflected an individual's failure to fulfill the demands of the work ethic. Society is at fault solely in establishing institutions that violate natural law in promoting vice through provisions such as the Poor Law. Conservatives agreed that the Poor Law must therefore either be abolished or radically reformed. If poverty is caused by the vice of the poor, the remedy for poverty must be to force the poor to practice virtue, to live up to the demands of the work ethic. Conservatives differed somewhat on which virtue was most necessary for the poor to practice. Priestley focused on frugality, Bentham on industry, Malthus on chastity, Paley on contentment (understood as the opposite of covetous envy of the rich). Thus, Priestley hoped to convert poor workers into virtuous bourgeois citizens through a legally mandated individual savings plan. Bentham favored a workfare system that turned the working poor into imprisoned debt peons of capitalist entrepreneurs. Malthus advocated leaving the poor to starvation, disease, and destitution, but offered them the hope that they could rescue themselves by postponing marriage and children. Burke and Whately agreed with Malthus, but attempted to put a liberaltory paternalist veneer on their view.[8] Uniting them all was the view that coercion was necessary to induce ordinary workers to practice the work ethic.

Priestley: The Cult of Independence

The path to secularization running from Baxter through Locke to Priestley amounted to a gradual relaxation of the demands of asceticism on the prosperous. Baxter takes a strictly instrumental view of the enjoyment of worldly goods: we should value them as God's gift to humanity, to be used to promote general human flourishing, not individual self-indulgence. Covetousness is strictly prohibited. Wealth must be given away to support public works and the poor.

One step down the path of secularization, Locke readily allows that workers are entitled to enjoy without guilt the rewards of their "honest industry" including the "comfort" and "conveniences of life." At the same time he rails against the luxury spending of the idle rich, which is ruining the nation by wasting money on fancy foreign imports. This money would be better dedicated to supporting industry and trade. While consumption in excess of need is no longer a sin, it remains confined to the modest proportions that are consistent with the good of society. Moreover, Locke also insists that the poor are entitled to charity. The duty of the able-bodied poor to work is equally shared by the rich. For the poor, that duty is matched with a right to a job with a subsistence wage, enforced by the state on private employers. Yet a harsh cast of mind toward the poor has crept in, a suspicion that they and even their children don't want to work and must be forced to do so.

Almost fully down the path of secularization, we find great chemist, Dissenter, and liberal political economist Joseph Priestley, writing a century after Locke. Priestley praises luxury. Individuals may harmlessly gratify their taste for luxury, as long as they can afford it. The quest for luxury is good, as a spur to industry. "The vanity of the French makes them industrious."[9] "Every individual wishes to rise above his neighbor."[10] A good society gives free play to this spirit of competitive acquisition by affording equal opportunities for all to rise through their industry.[11] The rich, provided they are educated in virtue, "are the greatest honour to human nature, and the greatest blessing to human societies."[12] Unlike Baxter and Locke, Priestley does not worry that wealth will tempt the rich into idleness. Rather, the danger is that they will hire too many servants, who while away *their* days in idleness, when their labor would be far more productive if otherwise employed.[13]

According to Priestley, the dangers of idleness are concentrated among the poor. (Baxter disagrees: the *rich* are especially prone to sloth, except for beggars, who are only "the *second* rank of idle persons in the land."[14]). State-mandated charity – the Poor Law – is to blame. Poor relief encourages idleness, profligacy, and lack of foresight among the poor.[15] It has "debased the very nature of man" and "defeated the purposes of providence," by freeing poor men to abandon their families and spend their wages on alcohol.[16] Where Baxter and Locke insist that charity is an obligation, Priestley explicitly contrasts charity, which must be voluntary, to obligation.[17] To spur industry, frugality, and foresight among the poor, state-run charity must be abolished. This would have the welcome side-effect of relieving the deserving and honorable rich from having to pay poor rates.

Priestley, however, does not believe that abolishing poor relief is sufficient to induce the poor to follow the work ethic. For the poor, lacking any realistic prospect of getting more, are satisfied with bare subsistence. So they quit work as soon as they earn enough to cover their immediate expenses.[18] To spur them to adopt the work ethic, they need a realistic hope of improving their condition. This is impossible without property. Priestley's solution is a state-mandated savings program, under which the working poor pay a wage tax saved in an individual account. Ultimately these savings are used to purchase an annuity that, at a specified age, will pay the individual an annual sum for the rest of their lives. Capital income will enable them to improve their condition, afford a little luxury, and thereby spur their industry. Under this individual mandatory savings plan, "all the poor" will "eventually provide for themselves."[19] Although the plan limits the liberty of the poor, it is just, because it makes "the idle and thoughtless ... do for themselves what the industrious and thoughtful are now compelled to do for them."[20] Thus, a combination of economic necessity and mandated savings will force the poor to adopt the work ethic. That will make them as virtuous as the bourgeoisie – by making them bourgeois.

Priestley's secular version of the work ethic promises three benefits for workers who follow it. First, workers will enjoy a dignified status. "[T]hey will feel a sense of *independence* and of *dignity* " arising from his plan.[21] Second, they will enjoy the fruits of their labors. Indeed, Priestley hopes that secularization, having removed all moral limits on material gratification, will encourage workers to engage in conspicuous consumption: they will "vie with their neighbors in acquiring every thing which is comfortable and reputable to them."[22] Third, they will be able to enjoy a leisured and comfortable retirement. The secularization of the work ethic pulls the saints' rest from the next life into this one. On top of his annuity plan, Priestley also proposes a system of public education for workers, which he believes will further motivate workers to adopt the work ethic, and enhance their sense of honor, thereby reducing the crime rate.[23]

It sounds like a good deal for workers, compared to their condition at the time. Yet Priestley's secularization of the work ethic contains a contradiction. Priestley recognizes that, in fact, the workers support the owners of capital and not the other way around: "[T]he labour of the husbandman, or the manufacturer, is the only source of all the gain and property in any country, even that of the merchant or the gentleman." So "in reality," even under the Poor Law, "it is their own labour that, more circuitously and ineffectually, now maintains them," although in a "wretched and dependent state."[24] Poor relief was funded by local taxes on the occupants of land, in proportion to its rental value. Locke had argued, and many in Priestley's day agreed, that the incidence of this tax fell on the landowner, even if it was paid by the leaseholder.[25] But, as Locke insists and Priestley acknowledges, the value of land depends on the workers. It would only acknowledge reality, and not in any sense reduce workers to a state of shameful dependence, to fund workers' retirement, along with social insurance against disability, sickness, and death of providers, with taxes on land, or on capital more generally.

In shifting provision for poor workers from taxes on capital to taxes on labor, Priestley's plan perversely turns the work ethic against poor workers, in four ways. First, it limits the scope of application of the work ethic to the working class alone. In contrast to Locke and Baxter, who insist that the rich also work, Priestley lets the idle rich off the hook. "Men will always live without labour, or upon the labour of others, if they can," he complains – while limiting his complaint just to those on poor relief.[26] This is despite his acknowledgment that workers are impoverished in part due to the fact that some of the fruits of their labor support the owners of capital.

Second, it places unjust conditions on the dignity of labor: only the supposedly "self-sufficient" workers are entitled to this dignity. This condition demeans not just the poor overall, but the nonmarket domestic work of women in general, notwithstanding its importance for sustaining families and children. By contrast, Baxter tells the poor that God values their work "the more, by how much the meaner work thou stoopest to at his command."[27] He regards women's unpaid childrearing labor, particularly their work "bringing up children for God" as an honorable calling in service to God.[28] When he considers which women were failing to take up this calling, he singles out the daughters of the gentry, who left childrearing and domestic tasks to servants so they could live in leisure.[29]

Third, in shifting the financing for support of the poor from taxes on capital to taxes on labor, he in effect lets passive capital owners take the first cut of the distributive pie, making it all the more difficult for workers to save for themselves. Finally, Priestley's individualistic cult of "independence," manifested in his insistence that poor relief be abolished and workers' taxes be kept in separate privately invested accounts, undermines the insurance aspects of the Poor Law. Numerous calamities regularly threw working-class people into destitution, including sickness, disability, death of a household wage worker, crop failure, and recessions leading to involuntary unemployment. These were not the workers' fault. Nor were they able to self-insure against them. Even their maximum feasible savings at any given time would be quickly exhausted by a large-enough catastrophe. Multiple small misfortunes, of the sort any poor person would likely encounter, would also drain the savings and accumulated interest needed for old age.

Only some kind of socialization of risk could shelter individuals, other than the very wealthy, from the diverse causes of blameless misfortune. The Poor Law, admittedly, did not do a great job of this. But it did a better job of pooling risks than personal savings could ever do for the vast majority of wage laborers. At the same time Priestley was writing, Thomas Paine and Marquis de Condorcet advanced proposals for comprehensive social insurance schemes – in Paine's case, by means of estate taxes, along with universal stakeholder grants for young adults.[30] They developed the work ethic in a progressive direction (see Chapter 8).

Priestley, however, insists on *individual* savings plans, in line with his abhorrence of any notion of collective responsibility for taking care of each other. His ideal of individual independence conflates at least three ideas: (1) the political condition of not being subordinate to another's will; (2) the moral-psychological condition of lacking initiative and self-reliance, of expecting others to do what one can do for oneself; and (3) the economic condition of being independently wealthy – of not having to rely on work, poor relief, or private charity for one's subsistence.[31] In fact, to be independently wealthy is precisely a condition in which one enjoys leisure by relying on others to do what one could do for oneself. That was why the original work ethic condemned the idle rich. For Priestley, however, because the rich buy their leisure by using their property income to pay hirelings to serve them, they are independent in the first sense of commanding others, rather than being commanded. Yet wage laborers had so little left to help themselves precisely because, on his own analysis, they had to spend their time and energy propping up the purported independence of property owners before they could help themselves. Far from failing to take responsibility for themselves, poor workers were assigned responsibilities to take care of the rich as well as their own needs, without sufficient resources to do both. William Hazlitt made the same complaint about Malthus's call to end poor relief. Has not the increase in spending on poor relief "been occasioned by the additional exorbitant demands, which have been made upon the poor and industrious, which without some assistance from the public they could not possibly have answered?"[32] Ricardian socialists concurred (see Chapter 5). The moral accounting that assigns responsibilities to individuals without regard – and even in *inverse proportion* – to the means they have to fulfill them remains a touchstone of conservative thought to the present day.

Priestley rightly recognized the importance of workers' access to capital as a condition of securing the promise of the work ethic for workers. Yet he represents a first step in a line of thought that turned the secularized work ethic against workers. Conservatives aimed to abolish workers' rights to income from capital not purchased through their own savings. These were rights they otherwise had through welfare financed by taxes on land, or could have through social insurance financed by estate taxes. The right to capital not created by one's labor, or purchased with the fruits of one's labor, and to income not ultimately derived from one's labor, was a privilege reserved for passive owners of capital, their heirs, and assorted schemers. In whichever way they develop it, the conservative version of the work ethic consistently places the interests of capital ahead that of workers. It thereby subjects many workers to poverty, precarity, and tyranny. Now only some must work to earn their bread, all for the sake of maximizing the share of income and wealth claimed by passive or merely extractive capital owners.

Bentham: The Dictatorship of the Bourgeoisie

Boots Riley, in his film *Sorry to Bother You* (2018), portrays a company that calls itself "Worry Free." Its commercials promise poor workers a job that will support their families in comfort for the rest of their lives. The trick is that they must sign a contract binding themselves to drudgery in company-operated prisons, where they are consigned to live and labor for the rest of their lives. I will show in Chapter 9 that Riley's depiction of what some contemporary capitalist businesses do is less hyperbolic than one would wish. His fantasy has historical roots. For Bentham seriously advanced a similar idea two centuries ago, promising "tranquility" to workers who took it up.

Michel Foucault remade Bentham's reputation by highlighting his panopticon prison design. Foucault also noted Bentham's passing claim, in the work introducing the panopticon, that its principles are equally applicable to the factory, school, hospital, insane asylum, and poorhouse.[33] Hence it is surprising that Foucault did not cite Bentham's *Pauper Management Improved*, in which he comprehensively described and defended the extension of his prison plan to cover the working poor, along with orphans, the aged, and the disabled. Bentham was so enthusiastic about *Pauper Management Improved* that he reprinted it twice after its initial 1798 publication, and stood by it for the rest of his career.[34] Foucault represents the panopticon as embodying a technology based on, and generating, a new type of scientific knowledge of human behavior. Bentham represents his scheme likewise. The Protestant work ethic also profoundly influenced Bentham's plan by comprehensively tilting his estimates of utilities. I don't claim that Bentham, an atheist, would have recognized this fact. But without empirical measures of utility, all utilitarians have to go on are their own ethical intuitions, which are feelings they have on imagining various states of the world. I shall argue that Bentham's claims on behalf of the utility of his scheme make no sense other than as expressions of unacknowledged nonutilitarian normative attitudes – *Puritan* attitudes – toward work, leisure, and discipline.

Bentham styles his plan as "a Romance – the Utopia," which he hopes will be enacted into law.[35] It advances two ideas familiar in neoliberal thought today: (1) outsourcing state functions to private, for-profit enterprises, and (2) punitive workfare for the poor.[36] It addresses the problem as Bentham sees it: that paupers, including their children, the insane, and the disabled, are a net burden on society, being supported by provisions of the Poor Law, financed by taxes. The solution is to force paupers to work, earning their own way.

Publicly operated workhouses designed to instill the work ethic in the poor had long existed in England, and proliferated over the course of the eighteenth century. Nearly 2,000 workhouses were operating in England by 1777.[37] But they were never able to cover their expenses by selling what their inmates produced. They were supported by tax revenues. Bentham blamed this inefficiency on the lack of incentives and business acumen of government managers. Let a private, for-profit enterprise put the poor to work. The managers' incentives can be aligned with the public interest by a contract that allows them to pocket the difference between the costs of maintaining the poor and the value of their production. Private enterprise would minimize the costs of maintenance and maximize the profits "extracted from [paupers'] labour," to the relief of the taxpaying public, which would now receive a share of the profits.[38]

The poor themselves would be relieved through the provision of subsistence and medical care.[39] They would receive training in disciplined labor, acquiring a work ethic by habituation and incentives. "Man must be new made, before [providence] can be made universal."[40]

Bentham proposes that a single for-profit company, the National Charity Company, have exclusive responsibility for maintaining paupers, and a monopoly on their labor. The Company would build

500 panopticons situated 10⅔ miles apart across England and Wales. Each would house 2,000 paupers, mostly in prison cells.[41] It would be required to accept all paupers who voluntarily entered. More importantly, it would be authorized to seize and imprison "all persons, able-bodied or otherwise" caught begging or without visible legitimate means of support, including orphans, sex workers, fortune tellers, debtors, delinquents, and numerous other categories of individuals, whom Bentham classifies in a typology of 33 classes.[42] Employers, husbands, and fathers could respectively force their lazy servants, unfaithful wives, or insolent children into a panopticon to reform them.[43] Once imprisoned, paupers would be forced to work until they paid off the cost of their maintenance. They would be entitled to continue to work there as long as they wished.[44]

In fact, Bentham imagines that paupers would be forced to work off considerably more than the costs of their maintenance. The Company's "end in view" is "the extraction of labour, to as great a value as may be."[45] He calculates that able-bodied men would generate 300 percent profits, able-bodied women, 200 percent. But the greatest profits of all would come from child labor.[46] Apprentices "constitute the chief basis of the Company's profit-seeking arrangements."[47] The Company could extract high effort from all workers by enticing them to compete for prizes awarded only to the most productive. The prizes themselves need cost the Company nothing. They could consist in such things as getting first place in line for meals.[48]

The profit motive would induce Company managers to test ways to minimize the cost of maintaining its inmates. It should provide the cheapest quality food consistent with survival. Managers should especially experiment on children, to see how little food they could be fed without dying or falling ill. They should record their findings for use by other caretakers.[49] According to Bentham's "earn-first principle," inmates would be denied a meal until they performed their assigned task.[50] This principle echoes the Puritans' Biblical refrain, "if any would not work, neither should he eat." Men could be encouraged to save their wages by eating only oatmeal and potatoes.[51] Inmates would wear wooden clogs (not leather shoes), and uniforms patched together from cast-off clothing.[52] The stigmatizing implications of this attire are evident. Just 20 years before, Adam Smith observed that "[t]he poorest creditable person of either sex would be ashamed to appear in public" without leather shoes and a linen shirt. Others would infer from the lack of such items "that disgraceful degree of poverty, which, it is presumed, no body can well fall into without extreme bad conduct."[53]

Inmates would enjoy no privacy. In the panopticon architecture, paupers would be confined to cells arrayed in an annulus visible to supervisors in a central tower. They would be subject to continuous surveillance to ensure good behavior.[54] Supervisors, too, would be subject to comprehensive surveillance by members of the public, who would be free to inspect the panopticon's operations and account books. Public inspection would provide appropriate incentives to managers not to abuse the inmates or let them die.[55] Disinterested humanity is an illusion. Only incentives will motivate people to maximize utility. Hence caretakers would be fined for deaths of inmates, and awarded bonuses for minimizing death rates.[56]

Polka-dot panopticons distributed across the landscape, housing imprisoned paupers forced to work for maximum profit to Company managers: this mad totalitarian vision, which Bentham enthusiastically calls his "romance," amounts to the fullest expression of the dictatorship of the bourgeoisie.[57] He represents his vision as a purely scientific application of utilitarianism. Yet the background normative assumptions of the conservative work ethic, including a legacy of characteristically Puritan attitudes, saturate his plan. "Habits of *industry*" are to be "maintained without relaxation."[58] Nothing may be wasted. The Company director must swear an oath "to adhere, with unremitting strictness, to ... principles of economy."[59] As far as possible, materials should have more than one use.[60] Beds double as tables. Inmates are to be assigned "the same room for all purposes – work, meals, and sleep."[61] Bentham cannot tolerate spontaneous motions not put to any further purpose. Even the feeble can have their tremors put to work by making them rock infants' cribs.[62] "Not the motion of a finger – not a step – not a wink – not a whisper – but might be turned to account, in the way of profit." "Every *fragment* of ability, however minute" of every inmate, even the bedridden and the insane, must be put to work.[63] Following the Puritans' ascetic rejection of frivolous pleasures as a waste of time, Bentham insists that "no portion of time ought to be directed exclusively to the single purpose of comfort." Allowable comforts are only those taken in the course of work, or to enable it.[64] So much for the official utilitarian doctrine that pleasure is the only end in itself. When Bentham thinks of the poor, the only permissible pleasures are those with an instrumental rationale – just as Puritan ascetics such as Baxter preached. In line with Puritans' suspicion of people shifting for themselves without a calling, Bentham calls for irregular workers, such as unlicensed street hawkers, to be forced into panopticons.[65] Like the Puritan advocates of the work ethic and their secular successors, Bentham promotes the goal of maximizing profits, based on hardheaded calculations of objective results.

Puritans were obsessed with keeping "account-books in which sins, temptations, and progress made in grace were entered or tabulated."[66] Bentham similarly insists that the Company keep account books tabulating not only finances but the health, comfort, industry, mortality, and discipline of inmates.[67] John Wesley, the founder of Methodism and a late advocate of the Protestant ethic, delivered a sermon in 1778 in which he famously pronounced that "[c]leanliness is ... next to godliness."[68] Bentham similarly obsesses over provisions to keep the panopticons clean and tidy.[69] As Baxter worries that wealth would tempt people to sin, Bentham worries that high wages for workers would undermine the morality of the "improvident and uncultivated," leading them to "sensual excesses."[70]

Puritans were notably severe and contemptuous of sentimentality. Weber notes that the hero of Bunyan's *Pilgrim's Progress*, the most widely read Puritan book, abandoned his wife and children to seek his own salvation.[71] A life comprehensively driven by the impersonal duty to glorify God doesn't sit very well with sentimental partiality toward loved ones. Bentham was similarly unsentimental. He even revels in his contempt for human feelings about others that resist reduction to cold calculations of their instrumental value. He describes paupers as the "refuse" of the population and "that part of the national live stock which has no feathers to it, and walks upon two legs," equally subject to market valuation as slaves.[72] Orphans are especially valuable to the Company because they have no "natural connections" to anyone else, so can be assigned "without hardship" to any place where their labor would be most useful and the cost of their maintenance minimized.[73] He suggests that poor parents living on their own could profitably hire the Company to educate their children on borrowed tuition. If they can't pay off the debt by the end of the year, the child would be forfeited to the Company, bound to serve it until age 21.[74] Against the objection that it is cruel to separate the poor from their friends and family, and especially hard to separate children from their parents, Bentham coldly observes that the children of the rich share the same lot when their parents send them to boarding school.[75]

One might plead that all of this could be made consistent with utilitarianism, if one inserts certain empirical assumptions about how the utilities work out. But this is the weakness rather than the strength of utilitarianism. It can deliver any conclusions one wants with the "right" utility assumptions. In Bentham's case, these are massively implausible. He imagines that paupers need only their minimal physiological needs served. He doesn't count the massive suffering entailed by the fact that pauper adults are deprived of dignity, civil rights, freedom, privacy, and opportunities to form friendships and intimate relations with others, nor that children are deprived of loving attachments to parents and siblings. He argues that even when children live in the same panopticon as their father, they should only be permitted to see and not converse with him, except under the supervision of an officer or guards, lest the father corrupt them.[76] He stigmatizes dependent poverty to the extent of effectively criminalizing it, without deducting the disutility of shaming the poor from his utility calculations.

His calculations of profitability make no sense. Bentham imagines that panopticons will be self-sufficient because inmates will grow their own food. This will consume two-thirds of the inmates' labor.[77] Much of the remaining labor would have to be devoted to maintaining the panopticons, sewing and repairing inmates' clothes, and so forth. The more panopticons constitute complete, self-sufficient communities, the less able they are to gain from trade with outsiders. With so little labor available for production for the market, and so many infirm and infant inmates, how could the Company expect profits exceeding 200 percent?[78] If child labor is so profitable, then why are working parents with many children so poor? For their entire history, workhouses were unprofitable, despite the wretched food, clothing, housing, and other goods they provided their inmates. It was always much cheaper for parishes to provide relief with cash. Bentham's fantasies of more efficient business management driven by the profit motive fail to identify significant opportunities either for saving costs or increasing revenues relative to existing workhouses.

Bentham's motivational assumptions are also contradictory. Because disinterested benevolence is an illusion, incentives must be rigged to deliver socially optimal results. This is why panopticon managers must be subject to surveillance by the public. Yet Bentham doesn't explain why members of the public would have incentives to inspect the work of Company managers, nor why they would care if the poor died from starvation, given that the Company would be distributing some of its profits from exploiting pauper labor to taxpayers:

Adam Smith provided further grounds for questioning Bentham's incentive case for outsourcing government functions to for-profit enterprises. Tax farmers, Smith complained, insist on, and receive, "the most sanguinary" tax laws. Unlike the sovereign, whose dynastic "grandeur . . . depends upon the prosperity of his people," the grandeur of the tax farmer depends on extracting wealth from the population even to the ruin of the country, which they not infrequently cause.[79] By parallel reasoning, "farming of the poor," as Bentham called his outsourcing proposal, would come to the ruin of the poor, and of the ratepayer. Bentham sniffed in "Farming Defended" that Smith had "drawn his hobgoblin."[80]

Bentham should have worried more about Smith's blistering critique of the misrule of the East India Company (see Chapter 5). For Bentham modeled his plan for the pauper-farming National Charity Company after the East India Company.[81] The latter was no model of fiscal responsibility. Despite its government-granted monopoly, and its power to extract tax revenues from its colonial subjects, the East India Company faced bankruptcy in 1772 and successfully begged the government to bail it out. Nor did it show much regard for the colonial subjects it was supposed to be uplifting with its rule. Its extortionate tax farming, interference with the grain trade, diversion of tax revenues from domestic investment (e.g., in maintaining irrigation systems) to Britain, and other ruinous policies turned a partial crop failure in Bengal into a famine in 1770.[82] Bentham certainly knew about this, as the Company's role in the famine and its bailout were leading controversies of the day.

Bentham's utility calculations are all the more absurd given his commitment to purely secular reasoning. Baxter could argue that the poor should feel lucky to not be exposed to the sensual temptations to which the rich are exposed, because they thereby avoid sins that could lead to eternal damnation. Bentham wants them to feel lucky just to be alive. We should worry about any moral system that can be so easily gamed through calculations founded on ruthless instrumentalization of the people whose lives are at stake. Yet there is no practical way to objectively constrain utility assumptions so as to exclude nonutilitarian moral intuitions.[83]

There is a deeper contradiction in Bentham's calculations. Utilitarianism is supposed to be an egalitarian moral system: everyone to count for one, nobody for more than one. Or, more precisely: every util counts exactly the same, whether enjoyed by the rich and powerful, or the poor and downtrodden. Since, in any hierarchical system, those at the bottom of the pyramid are vastly more numerous than those at the top, utilitarianism should not only be formally egalitarian, but move societies toward substantively more egalitarian outcomes. Moreover, Bentham's refusal to grant distinctions between higher and lower pleasures was explicitly designed to poke holes in the pretenses of the privileged that their pleasures should count for more: "Prejudice apart, the game of push-pin is of equal value with the arts and sciences of music and poetry."[84] Bentham also gleefully levels the ranks with his pen:

> Never is the day labourer, never is the helpless pauper, an object of contempt to me: I can not say the same thing of the purse-proud aristocrat: I can not say the same thing of the ancestry-proud aristocrat: I can not say the same thing of the official bloodsucker: I can not say the same thing of the man covered with the tokens of factitious honor: least of all can I say the same of a King.[85]

Yet it is impossible to read Bentham's calculus of utilities in *Pauper Management Improved* as anything other than contemptuous of the poor. *His* calculus of their utilities, not theirs, are all that counts. His leveling of pleasures is a double-edged sword. While it cuts down the pretenses of the rich and powerful to be living more valuable lives, it also rationalizes the elimination of pleasures beyond bare physical comforts from the lives of the poor. Bentham shares with Locke an epistemology of suspicion about the poor. He claims that panopticon agents may infer with "perfect certainty" that anyone without property or a job must be a criminal, who may therefore be forced into a panopticon.[86] In line with Priestley, it doesn't cross his mind that passive owners of property, extracting income produced by others, are a burden on society, or that the Poor Law distributed unearned rents more fairly. His work ethic applies only to those who cannot live idly off their property. Bentham can barely stand the idea that the poor might enjoy anything they have not earned through hard labor. If those living outside the panopticons suffer accident or hardship, they should get loans, which keep up "the spirit of industry and frugality," not gifts, which undermine the work ethic.[87] But he also can't stand the idea that their panopticon masters might not profit from even the most minute exertions of their slaves. Who are the parasites here?

Malthus: Chastity and Personal Responsibility Will Set the Poor Free

Thomas Malthus is best known for his pessimistic population theory. In the first edition of his best-selling *Essay on the Principle of Population* (1798), Malthus argues that humanity is doomed to permanent misery, because ordinary workers will breed like rabbits, without foresight or self-restraint, as soon as they get access to food above subsistence. They will thereby rapidly exceed the available food supply, which cannot grow as fast. Famine, disease, and competitive warfare over scarce resources – the positive checks on population growth – will inevitably follow, bringing the population back to subsistence level. Hence there is no possible "society, all the members of which, should live in ease, happiness, and comparative leisure; and feel no anxiety about providing the means of subsistence for themselves and families."[88]

Malthus's purpose in writing the first edition of *Principle of Population* was to quench the revolutionary sentiments of England's working classes, which were being aroused by the French Revolution and radical sympathizers such as William Godwin.[89] He is telling the rabble to settle down because they are already living in the best of all possible worlds. He also argues that England's Poor Law was self-defeating. Covering the gap between what the working classes can earn and what they need to survive only leads the poor to have *more* children who suffer destitution. Poor Laws thus "spread the general evil over a much larger surface."[90] "No possible contributions or sacrifices of the rich ... could for any time prevent the recurrence of distress among the lower members of society."[91] So the system of poverty relief should be abolished.[92]

It is one of the great ironies of intellectual history that Malthus may have been basically right about populations living at subsistence until the time he published his theory.[93] Yet the empirical basis for Malthus's attacks on the Poor Law was weak. England was in his day the only country in Europe that recognized the duty to provide for the poor as a national obligation. It had done so since the Tudor era.

Malthus concedes that England's poor were significantly better off than the poor in any other European country.[94] To explain away this embarrassment, he pleads that England has other advantages that counteract the purportedly bad effects of the Poor Law. Even in the first edition of *Principle of Population* he argues that all ranks of English society delay marriage until they can afford to raise children at their accustomed standard of living – a practice he also acknowledged to be prevalent in Western Europe. He also claims that cleanliness, another virtue of the work ethic, had ended epidemics in London.[95]

Perhaps, then, the working classes were not doomed to misery after all. Malthus develops this happier thought in subsequent editions of the *Principle of Population*, concluding in the sixth, published in 1826.[96] By following the work ethic – working hard, saving for the future, and above all, practicing ascetic self-denial in delaying sex and marriage until they were financially able to raise their children – the poor could rescue themselves from misery. If it were true, however, that the poor could avoid demographic self-defeat by following the work ethic – what Malthus called the "preventive checks" on population – then why not give them an additional boost by providing poor relief?

Malthus's answer to this question set the terms of virtually all subsequent conservative critiques of the welfare state: he blames poor relief for creating a culture of poverty. On Malthus's view, giving the poor goods that they haven't earned through their own hard work corrupts them by rewarding vice – that is, dispositions opposed to the work ethic. The Poor Law gives the poor incentives to quit work, fail to save for the future, waste their wages on alcohol, indulge in lust and thereby have children they are unable to support, and abandon their wives and children. Poor relief demoralizes workers by undermining their spirit of independence and indulging their sloth and lack of initiative.[97] The culture of poverty spreads misery by discouraging the virtues that enable people to escape poverty and take responsibility for themselves and their families.

Malthus's answer is notable for how little it depends on his population theory. It is true that he also claims that poverty relief will lead the poor to have more children until they are driven back to subsistence, because they exercise no self-restraint. Yet in an 1807 appendix to *Principle of Population* he concedes that the effect of the Poor Law on population was unclear.[98] What really drives his thinking is his commitment to the work ethic. The same point applies to his other criticisms of the Poor Law. Poor relief is unjust, because it puts the interests of the undeserving dependent poor ahead of the worthy, hard-working, independent poor. Inefficient workhouse production, subsidized by the state and run by incompetent government officials, unfairly competes with the production of more industrious and worthy independent workers, throwing them into poverty and dependence.[99] Moreover, the taxes paid to support poor relief, although assessed on occupants of the land (mostly farmers, whether they owned or leased), ultimately come at the expense of the industrious working classes.[100] In an apparent double-counting of the incidence of poor rates, Malthus also argues that "the landed interest" needs relief from poor rates, echoing the common complaint of the time that the rates forced rents down.[101] They threaten the "perfect security" of private property that is essential to promote "prudential habits."[102] Never mind that Parliament had been *attacking* security of property for the poor through coercive enclosures since 1750. In Malthus's system, it appears, only the rich are entitled to security of their property.

Malthus is on stronger ground in complaining that poor relief tyrannized over the dependent poor themselves. Relief was tied to settlement in one's birthplace, and to the oppressive meddling and discrimination of overseers of the poor and local magistrates, who exercised discretion over who would get relief and on what terms.[103] In contrast to Bentham, Malthus does think the liberty of the poor counts for something.

Malthus argues that the solution to these problems is the abolition of legally instituted poor relief.[104] The obligation to charity, a core duty of the original Puritan work ethic, which Locke raised to an entitlement of the poor, must be abandoned. In later editions, Malthus advocates a very gradual abolition, so as not to cast those who had grown dependent on it into starvation.[105] Ending poor relief will liberate the poor from its tyranny so they can take responsibility for themselves. He also cautions against liberal and indiscriminate private charity. The poor must never feel assured that they can count on private charity lest it corrupt them. Dependent poverty must be stigmatized.[106]

Wouldn't ending poor relief throw future generations of poor workers into desperate poverty? Malthus replies that the remedy for poverty lies entirely in the decisions of the poor themselves. The sole effective means of avoiding poverty is for the poor to practice chastity – to delay sex, marriage, and childbearing until they can afford to support their children on what they can earn. Collectively, this will restrict the growth of the labor supply below the growth in food production, enabling the working classes to enjoy higher real wages.[107]

Malthus also sees such "moral restraint" as an effective *individual* strategy for avoiding poverty, which applies independently of the aggregate effects of the population principle. By practicing the virtue of chastity, "it is in the power of *each individual* to avoid all the evil consequences to himself and society resulting from the principle of population."[108] No institutional changes, other than ending poor relief, and no cooperation of others, is necessary for a poor worker to avoid his and his family's misery.[109] He doesn't explain how an individual chaste poor worker could avoid the depression of wages below subsistence due to *others'* imprudent reproduction. Nor does he explain how practicing individual chastity, frugality, and industry could protect workers from the faultless disasters that so frequently struck them. These include disasters due to the economic system itself, such as industrial accidents, sickness from air and water pollution, and economic recessions. Rather, he blames the victim. "Diseases ... [are] indications that we have offended against some of the laws of nature."[110] The poor have only themselves to blame for their misery.[111]

Malthus argues that the poor must live in awareness of their precarity in order to acquire virtue. Hence, the insurance functions of the Poor Law are corrupting. The poor would save rather than dissipate their income on pleasures if they knew they could not depend on poor relief in case of accidents or the bankruptcy of their employer.[112] Men waste their wages on ale because they know their wives and children can depend on poor relief.[113] Malthus is certain that precarity is justified from a utilitarian point of view. Yes, some children will die if they can only rely on their parents for support, and their parents desert them. But this is no great loss: "The infant is, comparatively speaking, of little value to the society, as others will immediately supply its place." Moreover, if "the man were convinced that the woman and the child depended solely upon him for support, I scarcely believe that there are ten men breathing so atrocious as to desert them."[114] Children must be vulnerable to suffering, that their fathers may be spurred to virtue.

But what of the fact that children are innocents? Surely they do not deserve to suffer for their father's vices! Malthus replies that it is a "law of nature," instituted by God, that children are affected, for good or ill, by their parents' conduct. God is not unjust for "visit[ing] the sins of the father upon the children." For if this were not so, many more fathers would fail to fulfill their family responsibilities.[115] The harsh consequences visited on children are for the greater aggregate good.

Here we arrive at the crux of the matter. Malthus's utility calculations, like Bentham's, are driven by background nonutilitarian normative attitudes of the conservative work ethic. Although he presents his theory as empirical science, what really drives him is the need to "vindicate the ways of God to man."[116] The purportedly empirical laws of nature are God's laws. Since God is just and benevolent, somehow these laws must maximize utility, even when they cause suffering, whether to the blameworthy or the innocent. If we interpret the law of population in this light, we will discover what God is telling us to do. Humanity's original sin is "torpor," or sloth – our lack of a work ethic.[117] The misery caused by the fact that we tend to reproduce faster than we can increase food production is God's way of stirring us to adopt the work ethic. Our minds develop, our initiative is spurred, only under the threat of suffering.[118] "The laws of nature say, with St. Paul, 'If a man will not work, neither shall he eat.'"[119] Poor relief – or indeed, social insurance[120] – violates this law of nature, and so must be abolished.

This argument proves more than Malthus wished. It entails that property rights in any means of production other than labor, or held by anyone other than workers themselves, equally well violate this law of nature. For such rights create a class of independently wealthy landlords, who choose not to work to support themselves, because they get all their income from rents. If the threat of misery is needed to spur learning and virtue, shouldn't we think the idle rich, insulated by their property from such threats, are stupid and vicious, and undeserving of property they merely inherited? Locke, with Baxter, Sanderson, and other Puritans, insists that rich and poor alike are properly subject to the *same* moral and legal duties. *All* classes must practice the work ethic. There must be "one rule for rich and poor, for the favourite at court, and the countryman at plough."[121]

For Malthus, the laws of nature, and hence human laws, must be different for rich and poor. For

> [i]t is to the established administration of property, and to the apparently narrow principle of self-love, that we are indebted for all the noblest exertions of human genius, all the finer and

more delicate emotions of the soul, for every thing, indeed, that distinguishes the civilized, from the savage state . . . . In every society that has advanced beyond the savage state, a class of proprietors, and a class of labourers, must necessarily exist."[122]

Here Malthus appeals to the ancient theory that a leisure class, maintained by laborers, is needed to create the great works of the arts and sciences.[123] A class must exist that must depend on its labor alone to survive, for only under the pain of necessity will they be willing to produce more than their own subsistence. They must be held property-less, lest they quit working before producing the surplus needed to support the leisure class.[124] Malthus rejects the possibility that the working classes can be induced to produce a surplus by higher pay. Look at the manufacturers, who complain that "high wages ruin all their workmen."[125]

For this argument to work, there must be innate class differences in human nature. Somehow, the rich must be able to learn and create in leisure, without the threat of misery hanging over them. And only the poor, it now appears, are subject to the original sin of sloth. So they will work and learn only under the threat of misery. But if that were true, then Malthus would have to wish that the working classes will never be able to attain security from their own industry, frugality, and prudence, and never be justly rewarded for exercising virtue, lest they slack off and cause the collapse of civilization.

After the first edition of *Principle of Population*, Malthus offers some hope to them. By following the work ethic, including sexual restraint, the working classes *can* escape poverty and enjoy the just rewards of their toil. Indeed, he observes that they have been prudently postponing childbearing at increasing rates, and expects that improvement to continue.[126] Yet this improvement was happening even while the proportion of workers on poor relief was increasing – a fact that Malthus knew and lamented.

Only by special pleading could the different parts of his system hang together. For his theory to work, free stuff must not be corrupting when it takes the form of passive capital income and inherited property, even while it corrupts when it takes the form of welfare entitlements or social insurance. It is hard to tell the difference. No wonder Malthus implicitly assumed that human nature itself is differentiated by class. Ultimately, the contradictions, empirical inadequacies, and rigged utility calculations needed to vindicate Malthus's preferred social system reflect the difficulties that arise from a moral system that gives different moral laws to the rich and the poor, reserves most of the rewards of the work ethic to those not doing the work, and allocates the burdens to those consigned to work.

Paley: The Virtue of Contentment

The French Revolution inspired thousands in England to organize radical associations, debating societies, and public demonstrations. Working-class people enthusiastically participated. In 1792, shoemaker Thomas Hardy founded the London Corresponding Society, which agitated for universal male suffrage and annual Parliaments. The same year, 5,000 "republicans and Levellers" marched in Sheffield, celebrating revolutionary France's victory over Prussia at the Battle of Valmy. They carried posters depicting Edmund Burke, an opponent of the Revolution, riding a pig, and the Angel of Peace presenting Tom Paine's *Rights of Man* to Britannia.[127] Although such radical activity focused on constitutional demands, Paine and other radicals articulated the links between political and economic power: the propertied classes deployed their monopoly on political power to secure their economic domination at the expense of ordinary workers.

William Paley, Archdeacon of Carlisle, was eager to dissuade workers from such agitation. In 1792 he wrote "Reasons for Contentment," a short pamphlet widely reprinted well into the nineteenth century. He intended to persuade the working classes that they had no reason to envy the rich, because they were actually better off than their superiors. They envied the rich because they imagined that wealth led to a carefree life. In reality, the rich bear heavier burdens than they do. Workers should reject covetousness and count their blessings.

Addressing the working classes, Paley offers what he takes to be helpful advice. The work ethic is a cure for the distress that envy of the rich arouses. If only the working classes kept their noses to their grindstones, they wouldn't have time or mental energy to compare their lot to others.[128] Acknowledging that they *do* have the time and use it to compare, Paley offers them some comparisons he claims are more fair to the rich than what workers imagine.[129] In truth, the rich are miserable, because they are on the wrong end of the work ethic. They are "exceedingly oppressed" by idleness, because they have nothing interesting to do.[130] Their freedom to choose how to occupy themselves gets them "lost in the perplexity of choosing" and sunk into "irrecoverable indolence."[131] They suffer anxiety over their difficulty in placing their children in situations that would "support them in the class . . . and habits in which they have been brought up."[132] Because they wallow in pleasures, they are so satiated that "their desires are dead." Nothing amuses them anymore. "The epicure must be sumptuously entertained to escape disgust."[133] They get no pleasure in being free from the necessity of working.[134] Even genuine rest is beyond their reach, since "none can rest who have not worked."[135]

By contrast, the working classes have it easy! They enjoy the pleasures of being fully occupied with work. Because they have little choice over their occupations, they suffer no perplexity about what to choose. Because they are poor, they enjoy the pleasures of successful frugality.[136] Since they are already at the bottom of society, they need not worry that their children will fall in rank. They can give their children the education they need to succeed in their class "without expense," because they need only convey "industry and innocence" to them by their "authority and example."[137] Because they work so hard, "every pause is a recreation."[138] Because they haven't already been there, done that, they can still feel the pleasures of novelty.[139]

Paley drew from a line of thought begun by his Puritan predecessors. Baxter declared, "let others pity the poor: I will pity the rich, who seem to be pinched with harder necessities than the poor" in having to waste their time with frivolous entertainments in the course of public service or business, while "the happy poor" get to spend their time "in the honest labours of their callings."[140] Yet Baxter's moral premises differed from Paley's. Baxter was worried that wealthy officials put their souls at risk in having to indulge in luxury and expose themselves to temptations at parties in the course of their duties. By the late eighteenth century, as we have seen with Priestley, such other-worldly worries had vanished. Luxury was in. Asceticism was not a soul-protecting discipline. It was merely prudent for those who couldn't afford luxuries, but aspired to get them.

More fundamentally, the Puritans insisted that the work ethic also applied to the rich. They were not entitled to expect pity from the poor for problems wholly within their abilities to solve. If idleness is an affliction, the rich should get to work. If choosing an occupation perplexes them, they should consider Sanderson's advice on how to discover their calling. If indulging in gratification deadens their souls, they should enliven themselves with ascetic discipline. If luxury bores them, they should give away their fortunes. If workers can take pleasure in successfully mastering the anxieties of making frugal choices in the face of tight budget constraints, then the rich can take pleasure in mastering the anxieties of figuring out how to place their children in good situations. For conservatives such as Paley, however, the duties of the work ethic were for workers alone, while the rich reaped the fruits of the workers' labor.

In 1817, William Hone, former member of the London Corresponding Society (until Parliament banned it in 1799), launched the *Reformists' Register*, in which he promoted constitutional reform, attacked corruption, and excoriated conservative ideology. That April he examined "Reasons for Contentment," a reprint of which the *Times* had just advertised as an "Excellent Tract, for present distribution." In the 25 years since its original publication, the working classes had suffered from highly regressive taxes levied to pay for protracted war with France, several bad harvests, and a deep recession caused by the government's attempt to restore the pound's prewar value in gold.[141]

Such protracted working-class distress was on Hone's mind. To recommend "Reasons for Contentment" for *present* distribution "is mocking the poor man's sorrow – jesting upon his misery."[142] It is a "lying insult" to claim that the poor can easily provide for their children. It is "dreadful trifling with distress" to claim that "in the luxuries of eating and drinking ... the advantage is on the side of the poor"[143] when they and their children are dying from lack of food.[144]

Malthus claimed that the poor had it entirely within their grasp to solve their own difficulties by following the work ethic. Hazlitt's complaint about Malthus, that his "gospel is preached only to the poor!"[145] applies as much to Paley. Like Hazlitt, Hone recommends that the rich accept Malthus's instruction for themselves:

> The rich have the means of consoling themselves for disappoint-
> ment; they have money – and if money is unequal to answer all
> the wants of their families, and provide for them, they must take
> the advice to themselves, which Mr. Malthus gives to the poor –
> they must neither marry nor get children.[146]

Hone complains that "Reasons for Contentment" was even less fit for distribution in 1817 than in 1792. Paley claimed that the laws of property impartially benefit rich and poor alike, and so must not be altered. "Fixed rules of property are established ... without knowing, before hand, whom they may affect ... it is the law which defends the weak against the strong."[147] The claim was preposterous in 1792, given the ways property laws were rigged to favor landlords, and how Parliamentary enclosures were steadily extinguishing the customary property rights of agricultural workers through the eighteenth century. This process of redistributing property to benefit landlords at the expense of rural workers accelerated during the French Wars, when 43 percent of all Parliamentary enclosures took place.[148] Conservatives were happy to alter property rights as long as this benefited the rich. They held property rights sacred only when the poor wanted to change them.

Paley echoes Adam Smith in claiming that people overrate a sudden uplifting of their condition, and that the pleasures truly critical to happiness – the love and companionship of family and friends – are also accessible to the poor.[149] In supposing that these considerations address the concerns of the working classes, Paley reveals some characteristics of the reactionary cast of mind. He perceives every demand for relief from oppression as seeking to reverse the fortunes of rich and poor. But the working classes in his day were not demanding the confiscation and division of estates. Like the Levellers, they were demanding the franchise and other constitutional reforms that would make their interests count for something in the political order. More importantly, that the pleasures critical to happiness are in principle accessible to rich and poor alike neglects the negative side of the utility ledger. The poor were not complaining that they lacked pleasures, but that they suffered from injustice and extreme want. That Paley failed to sympathize with their plight, but made light of it, expressed precisely the bias in moral sentiments that Adam Smith thought was unjust: that people grant "ten times more compassion" to "every calamity that befalls" the great, compared to what they grant ordinary people.[150] That the rich expect the poor to hide from public view and feel ashamed of their condition, that the poor are acutely aware that others fail to sympathize with their suffering, are injuries of poverty over and above its material deprivations.[151] Smith would have endorsed Hone's complaint that Paley's comparisons mock the poor in trifling with their distress.

Burke and Whately: Aristocratic Paternalism

It is difficult to believe that any among the working classes would have taken Paley's arguments seriously. That Paley did reflects a maudlin vision of how some of the rich in his day preferred to see themselves. The relation of masters and servants is, Paley claims, "the foundation of so much mutual kindness and attachment, that very few friendships are more cordial, or more sincere," which leave "nothing in servitude, except the name."[152] This notion of tender relations between the rich and the poor was more likely among the landlords than among the rising manufacturers; more likely among Tories than liberals. Liberal political economists such as Priestley, Bentham, and Malthus inherited the Puritans' contempt for sentimentality. While this contempt was widespread across British society, some advocates of aristocracy aimed to legitimate the authority of the rich over the poor at least in part on claims of beneficent paternalism.

This position encountered difficulties, because many of the great landlords had taken up Locke's call to adopt a commercial orientation to their estates. In the eighteenth century, this went hand-in-hand with an aggressive policy of enclosures forced by Parliament at the behest of landlords. Enclosures, along with the adoption of labor-saving technology, threw agricultural workers into poverty and precarity. Many workers responded by rejecting the landlords' authority.

Landlords split over how to deal with this crisis. Some resisted commercialization in order to return to their traditional paternalistic claims to authority. Others, known as "liberal tories," embraced capitalist policies and advocated enhanced criminal enforcement to secure their authority. In practice, however, the two strategies overlapped.[153] Liberal tories did not wholly dispense with paternalistic claims. The challenge, then, was to combine a paternalistic claim to authority over agricultural workers with advocacy of capitalistic policies that made these workers worse off.[154] Edmund Burke and Richard Whately offered two ways to do this.

Edmund Burke, MP from 1766 to 1794, is best known for his critique of the French Revolution. Burke casts the aristocratic system of ranks, founded on dynastic wealth, as a beneficent order. Calling for "some decent regulated pre-eminence, some preference ... given to birth," Burke claims that "[t]he power of perpetuating our property in our families ... grafts benevolence even upon avarice."[155] "The spirit of an exalted freedom" is "kept alive, even in servitude itself" by "that generous loyalty to rank and sex, that proud submission, that dignified obedience." The sentiments, opinions, and chivalric manners that uphold this system

> had produced a noble equality, and handed it down through all the gradations of social life. It was this opinion which mitigated kings into companions, and raised private men to be fellows with kings.[156]

One might think Burke should have asked the servants how free and equal they really understood themselves to be in all this subordination. But their lot – especially, the lot of agricultural workers – was not to think. It was only to take orders from their superiors, the thinking part of society, in a humane "chain of subordination."[157] Burke admits that the legitimation of social hierarchy is based on "pleasing illusions." Government based on abstract, dogmatic principles of reason – exemplified by the recently ratified French Declaration of the Rights of Man and Citizen (1789) – strip away the illusions that "make power gentle, and obedience liberal." Without them, state authority is secured only by terror.[158]

Yet Burke himself eagerly resorted to abstract, dogmatic principles of reason to denounce a pragmatic attempt to fulfill the claims of benevolent protection on which the traditional authority of the landlords was based. His principles were that markets must be left absolutely free to set prices, even if they set wages below subsistence, and that the state must not fill the gap between wages and subsistence. The policy he denounced came to be known as the Speenhamland system, a set of ad hoc measures adopted by certain parishes in 1795 to provide relief for distressed agricultural workers in a year of poor harvests that made food unaffordable. One measure provided subsidies to some agricultural workers' wages so they would not starve.

Opposing this measure, Burke declares that it is the workers' job to maintain those in government (mostly landlords), not the other way around. The poor must produce a surplus for the rich to consume, for the rich "are under an absolute, hereditary, and indefeasible dependence on those who labour."[159] Like Priestley, Burke recognizes who is really producing the wealth of society, but condemns dependence – that is, receiving income without having to work for it – as a vice only in the poor. Never mind that the Speenhamland system mostly functioned as a subsidy to income obtained through work.

Burke claims that to tax the rich to feed the working poor is "plunder." Redistribution of their wealth by leveling down is useless. The rich are so few that an equal distribution will not significantly improve anyone's lot. The program amounts to "the poor ris[ing] to destroy the rich." Instead, workers should simply practice the work ethic – "patience, labour, sobriety, frugality, and religion" – more assiduously.[160] It's all on them to deal with hunger. The state, primarily representing the landed interests, as he claimed it ought to do in *Reflections on the Revolution in France*, has no responsibility to help them.

In this diatribe, Burke projects revolutionary intentions onto the Speenhamland system. Of course, the Speenhamland system parishes were not engaged in a radical egalitarian redistribution. Nor were they engaged in anything novel or irregular. They were acting in accordance with Gilbert's Act, passed in 1782 under Prime Minister Rockingham. Burke was an MP at that time and belonged to the Rockinghamite faction of Whigs. Gilbert's Act rolled back the harsh provisions of Knatchbull's Act (the Workhouse Test Act) of 1723, which had permitted parishes to require able-bodied recipients of relief to reside and work in a workhouse. MP Thomas Gilbert decried the inhumanity and high costs of the workhouses. Under his Act, participating parishes would provide able-bodied paupers work near their homes or "outdoor relief" – payments in cash or in kind outside workhouses to subsidize their wages. Gilbert's Act, as many Poor Law statutes had done, merely authorized for the whole nation practices already underway in certain parishes.[161] As I discuss in Chapter 4, the Speenhamland system was a very modest program primarily adopted in a few arable regions of England. In these regions, the local justices of the peace who set Poor Law rates and relief policies were selected by the gentry, and were typically landowners themselves.[162] It is absurd to suppose that they would have enacted policies that would lead to their own ruin.

Yet according to Burke, any tinkering with prices dictated by the free market is a gross violation of abstract principles of natural justice and liberty. For "[l]abour is a commodity like every other, and rises or falls according to the demand. This is in the nature of things."[163] Just wages are those set by the free market, through voluntary contracts between employers and workers. The sole job of the government is to enforce contracts already made, not to regulate their terms.[164] Government exercises arbitrary power in setting wages above their free-market price.[165] The survival of the workers is irrelevant to the workings of the market. Indeed, the more desperate they are, the lower are their just wages.[166] No one should condemn the market for working in this way, for "the laws of commerce ... are the laws of nature, and consequently the laws of God."[167] Tinkering with market outcomes will lead to "the very destruction of agriculture itself," by making it unprofitable. This will ruin everyone, including the workers.[168] Any attempt to regulate market prices only expresses an envious desire to tear down the rich.[169]

But what if market wages threaten famine? The workers' only recourse should be to throw themselves at the mercy of the charity of the rich. Their charity must not be compelled, but be at their complete discretion. Never mind that some may starve as a result.[170] Malthus incorporated Burke's argument into his own: "[T]he laws of nature, which are the laws of God," dictate that the worker has "no claim of right on society for the smallest portion of food, beyond that which his labour would fairly purchase," and must appeal to the "pity of some kind benefactor" for help if his wages fall short of subsistence.[171]

Burke attributes to nature what was the product of massive social engineering. It was not "in the nature of things" for labor to be a commodity. In agricultural regions, the commodification of labor was occurring only with the systematic expropriation of workers' traditional rights of access to land. This process took more than 300 years and was still ongoing in Burke's day. Burke's deification of the purportedly natural free market also masks the reality that capitalist markets rely on a complex system of laws that establish the constitutive rules of the market.[172] These rules are not neutral among the parties. The choice of rules has enormous distributive consequences even if they don't directly regulate market prices.[173]

In Burke's day, the common law of master and servant rigged the rules with a heavy thumb on the scales in favor of the masters. Able-bodied men and women without property could be compelled to work for a wage. They had no right to quit, and could be punished for deserting their post. Officials could impose penalties on employers who offered wages higher than those set by magistrates.[174] Indeed, it appears that Burke alludes to the fact that the state did regulate wages in the eighteenth century ("wages have been twice raised in my time"[175]).

But he fails to note that such regulations, which were set by local justices of the peace, put *ceilings* on wages in the arable regions.[176] (Attempts to get a minimum-wage law through Parliament had failed due to Pitt's opposition. The Speenhamland system offered a patchy substitute.[177]) Rather than complain about the injustice of such regulation by appealing to free-market principles, Burke claims that the wage levels thus set "bear a full proportion to the result of their labour." For Burke, free-market outcomes were divine only when they put workers in the subordinate place to which he thought they should be assigned, not when they enhance workers' bargaining power.

Burke's condemnation of state intervention to provide for the poor, and to prevent famine, repudiated centuries of state policy. England was the first European country to recognize provision for the poor as a state responsibility, not a matter to be left to arbitrary private charity. It also had long-established practices of state intervention to prevent famine. These were no revolutionary ideas, enviously tearing down the rich in egalitarian tyranny. They were modest and sober policies to ensure minimal subsistence to the least advantaged, adopted and endorsed by the propertied classes, who elected and served as members of Parliament and administrators of the Poor Law. Behind the mask of a genteel, sentimental, and beneficent traditionalism was a program to radically remake its very foundations in the name of an abstract, dogmatically held principle, consequences for workers be damned.[178]

Richard Whately, Archbishop of Dublin in the Church of Ireland, offered a different way to combine liberal principles of political economy with a quasi-paternalistic defense of the landlords' authority. Whately was the most widely read political economist of the first half of the nineteenth century.[179] He belonged to a school of political economy known as the Noetics, based in Oxford University. The Noetics developed a brand of Christian political economy, supplying an interpretation of natural theology that offered a vision of human progress by means of liberal economic principles. Their thought broadly supported the liberal tories, exemplified by Robert Peel (Prime Minister, 1834–35, 1841–46), who embraced commercial agriculture and liberal principles of political economy along with traditional lordly authority.[180] Like Malthus, they evaluated institutions at least as much for their impact on virtue and vice, understood in terms of the work ethic, as for their material results. They stressed the higher virtue of the independently wealthy and the necessity of property inequality and social hierarchy.[181] They also believed that the wealthy could "civilize" the lower orders, simultaneously promoting their moral and material progress. By imposing a liberal economic order on the working classes, they functioned as their moral tutors, teaching the working classes to internalize the work ethic and thereby also raise their material standard of living.

The hopeful idea that the history of humanity was a history of progress was a major feature of European thought starting in the mid-eighteenth century. Enlightenment figures such as Turgot, Kant, Condorcet, and Adam Smith's student John Millar offered progressive views of human history, followed in the nineteenth century by Hegel, Marx, Herbert Spencer, and many others. Malthus's pessimistic population theory cut against the grain of turn-of-the century thinking. Yet even he allowed a narrow path to progress for the poor, conditional on their following the work ethic, in later editions of the *Principle of Population*. The Noetics developed a similar line of thought in a more hopeful vein, in some cases even before Malthus.

Recall that Malthus implicitly assumes a deep class difference in personal morality. He assumes that the working classes have what economists call a "backward-bending supply curve of labor": they have a target income that would support their basic subsistence, and quit working as soon as they meet it. Hence, workers will not willingly produce the surplus needed for anyone else to survive. If they don't produce a surplus, then government, churches, schools, commerce, the arts, sciences, and manners – all the institutions and practices that distinguish civilization from barbarism – are impossible. The classes engaged in distinctively civilized practices do *not* engage in them only under the press of necessity. Indeed, they can undertake these practices only if they have enough property and leisure to release them from necessity. Unlike ordinary workers, for whom the threat of misery is needed to spur learning and virtue, they pursue learning and virtue without such threats. But for them to be free to advance civilization, ordinary workers, especially in the agricultural sector, must be coerced by law or physical necessity to produce a surplus beyond their personal needs. It is futile and dangerous to raise their wages, for that would only induce them to quit work sooner, thereby threatening the material basis of civilization.

Malthus's theory justifies the ways of God to man in a way that rationalizes the suffering of working people as a class, while offering its members only a narrow individual path to escape this fate, via the work ethic. Whately broadens that path by rejecting the assumption of inherent class differences in virtue, and by refiguring the relation of the rich to the poor. In Malthus's picture, the rich relate to the poor primarily as a class that lives off the surplus the poor produce, while excluding the poor from most of the benefits of civilization, since only under the threat of misery will they work hard.

Whately argues that the rich as a class have a tutelary duty toward the poor to civilize them by teaching them the work ethic. Once they have internalized it, they will willingly work harder for additional material rewards, and thereby willingly produce ever-greater surpluses that enable civilization to progress. Moral and material progress for *everyone* thus go hand-in-hand. In terms of modern economics, the rich must teach the poor to internalize a "forward-sloped" supply curve of labor, in which higher wages induce greater effort.

Like Baxter, Whately cagily departs from the traditional doctrine of original sin, according to which humans are inherently depraved and utterly incapable of doing anything to redeem themselves. To the contrary, a "capacity of improvement" is inherent in humans, both individually and collectively.[182] However, Whately also rejects the conventional eighteenth-century theory of historical progress, according to which all humans began as "savage" hunter-gatherers, and steadily learned to lift themselves out of that state, through the invention of animal husbandry, agriculture, and manufacturing technologies, ending in a fully civilized commercial society. There is "[n]o reason to believe that any community ever did, or ever can, emerge, unassisted by external helps, from a state of utter barbarism, into any thing that can be called civilization."[183] The first civilization to arise got started with the help of God's revelation. God instructed humans in the basic arts of herding and agriculture, after which people had enough stimulation to invent the other arts on their own.[184] "Savages," who lack these arts, have degenerated from a higher earlier state, and need the help of the civilized to make progress.

"Savages" lack not only productive technology, but secure institutions of private property. Living in a state of equality and common property, they lack incentives to produce a surplus. They need to be taught both the institution of private property and the "spirit of emulation" or competitive acquisition of material goods. Together, these will inspire industry by offering a "reward proportioned to its exertion."[185] Progress in civilization requires that people desire more than basic necessities. Whately magnifies Priestley's praise for competitive acquisition by turning that motive into the central driver of civilization. The effort of each individual to rise above the others through their own industry and frugality causes the whole society to become richer. "The race never comes to an end, while the competitors are striving, not to reach a certain fixed goal," but to get ahead of others. The material progress of civilization is thus potentially unlimited.[186]

We are a long way from Baxter's sin of covetousness. Bernard Mandeville had insisted that economic growth would only be spurred by "private vices" of greed and selfishness.[187] Whately replies, following Adam Smith, that honest industry in pursuit of honorable ends is no vice, even when the agent seeks merited esteem.[188] While wealth leads some of the rich into sloth and dissolution, the leisure it affords frees others to noble pursuits in the arts, sciences, government, and philanthropy.[189] From a collective point of view, progress in wealth and virtue are joined. "A rich individual may be idle, but a rich nation is always industrious," and more so than a poor nation.[190]

Whately thus offers the core justification for imperialism – for European nations to civilize "savage" nations, and indeed all nations that Europeans deemed less civilized. His theory set the key terms for the content of racist stereotypes that rationalized imperialism – the notions that the non-European subjects of colonial rule were lazy, improvident, promiscuous, and incapable of autonomous self-improvement. In short, he argues that they were inferior to Europeans in lacking the work ethic.

Whately applies the same argument to "the dregs of a civilized community." "[T]hey are idle, thoughtless, improvident," lacking "self-command."[191] The rich, by employing the poor, set them to work. By rewarding them in proportion to their efforts, as the market dictates, and by teaching them the appeal of material acquisition and emulation, they civilize the "dregs." Although the rich are mostly moved to do these things out of personal ambition, they thereby benefit the poor and promote human progress. Whately approvingly quotes his student Nassau Senior, another Noetic, on the results: "That state of society ... in which the productiveness of labour ... secure to the labouring classes all the necessaries and some of the conveniences of life ... [is] essential, both to their morals and their happiness."[192]

Whately had a class of British dregs especially in mind: the Irish peasantry. An Englishman appointed to church office in Dublin since 1831, Whately viewed Ireland as in a "state of semi-barbarism."[193] The question was how to lift Ireland to the same level of civilization as England. We shall see in the next chapter that the views of Burke, Whately, and other Noetics on this subject, along with other advocates of a conservative work ethic, were to have catastrophic consequences for the Irish poor. Noetic thinking about poor-law reform also seriously harmed the poor of Great Britain.

4 WELFARE REFORM, FAMINE, AND THE IDEOLOGY OF THE CONSERVATIVE WORK ETHIC

Applications of the Conservative Work Ethic (1): English Welfare Reform

Conservative discourse about the Poor Laws at the turn of the nineteenth century was not purely theoretical. British policies toward the poor in the nineteenth century were deeply informed by the conservative work ethic. This chapter will consider the New Poor Law of 1834, a welfare reform for England and Wales, the Irish Poor Law Act of 1838, and British policy toward famine relief in Ireland during the potato blight and its aftermath, from 1845 to 1852. In each case, the results were disastrous for the poor. These consequences, which were known and welcomed by proponents of the conservative work ethic, illuminate how this ethic functioned ideologically, rationalizing systematic suffering behind masks of progress and paternalistic beneficence.

These policies must be understood in historical context. In this period, conservatives were alarmed by rising radicalism among the working classes, who were inspired by the French Revolution to demand political rights at home. Political ideas were not the only factors leading to working-class agitation. Britain was at war with France almost continuously from 1793 to 1815. War led to restrictions on grain imports from Europe. Britain also suffered poor harvests in 1795, 1811–12, 1816–17, 1823–25, and 1828–31. Grain prices soared. Wages did not keep up. After 1813, rising rural unemployment caused by the introduction of threshing machines led to further distress.[1] The economy went into recession in 1814. In 1819, economist and MP David Ricardo persuaded Parliament to return to the gold standard after its suspension during the Napoleonic Wars. This deflationary move caused mass bankruptcies of rural banks, which reduced farmers' access to credit.[2] Farmers cut their demand for agricultural labor in response. Given such diverse troubles, it is not surprising that increasing numbers of working people sought poor relief to survive. From the 1790s to 1834, about 10 percent of the English population resorted to relief.[3]

The radicalized working classes blamed their immiseration on a corrupt state, which imposed steeply regressive war taxes, destroyed rural life through employment-reducing enclosures, and oppressed all workers through the system of aristocratic privileges and sinecures for the idle rich.[4] As the Industrial Revolution proceeded, workers also denounced machinery for eliminating their jobs. In the 1830 Swing Riots, agricultural workers smashed threshing machines that reduced the demand for their labor during wheat harvests. For the workers, unjust institutions were responsible for their misery.

In a moral panic, ideologues of the conservative work ethic blamed the rapidly increasing numbers of able-bodied people on relief, which coincided with a rising population, on the supposed corrupting influence of the Poor Law. This increase should be put into perspective. Hysteria is the characteristic emotional tone of reactionaries. They regularly imagine that unwelcome trends, however small in the larger scheme of things, portend a slippery slope to catastrophe for the privileged. In this period, the Industrial Revolution was dramatically increasing both GDP and the share of income taken by capital owners. Poor Law payments were therefore not taking an ever-increasing share of the national product. Although they increased after 1795, with the introduction of wage supplements, they were always well below 3 percent of GDP from 1783 to 1834. Indeed, they were *falling* in the decade preceding welfare reform, from a peak of 2.66 percent of GDP in 1820–21 to 2.0 percent of GDP in 1830–32.[5] These realities were not so evident to contemporaries. National income accounting had not yet been invented. Wealthy conservatives could see the rising relief rolls and expenditures. It was harder for them to compare relief to total economic growth. However, it wasn't so hard for most of them to check their rapidly rising personal wealth.

By the 1830s, saturated with Malthusian anxiety about the growing ranks of paupers, the propertied classes called for an investigation into the Poor Law. The government appointed a Royal Commission into the Operation of the Poor Laws in 1832. That the Commission was to recommend major reductions in the rolls was predetermined. It is often assumed that their choice was between Malthus or Bentham: would they recommend that the destitute be left to starve, or consigned to labor in workhouses? Nassau Senior, an Oxford political economist and former student of Whately, and Edwin Chadwick, Bentham's assistant, wrote the Royal Commission's report. Senior and Chadwick distributed questionnaires to thousands of parish officials responsible for administering the Poor Law, asking them how it operated in their locality. Their answers were published in nine volumes totaling nearly 5,000 pages. However, Senior and Chadwick never quantified this information or subjected it to statistical analysis. Their questions were ambiguous; the answers unstructured, incomplete, vague, and often irrelevant.[6] Senior and Chadwick cherry-picked officials' anecdotes to support a critique of the Poor Law driven by Malthusian theory.[7]

The Commissioners' Report focused critical attention on a system of poor relief begun in Speenhamland, Berkshire, in 1795, to deal with hunger among rural workers. To the Royal Commissioners, the scandal of the Speenhamland system consisted in the fact that it offered "outdoor relief" – poor relief outside workhouses – to some able-bodied working men, by supplementing their wages according to the cost of bread and the number of children in their families. By establishing an income floor based on the cost of living and family size, the Speenhamland system purportedly broke the causal connection between vice and misery. It paid a "bounty on indolence and vice," promoting improvidence and drunkenness.[8] Echoing Malthus, the Report complained that outdoor relief repealed "the ordinary laws of nature; to enact that the children should not suffer for the misconduct of their parents."[9] It thereby removed the incentive for fathers to support their children, corrupting their natures even below that of "savages."[10] Senior and Chadwick fantasized that life in the workhouses was so good that pauper children misbehaved in order to be returned to them. They catastrophized that rising costs would consume all the rents.[11]

To address these problems, the Royal Commissioners recommended several reforms of the Poor Laws. They did not question relief for orphans, or for adults deemed unable to work – the disabled, ill, insane, or elderly. They focused on sharpening the moral distinction between two groups of able-bodied workers: the deserving independent poor, and the undeserving dependent poor. Partial relief – wage supplements to the working poor – blurred the lines between the merely poor and the utterly destitute. Mere poverty should not be relieved. The only aim of relief should be to rescue people who would die without it.[12] To this end, the Commission recommended the abolition of outdoor relief. The destitute should have to enter a workhouse to obtain assistance.[13]

The Commissioners' insistence on drawing a sharp distinction between the deserving and undeserving poor reflects a major step backward in both normative and sociological sophistication. Poor Law reforms at the turn of the seventeenth century had been drafted partially in response to the discovery of a large class of poor who were neither the impotent deserving poor (unable to work) nor the able-bodied undeserving poor (unwilling to work). This third class of poor – the "laboring poor" for whom Adam Smith had great sympathy, and Burke such contempt – consisted of the involuntarily under- and unemployed. They were by far the most numerous among the poor. For this reason, the original priority of the seventeenth-century Poor Laws was to provide employment or the materials for work in home-based industry. Parishes quickly learned by experiment how difficult it was to make such schemes work. Hence, over the course of the seventeenth century, relief in cash or in kind came to prevail. At no time during the administration of the Poor Laws was more than a tiny fraction of the laboring poor able to obtain relief. And relief never amounted to more than a supplement to other sources of support. For the most part, the laboring poor had to shift for themselves, cobbling together diverse subsistence strategies to get by. These strategies included day labor, cottage gardens, gleaning, digging peat or coal, mutual aid, kin support, the dole (quasi-formal private charity), borrowing, selling or pawning possessions, begging at neighbors' doors, petty thieving and other "crimes of necessity." In the face of such complexity, the parish overseers and magistrates who administered and adjudicated claims of poor relief regularly encountered great difficulty in applying simple dichotomies between the deserving and undeserving. The difference between those who were granted and denied relief often turned on minute differences in the obsequiousness of the applicant's request.[14]

The Commissioners' recommendation of a workhouse requirement reprised the Workhouse Test Act of 1723. They seemed to have learned nothing from the debates over Gilbert's Act in 1782, which rejected the workhouse requirement due to its high cost and cruelty. Meanwhile, enclosures and the Industrial Revolution eliminated or sharply limited opportunities for numerous makeshift subsistence strategies. The Commissioners confused objective reductions in opportunities with skyrocketing rates of vice.

The workhouse requirement instituted the Benthamite principle of "less eligibility." According to this principle, the relief provided to the dependent able-bodied poor must always be less desirable than what the lowest-paid independent worker could earn. The principle did not mean that workhouse paupers must be fed less than independent workers. Since market wages sometimes paid below subsistence, that would have turned workhouses into starvation houses. Rather, because workhouse inmates lost their freedom and civil rights, and because their physical segregation and confinement stripped them of dignity and branded them as vicious, they would be inherently worse off than the independent poor even if the workhouses fed them enough to survive.[15]

The workhouse requirement served three purposes. First, it ensured that workers would have an incentive to comply with the work ethic rather than rely on relief. Senior and Chadwick argued that only 5–6 percent of current claimants would receive relief if they were subject to the "correct principle" of relief entitlement – absolute destitution. They noted that parishes that abolished outdoor relief for the able-bodied saw claims plummet. This supposedly proved that ample opportunities were available for the able-bodied to provide for themselves by practicing the work ethic. Second, the workhouse requirement functioned as a severe test of genuine need, which was required to overcome the strong presumption that anyone seeking relief was a lazy welfare cheat. The workhouse test would end fraud and discretionary favoritism by relief administrators, and eliminate the costs of investigating the legitimacy of claims for relief, along with appeals. It was thus the most efficient way to enforce the correct principle of entitlement.[16] Third, the workhouse requirement sharpened the moral distinction between paupers and independent laborers, by inflicting the shame of the workhouse on the former.[17]

By abolishing outdoor relief and offering relief only to the destitute, the Poor Law Commissioners' reforms made the working poor materially worse off. But it claimed to raise them above the destitute by casting disgrace on the latter. In reality, the reforms stigmatized all the poor through its virtual criminalization of poverty. This reinforced the presumption of the conservative work ethic that one's level of virtue could be inferred from one's wealth.[18] The reforms also reinforced the essentially antagonistic model of social order inherent in the conservative work ethic, which was based on a competitive esteem hierarchy. Each class except for the lowest got to satisfy its own vanity by stigmatizing its inferiors.

It might seem that, in choosing workhouses over the abolition of poor relief, the Royal Commission chose Bentham over Malthus. In fact, Peter Mandler persuasively argues that its recommendations reflected a partial convergence between Benthamite utilitarianism and the more dominant ideology of liberal toryism, which aimed to restore the landlords' authority via liberal economic principles.[19] Noetics such as Whately and Senior justified this strategy in terms of Christian political economy (see Chapter 3). Whereas the Benthamites believed that the rational administrative state could advance human happiness, the Noetics held that it could only deter sin. The Noetics' vision of the workhouse triumphed in the Royal Commissioners' Report. Workhouses were not to aim at the improvement or happiness of their inmates. Their primary purpose was to punish and degrade them, to deter the able-bodied poor from applying for relief.[20]

Parliament passed the Poor Law Amendment Act of 1834 (the New Poor Law) with the intent of implementing the Report's core recommendations. The act empowered a Poor Law Commission to issue workhouse regulations, to order any parish to construct and operate a workhouse, or outsource its operation to a private contractor. However, it also granted the Commission discretion to authorize outdoor relief to able-bodied workers.[21] Contrary to Bentham's fantasy that workhouses could generate huge profits, in practice indoor relief cost 63 percent more per recipient than outdoor relief. It is no wonder, then, that only a fraction of recipients were consigned to workhouses. By 1842, about 16 percent of recipients were forced into workhouses, compared to 8 percent under the Old Poor Law in 1802. The main effect of the New Poor Law was to reduce relief. Real benefits per recipient were cut in half.[22]

The consequences of the New Poor Law were especially ghastly for workhouse inmates. Workhouse rations were less than half that afforded to prisoners. Inmates had to eat with their hands, as no cutlery was provided. Private charities were banned from donating anything to improve conditions. Segregation of men, women, and children destroyed all possibility of family life. Inmates were forbidden to leave the workhouse, even to attend church.[23]

Scandal over the administration of workhouses broke out in 1845 with reports that famished inmates in the Andover Union workhouse resorted to eating the marrow from putrid bones they were assigned to crush for fertilizer. The House of Commons appointed a select committee to investigate. Newspaper reports of mounting abuses inspired public outrage. The select committee found that the master of the house was cruel and unfair toward inmates, forced them to eat raw potatoes and refuse meant for hogs and chickens, denied the sick health care, and fraudulently appropriated workhouse stores, among many other abuses. Andover Union officials denied applicants for relief their right to present their case and answer challenges in person, failed to maintain adequate books, engaged in self-dealing, and tried to cover up the scandal. The committee also found abuses at other workhouses.[24] The Andover workhouse scandal exhibited a pattern of maltreatment that has been endlessly repeated wherever vulnerable people are confined to total institutions, especially when the operators are able to profit from this arrangement.

All of the empirical and theoretical assumptions underlying the Royal Commissioners' Report were mistaken. The Speenhamland system, far from spreading across England as the Royal Commissioners claimed, had virtually disappeared by 1832. Patterns of use had always reflected local economic conditions, not general laws of human nature. It had existed primarily in wheat-growing counties in Southeast England. Even there, only 10 percent of parishes in Speenhamland counties paid wage supplements, mostly only to fathers with four or more children, and mostly only when grain prices were high. Child allowances were far too low to incentivize having additional children.[25] Speenhamland counties typically resorted to other forms of relief that could not have reduced incentives to work. These include unemployment insurance contingent on work unavailability, public works, and subsidies to employers to hire workers.[26] Such measures to promote work were consistent with the Poor Law reforms at the turn of the seventeenth century, which were based on the discovery of a class of laboring poor that suffered from involuntary under- and unemployment.

In practice, wage supplements partly made up for structural losses of opportunity to gain subsistence that were prevalent in wheat-growing counties. Zealous enclosures there had deprived agricultural workers of access to common pastures and garden plots they had formerly used to supplement their diets. Factories had wiped out rural cottage industries at which women worked. Threshing machines had reduced demand for agricultural workers at harvest time. In addition, over the course of the eighteenth century, farmers changed their hiring practices. In the seventeenth century, farmers hired agricultural laborers as servants on one-year contracts provided with room and board. Farmers scheduled work to keep them busy throughout the year. By 1851, servants had been entirely replaced by day laborers. This enabled farmers to concentrate work in shorter periods and to throw the seasonally unemployed onto the rolls for the rest of the year. Landlords gained from this practice. Enclosures, amalgamation of farms, and reduced labor costs all enabled landlords to raise rents on farmers. Increased rents greatly exceeded the rise in poor rates due to increased agricultural unemployment. Poor relief spending rose because of labor income losses mostly imposed by landlords' enclosures and farm amalgamations, not because the availability of relief encouraged sloth.[27]

Much relief functioned as seasonal unemployment insurance, or as wage supplements to low-intensity work, when demand for agricultural labor was low. It made sense for farmers to participate in such winter programs, to retain the labor force they needed in spring and summer.[28] There is no evidence that relief reduced workers' productivity. Agricultural productivity rose from 1795 to 1834.[29] From a theoretical point of view, too, the Royal Commissioners' reasoning was defective. If workers could rely only on the sub-subsistence wages common in Speenhamland system parishes in bad harvest years, they would have lacked the energy and strength to work productively.[30]

Given these empirical and theoretical weaknesses of the conservative critique of the Old Poor Law, it is no surprise that the cruelties inflicted on the poor under the New Poor Law yielded no economic benefits.[31] Yet the fault for this should not be placed entirely on a pure version of laissez-faire market fundamentalism. For the New Poor Law did not liberalize labor markets as Adam Smith and his successors desired. It didn't fully abolish the Settlement Act of 1662, which inhibited labor mobility by empowering local officials to force the poor to return to their birth parish if they could not prove that they would be unlikely to need relief.[32] This failure reflected the interest of the landlords in tightening their authority over the rural workforce by limiting its mobility. The Corn Laws, which artificially raised the price of bread, also helped the landlords at the expense of workers. Market discipline was reserved for workers, not the rich.

This failure to liberalize markets in a way that would enhance workers' bargaining power and access to subsistence makes sense in light of the liberal-tory basis of Poor Law reform. What fundamentally drove reform was not concerns over market efficiency or individual liberty, but a conservative work ethic that moralized class differences in order to legitimize the dominion of landlords over workers. It was a logic that recognized no limiting principle. Its appeals to natural law could justify any degree of engineering of positive laws to strip the poor of access to property and opportunities for subsistence, while swelling the coffers of the idle rich.

Applications of the Conservative Work Ethic (2): The Irish Poor Law

In the Acts of Union of 1800, Ireland joined Great Britain to create the United Kingdom of Great Britain and Ireland. Previously, Ireland and Great Britain shared the same monarch, but Ireland had its own parliament. With union, much of the Irish ruling class left Dublin for London. Shortly thereafter, discussion of the merits of passing a Poor Law for Ireland began. The government worried that union would lead many of the Irish poor to migrate to England, where they would swell the ranks of those seeking relief, at English taxpayers' expense, and drive down English wages.[33] However, government officials, under the sway of the conservative work ethic, had much greater ambitions for Irish economic reform than simply stemming the flow of Irish migration to England.

At the turn of the nineteenth century, Ireland was much poorer than England. This fact was reflected in their very different class structures. More than three centuries of enclosures in England had virtually eliminated the peasantry – small farmers who subsisted by growing their own food. Former copyholders had been turned into wage laborers, either in agriculture or factories. By contrast, most mid-nineteenth-century Irish agricultural workers grew their own food in small plots planted with potatoes. Because they earned hardly any money wages, their material standard of living, other than their nutritional status, was very low. They lived in hovels with very few possessions. Because potatoes were highly nutritious and took little labor to grow, Irish peasants had considerably more leisure than other poor workers. The Irish population was also booming. Even very poor peasants could maintain large families on potatoes.

From the point of view of the conservative work ethic, this situation was a moral disaster. Irish poverty was viewed as a product of Irish sloth, improvidence, and lust, portending Malthusian collapse. Potatoes were derided as "the lazy crop."[34] From the point of view of Whately's version of the conservative work ethic, Ireland was barbaric due to its primitive division of labor. To raise productivity, the division of labor had to be more fine-grained. Instead of growing their own food, each worker should specialize in some narrow occupation, and buy what they needed from the market. This required converting the Irish peasantry into wage laborers. To civilize them, the Irish must trade their autonomy and leisure for a life driven by the work ethic, which would be rewarded by higher material consumption.

The government appointed a Commission for Inquiring into the Condition of the Poorer Classes of Ireland in 1833 and charged it with investigating the feasibility of establishing a poor law for Ireland. Richard Whately chaired the Commission. The *Third Report* of the Commission presented its recommendations in 1836. It argued that the New Poor Law of 1834, which established a right to relief in the workhouses, would not work in Ireland. The Report expressed the Noetic view that the fundamental point of workhouses was not to put the poor to work – not, in other words, to fulfill Bentham's vision – but to deter dependence and force the poor to rely on their own efforts. Because Ireland had no poor law, the poor were already forced to rely on themselves. So workhouses were not needed to force them. Moreover, Ireland was too poor to recognize a right to relief. The Commission estimated that there were 585,000 Irish unemployed, and 1,800,000 dependent on them. Relieving them all would cost half the gross rents of Ireland and five-sixths of the Irish landlords' net income. No system of workhouses could possibly accommodate such large numbers. And outdoor relief would encourage idleness, dishonesty, and moral corruption, with handouts wasted on alcohol.[35]

Instead, the Commission recommended a program of subsidized emigration and economic development, focusing on public works, drainage projects, and recovery of waste land for agricultural production.[36] This would provide employment for the Irish poor and increase agricultural productivity. In addition, the "habits and conditions of the people" must be improved so they respect the "security of property."[37] This responsibility falls to the Irish ruling class, because "[t]hose who are uncivilized cannot civilize themselves." The rich must put the poor "into proper courses of industry," and teach them "the value of comforts" to spur their industry and draw them away from wasting their wages on fleeting gratifications. Landlords and manufacturing employers will civilize them by teaching them the work ethic and fulfilling their responsibility to treat the Irish poor with kindness and attention.[38]

The Commission suspected that opposition to subsidized emigration arose from English farmers. If the Irish were kept home, they would eat a greater proportion of the food Ireland grew, leaving less to export to England. This would help English farmers by keeping their prices high, at the expense of Irish farmers. (Corn laws blocked most grain imports from outside the UK. But the Act of Union had eliminated tariffs between Ireland and England.) It was unjust for the government to favor one group of farmers over another. Moreover, without agricultural exports, "civilization must end" in Ireland. Only by producing a surplus could an Irish agricultural worker earn money to buy clothes and be "a profitable member of society."[39]

The government received the Commission's recommendations with displeasure. By then, Whigs were in power. The government's response offers insight into the difference between liberal tory and Whig interpretations of the conservative work ethic. Liberal tories aimed to shore up the landlords' authority by using market discipline to tie agricultural workers in subordination to them, and to make those workers more productive. The work ethic gave duties of industry to the workers, not to the propertied leisure class. Whigs, following Locke, distinguished between lazy and industrious landlords. The latter relied on their own funds to invest in and commercialize their estates. From the Whig point of view, Whately's commission was not nearly demanding enough of the Irish landlords, who left so much of their land to waste, and rented out so much to Irish peasants who were producing for mere subsistence. The demands of the work ethic should apply to the landlords, too.

Lord John Russell, the Home Secretary, appointed George Nicholls, a Commissioner of the English Poor Law, to reinvestigate the Irish poverty question in 1836. Nicholls's report, submitted in 1838, made two major arguments. First, the introduction of a poor law to Ireland would not really cost more than the existing system of private almsgiving. One way or another, the destitute had to obtain the means of survival. A workhouse system on the English model, paid by taxes on Irish land, would have two major advantages over private charity. By enforcing the principle of less eligibility, it would deter begging, grifting, and idleness, and encourage self-reliance.[40] By supporting relief through taxation, it would spread the burdens more equitably. The existing system of begging from door-to-door in practice let the idle absentee landlords (who had decamped to London) off the hook entirely. And begging at the door only slightly burdened the resident landlords. Nearly all the burden of almsgiving was born by the Irish poor themselves, who were barely better off than their begging neighbors, but felt a moral obligation to give.[41] Nicholls had no patience for the self-flattery of Irish landlords, who falsely imagined (along with Malthus[42]) that the wealthy practice the higher virtue of charity more assiduously than the poor. The reality in Ireland was quite the reverse.

Nicholls's second argument was to prove even more consequential. The lazy Irish landlords must be compelled to invest in their estates, and to reform their agricultural system on the English model. This requires the consolidation of estates into large holdings that could profit from intensive investment. Consolidation requires elimination of the prevailing system of subdivision into tiny plots rented out to Irish peasants. The estates must be cleared of peasants, who must be converted into day laborers. Without the means to grow potatoes for their own consumption, day laborers, in a state of precarity, will have to work every day for wages to survive, rather than only a few days per week. A poor law for Ireland will assist this transition by offering relief for the truly desperate who are no longer able to grow their own food.[43] Here Nicholls followed Malthus in attributing Irish poverty, indolence, and overpopulation to excessive subdivision of farms and the ability of Irish peasants to eke out a living on the potato, with no money to spare for comforts.[44]

Parliament adopted a Poor Law for Ireland in 1838 along the lines of Nicholls's recommendations. There would be no general right to relief. Outdoor relief was prohibited. Ireland would be divided into 130 poor-law unions. Each would build a workhouse for provision of relief. Ominously, Nicholls warned that it would be "impossible to contemplate" the case of a general protracted famine.[45] It was obvious that 130 workhouses could not accommodate the numbers who would need relief in a general famine. However, the connection Nicholls made between an Irish Poor Law and measures to commercialize Ireland's agricultural sector were to lead the next Whig government down a fateful path. The government would use the Poor Law not merely to relieve distressed workers, but to force Irish landlords to clear their estates of peasants in the middle of a general, protracted famine.

Applications of the Conservative Work Ethic (3): Irish Famine Policy

On the eve of the Great Famine, Ireland had over eight million people – 40 percent of the UK population. Three million subsisted primarily on the potato. Blight repeatedly struck the crop between 1845 and 1850. By the end of 1851, Ireland had suffered more than a million excess deaths. Excess mortality continued for years after the blight had disappeared, due to the weakened state of many survivors. Over a million had emigrated, mostly to the US.[46]

This calamity did not result entirely, or even primarily, from crop failure. Some distress was inevitable given the scale of destruction. The government's responses inflicted immense additional suffering that could have been avoided. Its policies can be divided into four broad phases: (1) grain imports, (2) public works, (3) temporary soup kitchens, and (4) workhouses and evictions. The conservative work ethic shaped each policy, with especially devastating effects in the second and fourth phases. Sir Charles Trevelyan, assistant secretary and then head of the Treasury, micromanaged famine policy during the entire crisis – with the concurrence of Charles Wood, Chancellor of the Exchequer, and Prime Minister Lord John Russell for most of that time. These advocates of laissez-faire and the conservative work ethic assumed that the Irish poor preferred handouts to real work and suspected them of trying to cheat the recently established welfare system. They also suspected Irish landlords of evading their responsibilities to pay for relief. At every policy phase, Trevelyan was extremely stinting. He repeatedly insisted on delaying or ending relief on arbitrary deadlines.

He relented only in response to moral pressure from local relief officials who provided overwhelming evidence of need and incapacity to pay, and bad publicity from news reports on the catastrophic effects of government policies.

Grain Imports. In response to the partial crop failure of 1845, Conservative Prime Minister Sir Robert Peel ordered the government to secretly import Indian corn from the US and sell it at cost to voluntary local relief committees, who paid for it with private donations partially matched with government funds. From March to August 1846, they sold this corn to distressed individuals, or paid the very poor in food in return for their labor on public works. This policy of bulk government purchases for distribution in distressed areas was consistent with policies for dealing with crop failure that had been followed since the late sixteenth century.[47] Peel's policy successfully averted famine, mainly by preventing a spike in food prices. However, it did not prevent hunger. In line with the conservative work ethic, the government postponed food distribution to the last moment, to avoid discouraging the Irish from taking every means to support themselves.[48]

Public Works. Lord Russell, a Whig, was Prime Minister from July 1846 to February 1852. A free-market advocate, he resisted traditional famine-relief measures such as state-directed grain imports and restrictions on exports and brewing alcohol. Ireland continued to export massive quantities of food, including wheat, oats, barley, cattle, pigs, and butter, throughout the Famine.[49] Trevelyan sent copies of Burke's "Thoughts and Details on Scarcity" to members of the Irish Relief Commission, to justify the government's refusal to interfere with market prices.[50] Instead, from August 1846 to June 1847, the government employed distressed Irish on projects. The Irish must labor for their food, which they would buy at market prices with their wages. Public works employed about 10 percent of Ireland's working population during most of this period.[51]

The results were disastrous. Blight destroyed almost all of the 1846 potato crop. Potato prices quadrupled, and other food prices soared.[52] Wages for public works did not nearly keep up. To obtain any food, distressed workers had to toil at hard labor for below-subsistence wages. Obsessed with stereotypes of lazy Irish workers, the government insisted on paying by the task rather than the day, and delayed wage payments until the quality of work was confirmed.

Severely weakened by hunger exacerbated by waiting for their wages, workers could barely perform the tasks required. This reduced their pay. Applicants far exceeded the supply of jobs. Administrative costs consumed up to 25 percent of funds devoted to roadbuilding. It took weeks for public works plans to be developed and approved in the most distressed poor and potato-dependent districts. Meanwhile, the poor starved.[53] The year 1847 is known in Ireland as "Black ' 47" to mark the peak of the Famine.

The public works policy set Ireland up for further catastrophe in 1848. Because only those who had exhausted all means of self-support qualified for employment on public works, small farmers could not obtain relief until they had eaten their seed.[54] Roadbuilding also diverted labor from the far more important work of planting the next year's crop. The number of acres planted with potatoes dropped from 2.5 million in 1845 to 284,000 in 1847.[55] Hence, even though the blight receded in 1847, total potato production was very low. So the Irish faced famine again in 1848.

Ironically, a government officially dedicated to laissez-faire had grossly misallocated labor in a bout of centralized economic planning. Its dedication to an extremely harsh conservative work ethic helps to explain this contradictory policy. Whigs had long resented the fact that the Irish poor could attain self-sufficiency – perhaps even make themselves the best-fed population in Europe, if we take height as a proxy for nutritional status[56] – on a highly nutritious crop that required little labor on tiny plots. With the help of the potato, the Irish not only fed themselves, but exported enough food to the rest of Britain to feed two million people.[57] The stereotype of the lazy Irish was so deep that Senior blamed Irish distress on "the carelessness, the inactivity, and the improvidence of the sufferers." To support this judgment, he cited observations of Irish unemployment and untilled fields in 1847 and 1848 – two of the worst famine years. It didn't cross his mind that government policy left farmers with no seed to plant in 1848, or that listlessness is a symptom of starvation. Rather, he took at face value a false report that the government was "lavishly supplying all their wants as to food."[58] To such minds, the idle Irish had to be punished through subjection to onerous, externally imposed labor as a form of ascetic discipline – even if it was practically useless, as many of the poorly constructed roads built by emaciated workers were, and even if it diverted them from urgent but self-directed tasks.

Soup Kitchens. The government, belatedly recognizing the failure of its public works program, authorized temporary soup kitchens from spring until August 1847. Its main objective was not so much to rescue the starving. It was to force the costs of official relief onto Irish landlords. The plan was to ultimately fund the soup kitchens by poor rates assessed on Irish land. If not every Irish individual were self-reliant, at least Ireland as a whole would be. Soup kitchens dramatically reduced excess mortality for a few months, during which 36 percent of the population relied on them. Nevertheless, enforcement of the conservative work ethic reduced their effectiveness. Driven by the baseless idea that the starving Irish had been treated too liberally by prior measures, the government imposed burdensome and costly bureaucratic requirements on relief. As a result, some soup kitchens could not open until mid-June. To accelerate the transition to local responsibility, and to stop the diversion of labor from agriculture, the government ordered the end of public works in the poorest unions before soup kitchens were established. These delays and gaps increased mortality. Yet Temporary Relief Commissioners constantly complained that local relief committees were too generous. Portions had to be "miserable and scanty" to avoid demoralizing the hungry. Provision of cooked rather than uncooked food was a deliberate humiliation, designed as a test of desperation, lest some able to feed themselves seek handouts.[59] The resulting destruction of normal family life centered on home-cooked meals counted for naught.

Workhouses and Evictions. In mid-1847, Parliament passed laws designed to transfer all responsibility for famine relief to Ireland's 130 poor-law unions. This measure aimed in part to force "Irish property" to support "Irish poverty," relieving the rest of Britain from this expense. However, as Nicholls's report had warned the government in 1838, the workhouses were not equipped to manage mass distress due to crop failure. They rapidly filled during the famine, and could not come close to accommodating all applicants, even when several slept to a bed. The 1847 reforms increased the responsibilities of the unions by making relief, for the first time in Ireland, an individual right not limited to workhouse capacity, and by permitting unions to administer outdoor relief.

Richard Whately spoke before the House of Lords to denounce this policy, repeating the arguments he had made in the *Third Report of the Commissioners for Inquiring Into the Condition of the Poorer Classes in Ireland*, and echoing Burke. His chief concern was to protect the Irish landlords from the "blind indiscriminate rage" of the English, who he saw as aiming to punish them.[60] Enforcement of a right to relief would amount to confiscation of private property. A right to relief would inevitably lead to granting outdoor relief to the able-bodied – the very practice that the 1834 English New Poor Law had aimed to suppress for its corrupting effects on the poor. If outdoor relief were permitted, Whately predicted that "almost the whole labouring population" would "throw themselves upon the poor-rates, leaving the land untilled," while "the entire rental of Ireland" will be "swallowed up by the poor-rates," and pauperize the rate-payers.[61]

Liberal political economist G. Poulett Scrope denounced Whately's assumptions about the laziness of Irish workers as "dogmatic" and "uncharitable." In fact, the evidence showed that they were *agitating* for employment. The Famine was caused not by an absolute shortage of food but by the lack of employment.[62] The landlords, not the workers, were the lazy ones. The reform, by raising the poor rates, would rouse them from their "lethargy" by penalizing "those who continue to allow the resources of land and labour which are at their disposal, to lie idle through their apathy and neglect." High poor rates would stimulate them to employ the workers to improve the productivity of their estates, "to the infinite advancement of their own pecuniary interests."[63]

Scrope concisely expressed the ultimate aim of the 1847 reforms. It wasn't fundamentally about rescuing the starving. The real battle was over the fate of the Irish landlords. Whately rightly objected that the scale of the Famine exceeded Ireland's capacity to cope on its own resources alone. It became a net food importer in 1847, and could supply even the scanty relief offered only with massive loans from the Treasury. Although Whately's claim that an entitlement to relief would induce the Irish poor to quit work was absurd, he correctly predicted that the requirement to finance relief locally would bankrupt many landlords and pauperize small farmers with high poor rates. From Scrope's point of view, that was the point – to force the landlords to raise the productivity of their estates, or replace them with owners who would.

The reforms embraced three core principles: (1) that relief must be made a local responsibility, supported by local taxes; (2) that utter destitution be a condition of receiving relief; and (3) that the workhouse test of destitution for purportedly able-bodied men take priority over relieving the poor who were certainly unable to provide for themselves. Each of these principles had catastrophic effects on the Irish.

By making famine relief a local responsibility, the government put the greatest tax burdens on those least able to pay for them. From 1846 on, blight most affected the poorest regions of Ireland, in the west and south. The local poor rates that supported each union were assessed on the occupants of land, if they paid more than £4 annual rent, and on the landlords, if their tenants paid less. Demand for relief in the poorest regions of Ireland was high, because they were densely populated, with heavily subdivided estates dependent on the potato. This led to sky-rocketing rates on small farmers and large landholders alike. As Whately predicted, many small farmers were thrown into destitution by the rates, while many larger ones were threatened with bankruptcy, as their starving tenants were unable to pay rent.

To forestall bankruptcy, Irish landlords won a provision in the 1847 reforms known as the Gregory Clause, which tightened the means test for relief. This required occupants of more than a quarter-acre of land to relinquish it as a condition of relief. The Whig government welcomed this clause, because it would accelerate the clearance and consolidation of estates, and the conversion of the surviving peasantry into wage laborers. Now only the absolutely destitute were eligible for relief. Upon giving up their land, their homes were torn down to ensure they would not return. This forced thousands to seek shelter in the workhouses. More than a quarter-million tenants were evicted under the Gregory Clause from 1849 to 1854.[64] This reduced the rates assessed on large landlords. To save the biggest landlords, the Gregory Clause subjected the poorest in Ireland to mass homelessness and more deeply entrenched pauperization, as the homeless had no prospects of returning to independence.

Blight, unemployment, and evictions increased the number of purportedly able-bodied men who sought relief. Suspicion of these applicants was so extreme that, although outdoor relief had been permitted by the 1847 reforms, the government insisted that they be subject to the workhouse test to prove their lack of alternatives. However, the workhouses were already overcrowded with the ill, disabled, orphans, and widows with small children. To enforce the test, those unable to work were expelled from the workhouses to die in the streets, while able-bodied men, who vastly preferred outdoor employment, were admitted. This was not necessarily to their advantage. Due to gross overcrowding, poor sanitary conditions, and the weakened state of malnourished inmates, infectious diseases raged within them, killing many thousands.[65]

At every phase of relief policy, the British government knowingly inflicted avoidable suffering and death on the Irish. Administrators of relief in Ireland repeatedly informed them of the dire consequences of their policies. The dogmas of the conservative work ethic, tinged with anti-Irish racism,[66] drove the government's callousness. English Whigs believed that the Irish – laborers and landlords alike – were innately lazy and improvident, and that the poor threatened Malthusian disaster with their large families. In fact, although this was not known at the time, Irish birth rates were already falling before the Famine. But a combination of moral panic and ideologically driven opportunism made the government impatient.

Since they imagined that catastrophe for the peasants would come sooner or later, the Whigs decided that it may as well come sooner. They seized the opportunity of famine to remake Ireland's agricultural sector on the English model. It had taken England more than 300 years of enclosures to clear the land of surplus peasants and concentrate it in the hands of a small number of large landlords. They hoped that draconian relief policies would clear Irish estates of their surplus tenants in just a few years, convert the survivors to wage laborers whose landless precarity would force them to work hard, and compel the Irish landlords to either follow the English capitalist model, or sell their bankrupt estates to such capitalists. As the debate between Whately and Scrope demonstrated, neither liberal tories nor Whigs took the urgent interests of the Irish poor seriously. This was an ideological battle over the future of the Irish economy, in which the poor were mere cannon fodder. Many were destined for death, destitution, or exile, whichever side won.

Nassau Senior viewed British policy toward Ireland as a grand experiment in political economy, the findings of which justified the suffering it inflicted. In 1849 he wrote to Alexis de Tocqueville: "Experiments are made in that country [Ireland] on so large a scale, and pushed to their extreme consequences with such a disregard to the sufferings which they inflict, that they give us results as precious as those of Majendie" (who contributed to Senior's *Poor Law Commissioners' Report of 1834*).[67] More notoriously, Benjamin Jowett, Master of

Balliol College, recalled that Senior had told him that "he feared the famine in Ireland would not kill more than a million people, and that would scarcely be enough to do any good."[68] He meant that even a million deaths would not sufficiently clear the estates of enough people to permit modernization of Ireland's agricultural sector.

The Conservative Work Ethic as Ideology

The welfare reform of 1834, the Irish Poor Law, and British policy toward the Irish Famine reveal the deep structure of the ideology of the conservative work ethic. By "ideology" I refer in part to a set of explicit beliefs that rationalize some social or political ideal and its associated institutions and policies. I also refer to a system of representations, cognitive biases, attitudes, emotional and epistemic dispositions, and values embodied in the social practices associated with those ideologies. Institutions, policies, social norms, and so forth can embody these ideas and attitudes even if individual participants don't share them.[69] Some street-level bureaucrats might merely be following the rules for determining eligibility for some kind of aid. They may have given little thought to how stingy the aid is, how the rules disqualify clear cases of desperate need, or how the elaborate documentation requirements for proving eligibility make sense only on a prejudiced suspicion that applicants are likely to be lazy cheaters. Other bureaucrats may lament the injustice and callousness of the rules they have to enforce.[70] Even some true believers in an ideology and its associated practices might be unaware of the disastrous consequences of its associated practices, of the weaknesses of its empirical assumptions, and the biases in the attitudes they express. Hence, a critique of ideologies and the institutions and policies they support, on the basis of the attitudes and representations embodied in them, does not necessarily impugn their individual supporters or administrators. Some, such as Trevelyan and Senior, knew very well the disastrous consequences of what they were doing or advocating. One cannot say the same of Chadwick. Although the *Poor Law Commissioners' Report* he wrote with Senior reflects the cognitive biases of the conservative work ethic, it would be unfair to condemn Chadwick of a general callousness toward the poor. He devoted much of his career to improving public sanitation in London, focusing on its poorest residents, and advocated schooling for child factory workers against the wishes of the government he advised. The following comments therefore apply to the conservative work-ethic ideology and its associated social policies, and not necessarily toward all of its advocates or administrators.[71]

The ideology of the conservative work ethic is distinguished by a harsh orientation toward ordinary workers and the poor, and an indulgent one toward the "industrious" rich – those who occupy themselves with making money, either through work or investment of their assets, regardless of whether their activities actually contribute to social welfare. In practice, this orientation tends to slide into indulgence toward the rich, whether or not they are industrious even in this morally attenuated sense.

Indulgence toward the rich involves such policies as designing the laws of property, contract, economic regulations, and taxation to promote the consolidation of property into a few vast estates and the concentration of wealth in a few hands, to perpetuate this concentration through such measures as favorable tax treatment of inheritance and permissive attitudes toward anticompetitive activity, to enhance the bargaining power and legal authority of employers over workers, to favor creditors over borrowers, and to tax capital income and wealth very lightly. Harshness toward workers involves such policies as limiting workers' ability to quit and secure work from competing employers (or permitting employers to impose contracts that limit their mobility), repressing workers' organizations (or permitting employers to do so), opposition to workplace safety and other regulations that protect workers from abuse, opposition to policies that provide workers with effective access to affordable insurance, and regressive taxes – particularly measures that tax labor income and consumption more heavily than capital income and wealth. Such policies favor not just wealth accumulation, but widening inequality.

British welfare reform and famine-relief policies in the nineteenth century reflected the key features of poverty policies informed by the conservative work ethic. They offer extremely stinting levels of relief, typically insufficient to enable recipients to escape poverty, and sometimes even to survive. They observe the principle of "less eligibility," insuring that recipients, even if blamelessly unable to work, are worse off than the lowest-paid worker. They prefer to condition relief on the performance of wage labor, even if the recipient's activities would better promote social welfare if directed to education, self-employment, or dependent care. Work requirements are often imposed without regard to their interference with recipients' ability to fulfill duties to provide direct care for dependents. Recipients are subject to severe and intrusive means-testing, often requiring that they spend down all their assets. They lose their relief if they accumulate minimal assets. Policy favors humiliating forms of relief, and in-kind provision over cash relief, to ensure that the poor can't spend money on pleasures reserved for the purportedly more deserving. The fact of being on relief, and the process of gaining access to relief, is highly stigmatized. Relief regulations impose arbitrary delays in providing relief and time limits on relief that are unconnected to recipients' need and opportunities to secure employment or other means of subsistence. Eligibility rules impose burdensome bureaucratic requirements, the administration of which absorb a substantial share of relief expenditures, and result in the exclusion of many genuinely needy persons for failure to fill out complex paperwork correctly, meet deadlines, or satisfy other arbitrary procedures. To the greatest possible extent, the burden of providing relief is put on local communities rather than the whole state. Private charity is favored over state-based aid. Administration of aid, particularly if it involves in-kind provision, may be outsourced to private, for-profit enterprises.

Many of these features of conservative work-ethic poverty policy are more likely to keep or push people into poverty and precarity, rather than to enable them to escape from it. The problem arises not merely from the meager levels of relief. Policies that require recipients to give up their assets (for example, that farmers eat their seed, give up their acreage, and suffer their homes to be torn down) and prohibit them from accumulating new ones keep them in permanent precarity and may deprive them of assets they need to work productively. Money spent on excessive bureaucratic administration and punishing the poor, such as the workhouse, is money taken away from direct relief. Arbitrary bureaucratic requirements and cutoffs prevent the genuinely needy from getting access to relief. The insistence that recipients work for wages even if this entails depriving children of needed care undermines child development and thereby promotes the intergenerational transmission of poverty. The principle of local taxation ensures that the poorest districts face the highest tax burdens. It may also prevent the poorest taxpayers from accumulating the assets they need to escape poverty and precarity. Other provisions, such as settlement, may enable wealthier districts not only to avoid paying for relief, but keep the poor from getting access to opportunity. For-profit outsourcing may also prevent the poor from rising: to the extent that relief administration really does yield profits, administrators have an interest in keeping people on relief.

These poverty-promoting features of conservative relief policy obviously reflect ideological concerns other than tending to individual and community needs. These include (1) the requirements of capitalist class formation; (2) ideas about moral desert – in particular, purported causal connections between wealth and virtue, poverty and vice; (3) a resulting epistemology of suspicion toward the poor, and related cognitive biases; (4) associated attitudes toward the poor, including contempt, resentment, impatience, and fear; and finally (5) utopian fanaticism.

The first requirement of capitalist class formation, as Marx was later to theorize,[72] was to convert workers with capital or rights of access to capital into wage laborers, by appropriating their land. As we have seen, Whately rationalized this as part of the purportedly benevolent civilizing process that would lift autonomous but barbaric peasants up to the status of wage laborers and consumers. Of course, the peasants themselves would have chosen to work their own land if they could, to protect their autonomy. The same trade-off applied to manufacturing. Opportunities for self-employed and skilled work had to be destroyed to induce workers to accept the awful conditions and wages of factory labor in the first half of the Industrial Revolution. Throwing workers into poverty and precarity would force them to work long hours of mind-numbing, exhausting, and dangerous labor for bare subsistence wages, at great profit to their employers. Asset-stripping conditions on relief were instrumental to this process.

Even more influential in defining the conservative work ethic was the almost insuperable Malthusian and Noetic presumption that individuals' wealth is a product of their virtue, poverty of their vice. The relevant virtues are those constitutive of the work ethic – industry, discipline, self-reliance, frugality, chastity, temperance, and foresight – and the vices are their opposites – sloth, laxity, freeloading, prodigality, licentiousness, indulgence, imprudence. On this view, the purportedly free market rewards individuals in "full proportion to the result of their labour."[73] The market gives people what they deserve. Never mind that the rich rigged the rules of property and wage contracts to suppress market wages.

More generally, it could hardly be denied that how hard people work and save is a function not only of their inner moral dispositions but of background opportunities and incentives. Indeed, the supposed corrupting influence of the Poor Law was based entirely on this premise. And Whately had argued before the Famine that "we see that the [Irish] labouring class are eager for work, that work there is not for them, and that they are therefore, and not from any fault of their own, in permanent want."[74] This thought *competes* with Whately's hypothesis that workers are poor because they are lazy, and quit work as soon as they meet bare subsistence needs. In a context where grueling wage labor promised worse outcomes than working for oneself at a more leisurely pace, it was impossible to rationalize poverty- and precarity-promoting policies driven by the conservative work ethic as rewarding diligent labor with its just deserts. These policies were rather rationalized by the purported back-ward-bending supply of labor, which implies that labor had better *not* be well-rewarded, lest its supply be discouraged.

Here lies a central contradiction of the conservative work ethic. All the conservatives claimed that the key to overcoming poverty was to make the poor bourgeois in *attitude*. All they needed to do was adopt the work ethic, or be forced to adopt it, along with the spirit of competitive emulation, the desire to better others in the race for riches and ensure that one's children not fall beneath the standard of living in which they were raised. Poverty was proof that they hadn't adopted bourgeois virtues and aspirations. This presupposes that the poor suffered from no deficit in opportunities. The path to prosperity was open; the poor were simply failing to take it. Yet we have seen that, Priestley partially excepted, conservative policies knowingly reduced the opportunities of the poor to acquire or retain property, work for themselves, or escape precarity.

Ideologies function epistemically: they guide people's perceptions and understandings of their social world. If markets justly reward virtue and punish vice, then wealth and poverty may be taken as reliable *signs* of virtue and vice, respectively. This assumption explains the tendency to blame the disadvantaged for all their problems. Social psychologists view this tendency as an expression of what they call the "fundamental attribution error"[75] – attributing others' misfortunes to their internal dispositions rather than their circumstances. Some research indicates that this tendency is Western rather than universal, and that it targets low-status individuals.[76] It is plausible that the pervasiveness of the conservative work-ethic ideology in the West may have shaped people's cognition in this class-biased way.[77] This class bias explains the epistemology of suspicion toward the poor: the stubborn belief that if they make a claim of need on others, or are found without means of support, they are almost certainly lazy, improvident, and dishonest. (Recall Bentham's "perfect certainty" that everyone without property or a job is a criminal.) This attitude underwrites the insistence that any need-responsive welfare programs spend enormous resources and impose onerous bureaucratic procedures to screen out the undeserving. It explains humiliating and severe forms of relief, such as the use of the workhouse as both test and punishment. It explains the extreme priority given to denying relief to the undeserving over relieving those who are obviously needy through no fault of their own: let a million innocent Irish starve, lest one lazy one receive a bowl of gruel. It explains the extreme resistance to claims of need, even in the face of overwhelming evidence. It explains the pervasive Malthusian catastrophizing over poverty relief, as well as over the consequences of workers' independent agency – over their ability to make a comfortable living on their own, without being subject to the direction of an employer.

Ideologies may shape the emotions and attitudes of some of those who hold them. Prominent among these emotions is fear. With the French Revolution, terror of a working-class uprising inspired political and economic repression. Malthusian hysteria over the imagined consequences of caring for the needs of the poor – the fear of being demographically overrun, and of rents being "swallowed up" by famine relief – underwrote extremely stinting policies. The government's famine-relief measures from 1846 to 1853 cost the Treasury £7 million. This amounted to an annual 0.3 percent of the United Kingdom's GDP over that period. By comparison, the government paid £20 million to compensate 3,000 slaveholding families for the emancipation of their slaves. It spent £70 million to wage the pointless and bloody Crimean War from 1853 to 1856.[78] When it cared about the cause, the government's fiscal capacity was immense. It was not remotely threatened by the costs of famine relief. But panic is not a sound state of mind for doing math, or gaining perspective.

Power tends to breed contempt toward subordinates. But different ideologies inspire distinct understandings of the grounds of that contempt. Here is Senior's explanation of why the Irish, during the Famine, disliked the workhouses:

> Though the food, the lodging, and the clothing of the work-house are, and indeed must be, far superior to those of the cabin, or even the cottage; yet, such is the dislike among the Irish peasantry of cleanliness, of order, of confinement, and of regular work, however moderate – such their love ... of dirt ... that all but the really destitute avoided it ....[79]

Notable in this passage is not simply contempt for the starving Irish, but a grotesque claim about the quality of living conditions in the Irish workhouses, which lacked sanitation for inmates ravaged by disease. Was this fantasy to flatter the imaginary generosity of the ratepayers, or simply an expression of disgust at the Irish poor? Like Bentham, Senior exaggerated the material benefits of the workhouse while completely discounting inmates' losses of liberty, privacy, family life, and dignity. It also ignored the fact that the whole point of the workhouse was to make workers on relief worse off than those who could hang on in their own homes.

Now add resentment to this toxic mix. English Whigs openly resented Irish landlords as well as Irish peasants, the latter for laziness and suspected welfare cheating, the former for laziness, profligacy, and failure to take responsibility for their poor. No wonder Russell's government was so stinting, every penny toward relief begrudged. And no wonder it was so impatient to cut off support on arbitrary deadlines. Similar resentment toward the English poor drove the stinginess and punitiveness of the New Poor Law of 1834.

Yet callousness is not only driven by ideologically mediated fear, resentment, and contempt toward its objects. Ideologies may also promise spectacular rewards if only they are followed with sufficiently ruthless determination. Proponents of the conservative work ethic from Bentham to Whately were in the grip of a utopian picture of the transformative potential of inculcating the work ethic in those whom they saw as lacking it. Mass slavery, starvation, and brutal factory discipline now would ultimately civilize the working classes by bending their labor supply forward, and making them frugal, temperate, and foresighted. Enthralled by hopes of a glorious end, concern for the humanity and justice of the means taken was tossed aside.

Most importantly, in the rush to realize their utopia, proponents of the conservative work ethic destroyed decent human relationships, which must be constituted by nonconsequentialist norms of love, humanity, respect, and reciprocity. In the official ideology of this ethic, the harshness of leaving poor workers at the mercy of market forces was supposed to be tempered by the availability of voluntary private relief, conceived as virtuous so long as it was not required by law, but exercised at the perfect discretion of the beneficent. What supposedly corrupted the poor was not relief as such, but the *assurance* of relief provided by legal guarantees. Precarity, not actual destitution and death, was the essential condition for the poor to internalize the work ethic. Private charity, unlike public relief, blesses, purifies, and exalts the mind of the giver, and so should not be discouraged.[80]

In 1825, Irish socialist William Thompson criticized the advocates of the commodification of labor in the competitive market system as wanting "to make benevolence a crime, and *compel* [workers] to hate and undermine each other under penalty of starving!"[81] What may have seemed like a hyperbolic accusation at the time turned out to be prophetic. In the Irish Famine, even private charity was brutally punished. The great estates could not be cleared unless tenants were prohibited from taking in those evicted. In the early 1850s, while the blight was still affecting Kenmare, land agent William Steuart Trench, who managed the vast Lansdowne estate, decreed that any tenants who took in someone already evicted would themselves be evicted. Eviction amounted to a virtual death sentence. One evictee, 12-year-old Denis Shea, severely weakened from hunger, appealed to his aunt and uncle for shelter. In terror of eviction, knowing that his grandmother had already been evicted for taking Denis in, they beat him up and left him to die of exposure.[82] Such were the fruits of the ideology of the conservative work ethic.

5 THE PROGRESSIVE WORK ETHIC (1): SMITH, RICARDO, AND RICARDIAN SOCIALISTS

The Progressive Work Ethic in Classical Political Economy

The work ethic split into conservative and progressive versions in the late eighteenth century (see Chapter 3). In Chapter 4, I argued that the conservative version triumphed through the mid-nineteenth century, an era characterized by rapidly rising productivity and stagnant wages, and hence by an increasing share of income taken by capital owners.[1] This is what I call the hijacking of the work ethic by capital owners. The next three chapters examine the secularized progressive work ethic, developed by thinkers who sympathized with workers – not just in the sense of proposing policies they thought would help them, but also in taking seriously workers' experiences, perspectives, and aspirations. In the liberal tradition such thinkers include Adam Smith, John Stuart Mill, Marquis de Condorcet and Thomas Paine. In the socialist tradition they include the Ricardian socialists (a group of thinkers loosely connected to David Ricardo), Karl Marx, and Eduard Bernstein, the unjustly neglected pioneer of social democracy. Mill and Bernstein belonged to both traditions.

In the Cold War historiography that still dominates our thinking, Smith and Mill are heroes of so-called classical liberalism, a purportedly libertarian doctrine of nearly pure laissez-faire capitalism shared with other free-market advocates such as Priestley, Bentham, and Burke, and sharply opposed to the socialist ideas developed by Marx and partially instituted in the social democratic regimes of Western

Europe. My classification of work-ethic theorists as either "conservative" or "progressive" highlights a disagreement *within* economic "liberalism," understood as a view broadly friendly to free trade and competitive markets. It stresses shared values among the "progressives," even as they disagree profoundly about such matters as the role of markets in an ideal society. Theorists in the progressive tradition seek economic arrangements that emancipate workers from groveling subordination to superiors, and in which work is a meaningful domain for the exercise of varied and sophisticated skills. They reject the stunted conception of the good life as a matter of competitive acquisition in an essentially antagonistic zero-sum status game. They look forward to a society in which *everyone* can enjoy a life *beyond* the work ethic, one that recognizes a broader set of virtues and goods than those extolled by the work ethic. Such a society would offer plentiful goods for *all* to enjoy. It would not condition access to the goods fundamental to a dignified life, or to sharing in the common life of society, on "earning" them through individualistic striving. Such a society would be so arranged that individual fulfillment is inseparable from promoting the good of others, in which individuals are recognized for their contributions and take satisfaction in their contribution to the good of others.

I argue in the next three chapters that Smith and Mill belong to this progressive tradition and that Marx's thought is closer to Smith's and Mill's than Cold War historiography admits. Moreover, Marx planted the seeds of the democratic, nonrevolutionary branch of socialism that was to deliver historically unprecedented benefits to ordinary workers. We can see this more clearly if we read their texts through the lens of the values that united them: the values of the secular progressive work ethic.

The progressive work ethic includes the virtues of industry, saving for investment, and prudential planning. As a secularized ideal, it aims to bring the rewards of following the work ethic from the next life into this one. As with the conservative work ethic, this entails a rejection of Puritan asceticism with respect to consumption. A central tenet of the progressive work ethic is that workers are entitled to the fruits of their labor. This includes a high material standard of living that rises at the same rate as the growth of labor productivity. The progressive work ethic also rejects Puritan asceticism with respect to leisure. The saints' rest is to be enjoyed here on earth. Progressive theorists differ from conservative ones in insisting on the *universality* of leisure as a just reward of industry. Bentham's "utopia" is one in which every last bodily motion of the poor must be turned to the profit of a bourgeois dictator. Malthus and Whately view the division of society into a leisured propertied class and a relentlessly laboring class of poor as essential to civilization. Advocates of the progressive work ethic insist that *all* workers should have substantial time to enjoy the fruits of their labor in the leisured company of family and friends. They condemn any system that forces workers to slave away in mindless drudgery, living precariously from paycheck to paycheck, while capital owners subject them to tyranny and reap the fruits of the workers' labor. They also condemn Priestley's norm of competitive consumption and accumulation, because it constitutes an antagonistic economy of esteem. Beyond the instrumental benefits of work – consumption, leisure, and security – advocates of the progressive work ethic also seek to reform the organization of work itself, to advance workers' agency. Work ought to be meaningful and autonomously directed by workers themselves; enhance rather than degrade their powers; and uplift their status in society, to dignified people who command the respect of others.

Conservative and progressive advocates of the work ethic differ sharply in their explanations of market outcomes. Conservatives take it as axiomatic that wealth is a sign of virtue, poverty of vice. The laws of the free market are God's laws, distributing rewards in proportion to individual industry, frugality, and prudence. Tampering with them risks Malthusian (or else revolutionary) catastrophe. Trevelyan thought that God sent the Famine to teach the Irish a punitive lesson.[2] This purportedly divine point of view on markets, as we have seen with Senior's *Poor Law Commissioners' Report*, and with Trevelyan's response to the Irish Famine, relies at best on a highly selective body of evidence, and often on a flat refusal to consider counterevidence.

By contrast, advocates of the progressive work ethic insist on an unmoralized causal account of how markets work. In contrast to conservatives' endless handwringing over workers' purported lack of work ethic, they argue that habits of industry, discipline, saving, and so forth are a product of workers' incentives and opportunities. If workers are not working hard or saving enough, not planning far enough into the future or otherwise making imprudent decisions, this is a sign not of their vice, but of bad institutions that perversely constrain them, deprive them of the fruits of their labors, and undermine their cognitive powers. Real-world adverse market outcomes for workers do not reflect differential virtue. They are the product of institutions and incentives rigged by and for the rich and powerful. There is nothing divine about them. Because theorists of the progressive work ethic hold that behavior is the product of incentives and opportunities rather than moral exhortation, they don't *preach* the work ethic and conservatives do. Yet it takes only a little digging to reveal its operations in their theories.

Adam Smith: Sympathy for Workers

The conservative work ethic is not simply a set of doctrines. It embodies an extremely harsh set of *attitudes* toward the working poor: a nearly insurmountable suspicion of their claims of need and lack of opportunity to satisfy needs without assistance; contempt for their suffering and readiness to blame them for it; resentment of and desire to limit any pleasures or assistance they might enjoy; blindness to their virtues and merits; fear of their independent agency; an obsessive desire to control them for one's own profit; and a disposition to impose responsibilities on them, made in obstinate disregard for their physical abilities and opportunities, and for the costs they must bear in carrying them out. Such callous and imperious attitudes drive people to select and interpret evidence in ways that rationalize and reinforce them. The conservative work ethic, regarded as a set of doctrines, is the product of such self-justifying processes.

That's not just my view of the conservative work ethic; it's Adam Smith's. The critique of the conservative work ethic runs through Smith's major works. Indeed, the deepest, most consistent attitude he expresses throughout is a profound sympathy for the "laboring poor, that is, the great body of the people."[3] Burke condemns talk of the "laboring poor" as "base and ... wicked ... political canting language," and argues that the proper response to their condition is to tell them to practice "patience, labour, sobriety, frugality, and religion."[4] Although Burke claims to follow Smith, the contrast in their attitudes toward the working poor is striking: Smith refers to the "laboring poor" 10 times in his chapter on wages, consistently favoring their material advancement.[5]

By what standard can we adjudicate these sharply contrasting attitudes toward the working poor? A fundamental aim of *The Theory of Moral Sentiments* is to discern a point of view from which we can objectively evaluate our own attitudes toward others – their suffering, their pleasures, their merits, their conduct. From this perspective, we can evaluate our treatment of others. We can discern systematic biases that distort our attitudes, and correct those biases to arrive at impartial judgments of ourselves and others. From this point of view, we can also gain a more accurate understanding of our social world.

Smith argues that this point of view is that of an impartial and informed sympathetic spectator. To evaluate "our own sentiments and motives" we must view them through the eyes of a "fair and impartial spectator" who knows our situation.[6] If such a spectator's sentiments accord with (that is, are in sympathy with) our own, then the spectator approves of them; if not, then the spectator disapproves of them. The approval and disapproval of such an impartial spectator supplies the fundamental standard of the appropriateness of our sentiments and conduct.[7] The only "precise and distinct measure" of the "fitness or propriety of affection" lies "in the sympathetic feelings of the impartial and well-informed spectator."[8] The perspective of the impartial specta-tor also affords the standard for evaluating policies and laws, such as property rights, the obligations of contracts and promises, and punish-ments for wrongdoing.[9]

The most important moral discovery from viewing oneself through the eyes of an impartial spectator is that one is "but one of the multitude in no respect better than any other in it."[10] From this perspective we can come to recognize and discount sentiments that fail to accord with that judgment, and thereby learn to respect others as our moral equals.

Smith deployed his theory to undertake a critique of systematic biases to which our sentiments are prone. By far the most consequen-tial of his criticisms were of the biases people have in favor of the rich, and against the poor. "The disposition to admire, and almost to worship, the rich and powerful, and to despise, or, at least, to neglect persons of poor and mean condition ... is ... the great and most universal cause of the corruption of our moral sentiments."[11] Because of these biases, "we see ... the vices and follies of the powerful much less despised than the poverty and weakness of the innocent."[12] These biases systematically distort our judgments of virtue and vice. "In equal degrees of merit there is scarce any man who does not respect more the rich and great, than the poor and humble ... the presumption and vanity of the former are much more admired, than the real and solid merit of the latter."[13]

We are also far more disposed to sympathize with others' joys than with their sorrows.[14] This bias leads us to favor the rich and great with our attention, and to heap scorn on the poor. Smith invites us to consider and sympathize with how this feels to the poor:

> The poor man ... is ashamed of his poverty. He feels that it either places him out of the sight of mankind, or, that if they take any notice of him, they have, however, scarce any fellow-feeling with the misery and distress which he suffers. He is mortified upon both accounts; for though to be overlooked, and to be disapproved of, are things entirely different, yet as obscurity covers us from the daylight of honour and approbation, to feel that we are taken no notice of, necessarily damps the most agreeable hope, and disappoints the most ardent desire, of human nature .... The fortunate and the proud wonder at the insolence of human wretchedness, that it should dare to present itself before them, and with the loathsome aspect of its misery presume to disturb the serenity of their happiness.[15]

Because we sympathize more with the rich and powerful, we also care vastly more about their suffering than for the suffering of the poor. People are "indifferent to the misery of their inferiors." We feel "ten times more compassion and resentment" for "every calamity ... [and] injury" suffered by the great than if "the same things happened to other men."[16] Yet from the impartial spectator's perspective, we should have the same compassion for equal suffering, the same resentment for equivalent victimization, the same admiration for equal merits, the same contempt for equal vices, in rich and poor alike.

The biases in sentiment that Smith condemns are those of the conservative work ethic. These biases also affect our judgments of the nonmoral facts that underwrite this ethic. Because our disdain for the poor drives them out of public view, we also tend to be *blind* to their limited opportunities, physical abilities, and incentives. Such blindness facilitates the operation of the fundamental attribution error – the disposition to attribute the conduct of others to their inner dispositions, when it is really caused by their external incentives and constraints.[17] Smith systematically criticizes its expression in the core assumption of the conservative work ethic: that the working poor are lazy, imprudent, and licentious, while the rich are virtuous.

Against this assumption, Smith consistently argues that differences in behavior are due to differences in external constraints and incentives rather than inner dispositions. If workers aren't industrious, we should examine their circumstances. Food scarcity reduces the capacity of workers to labor.[18] Paying by the piece leads workers to work themselves to exhaustion in a few days, and hence hardly able to work the rest of the week. "The dictates of reason and humanity" tell masters to moderate their work demands, to preserve their workers' health as well as their productivity. Workers need "indulgence ... dissipation and diversion" to restore their capacity to work. They also need good wages. "The liberal reward of labour ... increases the industry of the common people."[19] "Independence" also improves productivity, because self-employed workers reap all the fruits of their labor and thus enjoy greater prospects of improving their condition. "Nothing can be more absurd ... than to imagine that men in general should work less when they work for themselves, than when they work for other people."[20] Apprentices don't work hard because they are unpaid.[21] The labor supply of common workers is decidedly forward-sloping. Frugality, too, predominates across society, as long as individuals stand to better their condition by saving for the future.[22]

If we want to look for vice, we are more likely to find it among the higher classes. The virtues of "patience, industry, fortitude, and application of thought ... are hardly ever to be met with in men who are born to ... high stations," since they enjoy esteem without displaying these virtues, and risk embarrassment if they fail at the tasks that require them.[23] African slaves are vastly more magnanimous than their masters.[24] Landlords are indolent.[25] Manufacturers are deceptive and oppressive, and constantly scheming against the public interest.[26] Kings and ministers are "always, and without any exception, the greatest spendthrifts," who are highly impertinent in "pretend[ing] to watch over the economy of private people" through sumptuary laws.[27] The "vices of levity" – intemperance, licentiousness, profligacy – are far more common among the rich than the poor, because the poor prudently take heed of the fact that these vices will ruin them, while the rich indulge in them as their privilege.[28]

Smith also rejects a second core assumption of the conservative work ethic: that wealth is due to virtue, and poverty to vice. In fact, there is nearly an *inverse* correlation between how hard people work and how rich they are:

> The labour and time of the poor is in civilized countries sacrificed to maintaining the rich in ease and luxury. The landlord is maintained in idleness and luxury by the labour of his tenents .... The moneyd man is supported by his exactions from the industrious merchant and the needy who are obliged to support him in ease by a return for the use of his money .... The rich and opulent merchant who does nothing but give a few directions, lives in far greater ... ease and plenty ... than his clerks, who do all the business. They too ... are in a state of ease and plenty far superior to that of the artizan by whose labour these commodities were furnished. The labour of this man too ... has his livelihood in no uncomfortable way if we compare him with the poor labourer. He has all the inconveniencies of the soil and the season to struggle with, is continually exposed to the inclemency of the weather and the most severe labour at the same time. Thus he who as it were supports the whole frame of society and furnishes the means of the convenience and ease of all the rest is himself possessed of a very small share and is buried in obscurity. He bears on his shoulders the whole of mankind, and unable to sustain the load is buried by the weight of it and thrust down into the lowest parts of the earth, from whence he supports all the rest.[29]
>
> [W]ith regard to the produce of the labour of a great society there is never any such thing as a fair and equal division. In a society of an hundred thousand families, there will perhaps be one hundred who don't labour at all, and who yet, either by violence or by the more orderly oppression of law, employ a greater part of the labour of the society than any other ten thousand in it. The division of what remains, too, after this enormous defalcation, is by no means made in proportion to the labour of each individual. On the contrary those who labour most get least.[30]
>
> [T]he landlords, like all other men, love to reap where they never sowed, and demand a rent even for its natural produce .... [T]here is no country in which the whole annual produce is employed in maintaining the industrious. The idle every where consume a great part of it.[31]

In these passages, Smith is insisting that, to understand economic outcomes, we resist moralistic explanations that rationalize them as rewards for virtue and vice. Only then can we grasp the profound role of nonmoral as well as unjust causes of poverty and prosperity. Agricultural laborers are poor not simply because they must support the idle landlords, but because their productivity is limited by the small degree to which the division of labor has advanced in agriculture, compared to manufacturing. Artisans enjoy higher wages than agricultural workers not because they work harder or more intelligently – indeed, their work is far less demanding and skilled than farming – but because their productivity is greatly enhanced by a fine-grained division of labor joined with labor-saving technology.[32] They also enjoy higher wages because they keep prices high through unjust monopolies, a privilege inaccessible to agricultural workers.[33]

These passages highlight information about the conditions and behavior of different classes in Smith's day, moving his readers closer to the standpoint of an impartial and well-informed spectator. From that standpoint, one finds oneself in sympathy with the working poor, and perhaps also indignant toward those who disparage them. Many other passages in Smith's writings have a similar impact. Indeed, the Austrian economist Carl Menger observed that

> Smith placed himself in all cases of conflict of interest ... between the strong and the weak, *without exception* on the side of the latter .... [T]here is not a single instance in A. Smith's work in which he represents the interest of the rich and powerful as opposed to the poor and weak.[34]

In his day, Smith's writings profoundly influenced people's views of the poor, raising their respectability and discrediting the harsh attitudes and policies of the conservative work ethic.[35]

Free Markets for Workers

The work ethic – "habits of oeconomy, industry, discretion, attention, and application of thought"[36] – lies at the core of Smith's account of virtue. A habit counts as a virtue if it would be approved by an impartial spectator.[37] By this standard, prudence, which Smith identifies with the habits constitutive of the work ethic, is a virtue:

> In the steadiness of his industry and frugality, in his steadily sacrificing the ease and enjoyment of the present moment for the probable expectation of the still greater ease and enjoyment of a more distant but more lasting period of time, the prudent man is always both supported and rewarded by the entire approbation of the impartial spectator.[38]

Prudence involves foresight and "self-command," or the power to forego immediate pleasure or endure immediate pain for the sake of future gain.[39] Because the impartial spectator approves of self-command, everyone esteems the "steady perseverance in the practice of frugality, industry, and application, though directed to no other purpose than the acquisition of fortune."[40]

Like all advocates of the secularized work ethic, whether conservative or progressive, Smith holds that industry, frugality, and discipline ("application") are virtues critical for a prosperous society. Conservatives argued that, because the poor are inclined to vice, they will practice these virtues only if forced by poverty and precarity to submit to the dictatorial authority of their social superiors. As Smith's contemporary Arthur Young, an influential agriculturalist, put the point, "everyone but an ideot knows, that the lower classes must be kept poor, or they will never be industrious."[41] Smith replies that the poor are at least as disposed to practice these virtues as anyone else. We can trust them to exercise their agency in accordance with these virtues, so long as they are free to seek the best opportunities, educated to think for themselves, and rewarded with the fruits of their industry, frugality, and self-discipline. National prosperity follows from workers' "universal, continual, and uninterrupted effort to better their own condition ... protected by law and allowed by liberty to exert itself in the manner that is most advantageous."[42] The key institution required to promote the work ethic is "the establishment of a government which afford[s] to industry, the only encouragement which it requires, some tolerable security that it shall enjoy the fruits of its own labour."[43] Smith thereby joins an account of the liberation of workers to exercise their own judgments of how best to better their condition to a view of economic growth, the fruits of which are widely distributed across all sections of society. Sound institutions will lead to "universal opulence which extends itself to the lowest ranks of the people."[44]

Another sign that Smith endorses a progressive work ethic is his attitude toward leisure. Smith rejects the conceit of the conservative work ethic, that consignment of workers to drudgery is a valuable ascetic discipline. This attitude discourages productivity-enhancing innovation. Masters punish slaves for proposing labor-saving technology, because they view such proposals as attempts to indulge in laziness at their expense. This practice reduces the productivity of slave labor.[45] Smith celebrates a work boy's invention that freed him from tending a machine so he could play with his friends.[46] Economic growth requires increasing labor productivity. Doing so entails that far *less* work is needed to produce even more than before, a condition that promises both "universal opulence" and greater leisure for all. Smith also endorses education for poor children, to inspire their imaginations so they can amuse themselves.[47] Although, as already noted, he holds that ordinary people are more likely to practice the work ethic than their superiors, he worries that the attraction of so many to small religious sects preaching asceticism tied them to "disagreeably rigorous and unsocial" morals. To dispel their "melancholy and gloomy humour," the state should encourage frequent and joyful "publick diversions" to "amuse and divert the people" by granting complete freedom to entertainers of all sorts to practice their arts.[48]

Smith narrates a two-phase account of human progress since the Middle Ages in which workers' emancipation fuels economic growth and widely shared prosperity. The first phase moves from the subjection to landlords under feudalism to commercial society. Commercial society as it existed in Smith's day, however, limited workers' liberty and opportunities because it was hobbled by mercantilist principles defined by "the corporation spirit." The second phase moves from the forms of subjection crafted by mercantilists, along with some residual feudal property institutions, to greater emancipation of workers in a free-market society. The second phase awaits major policy reforms that Smith advocates in *The Wealth of Nations*.

Smith casts the first phase as a tale of delicious irony.[49] Under feudalism, the great landlords owned vast estates, but commerce and manufacturing were undeveloped. Hence, they could spend their wealth only on the maintenance of a vast number of "retainers and dependents," who could not offer anything to the lords in return other than their subjection to the lords' authority. The peasants also lived in subjection to the lords whose property they occupied, either as serfs or tenants at will.[50] The great proprietors indulged their vanity and love of dominion in arbitrarily governing their dependents, particularly in sending their retainers to war against neighboring lords.

The rise of commercial society eventually overcame this disorderly system of subordination and violence. "All for ourselves, and nothing for other people, seems, in every age of the world, to have been the vile maxim of the masters of mankind." Foreign commerce and domestic manufacturers gave the lords a way to spend all their wealth on themselves. Instead of spending their wealth on maintaining dependents, they could spend it on "a pair of diamond buckles perhaps, or for something as frivolous and useless."[51] To do so, they had to dismiss their dependents, who went to the towns to become artisans, shopkeepers, and merchants. Because the latter serve many customers, they don't owe obedience to any one in particular. The towns were also self-governing. So the inhabitants were free from the lords' dominion.

To slake their vanity with the purchase of even more luxuries, the lords also wished to raise the rents. Their tenants could afford this only if they could reap some long-term gains from investing in better agricultural technology. So they bargained for longer and more secure leases in return for paying higher rents. Secure from eviction, the tenants, too, gained independence from their landlords' authority. "[T]hus, for the gratification of the most childish, the meanest and the most sordid of all vanities ... [the lords] gradually bartered their whole power and authority."[52] This process made town and country alike more prosperous. The rise of commercial towns fueled by the vanity of the lords increased demand for agricultural products, and led the merchants to buy land to fulfill dreams of joining the gentry. Because the merchants, unlike the landlords, are driven by the work ethic ("habits ... of order, oeconomy and attention"), they spend their money on improving the productivity of their estates rather than just on conspicuous consumption[53] – a point Locke also stressed.

Smith concludes that "by far the most important" of the effects of the rise of commercial society is the introduction of

> order and good government, and with them, the liberty and security of individuals ... who had before lived almost in a continual state of war with their neighbours, and of servile dependency upon their superiors.[54]

Smith here claims that the liberation of workers from "servile dependency" on their superiors is an even more important effect of commercial society than rising prosperity. One is far more free from subordination to superiors as an artisan, shopkeeper, or farmer with a long-term lease than as a domestic servant, retainer, or tenant-at-will on a landlord's estate. In shifting their expenditure from "hospitality" offered in return for dependents' subjection, to childish vanities, the lords gave up much of their power of personal domination over others.

Smith's sweeping narrative requires some refinement. The agricultural side of his story best applies to the seventeenth century. This was the great era of the yeoman farmers. They were able to prosper due to the sixteenth-century legal strengthening of their tenures enacted in response to popular opposition to the first wave of enclosures. This enhanced legal security empowered the yeomen to bargain for long leases from their landlords – often as long as three lives (the yeoman and two successive heirs) or 99 years. Because rents could not be raised for the duration of their leases, the yeomen could reap all the gains from additional labor and investment in their farms. They bred better seeds, generating a doubling of grain yields over the course of the century. The yeomen's savings blunted the impact of enclosures on agricultural employment. The second wave of enclosures from 1575 to 1674 reduced agricultural employment (8 percent for men, 12 percent for women, 14 percent for boys) and thereby generated emigration. In the South Midlands, a center of enclosure activity, most emigrants went to the burgeoning commercial city of London, where they paid for their sons to obtain an apprenticeship in a craft. I have argued that the second wave of enclosures broadly conformed to Locke's principles and consequently was not bad overall for most ordinary agricultural workers (see Chapter 2). Smith concurs with this judgment. The move from country to city in this era increased workers' freedom and opportunities.[55]

In the eighteenth century, however, the landlords took advantage of financial innovations in mortgaging to expand their estates with borrowed money. They eliminated the yeomen by refusing to renew copyholds and beneficial leases when they expired. In 1750, they launched a third wave of enclosures that was to continue for a century. This time they forced buyouts of leases and small freeholds through acts of Parliament. The resulting very large farms employed fewer workers per acre. They employed them as precarious day laborers rather than servants on annual contracts. Agricultural employment and wages plummeted, forcing many to resort to relief in the off-season. Day laborers were too poor to buy apprenticeships for their sons, emigration to manufacturing towns was low, and rural industry did not grow to absorb them.[56]

Smith's confidence in an improving gentry from the merchant class is overstated. While they energetically invested in their estates and introduced new techniques, the yeomen were the ones responsible for the agricultural revolution that increased productivity (yields per acre). Smith's contemporary Arthur Young influentially argued, on the basis of incorrectly analyzed data, that large estates were more capital-intensive and hence more productive than small ones. Young thereby promoted the case for the purportedly improving gentry to expand their holdings. In fact, they, along with the sluggish aristocrats, were to wreak devastation across rural England by shedding agricultural labor that was not absorbed by industry. By 1831, half of the agricultural laborers in the South Midlands were unemployed for most of the year. The landlords' revolution in agriculture, which consolidated most agricultural land in a small number of large capitalist farms, "produced paupers, not proletarians."[57]

Smith cannot be blamed for not knowing events to come. It is unclear how aware he was of the extent of destruction of the yeomen that had already been wreaked in his day, or of the extreme poverty and precarity of agricultural laborers. Widespread public attention was to be focused on the acute distress of English agricultural laborers only during the French Revolution, nearly 20 years after the publication of *The Wealth of Nations*. Smith did know, however, that workers' prospects were far from optimal in his day. He proposes reforms intended to help rural as well as manufacturing workers. This is the point of what he hopes will be a second phase of progressive reform. It aims to improve workers' education and sweep away the remaining feudal as well as mercantilist institutions in British society. Not just the feudal lords but merchants and manufacturers instituted their own oppressive and inefficient forms of government – most importantly, various forms of unfree labor, colonies, and monopolistic corporations. Smith's reforms include (1) ending the feudal institutions of primogeniture and entails; (2) attacking all forms of unfree labor and restraints on labor movement; (3) ending dominion over colonies; and (4) establishing universal state-funded education. Each of these reforms aims to enhance the independent agency of workers, improve their opportunities to better their condition, and thereby to promote widely shared prosperity.

Primogeniture and Entails. Most arable land in Smith's day was tied up in inheritance arrangements designed to preserve dynastic wealth by keeping the great estates intact.[58] Under primogeniture, the eldest son would inherit his father's entire estate. Entails empowered owners to determine inheritance not only on their own death, but for successive generations. They typically limited the ability of heirs to sell off parts of their estates. Smith follows Locke in criticizing primogeniture, a "method of succession, so contrary to nature, to reason, and to justice."[59] He condemns entails as "the most absurd thing in the world" since "the earth is the property of each generation" and should not be controlled by the dead hand of the past.[60] In the Middle Ages, there was a legitimate interest in keeping large estates intact. The lords were constantly at war with one another, and only large estates, which could maintain numerous retainers, could keep their inhabitants secure against plunder.[61] The rise of commercial society ended the lords' warmongering, and the loss of their independent authority strengthened the power of the national government to make all estates secure under the rule of law, regardless of size. Hence, the public interest in keeping large estates intact has disappeared.

The survival of primogeniture and entails now serves only "the vanity of families." It hampers economic growth by preventing its purchase by those most able and willing to invest in its improvement – the yeomen, and enterprising merchants who want to enter commercial farming.[62] Of these two groups, the latter *follow* the yeomen or small proprietors in being "the principal improvers" of agriculture "in every country."[63] (As noted above, research in economic history vindicates Smith's judgment.) Again following Locke, Smith argues that land should not be locked up in the hands of lazy landlords. The great landlords are indisposed to applying themselves to the small details needed to manage their estates productively, and would rather indulge in conspicuous consumption.[64] The most productive farmers are those who can keep the greatest share of the fruits of their labor. Slaves have no incentive to work hard, because they gain nothing at the margin for their labor. Sharecroppers, tenants at will, and farmers on short-term leases have little incentive to invest in improving the land, because the landlord would take part or all of their gains. At the margin, yeomen, whether freeholders or on long leases, get to keep all of the fruits of their labor, and so are the most productive farmers.[65] Hence, agricultural productivity would advance most rapidly if the great estates were "divided into a number of small possessions each having a separate master."[66] The abolition of primogeniture and entails would usher in a free and competitive land market, which would tend to allocate land to the most efficient producers – those following the work ethic. A free market in land would thus simultaneously promote the independence and prosperity of those who work the land.

Free Labor. Smith tells the story of the transition from feudal to commercial society as a story of progress because he favors the freedom and independence of workers over their subjection to masters. "The pride of man makes him love to domineer, and nothing mortifies him so much as to be obliged to condescend to persuade his inferiors."[67] This is why people would rather get what they want by ordering slaves than by bargaining with inferiors who are free, even if they would gain more in material terms from the latter relationship.[68] Unfree labor, whether it takes the form of slavery, serfdom, feudal and indentured service, or apprenticeship, serves the vanity of masters. It subjects workers to misery, precarity, and abuse. It is always less productive than free labor. Smith favors market society precisely because it advances the independence of workers, and thereby forces the rich and powerful to condescend to bargain with them. This is the moral meaning of Smith's famous claim about market exchange:

> [G]ive me that which I want, and you shall have this which you want, is the meaning of every such offer . . .. It is not from the benevolence of the butcher, the brewer, or the baker, that we expect our dinner, but from their regard to their own interest. We address ourselves, not to their humanity but to their self-love, and never talk to them of our necessities but of their advantages.[69]

Smith isn't celebrating selfishness here. He is commending a norm of address to others that recognizes their dignity, as people who have interests of their own that must be respected. For Smith, the relevant contrasts to such an address are haughty domination on one side – the lord ordering his servants around – and servile dependency on the other. "Nobody but a beggar chuses to depend chiefly upon the benevolence of his fellow-citizens," he says in the same passage. For humiliating subordination always attends such dependence. By contrast, the butcher, the brewer, and the baker offer an ideal of free labor as self-employed labor.[70]

Like Locke, Smith accepts the legitimacy of wage labor. Yet much of his case for *free*-market society lies in what he takes to be its tendency to promote self-employment, the freest form of labor. Free markets would maximize self-employment both by raising less-free workers to this status, and by forcing indolent rentiers to work for a living. As noted above, Smith argues that creating a free market in land by altering inheritance law would increase the ranks of yeoman farmers and reduce the numbers of lazy landlords who could live off their rents. Similarly, Smith argues that large-scale enterprises enabled by joint-stock corporations are mostly creations of inefficient and corrupt mercantilist policies. These policies grant monopolistic privileges to joint-stock corporations and protect them with tariffs, export bounties, and other special favors. Because the managers of such firms are risking other people's money, they waste it and take reckless risks. Managers who own their firms risk their own money, and hence manage them with energy, attention, and prudence. Elimination of mercantilist favors to joint-stock corporations would level the competitive playing field. This would result in the triumph of many smaller, owner-managed firms, resulting in more opportunities for self-employment.[71] The high growth rates induced by fully free markets would also reduce interest rates, and thereby "render it impossible for any but the very wealthiest people to live upon the interest of their money." People "of small and middling fortunes" would have to run their own business to make a living.[72]

Smith declaims at length against two forms of unfree labor: slavery and apprenticeship. Slavery – a term he uses to include the serfs of countries in Eastern Europe, as well as colliers and salters who are bound to their mines – subjects workers to the most cruel and arbitrary treatment, and deprives them of basic liberties and the fruits of their labor.[73] Unfortunately, wealthy and republican societies treat their slaves even more cruelly than poor and despotically governed societies.[74] "The greater [the] freedom of the free, the more intollerable is the slavery of the slaves." A humane person would rather wish that "opulence and [political] freedom, the two greatest blessings men can possess," should never exist than that these blessings exist with slavery, since the latter state is "incompatible with the happiness of the greatest part of mankind."[75] Smith's opposition to slavery explains his ambivalence toward republican government, notwithstanding his affirmation that it is one of the greatest blessings.[76] He feared that the love of dominion was so great that slavery would never be abolished, especially in a state with a republican government.[77]

Apprenticeship would be easier to abolish. By law, apprentices were bound to work unpaid for many years as a condition of becoming journeymen. Their parents had to pay the master for tuition and living expenses while the master taught them a trade. Smith condemns this arrangement. Artisan labor does not require such skill that it would require protracted training. Apprentices acquire habits of indolence because they are unpaid.[78] "The property which every man has in his own labour, as it is the original foundation of all other property, so it is the most sacred and inviolable."[79] By this Lockean principle, Smith objects to the "plain violation" of workers' liberty by legal restrictions against their offering their labor to any employer willing to hire them. Employers are perfectly able to judge the skills of such applicants, without any need for apprenticeship certification. The real purpose of apprenticeship is not to ensure high-quality workmanship. It is to satisfy "the corporation spirit" – the tendency of special interests to obtain special privileges at the expense of others, through private collusion or state law. Apprenticeship laws, which permit tradesmen to limit the number of apprentices, artificially raise wages by restricting the supply of workers in a given trade. This practice exploits apprentices and forces consumers to pay higher prices. Limits on the number of apprentices also exploit workers who provide the materials for the trade, by restricting demand for their labor and hence lowering their income. By combining to limit their own numbers, a half-dozen wool-combers have managed to reduce "a thousand spinners and weavers ... into a sort of slavery to themselves."[80]

Workers have a vital interest not only in being able to enter any trade, but to practice their chosen trade wherever they wish. Yet incorporated towns sometimes obtained monopolies on particular trades, preventing workers in other towns from competing.[81] In the interest of maintaining a monopoly on knowledge, some trades secured a draconian law prohibiting artisans from going abroad to practice or teach their trade.[82] Smith condemns such mercantilist restrictions as unjust violations of workers' liberty.

Today, Smith's attacks on mercantilist policies are mainly remembered as defenses of consumer interests. While Smith has consumer interests in mind,[83] he also stresses how mercantilism amounted to a kind of class warfare on poor workers. Industries protected by mercantilist policies are "carried on for the benefit of the rich and the powerful." Industries "carried on for the benefit of the poor and the indigent," such as the work of spinners undertaken by poor women, are "either neglected, or oppressed."[84] Mercantilist policy amounts to hurting "one order of citizens, for no other purpose but to promote that of some other," a practice contrary to "justice and equality of treatment,"[85] and which invariably supports privileged classes.

Colonies. Smith argues that the colonies of North America provided workers with extraordinary opportunity. Workers from the mother country could easily acquire land to become self-employed farmers. Under these conditions, employers and capital owners had to treat workers well to retain them at all. Hence wages were very high, and profits and rents low.[86] Yet these benefits cannot justify "the injustice of the project." The foremost injustices of colonialism are the "plundering" and "cruel destruction of the natives," and the oppressive institution of slavery.[87]

Colonial policies were originally founded on a foolish quest for silver and gold. They eventually focused on establishing trading monopolies between the colonies and the mother country. Yet the mercantilist economic arguments for such monopolies are fallacious. None of the North American colonies paid enough taxes to support the vast military costs needed to secure them, much less to cover their share of maintaining the empire. Even if the monopoly profits of the merchants and the favorable balance of trade counted as benefits to the empire, they are less than the military and administrative costs of the colonies. More importantly, these are not benefits at all. The colonial trade monopolies reduce the opportunities and wages of workers in the North American colonies, by barring them from manufacturing and trading directly with other countries. This "is a manifest violation of the most sacred rights of mankind."[88]

Smith criticizes mercantilists for promoting the values of the conservative work ethic, which advocates harsh treatment of workers and low wages. His replies to their arguments express support for the progressive work ethic:

> Our merchants frequently complain of the high wages of British labour as the cause of their manufactures being undersold in

foreign markets; but they are silent about the high profits of stock. They complain of the extravagant gain of other people; but they say nothing of their own.[89]

Mercantilists claim that high wages are bad for the economy. Here is Smith's reply to "the common complaint" that even the laboring poor in Britain could afford luxuries:[90]

> Is this improvement in the circumstances of the lower ranks of the people to be regarded as an advantage or as an inconveniency to the society? . . . Servants, labourers and workmen . . . make up the far greater part of every great political society. But what improves the circumstances of the greater part can never be regarded as an inconveniency to the whole. No society can surely be flourishing and happy, of which the far greater part of the members are poor and miserable. It is but equity, besides, that they who feed, cloath and lodge the whole body of the people, should have such a share of the produce of their own labour as to be themselves tolerably well fed, cloathed and lodged.[91]

Mercantilists complained of high wages because they endorsed the conservative work ethic.[92] Later advocates of the conservative work ethic such as Burke, Malthus, and Whately claimed to be following Smith. In fact they are descendants of Smith's opponents, the mercantilists, in advocating property arrangements that keep the working poor in poverty and precarity. According to Smith, high wages are commendable. But high monopoly profits undermine the frugality necessary for sound business enterprises.[93]

Colonies were not always governed by the state. The East India Company was a joint-stock company that began as a trading company, yet came to govern British India in 1757. It imposed taxes, secured its power with a vast private army, and governed until 1858. It offers a cautionary tale of what happens when the government is run like a business. "The government of an exclusive company of merchants, is, perhaps, the worst of all governments for any country whatever," because the interest of monopoly merchants is directly opposed to the interests of the people they govern.[94] They rule despotically and by violence. The British East India company caused famine in Bengal.[95] Its Dutch counterpart "[b]y different arts of oppression" reduced the population of certain islands in Indonesia to just what was necessary to grow the spices it exported to Europe.[96]

Some who claim to follow Smith today read him as a proto-libertarian critic of state power, from which they suppose it follows that private governments founded on property rights and contractual relations should be free of regulation. Smith's account of the arbitrary power of feudal lords – which was founded on their ownership of land – and of slavery – founded on a property right over people – as well as of apprenticeship, joint-stock corporations, cartels, and private colonies, shows that he is at least as worried about private as about state power.[97]

Universal State-Funded Education. Smith's policy positions reflect the progressive work ethic in advocating high wages along with workers' liberation from the private government of landlords and monopsonistic corporations. Workers are most free when self-employed, so they can autonomously direct their labor rather than submit to the haughty dominion of a master. However, his economic theory implies a tension between raising wages and workers' freedom. Rising wages are made possible by increasing productivity, which is due to an increasingly fine-grained division of labor. Smith's famous discussion of the microdivision of labor in a pin factory shows how reducing the work of any given laborer to a single extremely simple operation, repeatedly executed throughout the day, vastly increases the productivity of labor over a system in which each worker performs all of the tasks necessary for producing a pin.[98] Manufacturing workers earn higher wages than agricultural laborers partly because of this microdivision of labor. However, spending one's entire working day repeatedly executing a single operation dulls the mind and thereby undermines the capabilities needed for autonomous action, not just while at work, but in the conduct of the rest of one's life. A worker reduced to such monotonous labor becomes "incapable ... of conceiving any generous, noble, or tender sentiment, and ... forming any just judgment" about either "the ordinary duties of private life" or the public interest. "His dexterity at his own particular trade seems, in this manner, to be acquired at the expence of his intellectual, social, and martial virtues."[99] By contrast, although agricultural workers' wages are depressed by the lack of specialization, their minds and capacities for autonomous judgment are enlivened by the variety of tasks they must undertake.[100] The even greater variety of work undertaken in "barbarous societies" that have almost no division of labor makes "every man" inventive and fit for judging all matters, even of the public interest of their society.[101]

To reduce the tension between high wages and capacities for autonomous judgment, Smith proposes a program of state-funded universal education. Children of even the poorest workers should learn reading, writing, and arithmetic, and may be required to attend school for this purpose.[102] Educated workers will gain a sense of self-respect, "and [be] more likely to obtain the respect of their lawful superiors." They will also be better capable of judging the public interest, and so less likely to be misled by "the interested complaints of faction and sedition." Universal education will thus improve both the status of workers and the order and stability of a free society.[103] Tellingly, on Smith's view, workers' personal and political freedom *support* an orderly society.

Smith died before his recommendations on education were adopted. They became the subject of debate early in the nineteenth century, when reformers attacked apprenticeship laws. Supporters of apprenticeship endorsed its extremely narrow education by invoking values of the conservative work ethic. To secure civilization, the poor must be kept in their place. Apprenticeship would keep the working poor from vagrancy and in subjection to their masters. By narrowing workers' minds to just the tasks their masters assigned to them, it would keep them away from thinking about politics.[104] In calling for general education to replace apprenticeship, Smith expressed confidence that an educated population of poor workers would make positive contributions to political discussion and be *more* likely to support sound policies.[105]

Pragmatism vs. Dogmatism

Outside the rarefied circles of scholars dedicated to interpreting his work, Smith is typically viewed as a leading proponent of unyielding laissez-faire, just as Locke is viewed as advocating nearly absolute property rights. Yet his policy recommendations regularly display a pragmatic orientation to progressive improvement, rather than rigid attachment to purported moral principles regardless of the consequences.

Consider Smith's views of paper money. In his day, banks would issue paper money as a promissory note redeemable for gold or silver on demand. This increased the effective supply of money by increasing its velocity or rate of circulation, because businesses would not have to keep permanent stocks of gold and silver on hand to pay their bills. However, banks would routinely issue more notes than they could redeem if too many holders presented their notes at once. This led to periodic bank runs and financial instability that undermined everyone's economic interests, especially those of the poor.[106] To reduce this risk, Smith proposes that banks be permitted to issue notes only in the large denominations needed to support business-to-business transactions. The retail trade should be supported by gold and silver coin alone.[107] Smith grants that such a regulation is a "violation of natural liberty." Yet

> those exertions of the natural liberty of a few individuals, which might endanger the security of the whole society, are, and ought to be, restrained by the laws of all governments . . . . The obligation of building party walls, in order to prevent the communication of fire, is a violation of natural liberty, exactly of the same kind with the regulations of the banking trade which are here proposed.[108]

Smith's view aligns with Locke, who also supported regulations for the public interest even if they restrict "natural liberty."

Smith also recommends regulations on interest rates. In contrast to Bentham, who opposed any caps on interest rates,[109] Smith argues that the rate should be capped slightly above what we today call the prime rate. That way, honest people without the best credit could still borrow money by paying a modest risk premium. His reasoning is based on work-ethic values similar to Locke's. If the law permitted much higher rates, most money "would be lent to prodigals and projectors" who would "waste and destroy" capital rather than "sober people" who would use it in ways that promote economic growth.[110]

The terms of the employment contract may also be justly regulated, provided they favor the workers. Smith claims that pro-worker regulations are "always just and equitable."[111] He reasons that, under prevailing conditions of plutocracy, in which legislators depend on employers for advice, every law will give employers no less than their due. Hence any law favoring the workers, such as one requiring employers to pay them in cash rather than in kind, can be counted on to promote the interests of both sides. Such a law protects workers against adulteration of their compensation by fraudulent employers, and also protects honest employers from being fraudulently outbid for workers. By contrast, we cannot depend on the justice of regulations, such as maximum wage laws, that favor the employers. For legislators only hear their side of the case.

What then accounts for Smith's reputation as a dogmatic advocate of laissez-faire? Emma Rothschild traces this to an attempt by conservative policy makers to claim Smith for themselves shortly after his death.[112] Smith, who died at the start of the French Revolution, was lionized by many of its advocates. This fact briefly made Smith a seditious figure in Britain. Dugald Stewart, professor of moral philosophy at the University of Edinburgh, recovered him for conservatives in his 1794 memoir of Smith.[113] In 1800, Prime Minister William Pitt wrote a preface to Burke's "Thoughts and Details on Scarcity" that claimed that Smith always paid "the greatest deference" to Burke's views in *The Wealth of Nations*.[114] This claim led many to suppose that "Thoughts and Details on Scarcity" was simply an exposition of Smith's views.[115] These representations permanently colored Smith's reputation.

MP Samuel Whitbread had sponsored a minimum-wage law in 1795 by citing Smith's support for regulations favoring workers.[116] Pitt's opposition, aided by Burke's "Thoughts and Details on Scarcity," led to the defeat of that measure. Ironically, this defeat led to the adoption of the Speenhamland system of outdoor relief for able-bodied workers as a desperate alternative measure. We can only speculate on what Smith would have thought of this system. It is telling that in all his works, Smith never said a word against the general principle of poor relief. He criticized England's Poor Laws in only one respect: he criticized the Law of Settlement, which effectively barred the poor from seeking better work opportunities outside their birth parish.[117] Settlement regulations gave parish officials an arbitrary power to "imprison a man ... for life" in a parish by denying him a certificate providing that, were he to settle in a distant parish and come to need relief, his birth parish would assume the costs of his removal and relief.[118] Justice resides not in compelling parish officials to provide a certificate, but in abolishing the whole settlement system, under which parishes would deport poor workers who needed or might need relief. "To remove a man who has committed no misdemeanour from the parish where he chuses to reside, is an evident violation of natural liberty and justice." Settlement regulations have "most cruelly oppressed" the working poor.[119] Officials barred the poor from settling in a parish only to avoid the burden of poor relief. Had Smith solely been concerned with ensuring the freedom of movement of the poor, he could have equally well advanced that objective by advocating the abolition of poor relief. That he did not is evidence that Smith accepted the legitimacy of relief.

Charles Trevelyan further cemented Smith's reputation as a dogmatic advocate of free markets, regardless of consequences. During the Irish Famine, he distributed some of Smith's writings along with Burke's "Thoughts and Details on Scarcity."[120] No doubt his selections from Smith included his "Digression Concerning the Corn Trade and Corn Laws,"[121] which discusses policies to prevent famine. Some passages in the Digression sound like doctrinaire laissez-faire:

> [A] famine has never arisen from any other cause but the violence of government attempting, by improper means, to remedy the inconveniencies of a dearth.[122]
>
> The unlimited, unrestrained freedom of the corn trade, as it is the only effectual preventative of the miseries of a famine, so it is the best palliative of the inconveniencies of a dearth; for the inconveniencies of a real scarcity cannot be remedied; they can only be palliated.[123]
>
> The natural effort of every individual to better his own condition, when suffered to exert itself with freedom and security, is so powerful a principle, that it is alone, and without any assistance, ... capable of carrying on the society to wealth and prosperity ....[124]

Much of Smith's discussion criticizes popular demands to restrict the domestic grain trade during bad harvest years.[125] Popular opinion blamed high prices in such years on conspiracies of inland grain dealers to raise prices. Smith argues that these fears are baseless. Inland dealers are too numerous and scattered to effectively combine. Nor do they have any interest in doing so, because their interest coincides with the people's. Moreover, popular demands for regulation of the grain trade to prevent hunger are counterproductive. Smith discusses three such demands: prohibiting exports, cutting out dealers by forcing farmers to sell their grain directly to the people, and capping prices. All of these measures increase the risk of shortages by reducing the grain supply. Restrictions on grain exports reduce acreage under cultivation by limiting the extent of the grain market.[126] Cutting out grain dealers forces farmers to divert some of their capital from grain production to supporting the retail grain trade. Capping prices puts farms at financial risk by making it unprofitable for dealers to offer farmers multiyear fixed-price contracts for their grain. Such contracts insure farmers against severe price drops during gluts. But dealers could bear the losses in glut years only if they could clear profits from high grain prices in dearth years. Price caps also suppress imports into areas suffering from bad harvests.

Smith also criticizes England's Corn Law regulations on foreign trade. The Corn Laws, which were repealed during the Irish Famine, placed tariffs on imports and bounties on exports of grain. These laws raised the price of grain. Smith argues that they helped the landlords at the expense of the workers – an evident injustice. Imports should be tariff-free. This measure would greatly benefit the vast majority at little real cost to landlords. That import tariffs are suspended in dearth years shows their impropriety at all times.[127]

Smith had strong grounds for optimism about free trade in grain. England's agriculture was so well developed that it had not suffered a serious famine in centuries.[128] He rightly argued that, in the long run, freeing up markets would increase global food production by extending the market, and that this would reduce the risk of famine. Yet he also carefully notes an exception to free trade when its consequences would be dire. Although the interest of grain exporters usually aligns with the people's, it may be opposed in dearth years, if another country offers a higher price.[129] A small country practicing free trade in a region filled with countries not doing so could not freely export to a large neighboring country in dearth "without exposing itself to the like dreadful calamity." Such countries could justifiably restrict grain exports in dearth years. England, Smith thought, was too large and rich to have to resort to such measures. Yet Smith clearly allows that in cases of "urgent necessity," the state may "sacrifice the ordinary laws of justice" – including the freedom of a farmer to sell his goods wherever it can fetch the highest price – to the public interest.[130]

Thus, even the section of The Wealth of Nations that might be construed to most fully support Trevelyan's draconian policies during the Irish Famine does not do so. Smith was no dogmatist about free trade. Nor did he write a word against the principle of poor relief. More generally, the *spirit* of Trevelyan and of his fellow advocates of the conservative work ethic is opposed to Smith's. These dogmatists, identifying free-trade principles with the divine law and insisting on their application regardless of the consequences – or, in Bentham's case, designing a vast totalitarian machinery for enslaving the poor – exemplify what Smith condemns as "the man of system." This man is

> so enamoured with the supposed beauty of his own ideal plan of government, that he cannot suffer the smallest deviation from any part of it. He goes on to establish it completely and in all its parts, without any regard either to the great interests, or to the strong prejudices which may oppose it.[131]

Libertarians commonly cite this passage to enlist Smith against socialist schemes of comprehensive state planning of the economy, and on behalf of pure laissez-faire.[132] They are certainly correct about comprehensive centralized planning, although it would be anachronistic to suppose that Smith had that case in mind. But Smith's complaint about the "man of system" falls equally harshly upon anyone who "insist[s] upon establishing ... in spite of all opposition, every thing" that his "idea of perfection of policy and law" requires.[133] Nor should we imagine that the aim of those conservatives who insisted on a rigid application of laissez-faire principles was simply to realize a "spontaneous order" of liberty whose ultimate contours were unpredictable. As we have seen, they had a very specific class outcome in mind: to push the working classes into poverty and precarity, so that they would be forced to submit to the dominion of their social superiors, in the name of imposing on them a harsh and exploitative version of the work ethic. They accepted the grim costs of achieving this objective, including that a million Irish die from famine, and that up to 6.5 percent of British citizens be consigned to despotic workhouses at any given time.[134] Their intransigence ensured that workhouses would persist until 1948.

Smith's reputation as an advocate of severe laissez-faire principles is due not only to his mistaken reception, but to bad timing. He died at the peak of Enlightenment optimism about the future, before the French Revolution descended into terror, before the working classes were largely proletarianized and consigned to labor in gigantic, mechanized factories, before the shocking series of crop failures culminating in the Irish Famine. Free-market principles that he thought would deliver greater autonomy, respectability, prosperity, and leisure to the working classes turned out to have much harsher consequences for them as the Industrial Revolution proceeded. It is wrong to attribute to Smith any endorsement of those consequences. No one writing before Smith's death did or could have predicted them. This is not least because, far from being dictated by impersonal laws of market economics, they were the product of policy choices made by Smith's ideological adversaries – the doctrinaire advocates of the conservative work ethic, who "reinstated a catastrophic view of the world" in view of the darker events following shortly after Smith's death.[135]

This gets us to the crux of the matter. Smith contrasted free markets to the interventions of a state entirely controlled by wealthy property owners – landlords and manufacturers – and run for their interests. The rich rigged property laws to concentrate land ownership in a few families and to establish slavery in the colonies. They rigged trade regulations to raise the price of food and to create monopolies and oppressive colonies run by private corporations. They rigged labor regulations to exploit apprentices and cap wages. They rigged taxes to fall on ordinary workers rather than themselves. Occasionally he criticizes popular demands for state regulation, which he (almost always rightly) thinks are based on faulty economic analysis. But the overwhelming bulk of policy analysis in *The Wealth of Nations* criticizes the vast extent of rent-seeking by the rich, and the corruption of a state that serves their interests at the expense of ordinary people. When advocates of the conservative work ethic such as Burke cite Smith to support the view that labor is a commodity like any other – that is, that workers should have to rely on market wages alone to support themselves, and thus that they must bend their knees to their employers – they disingenuously use free-market rhetoric to hide the landowners' own rigging of the laws to strip workers of their property and prevent them from accumulating any. Exposing the landowners to market forces was not what these people had in mind. Smith, by contrast, wanted the rules designed to dramatically expand ordinary workers' opportunities to accumulate property and thereby become independent of their superiors.

Smith is no dogmatic laissez-faire theorist. He is an advocate of the progressive work ethic. Yet even in his day, Smith was unable to envision real remedies for some of the worst injustices he denounced. He was pessimistic about the prospects for abolishing slavery and ending imperialism. His educational proposals, while helpful, did not resolve the seeming conflict between economic growth and escape from mind-numbing forms of drudgery that left workers "mutilated and deformed."[136] Advocates of the progressive work ethic still had a lot of work to do to make their vision viable.

Ricardo, Rent, and the Stationary State

David Ricardo (1772–1823), a leading political economist of his day and Member of Parliament in his last four years, is canonized as Smith's successor in the history of economic thought. In the history of the progressive work ethic, he is more important for what others – James and John Stuart Mill, and Ricardian socialists – made of his theories than for what he made of them. Ricardo was a conventional Benthamite utilitarian. "[M]y motto, after Mr. Bentham, is 'the greatest happiness to the greatest number.'"[137] In keeping with the normative priorities of the progressive work ethic, "the greatest number" in this classical utilitarian formula implies a distributive requirement. It isn't acceptable to maximize total happiness by means that concentrate its enjoyment in fewer people.[138] Rather, policy should focus on promoting the happiness of the most numerous class in society, the workers. They are "by far the most important class in society."[139]

As we have seen with Bentham, however, what policies this view generates for workers depends on one's empirical assumptions. Like Smith, Ricardo opposed mandatory apprenticeships as violating workers' rights.[140] He supported more frequent elections, expansion of the franchise, a secret ballot to protect voters from coercion by their superiors, and the right of workers to assemble and petition Parliament.[141] Most importantly for the history of the progressive work ethic, Ricardo made the distribution of income by class a central focus of political economy. His development of Malthus's theory of rent generated damning conclusions about this distribution. Yet, as a consistent advocate of free trade and an opponent of price regulation, including of grain, wages, and interest rates,[142] he opposed state interference in the distribution of income and wealth. As a proponent of Malthus's theory of population and critique of the Poor Laws, he opposed bills to support the children of the unemployed, and to provide land to hand-loom weavers displaced by power looms.[143] Despite this conservatism, Ricardo's theories inspired the first generation of work-ethic progressives to ground programs for a radical redistribution of property in economic theory. To sort this out, we must begin with Ricardo's account of the laws of distribution.

The Laws of Distribution and the Stationary State. Ricardo claims that the main task of political economy is to determine the laws regulating the distribution of national income among the economic classes – workers, capitalists, and landowners – or almost equivalently, its division among wages, profits, and rents.[144] Economists no longer believe that there are laws of distribution by class. But in an era deeply influenced by Malthusian population theory, it seemed possible to discern such laws. Britain undertook its first modern census in 1801, which revealed a surprisingly high population of nearly 11 million (excluding Ireland). The 1811 census reported a population of 12.6 million.[145] At this rate of growth, the population would double in 38 years. Britain was also rocked by an unusual period of bad harvests. And the number of very poor – cottagers (seasonally employed agricultural laborers) and paupers – rose from 9.6 percent to 14.9 percent of English and Welsh families between 1759 and 1798.[146] These trends were temporary. The share of very poor families dropped by half by 1846. At the time, however, political economists interpreted the combination of population growth, food shortages, and rise in the number of very poor as evidence that Britain was approaching Malthusian constraints. Ricardo developed a model showing that if population really was pressing against food supply, laws of distribution could be derived from Malthus's theories of population and rent.

At the turn of the nineteenth century, wage-earners and relief recipients (workers, cottagers, paupers, and the lower middle class) comprised 84.6 percent of English and Welsh families, capitalists (farmers, financiers, merchants, etc.) 14 percent, and the landed class 1.3 percent. Wages comprised 56.6 percent of national income, profits 25.4 percent, and rents 18.0 percent.[147] What laws determined these shares, and how do they change over time? Ricardo's one-sector "corn model" of the economy predicts trends in the real income shares of the respective classes. In this model, capitalists lease land from landowners, deploy most of their capital stock to advance wages to workers, and earn profits as the residual from the sale of their product – corn – after deducting rent and wages. To simplify further, assume that extra units of production arise from additional units of labor and capital applied in a fixed ratio.[148] Profits mainly amount to interest ("a just compensation" for waiting before receiving any returns, needed to induce the capitalist to employ his capital[149]). After deducting a small portion for their own consumption, capitalists reinvest their profits into their businesses and hire more workers to enable this additional capital to generate further profits. Capital accumulation thus leads to a rise in demand for labor, and hence a rise in wages.

Malthus's population theory predicts that workers will leave as many descendants as their wage can support. Any rise in wages leads to a rise in family size that tends to reduce workers' real wages back down to subsistence – the rate at which they will survive and exactly reproduce their numbers. This is the "natural price" of labor. As long as capitalists continue to accumulate capital, they keep pushing wages back above subsistence, leading population to grow.[150] As population grows, so does demand for food. To meet this demand, farmers extend cultivation to less fertile land, or farm the same land more intensively. Either way, farmers obtain diminishing yields on each additional unit of labor+capital applied to the land.

At this point, Ricardo applies Malthus's theory of rent. Rent is here defined as pure ground rents, or the share of the crop paid to the landlord for the use of "the original and indestructible powers of the soil," and for the land's advantageous "situation" (mostly its nearness to markets). Rent does not include payments for the use of buildings, fences, walls or annual manuring of fields. It does include payments for investments made long ago that increased the fields' fertility.[151] In a newly settled territory where anyone can appropriate land for free – the situation of Locke's original state of nature, and of frontier North America – rents are zero. Rent arises only once land becomes scarce. Even then, no rent is paid on the least fertile tract under cultivation. The price of corn is equal to the marginal cost of production on that tract. Because rents are zero at the margin of cultivation, the marginal cost of production consists only of wages plus profits on the least fertile tract. In a competitive open market, wage and profit rates are equal across tracts, because any tract returning higher profits or paying higher wages would attract more capital and labor until wage and profit rates are reduced to the prevailing level. (Hence the marginal productivity and marginal cost of the last unit of labor+capital applied to more intensive cultivation on more fertile tracts is equal to that on the least fertile tract.) It follows that landlords receive as rent the *entire* inframarginal product of land – that is, the difference between the higher natural productivity of more fertile land and the productivity of the least.[152] Farmers and laborers gain nothing from farming more fertile land.

As cultivation becomes more extensive and intensive, the marginal cost of production rises. This increases the price of food. Landowners gain twice from the "difficulty of production" – that is, from diminishing returns on investment of labor and capital. They gain once from their greater share of total produce as rents rise with the increasing extent and intensity of cultivation. They gain again from the fact that this produce fetches a higher price.[153] Wage rates also rise in nominal terms, because they must cover workers' subsistence, and total wages rise in real terms, because the population is larger. Because profits are the residual after rents and wages are paid, and since the profit rate is determined at the margin of cultivation where rents are zero, as wages rise, the profit rate must drop. In other words, the capitalist cannot pass on wage increases to the landlord by bargaining for lower rents. It follows that, as population and production grow, rent and wages take an ever-larger share of national income. Less and less is left over for capitalists to reinvest. Eventually, the profit rate drops so close to zero that reinvestment is not worth the effort. Capital accumulation, economic growth, wage growth, and population growth cease. The economy arrives at a stationary state.[154]

Normative Implications of Ricardo's Distributive Theory. Ricardo's model implies that England's system of private property and free markets amounted to an assault on the progressive work ethic. It rewarded lazy landlords at the expense of the classes that do all the work and undertake all the saving. At the ultimate end of economic development, hard work seems only to yield bare subsistence, and capitalists can't improve their position by saving and investing. This undermines incentives to practice the work ethic and violates the principle of reward according to desert.

Ricardo draws damning implications for landowners from his analysis. Because landowners have an interest in high food prices, "the interest of the landlord is always opposed to the interest of every other class in the community."[155] "What the landlord gains ... [from high food prices], he gains at the expense of the community at large." With rent "it is only one class profiting at the expense of another class."[156] Against Malthus, who claims that rent adds to the wealth of society,

Ricardo disparages it as "nothing more than a revenue transferred from one class to another," which hurts everyone else.[157]

Given this analysis, it would seem both just and efficient for the state to target rents for taxation. Smith had already argued that ground rents are a particularly apt basis for taxation, because the landowner receives rent "without any care or attention of his own," and taxing rents would neither discourage production nor divert resources to less valuable uses.[158] Ricardo's friend James Mill observed that under feudalism, the barons received grants of land from the king in return for providing him military support, funded exclusively from their rents.[159] Mill's observation slyly suggests the following question: now that the landed class has been released from the military and other feudal obligations that originally justified rent, and given Ricardo's argument that rent does not add to wealth or perform any economic functions, what could justify the landlords' continued collection of rent?

Mill's question was posed in France during the Revolution. The original justification of rent was that landownership was tied to the performance of governmental functions. The lords needed vast estates and the revenues they generated to carry out their duties. In France, the nobles gave up their feudal privileges and powers and hence the governmental duties attached to land in one fell swoop when the National Assembly abolished feudalism on August 4, 1789.[160] Private property thus emerged through the separation of ownership from governmental functions. A lively debate ensued over the justification of landowners' revenues. The former nobility offered contorted reasons for keeping them.[161]

James Mill, in his popularization of Ricardo's economic theory, argues that rents should be taxed away. Granted, when land was converted to purely private property divested of governmental obligations, its market value rose to reflect that fact. People who purchased estates would have their expectations unfairly disappointed if their rents were taxed away. Yet they have no just expectation of collecting higher rents. Hence they have no grounds for complaint if their post-tax rents were frozen at current levels, and all future increases of rent were taxed away, or redistributed to the people.[162]

Ricardo rejects this proposal. Although his analysis concurs with Smith's – that taxes on ground rents are efficient – he objects to special targeting of rents for taxation as a form of unjust class legislation. Everyone should pay taxes in proportion to their ability to pay. Yet this argument ignores the gratuitousness of rents, compared to the need to compensate workers for their labor and capitalists for their frugality and risk-taking. Ricardo also worries that the reduction of land values following the taxation of rents would lead to speculation and gambling over land "rather than sober trade."[163] It is hard to see the force of that argument: if rents are frozen, what is there to speculate over?

Ricardo's theory implies that, as society progresses, rents will gradually absorb nearly all of society's surplus. Capitalists will stop investing just short of that point, to maintain profit levels barely sufficient to compensate them for the "trouble and risk" of managing their enterprises.[164] Yet Ricardo worries that the poor rates would absorb "all the net revenue of the country."[165] Following Malthus, he favors the gradual abolition of the Poor Laws. Yet he concedes that economic growth has always stayed ahead of the predicted catastrophe, and that the stationary state where catastrophe might occur was yet far off.[166] (As MP he argued that, although the Poor Laws cause "mischief," the poor must be supported.[167]) Given his critique of the landowners, why was he not worried about ever-rising rents?

Ricardo answers that the stationary state is better than all other states, because it lies at the point of maximum wealth for society. "High rent and low profits, for they invariably accompany each other, ought never to be the subject of complaint, if they are the effect of the natural course of things."[168] This answer evades the question at issue. Ricardo's theory shows that as society progresses to the stationary state, profits will fall and rents will rise.[169] It does not show that it is "natural," much less desirable, that rents should be collected by the landowners, rather than distributed to workers or spent on public goods. That landowners benefited was the result of a historical decision to let landowners keep their rents even while they were relieved of the governmental duties that justified their collection of rents in the first place.

At the stationary state, wages are reduced to their "natural price," which is "subsistence." This suggests an image of a vast mass of workers – the great majority of the population – living at the edge of survival. This image is misleading for the same reason that Malthus's apocalyptic predictions were. "Subsistence" is defined as whatever standard of living leads people to reproduce at the population replacement rate. This standard of living includes not just food and other necessities, but *conveniences*. If, as wages rise with economic growth, workers get used to this standard of living and want to ensure that their children don't fall beneath it, they will restrain their family size. Ricardo concedes that this could keep wages permanently high. The "natural price of labor" is no more based on a law of nature than Malthus's principles of population. It was based rather on Ricardo's belief that "so great are the delights of domestic society" that workers would marry early and procreate with abandon.[170]

Such are the dangers of assuming that recent events reflect inexorable long-term trends rather than contingent conditions. Nevertheless, it is worth pausing to consider the conditions that led Ricardo to his gloomy conclusion about the tendency of rents to consume the whole social surplus.[171] What observations about rents in particular prompted Ricardo to think that his model captured the underlying dynamics of capitalist society? I suggest that the brazen aggressiveness of landowners in the eighteenth and early nineteenth centuries played a role. The last wave of enclosures, from 1750 to 1849, was the largest and by far the most consequential for ruining agricultural laborers. It also squeezed capitalist farmers. Rents per acre on enclosed farms were double those of open-field farms.[172] Because enclosed farms were so much larger, farmers had to borrow large sums to make rent and gamble on high prices and a bumper crop to pay off their loans. Only the luckiest and wealthiest farmers succeeded. Many were driven to ruin. As a result, by the middle of the nineteenth century the landlords did manage to appropriate the entire agricultural surplus, including all of the gains in productivity that had been created by the yeomen. Their land-grabbing and rack-renting really was nothing more than a redistribution of wealth from the laboring and investing classes to the landlords, as Ricardo judged and his model predicted.[173] A one-sector economic model based on agriculture, however, could not accommodate the continuous technological progress and profitability of the manufacturing sector.

Ricardian Socialists

Ricardo portrays the classes of society as having essentially antagonistic interests. The interest of the landlords is opposed to the interest of everyone else. The interest of capitalists is also opposed to that of workers. As profits are the residual after rent and wages are paid, profits can rise only if wages fall.[174] Capitalists therefore have an interest in labor-saving machinery, to cut the wage bill. The introduction of machinery, although it may increase national wealth, profits, and rents, often harms workers by throwing them out of work and reducing wage rates.[175]

Despite these opposing class interests, Ricardo rejected class warfare. Even the lazy landlords are entitled to their rents. In Parliament, he denounced class legislation.[176] And as noted above, he opposed a bill to purchase land for hand-loom weavers displaced by power looms. The government should promote economic growth by eliminating restrictions on trade, without compensating the losers. The bill would violate the "sacredness" of property rights, even though it proposed to purchase rather than expropriate the land for redistribution, on a plan that would provide a way for the unemployed to earn their living rather than depend on poor relief.[177] His opposition conformed to the priorities of the conservative work ethic, to sharpen class boundaries by depriving workers of means of subsistence other than wage labor. This makes sense if all that matters is maximizing total economic growth, and not, as Locke insisted, ensuring the good of each particular member of society.

Others were appalled by a system that, in dividing people by class, put people into inherently antagonistic social relations. Class and class conflict is an artifact of property arrangements. Shouldn't we seek alternative arrangements that provide for everyone, give workers their just reward, and promote cooperative rather than antagonistic social relations? The Ricardian socialists, a group of English radicals writing in the 1820s and 1830s, saw grounds in Ricardo's labor theory of value for radically altering economic institutions in favor of workers, and against landowners and capitalists.[178] Although called "Ricardian," the economic thinking of these radicals was only loosely related to Ricardo's. From the perspective of the progressive work ethic, their fundamental contribution was to place desert-based claims of distributive justice at the center of concern. They were united in holding that the workers are entitled to the whole product of their labor. They interpreted the labor theory of value to imply that labor is the source of all value; that workers produce all national wealth. Hence, workers are entitled to claim *all* national income. Profit, interest, and rent – any income accruing to mere passive ownership of property – are illegitimate forms of unearned income extracted from workers. Capital income, like Ricardian rent, is "only a transfer of the earnings of the industrious to the idle."[179] As the unearned income accruing to passive ownership increases, workers are impoverished and oppressed, forced to labor more just to maintain classes of idlers.

Consider Thomas Hodgskin, lecturer at the London Mechanics' Institute, which was dedicated to educating workers. Hodgskin rejects the legitimacy of charging interest. He cites Ricardo's theory of the inverse relation of profits and wages to support the view "that the exactions of the capitalist cause the poverty of the labourer."[180] Hodgskin anticipates Marx in arguing that all capital really amounts to labor. Fixed capital – machines, tools, buildings – is just the result of accumulated labor. Circulating capital, or advances on wages, is, in real terms, merely commodities such as food and clothing, which are also just the product of labor. The capitalist reaps interest – what Ricardo called profit – on nominal advances of wages to workers, but has not accumulated a stock of real goods to advance to them. The capitalist's role as financial intermediary is dispensable, since the entire real circulation of commodities is undertaken by workers alone.[181] The capitalist *qua* advancer of wages is not like someone who stores up water in the rainy season so that it can be released in the dry season, when it would be more valuable. He is more like someone who dams a river just to be able to charge people living downstream for the water. (The capitalist *qua* worker who actively manages his business and exercises entrepreneurial judgment is entitled to a share, since this component of his profit is really wages, a reward for his industry.[182])

John Bray reasoned similarly: if we consider workers as a whole, "capitalists and proprietors do no more than give the working man, for his labour of one week, a part of the wealth which they obtained from him the week before!" They therefore give him nothing for something – an unequal and unjust exchange.[183] Thus, Ricardian profit (interest income on wage advances) is illegitimate. Workers are entitled to the whole national income.

Ricardian socialists advance wildly different views of the institutional arrangements needed to secure to workers the whole product of their labor. Here I focus only on the end points of a spectrum of views. Hodgskin stands at the individualist extreme, presenting a version of natural property rights in a neo-Lockean state of nature. In his picture, society will evolve toward anarchist capitalism as workers gradually refuse to recognize the artificial property rights established by the state. Artificial property is the basis for the income claimed by the idle classes. These classes include landlords, passive owners of financial assets, government workers, and priests, who are respectively supported by rents, profits, taxes, and tithes. Because the state exists only to support an oppressive class system in which idlers live off the labor of workers, workers' resistance will lead it to wither away. They will come to accept only Lockean natural property rights, in which labor alone generates a claim to property. Landholdings will be roughly equal, since no one can own more than they could work using their own labor. Workers will exchange their products on an unregulated free market. Unlike Locke, he doesn't think through the inegalitarian implications of anarchist capitalism for those unable to work, or once money is introduced. This is perhaps because, like libertarians today, he rejects any duty to assist others. Each individual should enjoy complete liberty to dispose of their property for their own "selfish purposes."[184]

John Francis Bray and William Thompson stand at the other extreme, advancing a utopian socialist vision of common property in the means of production. Bray defends a principle of distributive justice that Locke left implicit: that the only just wealth inequalities are based on individuals' unequal "industry and frugality."[185] Everyone is entitled to equal pay for equal hours of work. Just trades must exchange goods of equal value. According to the labor theory of value, two bundles of goods are of equal value if it takes an equal number of labor hours to produce them (including the hours spent obtaining raw materials, the prorated share of hours it takes to make and maintain machines and tools used in producing the goods, etc.). Workers' poverty is due to pervasive unequal exchange with capitalists and landlords, who charge interest and rent on the basis of mere ownership, without having earned their share by working. Workers are thereby forced to undertake relentless labor to support the idle classes, on top of the work they must do to support themselves and their families. The remedy for this injustice is to make everyone a worker and turn the means of production into common property. To this end, let the workers establish a set of joint-stock corporations that cover all production, in which each owns one share. Let the joint-stock corporations issue a fiat currency to purchase, by eminent domain, all existing means of production. Henceforth use that currency to pay everyone an equal hourly wage. General and local boards of trade will regulate production and exchange, ensuring that all commodities trade at their labor values. Under this system, everyone becomes a worker because no one can claim an "unearned share" based on individual ownership of assets. Individuals may acquire unequal wealth only by working more hours or saving more of their wages. But they would have no right to bequeath their savings to others.[186]

Bray and Thompson also advocate communal living arrangements, to provide for orphans, the aged, disabled, infirm, and others unable to work, and to liberate women from dependence on their husbands, a condition that leads to their subjection. The community would educate children. This would free mothers to engage in other types of work. Relations of cooperation would thereby replace antagonistic relations. Individuals will only be able to benefit themselves by contributing to the good of others, rather than advancing at the expense of others in the class system.[187]

William Thompson goes further than Bray in promoting a collectivist vision, along the lines of Robert Owen's utopian communes.[188] (Thompson dedicated his estate to a similar communal experiment, but his family successfully contested his will after he died in 1833.) According to Thompson, the right of workers to the whole product of their labor can be realized only at the collective level. Due to the pervasive division of labor and consequent necessity of cooperative production, there is no credible way to attribute particular increments of production to the efforts of any individual worker, or to assign unequal merit to different labors. Thompson therefore dispenses with any desert-based notion of distributive justice. Individuals should receive equal shares of the goods produced by their community, by which he means shares in accordance with need. People would be motivated to work hard out of sympathy for their fellow commune members, pleasure in meaningful work undertaken in far better conditions, and regard for the good opinion of their colleagues.[189]

At this point, one may wonder what work the labor theory of value is actually doing to support this utopian vision. Esther Lowenthal complains that Thompson's deployment of the labor theory of value in support of a theory of distributive justice makes no sense, since he denies that the fruits of any specific worker's labor can even be determined, and detaches claims to income from the number of hours one has worked.[190] One might read Thompson as using the theory only critically, to dismiss any individual claims to income on the basis of passive ownership.

Bray's system of equal pay for equal hours of work fails to grasp the economic logic of the labor theory of value. For Ricardo, the labor theory of value is a theory of the long-run equilibrium ("natural") price of commodities based on their cost of production. Two commodities exchange at equal values if their costs of production are equal, as roughly measured in the number of hours required to produce them.

Unlike Bray, Ricardo allows skilled labor to count at some multiple of unskilled labor, due to the costs of training.[191] As Marx later stressed, following Ricardo, the cost of production of the power to labor – to restore the worker's capacity to labor, and to reproduce that power in the next generation – is subsistence. Hence, when workers receive a subsistence wage from their employer, they are not being cheated by an unequal exchange, as Bray argued. They are being paid at their labor value. The quasi-Lockean normative interpretation of the labor theory of value, understood as measuring each worker's individual deserts by their productive contribution to the total wealth of society, is also flawed in confusing wealth with the cost of production. If technological progress doubles the productivity of labor, society is richer than before. Yet, since it takes half the labor hours to make the same goods as before, the labor it took to produce them has dropped, and hence so has their value. Economic progress increases wealth but reduces value – that is, the cost of production.

Bray and the other Ricardian socialists advance a claim of what Marx called "surplus value." This is the idea that workers labor for more hours than required to support themselves, since they must toil additional hours to support the idle classes, who extract this surplus from the workers through their ownership of the nonlabor means of production. Yet it hardly took a *theory* to make that point. It was obvious to everyone. Whately and his fellow conservatives stress it too. The only difference between them is evaluative. For the Ricardian socialists, this fact is unjust and oppressive to workers. For the conservatives, it is the very foundation of civilization.

The Ricardian socialists focus so intently on questions of distributive justice that they neglect the allocative functions of market prices in signaling to producers the most advantageous employment of their factors of production.[192] Hodgskin's attack on charging interest is typical. He doesn't recognize the role of interest in allocating credit between short-run and long-run investments. Yet one sees interest and even rent sneaking back into their ideal systems, even though they are unearned.[193] At some level they recognize that any economic system will generate unearned income – that is, income not attributable to any particular individual's labor. As John Gray, another Ricardian socialist, observes, "if the landlords did not take rent, the tenants would."[194] From the Ricardian socialists' point of view, the problem was not really that some people received things they had not earned. Most recognized the claims of people unable to work. Injustice lay rather in the division of society into sharply distinguished classes of propertyless workers and idle property owners. This led to a system in which the latter lived parasitically off the former, like drones living off the worker bees.[195] For Bray, the solution to this problem was to turn everyone into workers. In Thompson's system, "all laborers become capitalists."[196] These formulas come to the same thing in a system of production based on worker-owned firms: the workers' income will incorporate returns on the firm's assets.

Ultimately the Ricardian socialists aim to realize the progressive work ethic by abolishing class distinctions and hence class conflict. Universal reciprocal sympathy and benevolence (all but Hodgskin insisted) would ensue. Such a sweeping utopian hope is less interesting than their critique of the ideology of their opponents, the advocates of the conservative work ethic. It is all too easy to dismiss their critique by pointing to the pervasiveness of self-interested motives. But the Ricardian socialists do not oppose the pursuit of self-interest in ways that benefit others. The point of so radically altering property and production relations is to ensure that people can *only* advance their own interest in such ways.

Thompson targets a particular conception of self-interest that lay at the heart of the conservative work ethic: Priestley's idea of life as a competitive race to display superior acquisitions to others. This was the view of life that drove the ambitious bourgeois class to aspire to join "the aristocracy of wealth." A race is inherently a zero-sum game: winners entail losers. What's worse, the pleasures of the competitive scramble to outdo others in the acquisition and display of wealth are essentially antagonistic. They consist in gloating over the defeat of one's rivals. To force hapless workers to compete "under pressure of want" for the "gratification of antipathy" involves a conception of one's own good in which "pain or evil to others forms an essential ingredient."[197] This, above all, was the view of life that Thompson and most of his fellow Ricardian socialists abhorred. John Stuart Mill, Ricardo's successor in the pantheon of classical economists, shared their revulsion. But he was better able than they to join rigorous economic analysis to their aspiration to overcome the ideology of the conservative work ethic.

6 THE PROGRESSIVE WORK ETHIC (2): J. S. MILL

John Stuart Mill, Civilization, and the End of Economic Growth

Since the late eighteenth century, European thinkers viewed history as a story of progress toward "civilization," in which stages of progress are defined in terms of distinct modes of production. Societies progress by moving from hunter-gatherer subsistence, to herding, to settled agriculture, to civilized states with cities, manufacturing, commerce, arts, sciences, and law. These thinkers regarded Europe as ahead of "savage," "barbarian," and "semi-barbarian" societies in the rest of the world. This idea of European superiority in progress was reinforced in the nineteenth century by the spectacular economic growth spurred by astonishing technological innovations in manufacturing, transportation, and communication during the Industrial Revolution. European thinkers asked: what accounted for Europe's rapid economic and technological progress, far ahead of the rest of the world?

Virtually all, whether conservative or progressive, agreed on the answer: the keys to progress were an advanced division of labor, and institutions to promote widespread practice of the work ethic. Indeed, given that the work ethic involves dedication to a calling or specialized occupation, which entails a division of labor, one might say that the *sole* key to progress was the work ethic with its supporting institutions. However, a Puritan calling typically involved dedication to the production of some complete marketable product or service – one could be a farmer, tailor, baker, carriage maker, barber, teacher, and so forth – or at least a calling that would produce some complete marketable input to another's production, as shepherds and weavers did. By contrast, Smith identified as critical to economic growth a degree of specialization of occupations – a *microdivision of labor* – far more minute than anything the Puritans had imagined. In Smith's famous account of a pin factory, the work of making a pin was divided into 18 simple, endlessly repeated mechanical operations.[1] It is hard to imagine that God would call one to dedicate one's life solely to cutting a wire to pin-length, grinding the top to receive a head, or pointing the tip.

Smith's analysis posits an awful trade-off between two great goods: a high material standard of living, and individual human capabilities. His worry is not simply that the microdivision of labor vastly increased labor productivity at the expense of turning the experience of work into tedious drudgery – although it certainly did that. It is that a worker whose life is spent largely on repeating "a few simple operations" lacks opportunities for developing and exercising intelligence, along with moral sentiments and virtues, such as public spirit and courage, not included in the work ethic.[2] The skills and virtues of the typical "savage" were *superior* to those of the typical worker of purportedly more advanced civilizations.[3] How could we call "progress" something that degraded the capacities of the great mass of individuals in society, even relative to supposedly backward societies? And how could these individuals be reconciled to such progress, which came at such grave expense to their capabilities?

Advocates of the conservative work ethic replied by focusing on peaks and aggregates. While economic and technological progress degraded the typical individual's capabilities, it afforded sufficient leisure to a few so that they could attain higher peaks of knowledge, invention, and skill in civilized countries than in backward ones. It also greatly expanded the aggregate economic, technological, military, scientific, and cultural powers of society. From the point of view of ethical theory, we should tie this conservative argument to the purely aggregative view of classical utilitarianism. Advocates of the conservative work ethic used aggregative utilitarianism to rationalize the sacrifice or exploitation of some for the sake of increasing total happiness. They thereby departed from the original Puritan version of utilitarianism advanced by Baxter and Locke, which insists that each particular individual in society needs to be taken care of and treated justly.

Conservatives argued that the prospect of ever-greater consumption of commodities would reconcile workers to the drudgery needed to produce them. It wasn't just that luxury was desirable. To spur workers to internalize the work ethic, they had to view success in life as a matter of *competitive* conspicuous consumption. As Priestley and Whately argued, along with many others of the era, life was a "race" with one's peers to show off *greater* accumulated wealth and consumption than they could.[4]

To what end was progress headed? For any given individual, the goal would seem to be winning the race. But if the point of life itself is competition, the race itself, and hence "progress" understood in economic terms, would never really end.[5] For ordinary workers, the saints' rest would again be postponed to the next life – or, for Priestley, to the very end of life if they managed to save enough for old age. For workers were consigned to almost perpetual running in this life. For society, restless industry would be for the sake of never-ending accumulation: aggregate economic growth as an end in itself.

By the middle of the nineteenth century – still in Engels's Pause – the decades-long promise of ever-growing prosperity dangled before the working classes as a reward for practicing the work ethic was looking fraudulent. To be sure, a new industrial middle class was growing and reaping the promised rewards. But the Industrial Revolution had ruthlessly ground proud, independent craftsmen down to deskilled, impoverished wage laborers. Working-class families had to send their children to work in the factories just to survive. Industrial work was grueling, dirty, dangerous, and destructive of mind, body, and spirit. Agricultural workers, deprived of access to land, cottage industry, and other independent means of subsistence, were even poorer than industrial workers.

In part, these conditions followed from a contradiction inherent in the conservative work ethic. Conservatives claimed that workers could only be taught to internalize the work ethic in conditions of poverty and precarity, under the despotic discipline of their employers. But if internalizing an ethic is tied to experiencing its rewards, it is hard to see how putting them in such conditions, where they neither earned enough to buy much more than subsistence, nor had enough leisure to enjoy surplus consumption, would ever lead them to voluntarily adopt the work ethic. No wonder conservatives never willingly loosened their grip. They always complained that workers' supply curve of labor was never bent forward enough. And no wonder workers were in revolt. Among other labor movements, the Chartists revived key Leveller and Lockean constitutional demands, including a universal male franchise, apportionment of MPs in proportion to district population, and frequent Parliamentary elections. The Chartists pursued democracy with the aim of directing state power to improve the lot of workers.

John Stuart Mill, the greatest liberal philosopher of the nineteenth century, and the last of the canonical classical liberal economists, was keenly aware of the costs to ordinary workers of the conservatives' methods – both disciplinary and ideological – for inculcating the work ethic. He objects to the conservatives' view of progress and its end:

> I am not charmed with the ideal of life held out by those who think that the normal state of human beings is that of struggling to get on; that the trampling, crushing, elbowing, and treading on each other's heels, which form the existing type of social life, are the most desirable lot of human kind . . . . [T]he best state for human nature is that in which, while no one is poor, no one desires to be richer, nor has any reason to fear being thrust back, by the efforts of others to push themselves forward . . . . I know not why it should be matter of congratulation that persons who are already richer than any one needs to be, should have doubled their means of consuming things which give little or no pleasure except as representative of wealth; or that numbers of individuals should pass over, every year, from . . . the class of the occupied rich to that of the unoccupied. It is only in the backward countries of the world that increased production is still an important object: in those most advanced, what is economically needed is a better distribution . . . .[6]

Mill's point is not simply that workers should get a bigger share of national income. It is that the whole conservative vision of progress in civilization is deeply flawed. Mill opposes any notion of progress that focuses on the accumulation of material goods at the cost of the development and exercise of human capabilities. "Human beings have faculties more elevated than the animal appetites, and when once made conscious of them, do not regard anything as happiness which does not include their gratification."[7] These faculties include intelligence, imagination, and the moral sentiments.[8] The existing wage labor system makes the majority of workers "slaves to toil in which they have no interest, and therefore feel no interest – drudging from early morning till late at night for bare necessaries, and with all the intellectual and moral deficiencies which that implies."[9] This is intolerable. People need not only opportunities for developing their faculties, as Smith's proposal for publicly funded education would start to do, but also ample fields for their exercise. These were lacking in lives consigned to ceaseless, mind-numbing toil.

Mill also rejects a purely aggregative view of progress, in which the flourishing of some is achieved at the expense of others. Civilization and progress should advance to a state in which "what is a benefit to the whole shall be a benefit to each individual composing it."[10] We shall see that, with respect to property rights, this ideal reproduces Locke's theory. With respect to the division of labor, it reproduces Sanderson's aspiration, that each person be called to an occupation in which they ardently develop and exercise their talents in ways that benefit others.

Finally, Mill rejects social arrangements that put individuals in fundamentally antagonistic social relations. Such relations limit individuals' concerns to their narrow self-interest. They block sympathy, the most important of the moral sentiments. Sympathy is critical not just for promoting the good of others, but for the happiness of the individual motivated by it. This underlies his abhorrence of competitive conspicuous consumption, a form of zero-sum esteem competition in which one person's elevation entails another's degradation. It also underlies his rejection of the hierarchical relationships inherent in the conservative vision of civilized social order. For Mill, progress entails casting off hierarchy. "[T]he only school of genuine moral sentiment is society between equals."[11] When perfected in the progress of civilization, sympathy, or "the feeling of unity with others," makes an individual "never think of, or desire, any beneficial condition for himself, in the benefits of which they are not included." Such progress requires "removing the sources of opposition of interest, and leveling those inequalities of legal privilege between individuals or classes" which enable the powerful to disregard the happiness of their inferiors.[12] Mill holds that hierarchies between landlords and tenants, and capitalists and workers, are antagonistic, contrary to the conservative conceit that these relations were paternalistically beneficent.

In all these values, Mill agrees with William Thompson. They met in 1825, in debates between Mill's group of young political economists, and Thompson's group of Owenites. "We who represented political economy had the same objects in view which they had." But they disagreed on how to get there, due to their disagreements about Malthusian population theory.[13] Mill saw promise in Ricardo's stationary state as a way to overcome the ills of the conservative work ethic. Where others viewed the stationary state as dismal, Mill took advantage of the giant loophole in Ricardian political economy – that what counts as a subsistence wage is determined by workers' decisions to limit their family size – to portray the stationary state as a great opportunity. A stationary state could be achieved at a reasonably high material standard of living for all. Once reached, it would be futile to seek endless profit accumulation and economic growth. The conservative work ethic – most importantly, the competitive scramble to beat others in the race for wealth – would die. The progressive work ethic would still have its proper place in maintaining a decent standard of living for all. But the stationary state would free people's minds and energies to focus on the cultivation of virtues and capabilities *beyond* the work ethic. The end of progress – its goal – would involve the termination of purely material progress, in favor of the continuing cultivation and exercise of human capabilities – "all kinds of mental culture, and moral and social progress"[14] – in egalitarian relationships fostered by laws "favouring equality of fortunes."[15]

Mill's conception of progress in civilization entails an ambitious agenda. Institutions must be reformed to promote a better distribution of wealth, to end poverty and abolish the inequalities of property that underwrite oppressive social hierarchy. The organization of production must be reformed to minimize drudgery, enable workers to exercise intelligence and autonomous judgment at work, and end antagonistic relations between capitalists and workers. Mill advances this agenda by further developing the progressive work ethic of Locke, Smith, and the Ricardian socialists.

Mill's Lockean Theory of Property, with Applications to Corn Laws, Inheritance, and Land Tenure in England and Ireland

The first premises of Mill's theory of property are fundamentally Lockean. This may seem surprising, since Mill's utilitarian framework is usually cast as opposed to any notion of natural rights, an original state of nature, or social contract. But those differences are superficial. Locke understood natural rights to be just those rights people would enjoy in a state of nature, which is simply a state of anarchy. The legal rights to which people are entitled in civil society are different from their natural rights, and are – like all sound laws – just those that promote the "public good," consistent with the constraint that they provide for "the good of every particular member of that society."[16] The social contract is simply an imaginative device for guiding moral reasoning so that its conclusions conform to this standard. Mill declines to speculate about the rights we would enjoy under anarchy. His standard for the rights we should have in civil society is equivalent to Locke's: like all other laws, norms, and practices, they must be such that they would "benefit the whole" in such a way that they also "benefit ... each individual composing it."[17]

For both Locke and Mill, activity in accordance with the work ethic promotes the public good. Laws that reward industry, frugality, and prudence encourage such activity and directly benefit those who conform to the work ethic. Laws that discourage laziness, profligacy, and imprudence guide the wayward to behave in ways that will benefit themselves while also benefiting the whole. Thus, it is not surprising to find Mill endorsing a Lockean labor theory of property. According to Mill, property is founded on individuals' rights to their own labor, to the products of their labor, and to their fair market price.[18] Every defense of property is based on "the guarantee to individuals of the fruits of their own labour and abstinence."[19] Like Locke and Bray, Mill endorses inequalities of wealth due to unequal industry and frugality – that is, to unequal practice of the work ethic – and *only* those.[20]

Like Locke, Mill holds that land "is the original inheritance of the whole species."[21] Because no one made the land, there can be no direct labor-based justification for legal rights to private property in land. A system of landed property can be justified only if it serves the interests of every particular person. This is difficult, because "it is some hardship to be born into the world and to find all nature's gifts previously engrossed, and no place left for the new-comer."[22] In other words, property in land may need to be reconfigured once Locke's sufficiency proviso is breached. The primary justification for property in land is that its fertility is mainly the product of labor.[23] Because investment in the land will be reaped over many years, permanent tenure will maximize the incentive to improve it.

The main difference between Locke and Mill is how willing they are to take the labor theory of property to its logical conclusion. For both, the justification for landed property applies only to those who actually improve it. Locke, by locating his scenario in the state of nature, only cagily suggests that idle landowners who let their crops rot may rightfully have their land taken by anyone who would not waste its produce.[24] Mill boldly advocates what the labor theory of property implies for existing property relations in Britain. Four prominent cases involve the Corn Laws, the laws of inheritance, the English land tenure system, and the cottier system of renting land in Ireland.

Repeal of the Corn Laws, which propped up the price of grain by limiting imports, was a leading cause of free-market reformers. The case for repeal was not based simply on an abstract principle of free trade. It was based on a critique of monopoly grounded in the work ethic. Granting domestic landowners a *de facto* monopoly on the domestic grain trade gave them a windfall for which they hadn't worked, and a license to consume their rents on living high rather than investing in their estates. These gains for landowners came at the expense of workers, who had to pay more for their bread, and, as Ricardo had shown, of frugal capitalists, whose profits dropped when rents increased. Tories objected that repealing the Corn Laws would cause rents to fall and force the great landowners to sell their estates. Mill acidly replied with a favorite Puritan metaphor: Tories advance "the doctrine that the working bees should be governed by the drones" in claiming that aristocrats should rule because they have the greatest stakes in the country.[25] Their profligacy and indebtedness leave them with no money to improve the land, demonstrating that they show little interest even in their own estates, much less in the good of the public. Repeal of the Corn Laws would be a positive good if it caused their estates to pass from the aristocracy to their creditors, the "real owners" of the land, because they will invest in it.

"Great landowners are everywhere an idle class."[26] Even if a few improve their estates, their heirs have usually done nothing to deserve them. Mill concludes that the law may limit how much individuals may inherit. The right to inherit is not inherent in property, even though the right to bequest is.[27] He is even more stringent than Locke in applying the work ethic to parental duties to support their children after their deaths. Locke, arguing against primogeniture, argues that parents have a duty to support *all* their children, not merely for bare subsistence but for comfort and convenience to the extent they can afford this.[28] Mill argues that no parents have a duty to leave their children so much property that they can live idly off it. All they owe their children is a fair chance to succeed by their own efforts.[29] They might even forfeit that if they are unworthy. Granting that owners have the right to bequest their entire estates, it would be desirable if the law limited how much any individual may inherit to only a "comfortable independence." Then the number of vast fortunes, which, beyond that level, have no personal uses besides the indulgence of vanity or "improper power," would decline.[30]

Some people attempted to justify primogeniture on work-ethic principles by claiming that the example of large fortunes would motivate younger children to work hard to acquire fortunes of their own. Such people, Mill replied, must think it "indispensable to the activity and energy of the hive, that there should be a huge drone here and there, to impress the working bees with a due sense of the advantages of honey."[31] It would make more sense to spur people to industry and frugality by limiting fortunes to those earned by exercising these virtues. Moreover, heirs under primogeniture rarely improve their estates, because they haven't studied agriculture. They typically lack the funds to invest, either because they borrowed money for high living, or because the nonlanded property of the estate was bequeathed to younger siblings for their support.[32] Primogeniture should be banned in the interests of improvement and the diffusion of wealth, and because it arbitrarily discriminates among offspring on the basis of birth order.[33] Entails, which limit heirs to a life interest in the estate, because successors to it were named by their ancestors, are also incompatible with improvement. They prevent mortgaging the estate to acquire funds for improvement, and selling the estate to improvers.[34] Both provisions for securing dynastic wealth should be abolished. Property should revert to the state in cases of intestacy, with provision made for children to the extent of parental duties of care.[35] Inheritances should be subject to a progressive tax.[36]

Ricardo argued that rents serve no economic function, and so could be taxed away without harm to national wealth.[37] Interest (contra Hodgskin) *does* serve an economic function in guiding the allocation of investment.[38] Ricardo's economic theory thus supplies a good fit with the normative priorities of the liberal (not socialist) progressive work ethic: wages are a just reward for the industry of the working classes; profits are a just reward for the frugality of capitalists; rents are a parasitic drain on the productive classes by the idle landlords, who draw income "without working, risking, or economizing." John Stuart supported his father James's Ricardian argument for taxing rents[39] and sought to make such taxes a reality in founding the Land Tenure Reform Association (LTRA). In his 1871 inaugural lecture to the LTRA, and his 1873 address as its president, Mill laid out its platform.[40] In addition to eliminating primogeniture and entail, he called for taxing away the landlords' rent above what was incorporated into the purchase price. Charles II had relieved the landowners of their feudal obligations of personal service in wartime without taxing their rents. The Glorious Revolution of 1688, "made by towns against country gentlemen," imposed a modest land tax that had not been raised since. Yet rents were steadily rising due to the growth of manufacturing and towns. Landowners "need only sit still" while their incomes rise due to "the labor of other men." Mill could just as well have cited Locke's list of town and country laborers to whom the landlords owed their wealth.[41] It was high time to tax away the "unearned increment of rent."

It was also high time to end enclosures. Every year, Parliament allowed a mere 30,000 landlords, who already monopolized nearly all the land of England, to enclose thousands of acres of common land without any pretense of right to it, and without compensation to the impoverished rural workers and cottagers who had customary rights to it. This is simply "robbery of the poor." Land "stagnates in the hands of the idler, the spendthrift, the incapable." The remaining waste should be nationalized without compensation to landowners who may have some rights to it, and allotted at reasonable rents to agricultural laborers, the worst-off sector of the working class.

Mill offered more radical proposals for land reform in Ireland. He wrote the first edition of *Principles of Political Economy* during the Famine. Recall that the chief objective of British relief policy was to force Ireland to adopt the English model of large capitalist farms employing wage laborers (see Chapter 4). By forcing starving peasants to give up their tiny plots and homes, relief policy cleared them from Irish estates. By requiring Irish landlords to bear the costs of relief, policy forced them to either improve their estates, or be driven into bankruptcy, where their land would be bought by improving landlords. Mill shared the judgment of most English policy makers that the landlords of Ireland were lazy spendthrifts. Because they failed the conditions for legitimate landownership, it was proper to redistribute the land to those who would improve it.[42]

Yet Mill rejects the English model as inappropriate for Ireland. That model was based on the assumption that Irish peasants were by nature slothful and debauched – prone to bearing more children than they could support – and that they could be made industrious and temperate only under the discipline of employers. Mill concedes that Irish peasants could work harder, and that they bred more children than they could support. He denies that their behavior was due to vice. "Of all vulgar modes of escaping from the consideration of the effect of social and moral influences on the human mind, the most vulgar is that of attributing the diversities of conduct and character to inherent natural differences."[43] Conduct is a function of incentives. Mill attributes the problematic conduct of Irish peasants to a system of land tenure known as cottier tenancy, which gave them perverse incentives.

Mill defines cottier tenure as one where rents are set by competition rather than custom. In much of Ireland, cottiers rented land under the conacre system, under which they had to bid for a plot every year, without security of tenure. Although they bid in monetary terms, most cottiers had little cash. So they paid for their plots with labor. Ireland's high population relative to arable land led to bidding wars. Because their survival depended on access to land, cottiers would often bid rents far higher than they could pay in a year. Perpetually indebted, they had no hope of personal gain from working harder. Whatever they grew above their family's bare subsistence would be taken by their landlord to pay off their debt. Cottiers also had nothing to lose from large families, because they would pay no more than what was consistent with subsistence. They had nothing to gain from self-restraint, because the cost of renting a plot depended on the total population bidding for land. Mill condemns this system for its perverse incentives.[44]

Landlords could not claim rights of justice to competitive rents on the basis of a doctrine of freedom of contract. Rents are just an unearned return on a natural monopoly. Cottier rents are even worse than the Ricardian rents paid by capitalist farmers. The latter would never pay rents so high that they could not earn the market rate of profit from farming. But cottiers bid rents far higher, out of a desperate need to survive.[45]

The distribution of property in land is itself a matter of expedience, not justice. States are free to periodically redistribute unimproved land as population increases. However, those who have invested their labor in increasing its productivity are entitled to security of tenure, so they can reap the fruits of their labor.[46] Mill even considers communism. Echoing Smith,[47] Mill complains that the current system of property distributes income in inverse proportion to labor. If private property entailed such a distribution, communism would be preferable.[48] Fortunately, property does not entail such a contravention of the just claims of those who practice the work ethic. The key is to distribute property so as to reward them.

The question of how to organize property in land turns on which system best rewards and promotes the work ethic. The answer to this question was the critical point on which conservative and progressive advocates of the work ethic disagreed. For conservatives, ordinary workers would work hard only under fear of starvation, and under the tyrannical discipline of property owners. Poverty and precarity stimulate industry, frugality, and self-restraint. The independence afforded by property leads to sloth, prodigality, and reckless reproduction. As we have seen, the conservative view was fraught with contradiction. It entailed that to promote the work ethic, those practicing it must *not* be rewarded. Rather, the fruits of their labor should be appropriated by wealthy property owners, who are somehow not corrupted by the receipt of so much income that they need not work, save, or practice self-restraint at all.

The only way to resolve this contradiction was to presume some kind of class difference in virtue, such that the rich and poor respond differently to incentives. As Baxter, Locke, Smith, and Mill observed, this presumption was contrary to the manifest evidence of aristocratic idleness, waste, and debauchery. The presumption was also encapsulated in the assumption that the poor, unlike their superiors, supply labor inversely with the wage rate. This was not a stable position. If mere receipt of unearned income makes one virtuous, why wouldn't a more equitable distribution promote virtue more widely? Moreover, conservatives understood that the work ethic could not ultimately be successfully promulgated without eventually promising to workers a decent external reward for their virtue. For it was obvious that virtue was not its own reward. It entailed ascetic discipline in ceaseless toil, saving, and sexual self-restraint. Priestley, Malthus, Bentham, and Whately agreed on that point. The dictatorship of property owners could only ever be temporary, until workers learned to enjoy surplus consumption so much that they would work harder for the chance to improve their condition. But that required that workers actually experience the rewards of hard work during the period of tutelary dictatorship. Conservatives were never able to determine when it was safe to let up on tyranny, poverty, and precarity so as to let workers enjoy external rewards of their virtue. They pretended that the "free market" would decide. But the market decided under rules that were regularly rewritten to redistribute property to the rich, to eliminate opportunities for the poor to independently support themselves, and to increase their precarity.

For Mill as for Smith, the conservative postulate that the poor supply labor inversely to its rewards is an absurd case of the fundamental attribution error. If people are not practicing the work ethic, the fault lies with the perverse incentives afforded by the organization of property, markets, and public goods. These should be altered so that workers are amply rewarded for their industry, frugality, and self-control. We should empower ordinary workers to exercise their agency well under institutions that align incentives properly.

Conservatives and progressives agreed that cottier tenancy in Ireland should be eliminated. They disagreed on what should replace it. Conservatives argued that cottiers should be converted to day laborers on capitalist farms. They seized on the opportunity of the Famine to redistribute property to this end. Mill argues that cottiers should be converted into independent peasants farming their own land. "[J]ustice requires that the actual cultivators should be enabled to become in Ireland ... proprietors of the soil which they cultivate."[49] The labor theory of property supports this judgment. Considerations of the public good recommend the same. Peasant proprietors are "superhumanly" industrious, prudent, temperate, self-controlled, and save much of their income.[50] This follows from the facts that when people own the property they work, they keep all the fruits of their labor and bear the costs of their imprudence. As long as they have farms large enough to supply some comforts, they also have an incentive to avoid excessively large families. This is proven by the behavior of peasant proprietors in other countries.[51] Day laborers lack such strong incentives to practice the work ethic.[52]

Like Smith, Mill supports institutions that promote the agency and autonomy of ordinary people. Peasant proprietorship serves this end well. Peasants who own property must exercise judgment and varied skills to make a living. They are comparable to the middle classes in their capacities to manage their own lives. By contrast, day laborers suffer from enervating anxieties that undermine their initiative.[53]

Mill condemns British policy toward the Irish during the Famine, because it refused to "make ... [Ireland] a place fit for them to live in."[54] To make it fit, Mill proposes that landlords should forfeit any waste land they own to anyone who improves it. This is an application of Locke's remedy for property left to waste. The state should also buy Irish estates put up for sale, divide them into parcels, and sell them to Irish laborers.[55] Peasants who continue to rent should be able to do so on long leases at low fixed rents. Only capitalist farmers should have to pay market rents.[56]

From 1870 to 1909, Parliament passed a series of Land Acts in response to Irish agitation over land and political independence. The Land Acts at first regulated rents below market. They ultimately established a land purchase and resale system administered by the government to redistribute ownership from landlords to peasants on terms favorable to both groups. By 1929, these laws effectively realized Mill's vision for Ireland. They virtually eliminated the landlord class and turned 97 percent of the occupants of land into peasant proprietors.[57] Land reform did not lead to the efficiency improvements Mill predicted, due in part to the ways its design hampered peasants' access to credit.[58] Its ultimate beneficiaries were yeoman farmers producing for the market, more than peasants producing for their own subsistence. Mill would nevertheless have approved of reform in the name of justice, understood in terms of a Lockean work ethic: distribution of land to its "real owners" – those who work it.

Promoting Workers' Agency: Division of Labor, Hours, Unions, and Cooperatives

The progressive work ethic is based on the following convictions. With appropriate incentives and opportunities for the free development of human capabilities, workers will freely exercise industry, frugality, and prudence for the benefit of themselves and society. Tyrannical production systems and antagonistic economic relations undermine the work ethic, productivity, and most of all, human flourishing. Human flourishing itself requires ample opportunities for the exercise of a wide range of human capabilities, including judgment, intellect, imagination, autonomy, and diverse virtues – such as sympathy, public spirit, and courage – beyond those extolled by the work ethic.

Smith's version of the progressive work ethic faced an apparently insuperable trade-off between prosperity, which he tied to the growth of industry based on a microdivision of labor, and the development and exercise of diverse human capabilities, which were stunted and stifled by the mind-numbing drudgery seemingly entailed by that microdivision of labor. This trade-off took different forms in agriculture and industry. Agriculture was not subject to a similarly minute microdivision of labor as industry. The seasonality of agriculture ensured that, over the course of a year, agricultural workers could exercise diverse skills to raise crops and animals – provided they had full-time jobs and were not forced into day labor while kept unemployed in the off-season. Hence, it was easier to ensure that agricultural labor would not be stultifying. However, it seemed that the lack of a sophisticated microdivision of labor in agriculture limited labor productivity, and hence kept wages low and agricultural workers poor. Smith and Mill saw that rural poverty could be alleviated or ended by policies that enabled agricultural workers to acquire the land they worked, and thereby keep all the fruits of their labor, including returns on investments in improving the land. Property ownership yielded additional advantages for agricultural workers, affording them a domain for the exercise of autonomy, foresight, and diverse skills in managing their farms.

Industry seemed to pose a starker trade-off of prosperity against individual capabilities. The content of work under the microdivision of labor in the Industrial Revolution, consigning each worker one simple motion, tediously repeated for a whole working life, offered no scope for the exercise of diverse or sophisticated skills. It so stultified and exhausted workers that they couldn't exercise such skills off-duty either. Nor did they have the leisure to do so. Factory workers often worked more than 12 hours per day, six days per week. This schedule left little time to do much off-duty besides sleep, eat, undertake basic childcare, and commute to and from work. Children, too, worked in the factories, without a chance for education or other activities vital to development. Mill addresses this apparent trade-off in two ways. First, he advocates workers' leisure. Second, he urges an alteration in the division of labor and labor relations to enable workers to develop and exercise their higher faculties at work.

Where conservatives promote luxury, Mill promotes leisure. Unlike Baxter, who accepts rest as merely instrumental to restoring the capacity to work, leisure activities for Mill are an essential part of human flourishing. Workers need leisure to be able to exercise higher faculties, such as aesthetic appreciation, not activated in the productive process. Mill's support for a steady-state economy is a way to end the culture of competitive conspicuous consumption to make room for the leisure needed for the exercise of higher faculties. Leisure is so important that Mill accepts state regulations on the length of the working day as a major exception to the principle of laissez-faire he otherwise advocates. During Mill's lifetime, Parliament passed several Factory Acts to regulate child labor by limiting work hours and requiring that factory owners provide schooling. These exceptions to free-market outcomes are justified because children are too immature to freely consent to the terms of their contracts, and are vulnerable to the exploitation of factory owners and parents.[59]

Some Factory Acts also limited women's working hours. Mill rejects these limits as unjust constraints on women's freedom of contract. Women are full moral agents, capable of making decisions for themselves and in no need of paternalistic constraint. Women also need to be able to compete on equal terms with men for work. Although subjection to factory tyranny is hard, subjection to their husbands is often worse. Women need full powers to earn wages to gain some independence from their husbands.[60]

Not all regulations limiting work hours amount to paternalistic interference with workers' freedom of contract, however. Mill allows that some regulations on employment contracts might be needed to give effect to the overwhelming preference of workers. Workers could face a collective action problem in an unregulated labor market. Under laissez-faire, any given worker will earn greater total wages if they work 10 hours rather than nine per day. However, if workers could enforce an agreement among themselves to never accept a contract to work more than nine hours, the resulting restriction of labor supply could raise hourly wages enough so that working nine hours under the agreement would earn the same total wages as working 10 hours under laissez-faire. Every worker would costlessly gain an hour of leisure per day in this scenario. Yet without state regulation, such an agreement would be impossible to enforce. Any given worker could get ahead of others in competing for jobs by accepting contracts to work 10 hours.

While a few might willingly work that long, everyone else would be forced by necessity to do so, because employers would not offer shorter contracts if they could impose longer ones. A general and equal regulation could better fulfill most workers' preferences for leisure without paternalistically substituting the state's judgment of what is good for workers for their own, or creating an unequal bargaining position for one group of workers relative to another.[61] Oddly, Mill offers this argument as only a hypothetical, although as we shall see in Chapter 7, workers were already demanding work-hour limits in his day.

Mill's second basic strategy for overcoming Smith's trade-off of prosperity against human capabilities in industrial work involves a fundamental reconsideration of the division of labor. He questions Smith's claim[62] that workers are more industrious if they are limited to one task, because this prevents them from wasting time "sauntering" from one task to another, as Smith thought agricultural laborers did. Consignment to a single task is enervating. Variety restores workers' "animal spirits." Women, who are busy with more diverse tasks than men, given their responsibilities for household management and child-rearing, reject the view that they waste time in the transition from one task to another. General opinion would be more accurate if women's views were taken seriously.[63] This feminist critique opens room for enriching industrial jobs with various and potentially skilled tasks.

More ambitiously, Mill argues that the industrial division of labor should be understood as a particularly sophisticated form of social cooperation.[64] He thereby shifts our focus away from the technical advantages of the division of labor that Smith stressed – that consignment to a single task saves time, improves workers' dexterity, and facilitates the development of specialized tools that increase productivity. The idea of cooperation turns our attention to the social relations involved in the division of labor. It opens the possibility that reconfiguring these relations could improve opportunities for workers to develop intelligence and exercise autonomy *as workers*.

Mill contemplates three ways of altering the social relations of production to enhance workers' capabilities as workers: labor unions, profit-sharing arrangements, and workers' cooperatives. No laws should limit the right of workers to voluntarily join a labor union, or to strike for higher wages. They don't interfere with the freedom of workers not to join, as long as they limit themselves to exerting moral pressure on other workers. Although Mill condemns monopolies, he denies that voluntary labor unions interfere with free markets. Strikes are just part of the bargaining process that generates the market wage. Unions "are the necessary instrumentality of that free market."[65] Mill's confidence on this point arises from his pessimism that unions are actually able to raise wages above the market rate. It would be fine if they could. But workers are too numerous to effectively raise the general wage rate above the market rate. Sometimes workers bargain for terms, such as banning piecework and prescribing equal wages regardless of work quality, that violate the just deserts of those who practice the work ethic more assiduously. Even so, they should be free to try. The "best interests of the human race . . . require that all economical experiments, voluntarily undertaken, should have the fullest licence."[66]

It may seem strange that Mill endorses organizations whose basic aim – to raise wages above the market rate – he thinks is doomed to failure.[67] In the course of trying, however, workers develop and exercise several sophisticated capabilities: self-organization for the common good, solidarity (sympathy) with fellow workers, intelligent planning and foresight, cooperation on terms of equality with coworkers, collective deliberation about ends and means. Even defeat serves educative functions. It is better for workers to learn the principle of supply and demand for themselves, in a futile attempt to raise wages above the market rate, than to submit to anti-union laws, which lead them to mistakenly blame the laws for unsatisfactory wages.[68]

Mill also views labor unions as a step on the way to a fully egalitarian mode of cooperation. Unions are learning from experience that strikes only succeed in raising wages when profits are rising. When they limit strikes to these conditions, workers are in effect bringing about a mode of association with capitalists in which both classes share in the profits of the enterprise.[69] Profit-sharing arrangements lead both sides to focus on their joint interests, in which gains to the whole firm are reaped by every worker and investor in the firm. Workers come to see that they have a personal stake in good work habits, while capitalists and workers alike learn to cooperate on terms of mutual respect.[70] Because workers are standing up for themselves, capitalists cannot treat them as hapless dependents who can be imperiously ordered around. They can gain workers' willing cooperation only by treating them as independent, self-respecting agents. Such an "association of interests" educates participants in the virtues of public spirit, generosity, and justice.[71]

Ultimately, even a profit-sharing partnership between workers and capitalists will not fully satisfy the ideal of cooperation. Mill questions the very existence of a rentier class as an offense to the work ethic and its labor-based conception of just deserts:

> I do not recognise as either just or salutary, a state of society in which there is any "class" which is not labouring; any human beings, exempt from bearing their share of the necessary labours of human life, except those unable to labour, or who have fairly earned rest by previous toil.[72]

The just society is a classless society. "All privileged and powerful classes, as such, have used their power in the interest of their own selfishness."[73] Mill excoriates the conservative conceit that the proper relation between property owners and workers is a purportedly benevolent relation of dictatorial tutelage, in which workers are dependent on the will of their masters, should mindlessly obey their orders in return for protection, and practice deference and religion. The warm sentiments that color such hierarchical relations may naturally arise in less advanced states of society, where people need to seek refuge from lawless violence by accepting subjection to a lordly protector. But even then, they rarely fit the brutal facts of dependent relations: to live at the mercy of someone with superior power is to be vulnerable to violence and abuse.[74]

Literate workers, free to think for themselves, quit their employer, and choose their newspapers and ministers, will not be snookered by conservative preaching about obedience and deference. Organized into unions and democratic social movements such as Chartism, they are educating themselves and demand the right to self-government.[75] There are two ways to achieve this in production: individual self-employment, and workers' cooperatives. Peasant proprietorship is one kind of self-employment. While this model promotes independence, intelligence, and the work ethic, its atomized mode of production fails to promote other virtues such as public spirit and sympathy. It also entrenches patriarchy, given that wives have no independent legal personhood from their husbands, and live in subjection to them. Finally, the limited division of labor available in this model limits labor productivity and hence opportunities for leisure.[76]

In a workers' cooperative, the workers own and jointly manage their firm democratically. This model most fully realizes the ideal of cooperation on terms of equality. It thereby realizes both the productive advantages of a complex division of labor, and the full range of virtues – not just independence, autonomy, and the work ethic, but also a concern for the common good, sympathy, and justice. Workers can undertake the mechanical tasks of production as well as take on some management responsibilities in collective decision making. Cooperatives thereby overcome Smith's dilemma. Smith wrongly assumed that the consignment of each worker to a single simple operation was necessary for high productivity.[77] Cooperatives realize the

> best aspirations of the democratic spirit, by putting an end to the division of society into the industrious and the idle, effacing all social distinctions but those fairly earned by personal services and exertions.[78]

Mill's hope that workers' cooperatives would supersede capitalist factories was not ultimately realized. His vision was limited by his assumption that governance rights within the firm need to be tied to ownership. He took for granted that investment of capital in the firm, but not investment of labor, was required for governance rights. This assumption was ultimately to be overturned by the social democratic innovation of codetermination, or joint management by capitalists and workers. Yet given Mill's thorough-going positivism about property rights, and his willingness to rewrite property rules to liberate and empower workers, there is little ground for thinking that he would have resisted the social democratic innovation.

Mill's Darker Side (1): Domestic Imperialism

From the start, the work ethic had a dual character, capable of supporting strong claims on behalf of workers, and of harsh and repressive measures against them. We have seen that Locke, although mostly an advocate of the progressive work ethic, advanced a Poor Law reform program that even his contemporaries deemed too harsh, and which contradicted his own theory of proper child development. Mill's progressive work ethic also has a darker aspect, tied to his imperialism. I speak of imperialism broadly, to include domestic welfare policies toward the working poor. Public discourse in the nineteenth century, influenced by thinkers such as Whately, rationalized policies toward the domestic working poor and the colonized in the same terms. They characterized both groups as "savage" or "barbarian," lacking the work ethic and hence needing to be "civilized" by their superiors by despotic means. Even Mill, by far the most ambitious of classical liberals in proposing policies to overturn social hierarchies of class and gender, was influenced by such arguments.

Mill defends the New Poor Law on Malthusian grounds. The argument turns on the wages-fund theory, which claims that the funds available to pay wages are fixed by the capital stock. The wage rate at any given time is determined by the ratio of capital stock to population. High wages therefore ultimately depend on population restraints in any fully occupied country, because, without unprecedented agricultural invention, food production cannot forever keep up with unchecked population growth.[79] Malthus claimed that population growth is less than the maximum possible in all old and hence fully settled countries.[80] Hence either his positive or his preventative checks on population exist in all old countries. While the preventive check prevails in England, Mill claims that this is due to the self-restraint of the middle classes and skilled artisans. He accepts the conclusion of Senior's *Poor Law Commissioners' Report* that agricultural laborers recklessly reproduced due to the perverse incentives of the Old Poor Law.[81] Those who criticize poor-law reformers of "hard-hearted Malthusianism" ignore "the law of wages." It is far more hard-hearted "to tell human beings that they may, than that they may not, call into existence swarms of creatures who are sure to be miserable, and most likely to be depraved" and forget that the cause of excessively large families is wives' "degrading slavery" to their husbands' "brute instinct" and "helpless submission to a revolting abuse of power."[82]

Against Malthus, however, Mill insists that the poor have a right to relief. They should not have to resort to private charity. To avoid offering incentives that undermine the work ethic, such relief must satisfy the principle of less eligibility – that the condition of those on relief must be worse than that of unskilled wage laborers not on relief.[83] Furthermore, "no one has a right to bring creatures into life, to be supported by other people." Society has a right to control the fertility of anyone on relief, to avoid Malthusian disaster. There is no "hardship in preventing paupers from breeding hereditary paupers in the workhouse itself."[84] The right to relief must be paired with the deprivation of liberty and strict discipline of the workhouses to avoid undermining the work ethic.[85]

It is difficult to reconcile Mill's support for forced labor under the New Poor Law with his opposition to G. P. Scrope's proposal to guarantee a right to relief in the form of a guaranteed job during the Famine. Scrope proposed public funding to hire Irish workers to create new farmland to distribute to the peasants by draining the wastes. Mill agreed with Scrope's ultimate aim of waste reclamation and distribution. However, he objected that, for this end to be achieved, a job guarantee would have to be tied to forced labor, since "even a much more industrious people than the Irish" would not work hard if they could not be fired. Mill doubted "whether we can compel them to be compelled."[86]

However coercive Scrope's outdoor jobs guarantee would have to be, incarceration in workhouses implies a far greater sacrifice of liberty. Mill concedes that any system that detains some people under the power of others will generate abuses. Hence, he is not surprised by the Andover Union scandal (see Chapter 4). There will be abuses under "any conceivable mode of pauper management." But this is no reason to dismantle the extreme discipline of the workhouses, as the sentimental critics of the New Poor Law demand. Everything written against the New Poor Law is worthless. The need to instill a sense of independence in paupers is the key to ensuring their future well-being, and overrides the risk of abuse. Abuses should be suppressed by more rigorous state supervision of workhouses.[87]

Mill's dismissal of critics of the New Poor Law on the basis of a dogmatic attachment to Malthusian population theory is difficult to credit. Hazlitt had shrewdly challenged Malthus to quantify the impact of overpopulation on the misery of the poor, compared to human institutions and follies not working through the population principle. Malthus could not answer this challenge.[88] His claim that attempts to remove the misery of the poor through relief would lead to demographic catastrophe was seriously damaged by his concessions that the effects of the Old Poor Law on England's population were far from evident, that England's poor were better off than the poor of Europe who had no right to relief, and that all ranks of English delayed marriage until they could afford children at their accustomed standard of living.[89] Without any quantification of the effects of different causes, Malthus's insistence that England had other advantages that outweighed the bad incentives of the Poor Law was just special pleading.

By the time Mill was writing the first edition of *Principles of Political Economy* at mid-century, the repeated crop failures of the turn of the century, which had prompted resort to the Speenhamland system, were long past. While the Irish Famine was current, this was obviously due to an unpredictable potato blight, not to the steadily rising pressure of population growth. Why attribute hunger to general laws of population and human nature, rather than to temporary natural disasters that Britain had ample resources to deal with? Moreover, by mid-century production was galloping ahead of population growth – that is, GDP per capita was growing. The Industrial Revolution really was massively accelerating labor productivity, as Smith observed at its threshold, and as everyone could see by the mid-nineteenth century. This put off the imagined Malthusian catastrophe well into the future. Hazlitt challenged Malthus to "give some better reason" for "thrust[ing] the poor man out of existence" "than that there is not room for an unlimited number."[90] His challenge applies equally well to anyone who would thrust the poor into the workhouse now, to prevent some speculative catastrophe generations hence.

In Chapter 3, I argued that Malthus's population theory was not the fundamental driver of his policy recommendations. That was merely the utilitarian window dressing around moral judgments founded on the conservative work ethic. Yet population theory loomed large in nineteenth-century political economy. Mill articulated the core issue, a truism: the standard of living of the great mass of people cannot improve unless production grows faster than population, so that production per capita is growing.[91] In Mill's day, Britain had a census, but national income accounting was not yet invented. Both total production and population were rapidly growing. One might think that without knowledge of the numerator, and with the total number of poor people growing, people might have been unable to grasp that Britain was not suffering economically from a population explosion. Yet Mill and his contemporaries could easily have deduced that production per capita was growing from other evidence. They observed that labor *productivity* was rapidly growing. This fact lay at the core of the much-discussed idea that society was progressing. They also knew that the great mass of workers were not reducing their hours. These facts imply that production per capita was growing.

So Mill had evidence that his obsession with population restraint as a key to ending poverty in Britain rested on a dubious empirical foundation. I conclude that, as with Malthus, Mill's utilitarian population theorizing was not based on evidence so much as a commitment to the work ethic. This was paired with his moral judgment that the working poor – specifically male workers – were not practicing it with respect to the virtue of sexual self-restraint. Rather, they were subjecting their wives to their "brute instinct." Still, Mill's version of the work ethic is vastly more progressive than Malthus's, or even Locke's. This is reflected in his proposals concerning poverty policy. Mill holds that, although the New Poor Law is defensible, it is not optimal. There is a far more generous way to ensure that the working poor adopt the work ethic.

The Poor Laws would barely be needed "if the habits of all classes of the people were temperate and prudent, and the diffusion of property satisfactory."[92] The work ethic is undermined not just by unearned plenty, but by deprivation, which discourages energy and independence by taking away hope of success through one's own efforts. The key is to give assistance in such a way as to inspire such hope.[93] In Mill's view, the two central virtues of the work ethic are industry and sexual self-restraint. Suppose the working classes practice industry under a just distribution of property – one that rewards hard work by securing to workers the fullest fruits of their labor. And suppose they adopt a social norm against imprudent childbearing, in favor of limiting family size to what can be supported on household income. This will raise wages by limiting the supply of labor.[94] The widespread practice of these two virtues will deliver for workers a sufficient income to enable them to be independent, rather than relying on poor relief.

Mill proposes three strategies intended to instill these virtues. First, women need equal rights to men and full citizenship. Wives need the rights to own property, make contracts, and keep their own earnings without asking their husbands' permission. They also need the right to vote.[95] With economic and political independence from their husbands, women will gain more power within the family to limit sexual intercourse and pregnancy. Poor women have a stronger interest in sexual restraint, to avoid additional burdens of domestic drudgery on top of the need to engage in wage labor. Second, the state must provide for working-class children to be educated, so they can develop sound practical judgment. Third, an entire generation of the working class should be brought up under a decent standard of living. This will promote their education because it is difficult for indigent children to learn. If an entire generation were to grow up in "tolerable comfort" and acquire "good sense" through education, they would do what is needed to avoid falling beneath the standard of living to which they had become accustomed. As adults, they would voluntarily limit their family size to what their income could afford. Once they acquire the habits needed to secure a decent standard of living, their children would also acquire them, perpetuating a change in working-class norms.[96]

To enable a whole generation to raise its standard of living, Mill proposes that the state subsidize poor workers' emigration to the colonies. Wages were higher there. Reducing the domestic supply of workers would also raise the level of British wages. In addition, Mill proposes for England a small-scale version of his Irish strategy: conversion of agricultural wage workers into peasant proprietors. All future enclosures of commons need to set aside some portions to be divided into small lots, allocated to laborers, along with a year's advance of tools and subsistence if required. Workers could pay a low fixed annual rent or purchase the land outright once they saved enough money to do so.[97]

Thus, while Mill defends the despotic workhouses, he views them as suboptimal and a temporary expedient. Alternative, liberating policies would make them obsolete in 20 years. These alternatives – equal rights, education, property, and real freedom to emigrate – would, by promoting the work ethic in the working classes, permanently raise their wages and thereby secure their independence.

How different is this from the proponents of the conservative work ethic? They, too, claimed that tyranny over workers to force them to adopt the work ethic was only temporary. Even if conservatives imagined the workhouses to be temporary, despotic factories were not. Against the conservatives, Mill proposes means for incentivizing workers' adoption of the work ethic that are liberating. Factory despotism should be replaced by democratically run workers' cooperatives; all workers should ultimately own the capital they work; all should enjoy free education; all should enjoy leisure. The laws of property, labor unions, work regulations, and more should be rewritten to promote opportunities for all to escape this fate.

Mill's Darker Side (2): Foreign Imperialism

With regard to overseas imperialism, the leading labor issue of Mill's day was the abolition of slavery. A case can be made that Mill acquitted himself well with respect to this issue. The bulk of Mill's writings condemn slavery unequivocally. He insists, with Locke, that no one is by nature born to subjection to anyone else.[98] There is no valid property right in other human beings.[99] There are no valid contracts into slavery because such contracts would defeat the purpose of freedom of contract, which is to secure people's liberty over the course of their lives.[100] Perpetual contracts should be unenforceable, because judgments of their worth are not based on experience, and they bar revocation once people have enough experience to judge.[101] Slavery in the United States oppresses both the slaves and free people because slaveholders monopolize political power to protect the institution of slavery, imposing despotism on everyone else.[102]

In 1849, historian Thomas Carlyle wrote a polemical tract excoriating Britain's 1833 abolition of slavery in the West Indies. He called for its effective reinstatement in the form of lifetime bonded labor. An expanded version with a racist title was published in 1853. Carlyle complains that the freed people grew all the food they needed with a half-hour of labor per day and were idle the rest of the time. This put white plantation owners, who "cannot work," at a grave disadvantage, because they supposedly could not induce the freed people to work for them.[103] Carlyle proclaims that

> with regard to the West Indies, it may be laid down as a principle ... that no black man who will not work according to what ability the gods have given him for working, has the smallest right to eat pumpkin, or to any fraction of land that will grow pumpkin, however plentiful such land may be; but has an indisputable and perpetual right to be compelled, by the real proprietors of said land, to do competent work for his living.[104]

"Heaven's law" decrees that whites are born masters and Blacks are born servants to whites, for they are only useful as servants.[105]

In his reply, Mill ridicules Carlyle's preposterous fantasy that the freed people were idle. White plantation owners were the idle ones, and were still exporting plenty of sugar grown with Black labor. Carlyle's doctrine that Blacks are natural slaves to whites is damnable. He is simply appealing to the "iniquitous dominion of the law of might." The history of human improvement is a struggle to rescue people from that law.[106]

For our purposes, the most interesting feature of Mill's essay is his appeal to the progressive work ethic. Carlyle's "gospel of work," justifying "the right to be compelled" to work, is perverse in two ways. First, he fails to apply it equally to Blacks and whites:

> Of [socially necessary work] each person is bound, in justice, to perform his share; and society has an incontestable right to declare to every one, that if he work not, at this work of necessity, neither shall he eat. Society has not enforced this right . . . . If this experiment is to be tried in the West Indies, let it be tried impartially; and let the whole produce belong to those who do the work which produces it. We would not have black labourers compelled to grow spices which they do not want, and white proprietors who do not work at all exchanging the spices for houses in Belgrave Square.[107]

Second, work is not an end in itself, but good only if it produces something worth the trouble:

> [T]he multiplication of work, for purposes not worth caring about, is one of the evils of our present condition . . . . How many of the so-called luxuries, conveniences, refinements, and ornaments of life, are worth the labour which must be undergone as the condition of producing them? . . . . In opposition to the "gospel of work," I would assert the gospel of leisure, and maintain that human beings cannot rise to the finer attributes of their nature compatibly with a life filled with labour . . . . To reduce very greatly the quantity of work required to carry on existence, is as needful as to distribute it more equally.[108]

So far, Mill's opposition to slavery is clear. However, Mill does not hold that slavery is always wrong. He believes that humanity is progressing toward higher levels of civilization, but that different parts of humanity are progressing at different rates. Some parts were stagnating. Different peoples can be ranked according to their level of progress.

This way of evaluating societies had a profound impact on Mill's normative views. All policies and institutions should be judged by their utility, "but it must be utility in the largest sense, grounded on the permanent interests of man as a progressive being."[109] Policies and institutions should thus be judged according to their tendencies to promote progress. People progress by internalizing the work ethic.

Hence, policies and institutions should be judged by their tendencies to instill the dispositions comprising the work ethic in the people subject to them. The tendencies of any given institution may vary, depending on the level of development of the people in question.

Conservatives held that the poor had to be subject to poverty, precarity, and despotism in order to acquire the work ethic. By contrast, the principal means Mill advocates for instilling the work ethic in the domestic poor do so by enhancing their wealth and autonomous agency. European workers are far past the point where poverty could make them more industrious or civilized.[110]

But what about people of non-European descent? Here Mill accepts key premises of the conservative theory. For those "in a semi-barbarous state, with the indolence and few wants of a savage ... the pressure of physical want may have been a necessary stimulus ... to the exertion of labour and ingenuity required" to advance to an industrial economy.

> Want, in that age of the world, had its uses, as even slavery had; and there may be corners of the earth where those uses are not yet superseded, though they might easily be so were a helping hand held out by more civilized communities.[111]

This acceptance of slavery is not merely a stray remark:

> [U]ncivilized races ... are averse to continuous labour of an unexciting kind. Yet all real civilization is at this price .... There needs a rare concurrence of circumstances, and for that reason often a vast length of time, to reconcile such a people to industry, unless they are for a while compelled to it. Hence even personal slavery, by giving a commencement to industrial life, and enforcing it as the exclusive occupation of the most numerous portion of the community, may accelerate the transition to a better freedom than that of fighting and rapine.[112]

Any theory that holds that the greatest moral imperative is to promote progress, that people can be ranked-ordered in their state of progress, and that the lower ranked need their superiors to move them along, courts slavery and despotism. Mill embraces Whately's view for *all* peoples at a primitive stage of development. That includes ancestral Europeans, who needed despots such as Charlemagne and Peter the Great to help them advance.[113] "[S]pontaneous improvement, beyond a very low grade, – improvement by internal development, without aid from other individuals or peoples – is one of the rarest phenomena in history."[114] That he also sees whites as once needing despotism does not absolve him of the charge of racism. While he denounces the attribution of purported differences of character among different "races" as a "vulgar error,"[115] he still holds that "barbarians" had inferior dispositions due to their cultures, and rationalizes their subjection to despotic rule by "civilized" peoples on that basis.[116] Mill and Carlyle were on common ground in accepting stereotypes of nonwhite peoples as lacking the work ethic – a view that remains at the core of anti-Black racism today.

Mill's reasoning rests on his reconceptualization of the division of labor as a sophisticated form of cooperation. "Civilization," understood as a society's advanced degree of wealth and power in industrial economies, is based on its ability to mobilize the energies of its members in a coordinated, disciplined fashion toward common goals. "There is not a more accurate test of the progress of civilization than the progress of the power of co-operation."[117] Industrial societies organize cooperation in more complex ways, and on a vastly greater scale, than hunter-gatherer societies. Mill credits this difference in part to deficiencies in "savage" characters. Cooperation involves disciplined application of one's energies to goals that are not wholly one's own, since they originate in compromise with others, if not in the commands of a master. Doing one's part in a cooperative enterprise thus involves self-restraint: overriding impulses in favor of action on collective rules and norms, resisting temptations to free-ride on others' efforts, subordinating selfish ends to collective objectives. But "[t]he savage cannot bear to sacrifice, for any purpose, the satisfaction of his individual will. His social cannot even temporarily prevail over his selfish feelings, nor his impulses bend to his calculations."[118] If savages remain at liberty, they will therefore never progress. Progress requires that they learn to obey the commands of another.

Mill hastens to add that his theoretical

excite for slavery is only available in a very early state of society. A civilized people have far other means of imparting civilization to those under their influence; and slavery is ... so repugnant to that government of law, which is the foundation of all modern life, and so corrupting to the master-class when they have once come under civilized influences, that its adoption under any circumstances whatever in modern society is a relapse into worse than barbarism.[119]

Indeed, he takes back his excuse almost as soon as he advances it. "A people of savages should be taught obedience, but not in such a manner as to convert them into a people of slaves." Enslavement teaches people to obey commands only, not general rules. This disables them from advancing to the next stage toward civilization, which requires "the capacity to act on general instructions." This capacity is a prerequisite to learning self-command, or the capacity to control one's own conduct by giving oneself general principles on which to act. Some less oppressive form of paternalistic despotism is more suitable for civilizing "savages."[120]

It is impossible to make sense of Mill's rationale for slavery, either empirically or theoretically. Mill's assumption that slaves cannot obey general rules or govern themselves contradicts the overwhelming testimony of slave narratives that were widely published in Mill's day,[121] as well as the common practice of assigning slaves skilled as well as unskilled tasks in both the West Indies and North America. Smith sees matters far more clearly in praising the superior self-command of the enslaved relative to their masters.[122]

Mill did not think that slavery was justified anywhere in the modern world. But he did think that despotism by "civilized" countries over "backward" countries was justified. "Despotism is a legitimate mode of government in dealing with barbarians, provided the end be their improvement, and the means justified by actually effecting that end."[123] That includes the "rule of a free people over a barbarous or semi-barbarous one."[124] Despotism is inherently the best form of government over "savages" and "barbarians" (that is, hunter-gatherers and tribal herders) because the next step they need to take in the march of progress is to learn obedience, a prerequisite for the complex forms of cooperation needed for civilization. However, some peoples have learned the lesson of obedience to rulers and custom too well, and have thereby lost the individualism and spontaneity needed for further progress. In the absence of a native ruler of unusual genius and energy, such as Peter the Great or Charlemagne, such peoples will best make progress under the despotic rule of a more advanced country.[125] Such is the condition of "Oriental people," including China and India.

Despotism brought them up to a certain level of civilization, whereafter they fell back into stagnation for lack of innovative native rulers.[126] Mill appears to classify this condition as "semi-barbarous." For he claims that "[i]t has been the destiny of the government of the East India Company, to suggest the true theory of the government of a semi-barbarous dependency by a civilized country."[127]

Outside imperialist contexts, Mill constantly stresses the gross injustice of relations of domination and subordination, as well as their corrupting effects on both the dominators and the oppressed. This is the great theme of *The Subjection of Women*, in which Mill argues that the condition of married women under the common law, in which they lacked legal personhood, is a form of slavery.[128] Occupying a position of unaccountable power over others renders one unfit to exercise that power beneficently, by fostering ignorance of subordinates, who cannot safely communicate their thoughts, and impeding sympathy for them.[129]

How can one explain Mill's incoherent excuse for slavery and imperialist despotism? Mill held a contradictory position. He was both a leading advocate of a free society of equals as the ultimate destiny for all of humanity, and an officer of the British East India Company from 1823 to 1858, during which it ruled India. These roles cannot be reconciled without representing the colonized as like children, needing tutelage at the hands of purportedly beneficent masters, who are imagined to prepare them for freedom with a plan to emancipate them once they are judged ready. People with moral consciences everywhere trust their own power over others by consulting their own self-image as good people. This requires that they invent stories that rationalize social relations they would otherwise condemn.

Mill made the challenge of inventing a persuasive story harder for himself, because he had already developed theoretical resources sufficient to condemn despotic rule of foreign powers over distant "barbarians." By his own lights, such despotism was most unlikely to be successful, even assuming good intentions. In 1857, Indian sepoys in the East India Company's army began a mutiny. Civilians – alienated from Company rule, feeling oppressed by its high taxes and Company meddling in Indian traditions, and not finding value in its purported civilizing mission – joined in a mass uprising. The Company army suppressed the rebellion with great violence, including reprisal killings and lootings. It burned down villages and destroyed the cities of Delhi and Lucknow. Parliament blamed the Company and prepared to dissolve it, with a plan to turn over the government of India to Crown and Parliament. The Company asked Mill, who occupied the very high position of Examiner of Indian Correspondence, to write a defense of Company rule. Mill submitted two documents to Parliament in 1858 – the "Petition of the East India Company," and a long "Memorandum of the Improvements in the Administration of India in the Last Thirty Years." He repeated his arguments for the superiority of Company rule over direct Parliamentary rule in *Considerations on Representative Government*.[130]

In contrast to Bentham's case for outsourcing state functions to private enterprise, Mill does not rest his case on, or even mention, the purportedly greater efficiency of organizations driven by the profit motive. The Company was founded in 1600 as a merchant monopoly with a private army it used to defend its warehouses in India. Beginning in 1773, Parliament began to gradually convert it into a privately owned company functioning as an agency of the British government. In its last decades, the Company was even developing a personnel system approaching a meritocratic professionally trained civil service.[131] It established a college where Malthus taught economics to its students. Mill's case for retaining Company rule turned on the superiority of an impartial professional civil service subject to arms-length Parliamentary oversight, over a colonial administration that reported directly to Parliament and would thereby be subject to partisan electoral politics. In the latter system, candidates for Parliamentary seats would campaign over colonial affairs, appealing to a British electorate that neither knew nor cared about the colonized.

> It is always under great difficulties, and very imperfectly, that a country can be governed by foreigners; even when there is no extreme disparity, in habits and ideas, between the rulers and the ruled. Foreigners do not feel with the people. They cannot judge, by the light in which a thing appears to their own minds, or the manner in which it affects their feelings, how it will affect the feelings or appear to the minds of the subject population. What a native of the country, of average practical ability, knows as it were by instinct, they have to learn slowly, and after all imperfectly, by study and experience. The laws, the customs, the social relations, for which they have to legislate, instead of being familiar to them from childhood, are all strange to them. For

most of their detailed knowledge they must depend on the information of natives; and it is difficult for them to know whom to trust. They are feared, suspected, probably disliked by the population; seldom sought by them except for interested purposes; and they are prone to think that the servilely submissive are the trustworthy. Their danger is of despising the natives; that of the natives is, of disbelieving that anything the strangers do can be intended for their good.[132]

A government of one people by another is impossible:

One people may keep another as a warren or preserve for its own use, a place to make money in, a human cattle farm to be worked for the profit of its own inhabitants. But if the good of the governed is the proper business of a government, it is utterly impossible that a people should directly attend to it. The utmost they can do is to give some of their best men a commission to look after it; to whom the opinion of their own country can neither be much of a guide in the performance of their duty, nor a competent judge of the mode in which it has been performed.[133]

Direct Parliamentary control will either wrongly "force English ideas down the throats of the natives," such as by proselytization, or promote the interests of English settlers at the expense of the natives:

[W]hen a country holds another in subjection, the individuals of the ruling people who resort to the foreign country to make their fortunes, are of all others those who most need to be held under powerful restraint . . . . Armed with the prestige and filled with the scornful overbearingness of the conquering nation, they have the feelings inspired by absolute power, without its sense of responsibility. Among a people like that of India, the utmost efforts of the public authorities are not enough for the effectual protection of the weak against the strong: and of all the strong, the European settlers are the strongest . . . . [T]hey think the people of the country mere dirt under their feet: it seems to them monstrous that any rights of the natives should stand in the way of their smallest pretensions: the simplest act of protection to the inhabitants against any act of power on their part which they may consider useful to their commercial objects, they denounce, and sincerely regard, as an injury.[134]

Mill's argument is abundantly supported by the evidence on how British colonialism actually worked. Yet it proves too much for his purposes, since it equally applies to any system of colonial administration. It was always an illusion to suppose that a professional civil service could overcome the epistemic obstacles to knowing what is best for the colonized, muster up sufficient motivation to serve them, or stand in the way of the mercenary ambitions of the domestic population, or the pride and arrogance of the imperial center, when their objectives were contrary to the interests of the colonized. British emigrants to settler colonies didn't "civilize savages." They committed genocide and ethnic cleansing against them. The Industrial Revolution was not simply based on the industry of free British workers. It was launched on the backs of brutally exploited American slaves who grew cotton for export to Britain. Mill was wrong to think that India and China had been economically backward and stagnant for millennia;[135] in fact, they were the manufacturing powerhouses of the world in the seventeenth and eighteenth centuries. Extremely restrictive British mercantilist and protectionist policies, enforced by the East India Company, played a substantial role in reducing their share of global manufacturing from 53 percent in 1800 to 5 percent in 1900.[136] Britain manufactured almost nothing of interest to China in return for its silk, porcelain, and other goods. Humiliated by having to pay silver for China's superior products, it chose to become the world's biggest drug-pusher, waging two wars (1839–42 and 1856–60) to force China to accept opium instead.[137] Mill complained that "barbarian" societies did not respect international principles of reciprocity.[138] Yet it was the system of international law devised by Europeans that justified gunboat diplomacy. This was the practice of threatening or committing indiscriminate murder of innocent civilians to extract tribute from weak states in order to compensate for trifling civil claims of Europeans.[139] This was nothing more than plunder and piracy dressed up as justice.

Others in the eighteenth and nineteenth centuries better understood the inherent violence and depredations of imperialism. Smith rightly blamed the East India Company for the 1770 Bengal famine,[140] which killed ten million people – more than the entire British population. This was a great scandal at the time, due to the Company's shocking extraction of tribute from a starving population, its gross disruption of the domestic grain market, and its destruction of traditional methods of providing for crop failures in the name of modernization, among other policy failures.[141] Under Company mis-rule from 1765 to 1858, including all the years of its professionalized civil service, Bengal experienced 12 famines.[142] In 1785, Burke denounced the Company for contributing to the destruction of the extensive reservoir system of the Carnatic province of South India, constructed over generations by the population to enable farming in a dry region.[143] His description of these magnificent waterworks refutes Mill's racist supposition that Asians were incapable of large-scale complex cooperation. In the 1820s, British abolitionists painstakingly collected demographic data to prove that slaveholders in the West Indies, far from "improving" the enslaved, were working them to death.[144]

Mill was too well-read to be unaware of these facts. Many more damning facts about the brutal realities of imperialism were well-known in Mill's day. Yet he was too caught up in the fantasy of the civilizing mission, needed to justify his own career in the East India Company, to integrate these facts into the damning indictment of the *inherent* character of imperialism that they were. Mill, the great advocate of the progressive work ethic for Europeans, was Smith's "man of system" for non-Europeans, "so enamoured with the supposed beauty of his own ideal plan of government," that he promotes it "without any regard ... to the great interests ... which may oppose it."[145] The system that enamored him was the conservative work ethic.

7 THE PROGRESSIVE WORK ETHIC (3): MARX

Marx's Ideal of Unalienated Labor as an Expression of the Progressive Work Ethic

In 1835, Marx sat for his graduation exam at the Trier Gymnasium. One of the assigned topics was "Reflections of a Young Man on the Choice of a Profession."[1] Marx writes that a suitable profession must be capable of inspiring one's enthusiasm, be suited to one's capabilities, so that one can perform its duties well, and be one "in which we are not servile tools," but autonomous agents. Above all,

> the chief guide which must direct us in the choice of a profession is the welfare of mankind and our own perfection . . . [for] man's nature is so constituted that he can attain his own perfection only by working for the perfection, for the good of his fellow men.

Robert Sanderson would have approved.[2] Marx lived by these principles throughout his work as a philosopher, economist, journalist, and political activist. They inform all of his writing about what ideal work would be like, and what is wrong with work under capitalism.

Marx's conception of human flourishing is broadly Aristotelian: it consists in the exercise of essential human powers. The good life for humans thus includes the following components.[3] It consists in activities that exercise a wide range of human capabilities. Such activity should be free, both voluntary and autonomous – self-directed, according to one's own ideas. It is social, in the sense of promoting others' welfare, and being motivated by that end. This activity is recognized by the agent and others as having this social character, such that it is common knowledge between the agent and beneficiaries that the agent acted for the beneficiaries' sakes, and that the beneficiaries appreciate that fact. Thus, in an ideally organized society, each person promotes the welfare of others in ways that also promote their own flourishing. This formula, we have seen, can be traced back to Locke and the Puritan originators of the work ethic.

Marx's understanding of the good life is very close to Mill's. Mill, too, holds that happiness requires the exercise of distinctively human capabilities,[4] in ways that freely express one's own ideas about how to live.[5] The progress of civilization should result in mutual sympathy, a motivational state in which individuals "never think of, or desire, any beneficial condition for himself, in the benefits of which ... [others] are not included."[6] We should seek a state of society in which "what is a benefit to the whole shall be a benefit to each individual composing it."[7]

Marx views work as the principal domain of activity in which people flourish by realizing their essential natures. In "Comments on James Mill, *Élémens d' économie politique*" (1844), Marx writes that in fully human production, "[o]ur products would be so many mirrors in which we saw reflected our essential nature."[8] In the *Economic and Philosophic Manuscripts of 1844*, he claims that "the productive life is the life of the species," its "life activity; and free, conscious activity is man's species character."[9] In *The Communist Manifesto* (1848), he and Engels extol the communist reorganization of production as realizing a society in which "the free development of each is a condition for the free development of all."[10] In the "Critique of the Gotha Program" (1875), Marx proclaims that labor should be "not only a means of life but life's prime want," a domain for "the all-round development of the individual."[11]

Marx's stress on work as the central meaningful activity in people's lives reflects a secular transformation of the Calvinist work ethic. For the Calvinist, work – practical activity advancing the welfare of our fellow human beings – was meaningful as a fulfillment of God's will, which it is our mission in life to obey. For nineteenth-century German atheists such as Marx, influenced by Young Hegelian Ludwig

Feuerbach, the idea of God is a projection of human qualities and wishes onto an imaginary divine figure.[12] Humanism recognizes this fact. It thereby poses a question: if the hope of salvation, of everlasting communion in the love of God, is really a projection of a wish that all humans, as a species, live in communion with one another, what would it take for us to realize that wish on earth?

Marx's answer is that work itself must be transformed into something wholeheartedly undertaken for the sake of others, in which one can find one's own fulfillment or completion in such labor, because it realizes one's own specifically human capacities and expresses one's own ideas. Work should not be a matter of ascetic self-denial for some external selfish end – whether that be salvation or competitive acquisition. Nor should it be performed out of duty alone. It should inherently merit one's enthusiasm and dedication. He depicts this ideal most clearly in his "Comments on James Mill":

> Let us suppose that we had carried out production as human beings. Each of us would have in two ways affirmed himself and the other person. 1) In my production I would have objectified my individuality, its specific character, and therefore enjoyed not only an individual manifestation of my life during the activity, but also when looking at the object I would have the individual pleasure of knowing my personality to be objective, visible to the senses . . .. 2) In your enjoyment or use of my product I would have the direct enjoyment both of being conscious of having satisfied a human need by my work . . . and of having thus created an object corresponding to the need of another man's essential nature. 3) I would have been for you the mediator between you and the species, and therefore would become recognized and felt by you yourself as a completion of your own essential nature . . . and consequently would know myself to be confirmed both in your thought and your love. 4) In the individual expression of my life I would have directly created your expression of your life, and therefore in my individual activity I would have directly confirmed and realized . . . my human nature, my communal nature. My work would be a free manifestation of life, hence an enjoyment of life . . .. [T]he specific nature of my individuality, therefore, would be affirmed in my labour . . ..[13]

Marx's stress on how work should express each worker's individuality amounts to an application to the domain of work of John Stuart Mill's stress on the importance of individuality for the good life.[14] That aspiration, in turn, can be traced back to the Puritan idea that one's calling must match one's individual talents and interests.

Marx's secularized progressive work ethic extolls an extremely high ideal of work. The vast gap between what Marx thought work ought to be and could become, and what it actually was for ordinary workers during the Industrial Revolution, lies at the core of his critique of capitalism.

Alienated Labor and the Critique of Capitalism

Marx casts his critique of work under capitalism in terms of alienation or estrangement, an idea he drew from Hegel's philosophy. To understand this, we need to make a brief detour into Hegel's philosophy of freedom.[15] Hegel, like so many other European thinkers of his era, believes that human history is a march of progress. He judges progress in terms of freedom, understood as autonomy or self-determination. To be free is to be determined by nothing alien to the self. It is to guide one's action according to an understanding of oneself, of one's desires and plans, with which one wholly identifies. However, all action takes place under natural and socially determined circumstances that have not been crafted by the individual agent. These circumstances determine what worldly consequences one's action will have, which may not be wholly anticipated or desired by the agent. These consequences redound on the self. In the course of acting, we shape ourselves – our capabilities, habits, desires, emotional reactions, and so forth. Given that external natural and social circumstances condition the actual consequences of our action, and hence the self, it would seem that Hegel's ideal of complete self-determination is unrealizable.

Hegel answers this challenge by arguing that, over time, people can realize full autonomy by coming to identify more fully with our natures as deeply social beings who live together in community. The social conditions of our action are the joint product of all of our individual actions, typically undertaken in response to the normative expectations we place on each other. In our joint action, we continuously modify the natural world and hence ourselves. Suppose, then, that we (1) acquire a full understanding of the causal consequences of joint action on the natural world, our social world, and ourselves; (2) develop means whereby we can determine modes of joint action with which the members of society wholeheartedly identify, knowing their consequences; and (3) act accordingly, in full consciousness of all of this. Then each individual, in doing their part in this joint willing, will have been determined by nothing alien to the self, because each identifies with others in their community, with their individual role in it, and with the ways their willing redounds on the self and others. What is impossible for the individual considered in isolation is possible for all of us working together. Critical to this process is mutual recognition and affirmation of everyone's role in such collective, social determination of outcomes, as well as mutual affirmation of the outcomes themselves. Such recognition and affirmation turns what originally seemed alien into identification with the other, into seeing oneself in the other, and seeing oneself completed by the other. By expanding the boundaries of identity to include others in society, we come to understand ourselves as determined by nothing alien or outside the self after all. In this way we can be fully free even when subject to social determination – at least when things go well.

We have seen that Marx regards labor – working with the material world – as the primary domain in which we should realize our freedom in autonomously realizing ourselves as individuals, as members of the human species, and as in community with others. When we can fully identify with the product and process of labor, its consequences for self and others, when there is mutual recognition and affirmation of the value of these consequences – that the workers have satisfied others' needs for the others' sakes, and the others manifest their appreciation of that fact – and all of this is freely willed, then labor is unalienated, and hence free. Failure of any of these conditions entails that we are engaged in alienated labor. Alienated labor is labor that we can't identify with or affirm as an expression of our autonomy. It is unfree labor.

Marx argues that work under capitalism fails all of these conditions. In the *1844 Manuscripts*, he famously argues that capitalist work alienates workers from the product and process of labor, from other people, and from their essence or "species being." This critique continues in *Capital*, with somewhat more emphasis on the terrible material conditions of work.[16]

Wage laborers are alienated from the product of their labor in several ways. (1) They don't own what they make, since the capitalist is the legal owner of their product.[17] This sense is not fundamental, however, since Marx regards the obsession with private ownership as a feature of societies that alienates people from others. In an ideal society, workers, in producing to satisfy others' needs, could still identify with their product even when another consumes it, because they identify with consumers and are fulfilled by the fact of helping others. (2) More importantly, among the products of labor are the machines that structure the work process – its pace, dangers, noise, and the human movements needed to tend them. In a reversal of the proper emancipatory relation of agents to what they make, workers find themselves dominated by machines, turned into their mere instruments, when machines should be the servants of workers.[18] Marx quotes Mill to support the judgment that, whereas machines should be able to liberate people from drudgery, they actually enslave them to it: "It is questionable if all the mechanical inventions yet made have lightened the day's toil of any human being."[19] Capitalism thus turns machines into an alien, antagonistic power over workers.[20] (3) Through labor, workers shape themselves. Under capitalism, however, they reduce themselves to mere commodities, impoverishing themselves even as they are evermore productive.[21] It's not just that their wages are falling. Quoting Smith, Marx laments the fact that consignment to a single simple mechanical operation stunts workers' minds. Where labor should be the occasion for the development and exercise of a variety of human capabilities, under capitalism, skilled craftsmen are reduced to deskilled, homogenized operatives.[22] (4) Because their labor is homogenized, and due to the separation of mental labor (creation and design) from manual labor, the product of labor does not express workers' own individuality and ideas.[23]

These modes of alienation from the product of labor are tied to the multiple ways workers are alienated from the productive process. (1) Productive processes do not express workers' own wills, but were designed by capitalists to serve the latter's interests. Workers have no choice in the matter, but are coerced into submitting to factory labor. Lacking independent access to the means of production, they have no alternative but to submit to capitalist production processes.[24] (2) Factory conditions are dangerous and unhealthy.[25] (3) The labor process ruins workers' minds through tedious drudgery, excessive hours, and an overwhelming machine-driven pace. It deskills them, suppressing their individuality by reducing them to one-sided, homogenized workers.[26] (4) Because the process of labor has no intrinsic value, workers feel free only after work, not at work. But work has so exhausted them that even after work they have no time or energy to exercise higher capabilities. They are reduced to satisfying merely their animal needs.[27]

Capitalism alienates people from one another by placing them in antagonistic relations. (1) Workers must compete against each other for jobs, because they are in chronically short supply.[28] (2) Quoting Smith's observations that landlords "love to reap what they have never sown," and that the interests of manufacturers are opposed to the public interest, Marx objects to the ways capitalism sets different classes at odds.[29] (3) Echoing Locke, Marx complains that capitalist firms take advantage of consumers by manipulative marketing, to artificially stimulate desires for frivolous things.[30] (4) Capitalists dominate workers as dictators, enforcing military discipline in the factory.[31]

Finally, capitalism alienates workers from their essence or species-being. The distinctively human essence is to freely shape oneself, to develop and exercise diverse human capabilities, and to express the self through work that fulfills others' genuine needs. Capitalist work stunts both these capabilities and the possibility that they could be expressed in work. Hence, under capitalism, workers work to live, instead of living to work.[32]

Marx's ideal of unalienated labor is strikingly nostalgic, reflecting a romanticized version of artisanal work. Within the craft and guild, labor "still [has] the significance of real community life."[33] Master craftsmen were not alienated from their products or the work process. They created a whole product[34] and owned what they made. Their workmanship reflected their own design and could express their individuality. They exercised a variety of skills, both mental and manual, engaging in interesting work.[35] They could take pride in their work, and in how well it served the needs of their customers. Customers would choose them for their excellent craftsmanship, showing appreciation for their individual skill and design work. Master craftsmen owned their own tools, which served them at their own self-directed pace, enhancing rather than degrading their skills. As self-employed workers, their labor was not a mere commodity sold to others. They enjoyed a decent standard of living for their day. They recognized no superior authority at work.[36] The workshop was a vastly less dangerous place than the modern factory. In the traditional guild system, masters did not compete with one another in a ruthless market, but combined in solidarity to protect their positions. It was not hard to imagine that such craftsmen often enjoyed their work and to a significant degree lived to work – much as many professionals do today, finding satisfaction in exercising varied skills to serve others' needs, with work that expresses their own judgment and individuality.

Marx's nostalgic view of artisanal work fit his social environment. He associated with radical artisans in Paris while writing the *1844 Manuscripts*. He regularly delivered lectures to radical German artisans in London in the 1860s. He worked closely with them as a leader of the International Working Men's Association in London from 1864 to 1873.[37] These craftsmen had recently lost their traditional work in the onslaught of capitalist industrialization, or expected to go under soon. Marx saw in them "the real brotherhood of man."[38] They longed for the world of work they had lost or were about to lose – work that was far more fulfilling than the tedious factory labor to which they were already or soon to be consigned.

From the radical artisans' point of view, it was all too easy to overlook the problematic features of traditional crafts. The Levellers had complained that, far from being an association of equals, the guilds empowered the wealthy masters to limit the freedom of less wealthy masters.[39] Smith lamented the ways masters dominated and coerced unpaid apprentices, and how the guilds were cartels that conspired against the public in limiting work opportunities and artificially raising prices.

Marx did not aim to restore the artisanal world that capitalism was destroying. *The Communist Manifesto* devotes many pages to commending the bourgeoisie for revolutionizing production, even at the cost of destroying treasured social relationships and modes of life. "The bourgeoisie, during its rule of scarce one hundred years, has created more massive and more colossal productive forces than have all preceding generations together."[40] Like Mill, Marx hoped to combine the immense productive power of modern industrial systems with a reorganization of work that would enable workers to exercise autonomy, skills, and judgment at work, in mutually affirming relations with fellow workers. Like Mill, he was struck by the contradictory directions taken by the collective powers of capitalism and the powers of individual workers:

> [T]he more the worker produces, the less he has to consume; the more values he creates ... the more unworthy he becomes; the better formed his product, the more deformed becomes the worker; ... the more powerful labor becomes, the more powerless becomes the worker. ... [Labor] replaces labor by machines, but it ... turns the other workers into machines. It produces intelligence – but for the worker, stupidity ....[41]

To both Marx and Mill, it was also obvious that these perversions are unnecessary. The vastly increased productive powers of labor could be redirected to make all workers better off. Machines could be redirected to lighten the burdens of labor and increase leisure. Ever-more sophisticated and larger-scale cooperation in production could intensify and enlarge the scope of people's affirmation of one another, rather than putting them at odds in a competitive struggle for superior position. The ingenuity of the production process and the division of labor could be reconfigured to enhance workers' minds and practical skills. For Marx, such changes are not only possible but necessary:

> Modern Industry, indeed, compels society, under penalty of death, to replace the detail-worker of today, grappled by life-long repetition of one and the same trivial operation, and thus reduced to a mere fragment of a man, by the fully developed individual, fit for a variety of labors, ready to face any change of production, and to whom the different social functions he performs, are but so many modes of giving free scope to his own natural and acquired powers.[42]

These changes would happen only when workers assume collective control of production.

Marx and Mill agree on what is objectionable about work in the Industrial Revolution, and on what goods progress should secure for ordinary workers. They agree that it is possible and vitally important to transcend the contradictory features of capitalism noted above. *They even agree that such transcendence would require the end of class-based society,* understood as a society divided between wealthy property owners who live idly on income accruing to capital, and workers, who do all the work. They agree that in the ideal society, every able-bodied person works in Baxter's inclusive sense of "work," which encompasses all socially necessary and useful labor, including domestic and dependent-care work that is unpaid under capitalism.

Marx and Mill disagree on two key points. First, Mill argues that the ideal society at the end of progress could and would be achieved by nonviolent, evolutionary means. Property rights may need to be reconfigured – sometimes dramatically, as in the cases of inheritance and Irish land tenure. Some state regulations may need to be imposed. Workers would need to apply their work ethic to save money so they can found cooperative enterprises. All of these changes could take place peacefully, at least within Britain, with the help of its evolving democratization. By contrast, for most of his adult life, Marx held that violent revolution was necessary to achieve the ideal society.

Second, Mill argues that workers can become prosperous, develop their capabilities, express their individuality, exercise autonomy, and enlarge their sympathies with others within an economic system founded on private property and competitive markets. Mill's ideal of a classless society, like that of the Ricardian socialists, is one in which everyone becomes both a worker and a capitalist, owning at least a share of the capital they work.

Marx insists on the abolition of private property and markets, and hence of anything resembling capitalism, because he holds that the perverse contradictions he identifies are inherent to the system. Private property is the source of class divisions and antagonism, and of an organization of work that maximizes profits at the expense of workers' freedom and well-being. Market-based economies lead people to relate to one another as egoists, suppressing mutual support and affirmation. The reduction of labor to a commodity pits workers against each other, subordinates them to dictatorship at work, and generates poverty, precarity, and a microdivision of labor that stunts workers' capabilities. In addition, "anarchic" market-based economies generate crises of overproduction and recession, which regularly lead to catastrophic mass unemployment. The entire system of private property and markets would need to be transcended to overcome the contradictions between the vastly improved collective powers of the economic system and their gratuitous and devastating consequences for individual workers and for the quality of social relations. Only a revolutionary overthrow of capitalism could achieve this.

Communism: Babeuf vs. Marx

Marx mainly characterizes communism in terms of the institutions it would eliminate. Private property will be abolished. Markets – not just for labor, land, and capital, but for all goods – will be eliminated. "Selling and buying disappears."[43] "In communist society with common ownership of the means of production, workers do not exchange their products."[44] The bourgeois family will vanish.[45] State power will be destroyed,[46] or simply "dies out."[47]

What institutions will serve the socially necessary functions that revolution sweeps away? One might expect that Marx and Engels would have devoted serious thought to this question. Yet they write almost nothing about the institutional structure of communist society. What they do write is ambiguous enough that later thinkers and activists interpreted it in contradictory ways. One side saw in Marx and Engels a rationale for a totalitarian society. Lenin took their thought that direction, with many communist party leaders across the world following in his wake. Cold War ideologues in the West agreed with the totalitarian reading, and thereby cemented the reputation of Marx and Engels as the architects of state-centered totalitarian communism, as practiced in Stalin's Soviet Union, Mao's China, and even Pol Pot's Cambodia. Another side of Marxism, originally called "revisionism," saw in Marx and Engels a rationale for a more fully developed democratic society, but one that should be achieved entirely through nonviolent democratic means. Eduard Bernstein was the most important early theorist of this interpretation, which ultimately led to social democracy (see Chapter 8).

These two interpretations became the most historically significant legacies of Marxism, because they were actually instituted in many states. But they were not the only interpretations that political activists tried to realize. Rosa Luxemburg defended violent revolution, but rejected Lenin's view that a tiny vanguard should indoctrinate and direct the mass of workers in authoritarian mode. The workers themselves should be free to experiment and spontaneously work out for themselves what the revolution will become, in a democratic way.[48] This view draws inspiration from nascent attempts of revolutionary workers to spontaneously organize society, as in the Paris Commune of 1871, and the soviets (workers' councils) of Russia's February Revolution. However, these attempts were rapidly crushed wherever they appeared. For this reason I shall set it aside.

It is pointless to argue over which interpretation of Marxism is "right." In the course of attempting to realize in the world what they saw as Marx's ultimate aspirations, different sides gave priority to different normative ideas in Marx and Engels's thought, and made fateful choices in view of their perceptions of the opportunities and constraints in a world Marx and Engels had not anticipated. Each side thus ended up rejecting core features of Marx and Engels's original views that could not be reconciled with the normative priorities they emphasized, or with empirical realities. Such is the fate of all utopian thinking when political actors attempt to realize it in practice.

To grasp the totalitarian reading, we must go back to the first modern theorist of totalitarian communism, François-Noël Babeuf. Babeuf was a radical during the French Revolution who led the "Conspiracy of Equals," a secretive group that plotted a coup to overthrow the government in 1796. The Equals had two ostensible aims by which they hoped to inspire workers to support their coup: to restore the never-implemented Jacobin Constitution of 1793, which called for universal male suffrage, and to restore price controls on bread. (France, like England, suffered from crop failures and high grain prices in this period.) In reality, they aimed to establish a totalitarian communist state. Babeuf and his coconspirators, most notably Philippe Buonarroti and Sylvain Maréchal, wrote extensively about how a communist society should be organized and why it was necessary. The contrasts between Babeuf's ideas and those of Marx and Engels help us to understand how the thought of the latter could lead – and in one branch of influence actually did lead – to social democracy.

Babeuf was captured and tried before the High Court of Justice at Vendôme in 1797. At his trial, in which he represented himself, he summarized his communist plan:

> [T]o establish a common administration; to suppress private property; to place every man of talent in the line of work he knows best; to oblige him to deposit the fruit of his work in the common store, to establish a simple administration of needs, which, keeping a record of all individuals and all the things that are available to them, will distribute these available goods with the most scrupulous equality.[49]

Babeuf's model of communist society is the army. He cites Revolutionary France's army of 1,200,000 men to prove the feasibility of his scheme. In an army, everyone is required to work an assigned job according to their ability. Everyone is supplied with their simple needs from a common store. Everyone is fed the same food and wears the same clothes. Everyone lives together in barracks. No markets are needed to satisfy needs, because everyone's needs are reduced to the lowest common denominator, without room for individuality. Nor are markets needed to allocate labor, because the entire organization is planned from the top down. Each individual is bound to follow their superior's orders.

Buonarroti spells out in detail the communist plan for running all of society like a giant army. The state would determine what is grown where, assign all jobs, and distribute all production from the common store in equal amounts to each. It would also enforce virtue. Greed and competitive consumption would be eradicated by several means. Only simple clothes would be worn, all luxuries and frivolous consumption ended.[50] As cities tend to corrupt morals due to the anonymity of crowds, the cities would be emptied and its inhabitants ordered to work in the countryside.[51] In face-to-face communities, no one could escape scrutiny. Socially necessary work would be done in groups, to ensure that everyone had someone looking over their shoulder. The people would be frequently called up to publicly censure those engaged in bad behavior.[52] The state would subject everyone to surveillance: "In a well-ordered society nothing would escape the searching mind of the legislator."[53] Paternal authority would be abolished. Children would be taken from their parents at an early age and educated in sex-segregated boarding schools, where they would be drilled in communist virtue and removed from the temptations that stimulate the passion of love.[54] "Living constantly together, they would soon learn to commingle their happiness with that of others, and removed from the contagion of self-interest and ambition" they would have no other desire than to serve their society. Schools would banish "everything that is not strictly necessary to the well-being of the Republic."[55] All writing opposed to strict equality and popular sovereignty would be banned. The arts and sciences would be suppressed as effeminate and tending to promote the pride and vanity of those who pursue them.[56]

Stalin, Mao, and Pol Pot implemented many of these totalitarian ideas. They instituted pervasive censorship and surveillance, and suppressed private passions and romance. Stalin staged show trials to purge those suspected of disloyalty to the regime. Mao standardized a common uniform for adults. He directed the people to bring purported class enemies before them for struggle sessions. During the Cultural Revolution, he prohibited traditional opera and other arts, closed universities, and sent students down to the countryside. Pol Pot emptied Phnom Penh and forced its inhabitants to work in the rice paddies. Uniquely in modern history, he even abolished money.

To justify their system, the Equals advance a radical principle of material equality. Babeuf claims that communism is the only way to satisfy the principle of luck egalitarianism – the doctrine that no one should have more or less than anyone else due to mere luck. The goal of his system is

> to bind together everyone's lot; to render the lot of each member of the association independent of chance, and of happy or unfavorable circumstance; to assure to every man and to his posterity, no matter how numerous it may be, as much as they need, but no more than they need; and to shut off from everybody all the possible paths by which they might obtain some part of the products of nature and of work that is more than their individual due.[57]

The last clause might appear to permit inequalities due to unequal desert. However, Babeuf argues that "The superiority of talents and of efforts is only a chimera and a specious trap." People who do intellectual work claim superior talent, productivity, and desert. But this is an arbitrary judgment, disputed by manual workers, who claim that hard physical toil is equally deserving. Need is the sole ground for claiming material goods. Intellectual work does not make one more hungry than manual labor.[58] Moreover, intellectual work depends on prior invention, which is due to the efforts of other members of society. Hence, it should all be considered the common property of society. The same reasoning applies to all work, since the productivity of each individual depends on the work of others. What about someone who is able to do the work of four others, and claims four times the compensation? Such a person threatens society by attacking the principle of equality. Society should "reduce him to a state whereby he can do the work of only one man, so that he will be able to demand the recompense of only one man."[59] As far as I know, this is the only case in the history of egalitarianism in which someone has actually advocated the monstrous scenario of Kurt Vonnegut's "Harrison Bergeron," in which society enforces equality by handicapping those with superior talents and industry.[60]

Babeuf's coconspirators reinforce Babeuf's rejection of desert claims. While a few poor people are poor due to vice, the vast majority of the poor are not vicious. They are poor due to misfortunes and the monopoly on property by the rich. Even individual vice is due to the corrupting effects of social institutions, which activate and then punish destructive passions.[61]

For the Equals, the fundamental case for holding all property in common and distributing production equally (that is, in accordance with need) is that private property inevitably leads to class oppression. No one can deserve to appropriate property in land. Once such a right is recognized, accidents will eventually concentrate all land in the hands of a few. The vast majority of people, lacking land, will be forced to work for wages, living at the mercy of the idle rich. The rich will run the state, establishing laws that oppress the poor. The result is the misery and oppression of the poor. Even "the laborious and economical man" cannot deserve opulence, since no one can have a right to "poison his country" with inequalities that lead to such consequences.[62] "Nature has given to each individual an equal right to the enjoyment of all the goods of life."[63]

The Equals' argument implies that there is a contradiction in the work ethic. If private property is justified as a reward for industry and frugality, and no limits are placed on individual accumulation and bequest, the private property system will ultimately destroy its own normative foundation. The rich and their children will be able to live idly off their property, while the poor do all the work. Exposed to innumerable accidents and misfortunes, the poor will have little hope of improving their lot. Eventually, inequality will be so great that it will be pointless to try to gain a fortune through hard work. The only paths to riches will be to inherit a fortune, or to marry into one. Property will be monopolized by the idle and foreclosed to most of the industrious. Two centuries later, economist Thomas Piketty identified the critical condition under which the Equals' scenario would occur: when the rate of return on capital exceeds the rate of economic growth. This happened in the nineteenth century, with cultural consequences corrosive of the work ethic as depicted in the novels of Jane Austen and Honoré de Balzac.[64]

For the Equals, no inequality can be tolerated, either in property or in the burdens of labor. To avoid this, not only must all property be held in common, but all must be required to work. People will still be willing to work hard without material incentives, because they will want to compete for glory and avoid public censure.[65] The Equals' argument reveals a peculiar obsession with strict material equality at the expense of equality of social relations of esteem and power. They claim that citizens will rotate in offices of public administration,[66] which presumably include positions of command in the military-style production system. But that isn't enough to undermine oppressive relations of domination and subordination. Giving every slave the chance to be overseer for a day does not abolish slavery.

We can certainly find similarities between the Equals' plan and Marx's ideas about revolution. The Equals aimed to fulfill what they saw as the aspirations of Robespierre. Marx modeled his communist revolution after the radical Jacobin phase of the French Revolution, including something like Robespierre's Terror, which aimed not only to eliminate the enemies of the revolution but also to instill revolutionary virtue. The 10-step revolutionary plan outlined in *The Communist Manifesto*, which Marx wrote as the platform for the German Communist League a few days before the 1848 Revolution, follows this idea.[67] Ominously, it includes "[e]stablishment of industrial armies, especially for agriculture," and "gradual abolition of all the distinction between town and country by a more equable distribution of the populace over the country."[68] These steps could be read as following the Equals' plan. Marx even exempts Babeuf from his criticisms of other socialists in the *Manifesto*.[69] The slogan of the "Critique of the Gotha Program" – "[f]rom each according to his abilities, to each according to his needs"[70] – summarizes the principles of labor allocation and distribution advocated by the Equals.[71] It isn't hard to read these passages as heading in the same directions that Stalin, Mao, and Pol Pot took.

Yet the Equals' communist plan contradicts many of Marx's core values. Marx criticizes the social relations of capitalist production for imposing autocracy and "barrack discipline."[72] This is incompatible with running production like an army. He celebrates the advance of industrial manufacturing and condemns the "idiocy of rural life." This is incompatible with forcing the industrial proletariat back into an agricultural labor force. Marx advocates scientific and technical progress, and commends the bourgeoisie for promoting it.[73] This is incompatible with the Equals' plan to suppress the sciences. He embraces the Enlightenment ideal of *Bildung*, the many-sided development of the individual, and a reduction in the length of the working day to make room for leisure time for individuals to develop their artistic capabilities.[74] This is incompatible with the Equals' plan to suppress the arts. In line with the secularized work ethic, Marx endorses freedom of occupational choice in accordance with a richly individualized conception of human development:

> [T]he vocation, designation, task of every person is to achieve all-round development of all his abilities, including, for example, the ability to think .... [T]he individual ... has been crippled by the division of labour at the expense of his abilities and relegated to a one-sided vocation against his own need to become different, a need which has been stated to be his vocation .... The all-round realisation of the individual will only cease to be conceived as an ideal, a vocation, etc., when the impact of the world which stimulates the real development of the abilities of the individual is under the control of the individuals themselves, as the communists desire.[75]

Marx wants communist society to enable workers to freely choose varied occupations that express their full range of capabilities and personal interests:

> [I]n communist society, where nobody has one exclusive sphere of activity but each can become accomplished in any branch he wishes, society regulates the general production and thus makes it possible for me to do one thing today and another tomorrow, to hunt in the morning, fish in the afternoon, rear cattle in the evening, criticise after dinner, just as I have a mind.[76]

This is incompatible with the Equals' conception of the top-down assignment of workers to jobs. It is also incompatible with their homogenized conception of citizens and their needs.

Above all, Marx's normative framework centers on freedom, not distributive justice. Where Marx and Engels offer a positive description of communism, it is overwhelmingly in terms of the end it is supposed to realize: freedom in the Hegelian sense. As Engels describes it, communism will realize Hegel's conditions for full autonomy and hence an unalienated social life:

> Man's own social organisation, hitherto confronting him as a necessity imposed by Nature and history, now becomes the

result of his own free action .... Only from that time will man himself, more and more consciously, make his own history – only from that time will the social causes set in movement by him have, in the main and in a constantly growing measure, the results intended by him ....

The proletariat seizes the public power, and by means of this transforms the socialised means of production, slipping from the hands of the bourgeoisie, into public property. By this act, the proletariat frees the means of production from the character of capital they have thus far borne, and gives their socialised character complete freedom to work itself out. Socialised production upon a predetermined plan becomes henceforth possible .... In proportion as anarchy in social production vanishes, the political authority of the State dies out. Man, at last the master of his own form of social organisation, becomes at the same time the lord over Nature, his own master – free.[77]

In such a fully autonomous mode of social life, everyone wholeheartedly identifies with social institutions, their individual roles within them, and the consequences of everyone's participation in them. Hence, labor under communism is unalienated. It "has become not only a means of life but life's prime want."[78] People perform it for the sake of promoting others' well-being, not out of necessity or for external incentives. Unlike in the Equals' scheme, they don't work hard to get more glory than others, or to avoid public censure.

For this reason, in Marx's communist society, no one cares about "bourgeois right" – that is, about getting their fair share for labor performed. Marx agrees with the Equals that, under communism, each will give according to their abilities and receive according to their needs. But for Marx, this state of affairs does not arise from the coercive enforcement of rules of distributive justice by the state. It is simply the natural outcome of a wholly autonomous, unalienated system of production that individuals will willingly fulfill others' needs according to their abilities, and will receive from others according to their needs.[79] Because each individual wholeheartedly participates in social institutions, and freely develops and expresses their individuality within it, there is no need for coercive measures to enforce the rules.[80] This is why the state, understood as the entity that asserts a monopoly on such coercive measures, "dies out."

Suppose that such a communist society of full Hegelian freedom is possible. Even if this society requires no *coercive* institutions, it still needs institutions to *coordinate* labor within productive enterprises, and to *allocate* resources to the provision of diverse goods and services so that all needs are met. What would these look like? Marx and Engels don't say. They do, however, write a few paragraphs about the institutional structure of the transitional form of society between capitalism and communism. They call this the "dictatorship of the proletariat."[81] The term "dictatorship" could be interpreted as suggesting that a single leader or a tiny cabal runs society by fiat, as Robespierre did during the Reign of Terror, or as Lenin ran the Soviet Union. However, "the proletariat" refers to what Marx and Engels thought would be, at the time of the revolution, virtually everyone in society, except for a small class of monopoly capitalists who own all the means of production. On another reading of "dictatorship," the proletariat organizes itself democratically. It functions dictatorially only in the sense that, like all states, it coerces those who resist the regime to obey its laws. In the beginning, most people will resist because they are corrupted by the egoistic and antagonistic dispositions fostered by capitalism. But Marx and Engels think that over time, as people come to identify with communist modes of collective decision making and their results, the need for coercion, and hence for the state, falls away. On this second reading of "dictatorship," the main difference between the purely coordinating institutions of the dictatorship of the proletariat and communist society lies more with people's attitudes toward them than with their organization. What dies out is the need for coercive or punitive institutions to assure people that everyone is following collective decisions.[82]

Marx and Engels do not offer a consistent view of these coordinating institutions. *The Communist Manifesto* suggests a centralized communist system. It envisions that "[t]he proletariat will use its political supremacy to wrest, by degree, all capital from the bourgeoisie, to centralise all instruments of production in the hands of the State, i.e., of the proletariat organised as the ruling class."[83] Land, credit, and industries would be nationalized. Child labor would be replaced by universal free public education. The economy will be run by "a vast association of the whole nation."[84] This sketch leaves the rules and organization of the vast national association completely unspecified. However, some kind of democratic or collaborative ordering is implied by the term "association" ("*Assoziation*"). Marx drew the idea of association from the radical artisans in his social circle when he was in France, writing the *Economic and Philosophical Manuscripts of 1844* and other works. These artisans deployed the rhetoric of "association" to justify their corporate organizations in terms intelligible within the individualist normative framework of the French Revolution, which had abolished the traditional guilds. Radical artisans cast their organizations – which functioned as mutual-aid societies, bodies for collective protests and strikes, and aspiring workers' cooperatives – as legitimate exercises of freedom of association. Their organizations were voluntary and organized democratically.[85]

The Civil War in France imagines a decentralized communist society. Every settlement, down to the smallest village, would be organized as a little republic. Marx took his model from the Paris Commune – the revolutionary government of Paris run by radical workers and National Guardsmen for barely three months upon France's defeat in the Franco–Prussian War in 1871. In *The Civil War in France*, Marx sketches how such a "social republic" might be scaled up. Municipal councillors in each settlement would be elected on short terms by universal suffrage. Each commune would send elected delegates to a district assembly to work out regional policies. District assemblies would send deputies to a national assembly in Paris. Because deputies would be bound by local instructions of the constituents, the national assembly would be weak. This amounts to the "destruction of state power,"[86] because the state's key institutions – a standing army, established church, and national police, magistrates, and civil servants – would be eliminated. Local municipalities would be free to run their own affairs. Each productive establishment would be run by a free association of workers. "United co-operative societies" would "regulate national production upon a common plan," thereby eliminating the periodic economic crises of capitalism.[87] Engels adds to this picture the claim that "[s]tate interference in social relations becomes, in one domain after another, superfluous, and then dies out of itself; the government of persons is replaced by the administration of things."[88]

Although these two visions differ in their degrees of centralization, both characterize communist coordinative institutions, however vaguely, as democratic, in the sense that they would be based on a collaborative system of collective decision making by workers. This follows from their view that communist society must realize freedom both in collective *and* individual decision making. "It goes without saying that society cannot free itself unless every individual is freed."[89]

The success of this vision requires that free individual choices – particularly of occupation – need to match collective decisions of what people need, and that those collective decisions track how each individual understands their needs. Marx and Engels assume that unalienated workers will want to fulfill social needs, and so will freely allocate their labor according to the requirements of the common plan, without the need for either coercive assignments or markets. The Equals argue that military-style centralized planning can replace markets. That is plausible only so long as the economy is confined to an administration of simple homogeneous needs imputed to a population that is given no other choices, either with respect to consumption or work. Once the economy is expected to satisfy highly individualized needs for both consumption and work, and to do so by free individual choices, it is hard to see how this can be achieved without markets. Even if we assume that everyone will want to satisfy others' needs as part of their own good, it is hard to see how democratic institutions, whether centralized or decentralized, can gather the vast amounts of information needed to ensure that the common plan produces and delivers the right amounts of every good to meet each individual's needs, and determine appropriate trade-offs among different needs.[90] Having decided to abolish all markets, Marx and Engels simply declare that the workers will figure out their functional replacement somehow or other, spontaneously creating institutions that will enable them to self-consciously control their own destinies, without running aground on unintended consequences.

It could be argued that the sketchiness of Marx and Engels's vision reflects their commitment to the autonomy of the revolutionary workers. It didn't cross their minds that the workers might autonomously decide to recreate markets – for lack of any workable alternative, and because markets did not lie at the root of their problems. The sketchiness of Marx and Engels's vision also reflects the likelihood that their ideal of freedom is so high that no plausible system of institutions could satisfy it. They may be faulted for unrealistic utopianism. They may also be faulted for advocating violent revolution as the means to emancipate workers. They failed to consider that the means used shape the ends likely to be achieved. In the case of actually existing communism, the resort to violence to completely overthrow existing institutions empowered the most ruthless megalomaniacs, who installed totalitarian regimes. Furthermore, an ideology that accepts terror as a means to instilling virtue, as Robespierre advocated, is liable to need permanent terror, if selfishness and group conflict are not mere products of class society but are liabilities in any mode of organizing society.

Nevertheless, Babeuf and his coconspirators' values differ fundamentally from those of Marx and Engels, in ways that make totalitarianism a better fit for the former. Marx and Engels envision communism as a broadly collaborative form of society whose members would enjoy full freedom to develop and express their individuality. Such a society would be one in which each individual's conception of their individual good would include advancing the good of others. In this profound respect, Marx and Engels's ideal is the same as Mill's, even though they had radically opposing views of how property, markets, and the state would figure in realizing it.

Marx and Engels were political actors as well as thinkers. Here, too, notwithstanding their revolutionary commitments, they ultimately launched a democratic path for workers' emancipation. Marx set the agenda for the 1871 conference of the International Working Men's Association in London (IWMA). The main item was a call for workers to create their own political parties and compete for seats in the representative assemblies of their respective countries. This radical change of strategy for the IWMA sparked an anarchist revolt within its ranks, led by Mikhail Bakunin. Marx won this battle in the IWMA's 1872 conference in the Hague. Although his maneuverings led to the collapse of the IWMA, his call inspired the formation of social democratic parties across Western Europe. A news report of an address Marx gave in Amsterdam that year even indicated that he thought that workers might come to power peacefully in Britain, the Netherlands, and the United States.[91]

8 SOCIAL DEMOCRACY AS THE CULMINATION OF THE PROGRESSIVE WORK ETHIC

Social Democracy as a Marxist Development of the Progressive Work Ethic

The progressive work ethic culminated in social democracy, a political program devised by the social democratic political parties that formed in many countries of Western Europe in the late nineteenth century. These parties began as the political arm of various national trade union movements, and aimed to represent the working classes more broadly. Sweden's SAP was the first to take power, in 1932. Most established their key programs after the Second World War.

It is telling that in the history of political thought, no social democrat has been canonized, despite the huge influence of social democracy in many wealthy capitalist democracies. The leading early theorist of social democracy was Eduard Bernstein, sometime member of the Reichstag, leader in the German Social Democratic Party (SPD), and theorist of "revisionism," the branch of Marxism that repudiated violent revolution and embraced democratic reform in the late nineteenth and early twentieth centuries. His most important work, *Evolutionary Socialism*, considered "the bible of early twentieth-century revisionists"[1] is little-read today. I suspect that the Cold War played a role in omitting Bernstein from the canon. Social democratic parties emerged from Marxism. During the Cold War, Marx was depicted as the pivotal ideologist of communist totalitarianism, a thinker who purportedly made a radical break from the entire tradition of liberal thought found in figures such as Smith and Mill. Cold War ideology represented social democracy as nothing more than a slippery slope to totalitarianism. The title of Friedrich Hayek's bestselling work in this vein, *The Road to Serfdom*, says it all.[2]

Decades after Hayek's wildly failed prediction, we are long past time for a serious consideration of social democracy. To do this, we need to examine its origins. The last chapter showed how Marx's thought could be taken in either totalitarian or democratic directions. I argued that Marx's thought, far from breaking with prior classical liberal thinking in political economy, is deeply continuous with it. In many ways he is a backward-looking figure.[3] His economic theorizing was still wrestling with problems set out by Smith and Ricardo, even as economics was moving past the classical paradigm. The first volume of *Capital* (1867), Marx's most developed work of economic theory, quotes Smith copiously and often admiringly. His evaluative concerns about the nature of work under capitalism are very close to those of Smith and Mill. For Marx, too, was influenced by the progressive work ethic. This ethic pervades classical economics in at least three important ways. The progressive work-ethic concern that workers receive the fruits of their labors led classical economists to focus on the causes of the distribution of income and wealth across classes. The concern that work fit into a flourishing life led them to consider the impact of work on workers themselves – on the skills, virtues, and dispositions constitutive of a flourishing life. The concern that people relate to each other in mutually supportive ways – for example, that *everyone* work for others' benefit, and that even the most menial workers be respected and treated well – led classical economists to consider how labor markets, property regimes, and class structures affect the quality of human relationships. Do they stigmatize or uplift the poor? Do they foster relations of domination and subordination, exploitation, and zero-sum status competition, in which some can rise only by pushing others down? Or do they rather promote relations of mutual respect, autonomy, and sympathy or solidarity? In focusing on such concerns, Marx is united with Smith and Mill, even though his political program is radically different.

Social democracy, too, has deep ties to pre-Marxist thinkers, and not only through Marx's influence. Comprehensive social insurance is a central plank of its economic agenda. That idea was developed during the French Revolution by Condorcet and Thomas Paine, important Enlightenment figures squarely in the liberal tradition. They advanced the idea of social insurance in defense of private property and against totalitarian communism as conceived by Babeuf.

The Origins of Social Insurance: Condorcet and Paine

Social insurance – state-organized universal retirement pensions, along with disability, health, and unemployment insurance – is a pillar of social democratic policy. In the United States, conservatives have long objected to social insurance as socialist or even communist. In 1961, Ronald Reagan recorded a speech for the American Medical Association attacking Medicare for endangering individual liberty. He predicted that it would lead to the state dictating to doctors what jobs they would have to take and where they would live. Republicans have attacked President Barack Obama's Affordable Care Act – a measure that falls well short of the universal health insurance plans implemented in every other rich country in the world – as communist. Ben Carson, President Trump's Secretary of Housing and Urban Development, tied Obamacare, which he called "the worst thing that has happened in this nation since slavery" to Lenin's purported view that "socialized medicine is the keystone to the establishment of the socialist state."[4]

Such thinking perpetuates the myth that social democracy represents a radical break from the classical liberal tradition, a collectivist threat to individualism, liberty, and personal responsibility. In fact, the idea of social insurance was developed within the classical liberal tradition by Condorcet and Thomas Paine – key liberal Enlightenment thinkers. Paine promotes social insurance as a *defense* of private property *against* Babeuf's communist plans. Condorcet and Paine promote social insurance as a property innovation continuous with other classical liberal property reforms within the progressive work-ethic tradition.

Condorcet and Paine advocate social insurance as a middle course between the conservative work ethic and communism. The conservative work ethic blames the working poor for their misfortunes and (in England) subjects them to the despotic control of Poor Laws as a condition of relief. Babeuf blames private property for the misfortunes of the working poor, but also aims to subject them to despotic control in his communist plan. Condorcet and Paine argue that a reconfiguration of private property rights can prevent poverty and secure workers' freedom.

The Poor Law regime assumed that poverty was caused either by vice – idleness, indulgence, and other deviations from the work ethic – or unavoidable natural causes – illness, accidents, disability, orphanage, old age. This was not true. Big landowners were idle, and many were drunken, ill, disabled, orphaned, or old. These conditions did not make them poor. Moreover, most of the poor were neither disabled nor idle, profligate, or unchaste. They were the "laboring poor" whose discovery in the late sixteenth-century surveys caused such a shock to English officials.

Condorcet argues that poverty is fundamentally caused by inequality of wealth and education. Workers live in precarity because they rely entirely on their labor to secure their needs, and have no property to fall back on if their capacity to work gives out due to old age or misfortune. (Later advocates would add job loss due to economic shocks or recessions to the causes of precarity.) By contrast, those with land or capital can live off rents, interest, and savings without having to work at all. Condorcet blames the precarity of workers on the ways the legal system is rigged against the working poor.[5] In addition, poor workers lack access to education and tools. This depresses their wages. Once we shift our focus from individual choices and events to the social structures that deliver such harsh consequences to workers as a result of such contingencies, the solution is evident. To cope with the risk of wage loss, institute an insurance scheme whereby families pool their risks of illness, disability, unemployment, death of a family wage earner, and outliving the capacity to work. To overcome the low wages of the working poor, institute a system of grants for young adults so that they can augment their productivity with further education or tools. And institute universal education to enable the free development of everyone's industry and capabilities, and to liberate them from "every species of dependence, whether forced or voluntary."[6] That is, educate everyone to the level necessary for each to stand in relations of equality with everyone else.

Condorcet never got the chance to work out the details of his scheme. He wrote *Historical View of the Progress of the Human Mind* during the Terror, while hiding from arrest for having criticized the Jacobin constitution. Warned that he was unsafe, he fled, wandering for days on foot without food or shelter. Famished, he ordered an omelet at an inn. He gave his aristocratic status away by asking that it be made with a dozen eggs. Condorcet was arrested and died under mysterious circumstances on his first night in prison in March 1794.[7]

Thomas Paine was the first thinker to work out the details of a social insurance scheme. With Condorcet, he participated in the French National Convention's Girondin constitutional project. He, too, was imprisoned during the Terror. Due to a jailor's error, he escaped execution on the appointed day. A few days later, Robespierre was executed. This saved Paine from the same fate. He won release on the strength of his claim to be an American rather than a British citizen.

Given their intimate experiences with Jacobin extremism, it is not surprising that both Condorcet and Paine wanted to show how equality can be advanced without destroying private property. Condorcet argues that reforming the system will enable a steady progress toward equality, but warns that attempts to create strict material equality will give rise to "more fruitful sources of inequality" and deliver a "more fatal blow" to the "rights of man."[8] His warning certainly applies to the Equals' scheme. Paine wrote "Agrarian Justice" in 1796. In it, he demonstrates the feasibility of universal social insurance and young-adult stakeholder grants based on English economic data. Paine's inscription to the Legislature and the Executive Directory of France notes that Babeuf attempted to make himself dictator, rather than proposing legitimate measures "useful to society."[9] He offers his plan as a superior alternative: poverty can be eliminated without the Equals' violent dictatorship, and without abolishing private property.

Paine offers a Lockean case for social insurance in reply to the Equals' critique of Lockean social contract theory. Recall that in Locke's theory, the sufficiency proviso is violated in the state of nature once all land is appropriated. This requires a remedy provided by civil society, including a poor law that provides for the survival of the poor under harsh conditions (see Chapter 2). The Equals argue that private property itself is unjust. Private property rights are entirely a product of law. In the state of nature, no one is poor, and no private property can exist. Because private property necessarily creates poverty, a legal regime that permits it leaves some people worse off than they would be in the state of nature. People would therefore refuse to consent to such a regime. They would consent to a communist political regime – that is, a regime in which all productive property is held in common – as the only way to ensure that each individual is better off than in the state of nature.[10]

Paine accepts the Equals' objection that existing property rights unjustly create poverty. He rejects their claim that private property *necessarily* causes poverty. It does so only because the existing property regime abrogates a rightful property claim that was overlooked in the original state of nature and in political society. In the state of nature, the earth is held in common while individuals own their own labor and its fruits. When individuals mix their labor with the land, it follows that they are entitled to the *value added* by their labor to the land. They are not entitled to the value of the natural product of the land, to which everyone retains a claim. To compensate everyone for their exclusion from the value of the natural product of privately appropriated land, landowners owe a rent to society.[11] This could be most conveniently collected through an estate tax imposed upon the death of the owner. This tax would be used to fund universal old age pensions and disability insurance, plus a universal grant to all members of society upon reaching adulthood. Pensions and disability insurance would prevent people from falling into poverty due to inability to work. Stakeholder grants would enable young workers to afford the tools and education they need to command above-poverty wages. Individuals would receive their rents in these forms to satisfy the Lockean requirement that any legal regime leave *everyone* better off than in the state of nature. This requires that the property regime secure all against falling into poverty over the course of their entire lives.[12]

Paine's proposal has several advantages over the poor-law regime. It prevents poverty, rather than merely ameliorating its worst effects. By framing social insurance and stakeholder grants as due to recipients as a matter of property rights, and hence of justice, rather than charity,[13] Paine's proposal destigmatizes recipients. They are not "dependent," as Priestley sneered. They are dignified property owners, akin to policyholders in a mutual insurance company with a real-estate investment portfolio comprising a share of all the land in the realm. By insisting that benefits be universal, rather than means-tested, Paine further destigmatizes recipients. Because payments are property entitlements, recipients do not have to submit to the despotic authority of overseers of the poor, workhouse managers, or even employers in order to claim them.

Paine's proposal is also superior to the Equals' scheme. Their system abolishes poverty only by subjecting everyone to despotic rule. Paine's system secures everyone's personal independence by ensuring that each individual – men and women alike – enjoys private property entitlements. Paine also avoids any suggestion of class warfare or fault of one class in relation to another. That was a framing central to Babeuf's argument for communist revolution. Paine argues that "[t]he fault ... is not in the present possessors. No complaint is tended, or ought to be alleged against them .... The fault is in the system" that permits uncompensated private appropriation of land from the commons.[14] Provided property institutions are well-designed, some degree of inequality can be beneficial. "I am a friend to riches because they are capable of good. I care not how affluent some may be, provided that none be miserable in consequence of it."[15] Condorcet advances a stricter criterion for justified inequality. It is not enough that inequality make no one miserable; it must actually benefit everyone. He wants "no other inequality subsisting but what is useful to the interest of all, because it will favor civilization, instruction, and industry, without drawing after it either dependence, humiliation, or poverty."[16]

Paine's proposal also enjoys advantages over Priestley's individualist alternative (see Chapter 3). Under Priestley's plan, workers can only accumulate capital from their own saved wages. Property owners are supported by the workers, but pay nothing into the scheme. Because, as Priestley acknowledges, workers start out with no capital and must support the idle rich as well as themselves, their wages are low. This limits their ability to save. Paine's wealth tax and stakeholder grants avoid these problems. In addition, Priestley's plan, in stressing individual self-reliance, lacks disability insurance. Paine's scheme offers lifelong support for people who become disabled at any age. Under Priestley's scheme, which fails to pool risks, disabled young and middle-aged adults could not survive on the annuities they could buy with the paltry savings they had managed to accumulate in the short period before they become disabled, and people disabled as children would have no support at all.

Yet Paine's scheme suffers from a vulnerability. How can he guarantee that the value of the natural product of the land – what it would produce without labor – matches what is needed to secure all against poverty? Paine assumes a 90 percent labor theory of value, attributing 10 percent of value added to the earth's natural output. He also argues that the social insurance and stakeholder grant tax base should extend to all personal property, not only to land. The remainder mostly consists in the value of housing. He justifies this extension of the tax base as follows:

> Personal property is the *effect of society*; and it is as impossible for an individual to acquire personal property without the aid of society, as it is for him to make land originally. Separate an individual from society, and give him an island or a continent to possess, and he cannot acquire personal property. He cannot be rich …. All accumulation, therefore, of personal property, beyond what a man's own hands produce, is derived to him by living in society; and he owes on every principle of justice, of gratitude, and of civilization, a part of that accumulation back again to society from whence the whole came.[17]

Paine's reasoning here follows the same logic as Babeuf's argument against desert-based claims to inequality with respect to intellectual labor – that one cannot claim to deserve all the value of one's intellectual production, since so much is based on ideas drawn from the intellectual commons supplied by society. He did not see that this reasoning undermines all theories of justice based on desert, understood as the individual's specific productive contribution to total output. For each worker's productivity is due not simply to their individual talent and industry, but to the social division of labor and its overall organization. The latter are public goods that contribute to the total product in ways that cannot be allocated to individual workers. Even the unemployed contribute to productivity, by serving as a pool of readily available labor to which firms can quickly resort in response to spiking demand for their product or service. They thereby enable firms to adopt flexible business plans in which they can rapidly increase production. As Thompson argued, the work-ethic notion of the fruits of one's labor, understood as an individually attributable quantum of production, makes no sense in economies based on cooperative and specialized labor.

Paine's aspiration to forge a path beyond class warfare and class paternalism was largely vindicated by the adoption of state-supported social insurance programs by virtually all developed countries starting in the 1880s. Social democratic and worker-based politics were vital causal factors behind the adoption of social insurance programs.[18] Their agitation persuaded conservatives to go along, to prove to workers that capitalism could offer them a better deal than socialism. A century after Paine warned the propertied classes that they might face communist revolution if they didn't offer workers a better deal, Otto von Bismarck, the Chancellor of the German Empire and Prime Minister of Prussia, heeded his call. Bismarck instituted the first social insurance programs in the world – for health care (1883), workers' compensation (1884), and retirement pensions (1889). These programs were initially targeted to the male industrial working class. Over time they developed into universal programs. Bismarck was no socialist. He also secured passage of a notorious Anti-Socialist Law (1878–90) that prohibited the socialists from meeting or distributing their publications, and authorized police to banish individual socialists from particular cities. While Bismarck instituted social insurance to undermine both the appeal of socialism and its independent labor organizations, the point was not merely strategic. Social insurance also appealed to employers as it promoted a healthier workforce, enabled them to pool the risks of liability for industrial accidents, and shifted costs from poor relief funded from general taxation to workers' contributions.[19]

It is therefore no wonder that European socialist parties were initially wary of social insurance. Their conversion to full support reflected their abandonment of the Marxist ideology of class conflict and revolution, embrace of cross-class coalitions and gradualist reform, and adoption of a normative perspective based on citizenship in the nation rather than membership in the working class. Other parties, notably the Christian Democratic parties, also came to embrace social insurance as an expression of society's obligation to secure a decent life for all. Across Europe, social insurance programs were therefore typically advanced by broad-based coalitions. The ideology of the conservative work ethic, which stressed that labor is a commodity and that workers should rely on free-market wages alone, never had nearly the sway on the European continent that it had in English-speaking countries. Catholic ideology also favored social provision[20] and shaped social insurance regimes in countries with significant Catholic populations.[21]

In the developed countries today, universal social insurance and publicly funded education – a functional analog to universal stakeholder grants, focused on ensuring that every young adult starts out with an ample fund of human rather than financial capital – dwarf means-tested welfare payments as poverty-reduction programs. Some countries, including France and the Netherlands, have reduced elder poverty to negligible rates due to their social insurance systems. Even the United States, which provides lower rates of income replacement than most of its peers, has dramatically reduced elder poverty by means of Social Security and Medicare.[22] And universal public investment in young people is of course key not only to preventing poverty among young adults but to securing a highly productive economy that serves everyone's interests. We may thank Paine for being the first to show how this could be done, and why it was just.

Eduard Bernstein and the Path to Social Democracy

By the late nineteenth century, radical and revolutionary workers' movements had largely died down. In Britain, the Chartists took their last significant action in 1848. In France, the Third Republic crushed the Paris Commune in 1871, marking the end of a revolutionary era. In Germany, while the Social Democratic Party (SPD) embraced revolution as a matter of orthodox Marxist theory, it did nothing to organize for revolution. It imagined that workers would somehow spontaneously overthrow the system in response to some ultimate crisis of capitalism in the indeterminate future. Instead, the SPD was running candidates for election to the Reichstag – even while Bismarck had banned the party in 1878, forcing its members to run as individuals.

What accounts for the decline of worker radicalism toward the end of the nineteenth century? Craig Calhoun offers the most persuasive explanation.[23] The most radical workers in movements across Europe were largely artisans, not the industrial proletariat. They were fighting to win back the world they had lost or were about to lose. This was a world in which they enjoyed the protections of a guild, a dignified life at a decent standard of living, a skilled trade in which they could exercise higher capabilities than mindlessly repeating a single physical operation the entire day, control over their tools, some measure of autonomous self-direction at work, often via self-employment, and a rich network of communal relations founded on the centrality of craft-based production. They saw that the factory system was ending their way of life forever. The only way to protect or restore it was to destroy that system. No wonder they smashed machines. Sometimes agricultural workers joined them, for similar reasons: capitalism was destroying not just their livelihood, but the rural communities that defined their lives and identities. For these workers, the Industrial Revolution was a catastrophe. No compromise with its capitalist leaders was possible, for the two sides were committed to utterly incompatible modes of production.

As the Industrial Revolution proceeded, generations of industrial workers grew up who knew no other life. At mid-century, Engels's

Pause ended. British industrial wages started growing. The gradual democratization of industrializing countries opened up prospects for workers to use the political process to win safer working conditions and limits on the length of the working day. Labor unions organized to get better wages and conditions within the system. Capitalism was not an existential threat to industrial workers, since they, unlike artisans, were indispensable to the system. From the point of view of most of the proletariat, the critical goal became not to destroy the system, but to get a better deal from it.

Marx's critical years of intellectual formation in the 1840s took place in close association with radical artisans. Their "reactionary radicalism," as Calhoun describes it, makes sense of much of the backward-looking, nostalgic features of Marx's ideal of unalienated labor, which he carried through to his critique of the division of labor and factory system in *Capital*. It also makes sense of his revolutionary theorizing, which always looked back to the French Revolution as a model.

Despite his revolutionary theorizing, all of Marx's *practical* activism after 1848 had a pronounced reformist bent. Marx channeled most of his activism through the IWMA. From its founding in London in 1864, the IWMA promoted industrial labor unions, made public declarations and defenses of workers' goals, and supported labor actions in pursuit of those goals, all within the capitalist system. The IWMA's 1866 Congress supported limits on the length of the working day, limits on women's and child labor, international investigations of workplace conditions, trade unions, and the right to strike. The last significant act of the IWMA was its call to form workers' parties to compete for parliamentary seats. Marx's main supporters within the IWMA were nonrevolutionary English trade unionists. His main enemies were anarchists, whose popularity was concentrated in the less industrialized Southern European countries, where radical artisans were still a significant force and trade unions were banned. The anarchists promoted violent revolution by secret societies, just as the most radical artisans in England had before 1848.[24]

When workers heeded the IWMA's call to form workers' parties across Europe, many of these parties incorporated the contradiction between revolutionary theory and reformist practice that defined Marx's course after 1848. Nowhere was this contradiction sharper than in Germany's Social Democratic Party (SPD), which emerged from the union of the Social Democratic Workers' Party of Germany, led by Marx's protégés August Bebel and Wilhelm Liebknecht, and the General German Workers' Association, led by Ferdinand Lassalle. Eduard Bernstein was the leading figure in the SPD who argued that the party should revise its theory to conform to its evolving democratic practice.

In his most important work, *Evolutionary Socialism*,[25] Bernstein methodically lays out a range of facts that undermine Marx and Engels's predictions about the course of history in their purportedly scientific theory of historical materialism. None of the key predictions of historical materialism were supported by trends in capitalist societies. By the benchmarks of the theory, the prospects for revolution were steadily receding. Moreover, with the advance of democracy in the leading capitalist countries, the prospects for improving workers' lives by peaceful democratic means were steadily advancing. Democratic means are more likely to lead to "lasting success" than a revolution following a catastrophic crisis of capitalism.[26] Most importantly, Bernstein argues that socialists should embrace the institutional framework of liberal democracy not merely as a means to the emancipation of workers, but as a constitutive feature of socialism. Even private property and markets, provided they are properly regulated, may play legitimate roles in a socialist society. Through the socialist movement, the working classes will "work out their own emancipation by changing society ... from a commercial landholding oligarchy to a real democracy ... guided by the interests of those who work and create."[27]

That quote expresses a commitment to the progressive work ethic. Locke could have accepted it. Bernstein's critique of the labor theory of value also returns its critical insight to its Lockean origins. Marx attempted to develop the labor theory of value into a theory of prices and profits for each individual commodity. The theory foundered on the fact that, by its logic, firms with lower capital investment per worker should enjoy higher profit rates. This contradicts the tendency of profit rates to equalize across firms, and makes it a mystery why capitalists would bother investing in machinery.[28] Bernstein argues that Marx erred in attempting to decompose aggregate surplus value into distinct quantities embodied in each commodity. This theoretical rabbit hole is a distraction. The fundamental point of claims about surplus value is simply that workers are doing all the work, while there is a class of idle property owners, much richer than the workers, who consume a huge chunk of what they produce. This fact is directly observed and needs no proof.[29] Baxter, Sanderson, Locke, Smith, the Ricardian socialists, and Mill already said as much. They said it with as much disapproval of that fact as any Marxist, since the fundamental roots of their disapproval lie with their shared commitment to the progressive work ethic.[30]

Marx and Engels's theory of historical materialism makes several key predictions about the development of capitalism over time. Workers' wages will decline to the point of near-universal immiseration. All classes other than large capitalists – artisans, skilled tradesmen, the self-employed, peasants, small business owners – will be cast into the proletariat. In all sectors of the economy, wealth will be concentrated in the hands of a small number of monopoly capitalists. Capitalism itself will be rocked by ever-more severe economic crises and a declining rate of profit. Eventually, the outrageous contradiction between the immense productive power of the means of production and the misery of the great mass of people will lead workers to mount a revolution, which will replace capitalism with communism.

Bernstein demonstrates, on the basis of data in the leading industrialized countries, that none of these predictions were coming to pass. Wages were rising. The rate of profit was not declining. Capitalism was generating a growing, prosperous middle class. Shareholding was spreading beyond the capitalist class. Class distinctions were proliferating. The skilled trades, self-employed, small businesses, and peasants were not going away. Economic crises seemed to be less frequent and severe. These were not just accidents. Capitalism had to grow a middle class to consume the things it was producing in ever-greater quantities. Nor could it be ruled out that capitalists might devise effective means of limiting crises. More sophisticated banking systems might do so. Capitalists could form cartels to limit overproduction. Any argument that they couldn't is equally much an argument that socialist planning cannot prevent economic crises.[31]

A working-class communist revolution is both infeasible and undesirable. It is infeasible, because the proletariat is only a small section of society, which would meet massive resistance from the other classes. Even the proletariat itself is highly differentiated. It has diverse interests and lifestyles shaped by occupational and other differences, and limited solidarity. It is hopeless to expect them to revolt as a unified body. The vast majority only wish to improve their condition.[32]

Communist revolution is undesirable because revolutionaries have no idea how to run productive enterprises. Nor could municipalities operate them competently. No one has any idea how to replace markets. The state lacks the capacity to run the entire economy. It is vastly more complex than any centralized state could manage.[33]

Bernstein is surprisingly skeptical of the egalitarian potential of democratically organized workers' cooperatives, on which Mill put so much store. Once an enterprise grows large enough, it will need a hierarchy of offices to function effectively. This will generate heterogeneous interests among the workers. Managers will need the authority to make decisions that some workers will not like. Managers will not be able to manage the enterprise well if holding their jobs depends on not ruffling the feathers of any worker. Moreover, worker-owned enterprises will still have all the same parochial interests that are in potential conflict with the public interest as any bourgeois business owner.[34] It is also hopeless to expect peasants to accept collectivized farming. They don't want to be an agricultural laborer on a large farm, even if they have a voice in running it. They want the autonomy inherent in operating their own farm in their own way, even if the plot is tiny. Socialists should not insist on expropriating their holdings in the name of communist dogma. Furthermore, experiments in communal agriculture show that the durable ones survive only in isolation from the larger society, typically under the sway of some strong religious ideology or similar bonds. Such communes function only by restricting the free development of the individual. Hence, they cannot offer a desirable model of associated labor.[35]

Bernstein's point is not to attack the very idea of cooperative or associated work. He insists rather that the optimal organization of work needs to be determined through careful and protracted experimentation. Various models of association should be tested, with the expectation of frequent failure.[36] That is not the kind of thing a revolution that suddenly overturns the existing economic order is equipped to do.

If the proletariat will not eventually include everyone, then it cannot represent the universal interests of humanity. The persistence of class differentiation in any foreseeable future entails a differentiation of human interests. Such differentiation is a natural outcome of the ways different modes of work appeal to and shape individuals with different dispositions. This fact need not lead to inexorable class conflict. Just because peasants are deeply attached to private property in their smallholdings, or artisans and small-businesspeople to property in their shops, does not make them reactionary enemies of the proletariat. Even Marx stressed this point.[37] It follows that a political order in which power is monopolized by the proletariat cannot be responsive to all legitimate interests. The same point applies to an economic order in which the proletariat monopolizes all authority over enterprise management.[38]

What kind of political and economic order could promote the common good, the interests of all, consistent with promoting the interests of each individual within it? That is the fundamental normative standard of the progressive work ethic, from Locke forward. Such an order would need to be responsive to the diversity of interests generated in a highly developed and differentiated economy. It would need to support the conditions for the free development of individuality. Only a fully democratic order is up to this task. This excludes any form of rule that privileges any particular class relative to the whole community. Pure majority rule, which permits majorities to trample on the vital interests of minorities, also fails to realize democracy. Individual rights to freedom and equality under the law must be secured, even at some cost to economic progress. It follows that social democrats should not repudiate liberalism, but embrace it. Although historically, liberals became the

> guardians of capitalism ... with respect to liberalism as a great historical movement, socialism is its legitimate heir ... as is shown moreover in every question of principle in which social democracy has had to take up an attitude .... The security of civil freedom has always seemed to it to stand higher than the fulfillment of some economic progress. The aim of all socialist measures ... is the development and the securing of a free personality.[39]

Even where socialism promotes laws that limit individual freedom, these are justified only as measures that open up greater opportunities for individual freedom. Bernstein illustrates this point by appealing to maximum-hours laws. Without such laws, employers can coerce individual workers into accepting longer hours than are compatible with their freedom, as a condition of getting any work at all. He could have cited John Stuart Mill in support of this position. This is evidence of Bernstein's claim that social democracy is the legitimate heir of liberalism.

Socialism develops liberal democracy further by extending its principles to the economic domain. Individual workers must not be forced to choose options that undermine their freedom out of material necessity. "The individual is to be ... free from every economic compulsion in his action and choice of a calling." This requires measures that decommodify labor, including social insurance, broad provision of education and other public services by the state (so that access does not depend on personal earnings), industrial courts to adjudicate disputes between workers and employers, and trade-union defense of workers' rights against arbitrary firing.[40]

Democracy should also be extended to productive enterprises, so that workers have a voice in managing the firm. Having already cast doubt on workers' cooperatives, on the idea that workers should be able to fire their managers at will, and on parochial class rule, Bernstein's argument leads naturally to some form of codetermination – that is, joint management of firms by workers and owners together. "[T]rade unions are indispensable organs of the democracy." Yet the trade union "can only further simultaneously the interests of its members and the general good as long as it is content to remain a partner" with the employer.[41] Codetermination became a hallmark of German social democracy in the post-Second World War era.

Bernstein reveals the common roots of economic liberalism and social democracy in the work ethic through "the principle of economic personal responsibility which belongs apparently so entirely to the Manchester School." This principle "cannot ... be denied in theory by socialism nor be made inoperative under any conceivable circumstances. Without responsibility there is no freedom." Under socialism, however, the principle does not amount to limiting individuals' access to the means of survival and freedom to just what their market income can buy. Rather, it is the recognition of the individual responsibility to live up to a principle of reciprocity: in return for the goods provided by society, everyone capable of work must do their fair share of it.[42]

Because class differentiation will exist for the foreseeable future, workers must make coalitions with other classes in order to gain political power and further develop democracy. Bernstein suggests that social democrats should ally with the peasants by advocating policies that would appeal to them. Peasants, too, are workers. They would benefit from the abolition of the last remnants of feudalism, including entails, the legal reduction of excessive rents, and promotion of peasant cooperatives to purchase supplies and obtain credit at reasonable cost.[43] Such an agenda requires recognition of a right to private property. A general expropriation "would only be robbery dressed up in a legal form." State entities may only take property with compensation, within the terms of the "inviolable" rights of property recognized in the law.[44]

The SPD must "make up its mind to appear what it is in reality today: a democratic, socialistic party of reform."[45] Revolutionary cant only alienates other classes and contradicts the commitments entailed by running for office – namely, to use the powers of office to promote the welfare of citizens. Bernstein warns against tendencies within the party to advance "hard-and-dry Manchesterism" against modest advances for workers within the capitalist system.[46] Those within the party who embrace the harsh implications of the Manchester School of laissez-faire capitalism hoped to thereby hasten the revolution. Marx himself was a lifelong free trader for this reason. He believed that laissez-faire policies would both promote capitalist economic development on a global scale and heighten the contradictions between aggregate pro-duction and the immiseration of the proletariat by concentrating wealth in the hands of a few monopoly capitalists.[47] From this point of view, any regulations of capitalism that improve workers' lives threaten to dampen workers' revolutionary ardor. Bernstein objects that the future of socialism depends on spreading wealth more broadly, not on concen-trating it in a few hands.[48] Workers can and should win their emanci-pation by assiduously promoting the development of democracy throughout society. This is a constitutive principle of socialism, not merely a means to preconceived objectives. Only through patient demo-cratic experimentation will we discover how to organize society so that it promotes the common good consistently with the freedom of each individual. For this reason, Bernstein declares, "I cannot believe in a final aim of socialism. But I strongly believe in the socialist movement."[49]

The SPD was unable to resolve the contradiction between revo-lutionary theory and reformist practice during the Weimar Republic. In the early Weimar years, it successfully promoted better working condi-tions, codetermination, social insurance, and other reforms. But at the decisive moment it could not get past apocalyptic laissez-faire thinking. The SPD was in power when the Great Depression forced millions of Germans out of work. The government fell in 1930 but was unable to agree on a relief program that could appeal to workers. Wladimir

Woytinsky, a trade union leader, developed a plan for the state to stimulate the economy and create jobs. He urged the SPD to abandon their faith in the "mystical powers of the market" and directly improve workers' lives without waiting for the revolution. This was both good in itself and necessary to avoid a catastrophic election loss to the Nazi Party, which was already promoting job creation through state spending. Rudolph Hilferding, the SPD's leading economist, attacked Woytinsky's plan as "un-Marxist." The SPD should let the "logic of capitalism" work itself out without intervention.[50]

Fritz Tarnow, a union and party leader, explained the SPD's dilemma in a speech at its 1931 congress:

> Are we standing at the sickbed of capitalism not only as doctors who want to heal the patient, but also as prospective heirs who can't wait for the end and would gladly help the process along with a little poison? .... We are damned, I think, to be doctors who seriously want to cure, and yet we have to maintain the feeling that we are heirs who wish to receive the entire legacy of the capitalist system today rather than tomorrow.[51]

While vaguely declaring that the time for socialism was imminent, the SPD offered no concrete plans to help workers in the 1932 elections. It suffered a crushing defeat. Hitler became Chancellor in January 1933. Shortly thereafter, he suspended civil liberties, arrested and murdered dozens of SPD deputies, forced many others to flee, and banned the party. Outside neutral Sweden, social democracy was suppressed throughout continental Europe until after the Second World War.

Social Democracy as a Culmination and Transcendence of the Progressive Work Ethic

The guiding idea of the progressive work ethic is to organize, recognize, and reward work so as to promote the welfare of the whole society in ways that promote the freedom, dignity, and welfare of each, along multiple dimensions of well-being. Over time, it came to adopt the following goals: securing the dignity and autonomy of workers at work along with safe and healthful working conditions; advancing real freedom of occupational choice through equal opportunity, including universal education and antidiscrimination laws; ensuring that workers are appropriately rewarded for their labors, are secure from poverty and precarity, and have significant leisure time to have a flourishing life outside work; ensuring meaningful work that promotes human welfare in ways that develop and exercise a wide range of skills and virtues; and promoting social relations of equality and fraternity over antagonistic relationships at work and in the wider society.

This ethic reached its culmination in Western Europe in the postwar era, when social democratic and allied parties, such as the Labour Party in the UK, adopted a suite of policies to achieve its goals. These include comprehensive social insurance, facilitation of labor unions and collective bargaining, codetermination, dramatic expansion of public higher education offered at low or no cost, and guaranteed paid vacations and family leave.

Beyond just a package of policies, social democrats adopted a broader normative vision that united its prescriptions under the ideal of democracy. This amounted to a profound shift of normative perspective, under which the work ethic transcended itself. We have seen that as it secularized, the work ethic divided into competing class-based perspectives that reflected the class divisions of English society. The work ethic shaped the discourse of class warfare: even the idle landlords had their reactionary Noetic version (see Chapter 3). The shift to a democratic perspective amounted to an attempt to transcend class warfare even while retaining some class distinctions. Instead of tying benefits to work, it tied them to citizenship through a rich conception of "social rights." In English sociologist T. H. Marshall's classic account of the evolution of citizenship, full membership in the nation gradually expanded from civil rights (guarantees of individual autonomy in speech, religion, contracts, property, and due process of law), to political rights (to vote and hold office), to social rights "to share to the full in the social heritage and to live the life of a civilized being according to the standards prevailing in the society."[52] In the comprehensive welfare state of postwar Britain, social rights included rights to education, health care, housing, child allowances, and even legal aid, along with social insurance for unemployment, sickness, disability, retirement, and survivors' benefits.[53]

Bernstein was a key thinker behind this democratic move. In the course of dispensing with virtually every Marxist doctrine, Bernstein began a process of shifting the normative perspective of social democracy from the working class to the democratic nation of citizens. The shift was practically necessary once it was recognized that the industrial proletariat would not become the universal class, but just one class among others. To win elections, social democrats would need to form coalitions with other classes. The Swedish Social Democratic Party (SAP) was the first to gain power in 1932, through a coalition of industrial workers and small farmers.

The shift was also theoretically necessary, given the aspirations of the progressive work ethic. The fundamental normative principle of the progressive work ethic is to structure the institutions of society such that they "benefit the whole" while also "benefit[ing] ... each individual composing it."[54] Its ethos, as Marx stressed, is for people to freely act on that principle, to receive the benefits of others acting on it, and for all to affirm each through common mutual recognition of that fact. This is a norm of fraternity or solidarity, founded on shared affirmation of reciprocity. In the classical vision, the way to achieve this was to create a classless (or single-class) society by situating everyone in the same relation to the means of production: everyone a worker (in Bray's view of cooperatives, a formula which might apply more accurately in the communist and Fabian socialist vision of workers laboring on national-ized means of production), or everyone a capitalist (in Thompson's and Mill's vision of worker-owned cooperatives).

Bernstein argued that class differentiation was a permanent feature of industrialized economies. Social democracy accepts class diversity in the sense that different people have different relations to the means of production. Business owners, including farmers, may own the capital they work, but the typical wage laborer does not. Workers' cooperatives may be encouraged, but exist along with other types of firm. Once class differentiation was accepted, a common perspective from the standpoint of which institutions could be justified could no longer be the perspective of any single class. Social democrats saw in equal democratic citizenship the practical basis for such a common perspective, at the scale of the nation. In the words of Per Albin Hansson, chair of the SAP from 1925 to 1946, the party's ideal is of

> a society of free and equal individuals in democratic cooper-
> ation, where common resources are used to ensure security and
> well-being for all. We Social Democrats do not accept a social
> order with political, cultural and economic privileges or one

where the privately owned means of production are a way for the few to keep the masses of people in dependence . . . . [Yet] we have no desire to interfere [economically] in such a way that will hold back or injure production . . . . Our main interest is in getting the most out of our nation's productive capacity . . . so that we can [ensure] a better distribution of welfare . . . . Sweden belongs to us all, it has resources for all and everything should be done for the good [of the whole].[55]

Articulating a basis for a shared normative perspective of equal citizens does not of itself overcome class conflict. To enable this perspective to gain practical normative authority, economic and political institutions had to be altered so as to overcome structurally antagonistic social relations. This was a priority of advocates of the progressive work ethic from the Ricardian socialists on.

In the version of capitalism advocated by the conservative work ethic, such antagonisms arise in at least four ways: (1) a class system in which propertyless workers toil in poverty and precarity to maintain idle propertied classes in luxury; (2) in which labor is a commodity treated like any other commodity, disposable at the whim of capitalists; (3) where workers must compete against one another in the labor market for scarce jobs, driving wages and working conditions down; and (4) where the ethos of society is driven by competitive acquisition – a toxic, zero-sum form of esteem competition. Social democrats advanced a suite of policies and institutions to overcome these antagonisms. A democratic perspective on distributive justice affords a starting point for considering this project.

Distributive Justice. During the nineteenth century, arguments about distributive justice were conducted in terms of class conflict. Radical workers and various Ricardian socialists denied the legitimacy of profits, rent, and interest. These types of income were unearned and undeserved because they accrued to passive ownership alone. They led to a division of society into oppressed workers and idle rentiers. By contrast, Malthus, Burke, and other conservatives viewed recipients of poor relief as the real idlers. Burke's insistence that labor is a commodity – that workers deserve no more than market wages, even if wages are driven below subsistence – was all about keeping workers in a state of precarity and dependence on the wills of their superiors. Capitalists such as Ricardo, who made his fortune in bond trading on the London Exchange, defended the legitimacy of interest as just deserts for postponing consumption,[56] while rejecting any desert-based or productive-contribution case for rents. Late in the nineteenth century, neoclassical economists justified the capitalist class system by claiming that each factor of production – labor, land, and capital – received its just deserts as measured by its marginal productivity.[57]

The irresolvable character of disputes over distributive justice conducted in terms of desert and merit confirmed Babeuf's and Thompson's arguments that such disputes are hopelessly subjective and cannot form the basis of any system of distributive justice. Marx, too, rejects desert-based claims of distributive justice – including the claim of workers to the whole fruits of their labor – as reflecting the egoism induced by capitalist society. He also argues that the claim neglects economic necessity: before the national product is distributed to individual workers, deductions must be made for replacing worn-out capital, new investment, disaster relief, accident insurance, public goods such as schools and health services, provision for the unemployed and those unable to work, and public administration of these programs.[58]

I would add that arguments about just deserts that reject whole types of payment also neglect the fact that factor prices are needed in a market system to ensure that factors of production are not wasted, but directed to their best uses. For prices to serve this function, they need to signal to producers where their resources are best deployed in the immediate future. This is incompatible with the backward-looking perspective of desert, which attempts to reward people on the basis of their past actions. Fulfillment of this function requires that money, land, and fixed capital bear prices reflecting their opportunity costs, a contingency that no one deserves. Moreover, as Ricardo showed, even where rent serves no economic function, it will accrue somewhere in any market system.

James and John Stuart Mill helpfully steered discussions of distribution away from attempts to abolish whole types of income such as ground rents, and toward taxation. By the end of the nineteenth century, Fabian socialists developed a theory of taxation from the argument of neoclassical economists that all factors of production earn "rents" on inframarginal units. They argued that all such rents are unearned and can be justly taxed and redistributed on an egalitarian basis without disturbing the allocative function of prices.[59]

The Fabians' symmetrical treatment of income types set the stage for the social democratic breakthrough, which set aside class-based disputes over desert. Instead, social democrats adopted a common national perspective on distributive justice founded on the shared ideals that underwrite democracy as a mode of social life based on equality, liberty, and fraternity. A community of equals, as Locke, Mill, Marx, and others in the progressive work-ethic tradition stressed, must be one in which the advancement of any individual's good advances the whole. If we start from a presumption of equal distribution and consider which departures from equality could be approved by all, regardless of their class position, the natural conclusion is that inequalities will be approved just so long as they redound to everyone's advantage, and disapproved as soon as they come at the expense of the less advantaged.[60] This was Condorcet's view,[61] and a natural interpretation of Hansson's. It supports the progressive income and wealth taxes characteristic of social democracies, along with predistributive policies that prevent pretax incomes from greatly diverging in the first place.

This principle makes no reference to considerations of desert. It rather expresses a kind of deep reciprocity across society. According to this principle it is impossible to justify a class system in which impoverished workers toil to maintain other classes in idle wealth. Reciprocity requires that all who are able should contribute to the common good. With permissible inequalities sharply limited, and an ethos of working for the common good of fellow citizens in place, a conception of life as a race of competitive acquisition against others also makes no sense. The shared perspective of citizens in a democracy thereby eliminates the first and fourth bases of antagonistic social relations noted above.

Labor Markets, Precarity, and the Decommodification of Labor. Burke, Whately, and other conservatives argued that labor should be treated as a commodity. This ensured the precarity of the labor force and forced workers to live at the mercy of property owners, who would employ them and supply credit at interest. Postwar social democrats promoted several policies to decommodify labor. First – an innovation only clearly conceived after Keynes – state fiscal policy and central banking monetary policy would work together to ensure full employment, so that there would not be a surfeit of workers competing against each other for scarce jobs. Second, comprehensive social insurance and generous provision of public goods would eliminate precarity and thereby the need to rely on market wages alone to satisfy needs. Third, workers would be unionized so they could undertake collective bargaining with employers. This system was most fully realized in Scandinavia, which implemented large-scale sectoral bargaining between groups of labor unions and groups of employers.[62] Fourth, some social democratic countries implemented dignitary minimum wages to ensure that no worker would toil in poverty. Together, these policies undermine the second and third bases of class-based antagonistic social relations.

Education, Upskilling, Codetermination, and Workers' Autonomy. In economics, the term "commodity" can be understood in a wide or a narrow sense. In the wide sense, commodities consist of any goods or services exchanged on a market. In the narrow sense, commodities are exchangeable goods or services with interchangeable units of uniform quality, such as grains, pure metals, and mass-produced chemicals. Because there are typically many producers of any given commodity, and minimal product differentiation, commodity producers market their products in highly competitive markets. This leads to extremely low profit margins.

The Industrial Revolution turned labor into a commodity in this narrow sense. Through the microdivision of labor, jobs were reduced to simple repetitive operations that nearly anyone could perform with minimal training. Such commodification increased the number of workers available to compete for any given job and thereby depressed wages. It also enabled employers to disregard dangerous working conditions, because workers could be easily replaced if some died or became ill or disabled at work.

From Smith forward, advocates of the progressive work ethic deplored the effects of commodification not only on workers' wages and working conditions, but on their skills, intellectual powers, and moral virtues. They promoted publicly funded education as a partial remedy for these effects. At mechanics' schools, such as the one in London where Hodgskin lectured in political economy, working-class adults eagerly took classes not only to improve their vocational skills, but to gain a wider understanding of their world. Unsurprisingly, this often had radicalizing effects.

From a social democratic perspective, free public education has decommodifying effects in conjunction with the policies just discussed.

When collective bargaining and full-employment policies raise wages, and workers are well educated, this gives employers an incentive to restructure the division of labor so as to include higher-skilled tasks – or at least a wider variety of tasks – in most jobs, so that each worker's productivity rises to cover the cost of their wage. Jobs thereby become more interesting and afford a field for the exercise of more sophisticated skills. These changes reduce the drudgery of work, enhance respect for workers, and enable work to be a domain of human flourishing rather than of dreary ascetic discipline and necessary toil.

A classic example of social democratic policy in this respect was Volvo's reorganization of its method of assembling cars in the 1980s. Under the assembly-line technology pioneered by Ford Motor Company in 1913, each worker was consigned to a single task, repeated on each car as it moved along the line. Volvo redivided the labor by creating small teams that would assemble whole cars together, deploying many skills. The system of codetermination also placed workers on the corporate board and in plant-level works councils that regulate local work processes and conditions. Having thereby acquired managerial skills, virtually all white-collar employees at Volvo's advanced assembly plants were recruited from the shop floor. Workers were enthusiastic about getting more interesting work and prospects for upward mobility, and productivity rose.[63]

Thus we see that achieving real freedom to choose an occupation involves not just effective access to the formal education needed to acquire vocational skills, but opportunities to learn at work, and to deploy that learning in more advanced jobs, through a robust internal promotion ladder. Redividing labor to incorporate more skills in any given job, along with works councils, promotes these goals. Such policies move production closer to the system Mill and Marx desired, in which greater total productivity also enhances the skills and engages the interest of each individual engaged in production. Codetermination enhances workers' collective autonomy in extending democratic principles to the workplace. It also offers some scope for workers to develop and exercise capabilities beyond those required for their particular occupation.

Beyond the Work Ethic: Education, Family Leave, and Leisure. Advocates of the progressive work ethic from Smith forward always look beyond the work ethic to a broader vision of life. They focus especially on the development of virtues besides those comprising the work ethic, and on expanding opportunities for leisure and play. Smith delighted in the work boy who invented a device that enabled him to play with his friends rather than tend a machine.[64] He worried that the factory system prevented its workers from cultivating intelligence, judgment of wider affairs, public spirit, and courage. Mill extolled "the gospel of leisure" to afford workers with free time in which they could exercise higher capacities and enjoy higher pleasures.[65]

France pioneered a breakthrough in 1936 when Léon Blum, head of the Popular Front government (an alliance of left-wing parties), brokered an agreement between the General Confederation of Labour and the General Confederation of French Production to establish by law a 40-hour work week, prohibition of overtime, and two weeks of paid vacation. Guaranteed paid vacations and holidays are so popular that they exist in all the rich democracies except the United States, where the conservative work ethic has retained a tighter grip than anywhere else.[66] Limits on working hours, guaranteed paid vacations, and social rights to paid family leave – another innovation of social democracy absent in the United States – ensure that workers have real freedom to pursue a flourishing life outside work, to spend time with friends, build families, pursue hobbies and interests, play, and rest.

Rights to free or very-low-cost public education, including at post-secondary levels, fit in here as well. From a social democratic point of view, vocational training plays critical roles in ensuring freedom of occupational choice, supporting the skill development needed to sustain a high-wage economy, and a flexible workforce that can adapt to dynamic markets. But education is not reducible to job training. A sound educational system also affords opportunities to develop intellectual virtues, enhance individual autonomy, pursue arts and culture, and forge habits of democratic engagement with fellow citizens from different walks of life. Rights to education, while serving work goals, also aim to develop and exercise capabilities beyond those required by the work ethic.

Thus we see that the package of policies advanced by social democracy always seek more than just a secure and relatively high material standard of living for all. Different policies work in conjunction with others to promote individual freedom and autonomy, a rich family and community life, social solidarity, a wide range of capabilities, and democracy itself.

Decommodification and the Persistence of Class Inequality. Social democracy aims at broad equality of citizens in a context of class differentiation. Decommodification of labor through the expansion of social rights is its core strategy. As Marshall explained, social rights, including a robust system of direct social provision – in the UK, most famously in the National Health Service – comprise a right to a real income sufficient to cover the "essentials of social welfare" independent of the market value of one's labor.[67] Thus, the rights of citizenship expand, while the need to rely on markets to make a living declines. Marshall hoped that education at common schools, and the experience of obtaining goods such as health care on a common basis from state providers, would also blur the cultural boundaries among the classes and help to forge a common democratic culture. At the same time, he acknowledged that some incentives to produce at a high-enough level to fund social rights would need to be retained, and hence that there were some ultimate if indeterminate limits to how far social equality could be advanced. Strict equality of income is not the point; equality of status is more important.[68]

Yet even here, Marshall argued that the imperatives of bureau-cratic administration of social rights would inevitably generate social stratification. In the English educational system, students' occupa-tional prospects are sealed with exams taken at the age of 16. Exam results determine whether a student can go on to advanced study and ultimately university. Intellectual abilities that vary on a continuum are thereby bureaucratically classified into strict divisions, to which dramatically different future prospects are attached. Even if it were possible to say that students enjoyed equal educational and occupa-tional opportunity up to age 16, educational differences after that point widen and sharpen class differences. Marshall accepted this meritocratic sorting and ranking on the principle that "unequal sta-tus" is "fairly apportioned to unequal abilities." In this way, "citizen-ship operates as an instrument of social stratification. There is no reason to deplore this." For in this case, democratic institutions and debates over social rights, rather than the market, settle what social inequalities are just.[69]

Today we have strong grounds for worrying that the intergen-erational transmission of educational advantages within the family will harden a purportedly meritocratic higher-education system into a new aristocracy of the highly educated, with little room for upward mobility of individuals born to less well-educated parents.[70] Instead of turning trivial differences in test scores into massive inequalities in educational and hence occupational opportunity, it would make more sense to expand higher education and open up a wide variety of modes of access, including some with a lottery element. For there are strong reasons to believe that a relatively closed, self-reproducing educated elite cannot serve a democratic society as well as one more representative of the full range of social positions within it.[71] In addition, any system that reserves a decent standard of living, social esteem, and political office for the highly educated is patently inconsistent with the progressive work ethic. As Baxter insisted, all workers must be honored and paid decently, regardless of their occupation. And democracy cannot work well if significant groups in society lack a seat at the table.

Social insurance systems also structure social stratification. This is inherent in the Bismarck system of social insurance established in Germany, Austria, France, Italy, and other European countries. They offer different pension schemes to different occupations, with benefits graded in accordance with occupational status and paid for by workers' contributions. Such a system minimizes interclass transfers. Beveridge-system social insurance, named after William Beveridge, the architect of the UK's welfare state, features universal flat benefits at a low rate, funded from general revenues.[72] In purely distributive terms and considered in isolation, such a system tends to equalize outcomes and is formally far more egalitarian than Bismarck-style social insurance. However, because benefits are low, they are unattractive to the middle classes, who purchase private schemes or bargain for better fringe benefits from their employers. The public insurance scheme becomes stigmatized, as mainly a resort for the poor, and reproduces in milder form the harsh treatment of the least advantaged in poor-law regimes. The Scandinavian social democracies discovered that, to draw the support of the middle classes for social insurance through a single universal system, benefits had to be graded to customary earnings. The key is to be generous enough to prevent middle-class defection to private insurance. This helps sustain middle-class support for tax rates high enough to enable significant interclass transfers. Such a scheme thereby maximizes decommodification, or the ability of people to lead decent lives not tightly coupled to market earnings. Notwithstanding the relative freedom from the market such regimes feature, labor-force participation rates are very high in these systems, putting the lie to the conservative assumption that people will opt out of work whenever they can.[73]

Social democracy aspires to a democratic system in which inequalities are limited to just those that benefit everyone, especially the least advantaged, and in which access to more advantaged positions is effectively open to all on a basis of equality of opportunity. Its success depends on striking a delicate balance in two internal tensions. First, social democracy is committed to making extensive use of markets, while also decommodifying labor. Decommodification requires a welfare state substantial enough that individuals can leave the workforce or go part-time without suffering severe reductions in their standard of living, or dropping below a decent standard, for a wide range of reasons – vacation, retirement, education, dependent care, illness, disability, etc. – that are at most lightly screened by the state. This points us beyond the work ethic to substantial freedom from paid work.[74] At the same time, social democracies typically promote high rates of laborforce participation to generate the high rates of taxation needed to support generous welfare policies.[75]

Second, class differentiation and consequently some degree of inequality is built into social democracy. The challenge is to retain the loyalty of the broad middle classes to solidaristic institutions that leave no one behind. This equilibrium is delicate, especially in market economies open to globalizing forces.[76] When those at the top are able to alter the rules of the global economic game, and have greater influence even over domestic rules, the equilibrium destabilizes. They may be able to buy off the upper-middle class by enabling them to break away from the rest. When the new rules redound to the disadvantage of those right in the middle, it is all too easy to deflect their resentment downward, onto those who are the most salient beneficiaries of social transfers. The least advantaged are typically not the recipients of the largest transfers. But the ways transfers are packaged may make it seem that way.[77] This creates the conditions for a cascade of inegalitarian and antidemocratic sentiment fueled by an interpretation of events deeply shaped by the conservative work ethic. As the next chapter argues, late twentieth-century and twenty-first-century neoliberalism, in ideology and policy, amounts to a modern-day version of the conservative work ethic.

9 HIJACKED AGAIN: NEOLIBERALISM AS THE RETURN OF THE CONSERVATIVE WORK ETHIC

The Rise of Neoliberalism and the Legacy of the Conservative Work Ethic

In Chapter 3, I argued that in late eighteenth-century Britain, lazy and predatory capital owners – the original targets of Puritan critique – *hijacked* the work ethic and turned it against workers. These were the great landlords, rentiers, crony capitalists (including the shareholders and managers of the piratical East India Company, colonial slaveholders, and other state-sponsored imperialist ventures), schemers, and monopolists. These were people who got rich not from hard work, saving, and prudent investment in the real economy, but from merely passive ownership of property, state favoritism, market manipulation, financial speculation, and oppression of the less advantaged, especially of workers, tenants, and needy borrowers. One measure of its economic effects is the gap between productivity growth and wage growth. During Engels's Pause, from the turn of the nineteenth century to mid-century, British wages stagnated even as productivity galloped ahead.

In the second half of the nineteenth century, workers successfully mobilized for democracy and organized trade unions. Their efforts led to the rise of social democracy. Social democratic policies and institutions enjoyed great success in the three decades following the Second World War. Even in the United States – which never had a major socialist party – progressive-movement, New Deal, and Great Society reforms included weaker versions of some social democratic policies. In the 1970s, however, social democracy began to lose ground to neoliberalism. By the turn of the twenty-first century, the battle had turned into a rout. The US and UK led the way, both ideologically and in policy terms, with the elections of Ronald Reagan and Margaret Thatcher. As I noted in the Preface, a huge battery of policies favoring capital interests and weakening labor have followed in most developed countries since then, sometimes even with the help of social democratic or center-left political parties. A partial list includes the following: Keynesian macroeconomic monetary and fiscal policies, aiming at full employment, have been replaced with policies focused on reducing inflation and budget austerity; taxes on capital income have been cut below taxes on wages, and their overall progressivity reduced; inheritance taxes have been cut or eliminated; international trade agreements stress the free flow of capital, intellectual property protections, and protections for foreign investors, with little or no protections for workers or the environment; financial deregulation has enabled the financialization of capitalist economies, especially in the US and UK, where banking, asset trading, and financial intermediation take growing shares of GDP; changes in bankruptcy laws favor creditors over borrowers; in the US, a dramatic weakening of antitrust doctrine and virtual suspension of enforcement has led to massive consolidation in many sectors, to the disadvantage of consumers and workers; labor laws and enforcement have also steadily weakened at both the federal and state levels.

Not just public policies, but business strategies also dramatically changed. Economist Milton Friedman is often credited with pushing an ideological shift from stakeholder to shareholder capitalism. Under the postwar stakeholder model, the job of business executives included not just seeking profits, but ensuring that all stakeholders in the firm – customers, employees, suppliers and vendors, investors, and even communities and governments – gain from the firm's activities. Friedman, by contrast, insisted that the sole duty of executives is to maximize profits within the constraint of the laws.[1] Executives rapidly adopted this model.

Especially in the US, this change in business models has led to an escalation of profits and skyrocketing executive compensation. This was rationalized by the supposed need for outsized compensation to align executives' incentives with shareholder interests. It has also led to a dramatic weakening of workers' bargaining power. Assisted by the systematic weakening of labor laws brought about by their own lobbying, finance of political campaigns, and other outsize influence on government, businesses have adopted union-busting strategies and defeated unionization drives across the economy.

Leading firms have also systematically shed employees, in a process known as the "fissured workplace."[2] They have outsourced work to temporary employment agencies and to small suppliers who compete against each other, driving down wages. They have converted employees into (often misclassified) "independent contractors" to avoid minimum-wage laws, training costs, unemployment insurance taxes, and other costs of formal employment. They have turned permanent employees into part-time workers with no benefits and irregular, unpredictable schedules. Jobs have been fragmented into tasks or gigs, sometimes solicited on tech platforms. Corporate promotion ladders and opportunities to move from temporary to permanent work have shrunk. "The corporate *career*, with a series of jobs bearing more responsibility (and pay) was replaced by the *job*, and now the job is being replaced by the *task*."[3] The result is the twenty-first-century equivalent to the microdivision of labor during the Industrial Revolution: a recommodification of labor in the narrow sense, with ordinary workers deskilled and reduced to interchangeable and disposable parts, without bargaining power. This process has led to a return of Engels's Pause: while US productivity rose 64.6 percent in the 42 years from 1979 to 2021, real hourly wages plus benefits for ordinary workers have risen only 17.3 percent.[4] Vast numbers of workers, even if not reduced to poverty, have been thrown into the ranks of the precariat.

These developments amount to a *second hijacking* of the work ethic by the targets of its critique. Call it what you will – neoliberalism, classical liberalism, libertarianism, free-market capitalism – the ideological rationale for these changes is at root a revival of the conservative work ethic. To be sure, advocates no longer claim that "savage" workers need to be "civilized" through subjection to their employers. Now "meritocracy" rules: the rich are simply being rewarded in accordance with their purportedly vastly superior merit or productive contribution to society.[5] Yet Malthus and Whately had already made similar claims, implicit in the idea that the rich were the founts of civilization. Priestley was not much different, although he focused more on wealthy industrialists than leisured landlords, more on narrowly economic than cultural contributions.

Social democratic and other center-left parties failed to counter this reversal. In part, they were victims of their own success. Expansion of educational opportunity has always been a core part of the center-left agenda. As the constituents of center-left parties gained access to a college education, the demographics of these parties shifted from the less to the more educated, from the working class to the professional-managerial class.[6] They lost touch with working-class concerns and were seduced by the meritocratic ideology that legitimized their status but replaced the quest for substantive equality with "the right to rise." This is a resurrection of Priestley's vision of life as a competitive race for superior status, which J. S. Mill had condemned.[7] It is a betrayal of the social democratic vision of a free society of equals. Center-left parties joined center-right parties in supporting neoliberal trade agreements, tax policies, and harsh welfare reforms, and failed to update their labor policies to meet neoliberal challenges to organized labor.

The rest of this chapter documents the return of the conservative work ethic in practice. My focus is on the United States. England was the original home of the work ethic. But today, its conservative version is most nakedly evident in the United States. The dominance of the conservative work ethic in the US is due in significant part to the continuing racist legacies of slavery. Puritans brought the work ethic to the US when they settled the Massachusetts Colony. Their constitution provided for the enslavement of captives in war, as well as contractual slavery, in accordance with Biblical law.[8] Struggles over slavery deeply shaped both the progressive and conservative work-ethic traditions in the US. Southern politicians and propagandists defended slavery by appropriating themes of the conservative work ethic. One leading defense was the claim that civilization requires a class of drudges to support it.[9] They even perversely argued that slavery was a form of free labor and consistent with a free-market society. After the Civil War, Southern evangelical ministers continued to appropriate the imperialist themes of the conservative work ethic to justify the domestic subjection of Black workers and a laissez-faire regime for workers more generally.[10] Such arguments fit well with continuing American importations of conservative work-ethic thinking from Britain in the late nineteenth century.[11] As we shall see in Chapter 9, US welfare policy today reflects both the continuing influence of racism and the thought of classical conservative work-ethic theorists such as Malthus and Whately.

There is also a rich progressive work-ethic tradition in the US. Black activists and thinkers, from W. E. B. Du Bois to Martin Luther King Jr. and Cornel West, have profoundly shaped this tradition. They stressed the importance of combating racism through cross-racial worker solidarity as an essential means toward constructing a just economy.[12] However, unlike in Europe, the American progressive work-ethic tradition did not lead to the formation of an electorally competitive socialist or social democratic party. This weakness was not due only to racism. Leading aspirational forms of the progressive work ethic in the US proved to be less viable vehicles for the growth and development of this ideal than the dominant forms in Europe. In the first half of the nineteenth century, the US was a wellspring of dozens of utopian socialist communal experiments that were deeply influenced by Ricardian socialist and allied lines of thought.[13] All of them, save the celibate Shakers, failed in short order. More importantly, the individualist dream of self-employment as a vindication of labor has captivated ordinary American workers to an extraordinary degree throughout US history. At its founding, the Republican party based its antislavery platform on a free-labor vision that stressed self-employment.[14] This vision remains strong despite the steady decline of self-employment as a viable option for making a living since the Industrial Revolution.[15] Workers who aspire to self-employment are liable to identify with business owners and to resist the collective institutions – labor unions, workers' parties, workers' cooperatives, an expansive welfare state – characteristic of the European progressive work-ethic tradition.

Couple American individualism with deeply entrenched racism, which casts the victims of settler colonialism as lacking the virtues of the work ethic, and it is easy to understand why the American progressive work ethic faltered. Hence neoliberalism exists in the US in its least diluted form among the rich democracies. For this reason, the rest of this chapter will focus on the ways neoliberal policies in the US today reflect ideas advanced by advocates of the conservative work ethic. Social welfare policies continue the poor-law thinking of Whately, Malthus, and other conservatives behind the Poor Law reform of 1834. Government outsourcing of services to private, for-profit firms, including carceral institutions for the poor, follow Bentham's ideas. Shareholder capitalism puts Priestley's vision of competitive acquisition on steroids. It does so in violation of every principle of business ethics that Baxter and Locke thought was required by the work ethic.

Neoliberal Welfare Policy: The Return of Whately, Malthus, and the New Poor Law

Whately's legacy hangs over US welfare policy in a specific racist form. Slavery in the US rested in part on the imperialist version of the conservative work ethic articulated by Whately. Advocates of slavery claimed that it was a means of uplifting and civilizing enslaved people, overcoming the purportedly natural indolence of Blacks through forced labor.[16] After emancipation, racist propaganda depicting the freed people as lacking the characteristic virtues of the work ethic – industry, frugality, sexual restraint, independence, and a sense of personal responsibility – was deployed to rationalize and stimulate resistance to Blacks' civil and political rights, and to state programs to help them or the poor generally. These prejudices continue to underlie opposition to means-tested welfare programs in the US, because their beneficiaries are stereotyped as Black (although more whites take advantage of them) and hence as undeserving by the standards of the work ethic.[17] Lavish state benefits directed toward those with higher incomes are often packaged in hidden ways, to shore up the conceit of independent self-reliance on which the pride of the better-off is based. For example, state subsidies for middle-class childcare, housing, retirement saving, and employer-provided health insurance are packaged as tax deductions, exemptions, and exclusions. Benefits packaged as such "tax expenditures" heavily favor the better-off: the top 1 percent of income-earners get a quarter of the benefits, and the top 20 percent nearly 60 percent of the benefits.[18]

It is no wonder, then, that US benefits targeted to the poor through means-testing are stinting, stigmatizing, difficult to obtain, and often keep people in poverty rather than enabling them to rise above it. The prejudices against the poor embodied in the conservative work ethic, and the welfare regulations that express it, are continuous with poor-law thinking. Let us count the ways.

Workfare over Welfare and the Denigration of Domestic Dependent Care for Poor Children. In 1996, President Bill Clinton signed the Personal Responsibility and Work Opportunity Reconciliation Act. The act replaced a means-tested entitlement to cash benefits for families with dependent children (Aid to Families with Dependent Children [AFDC]) with benefits tied to work (Temporary Assistance for Needy Families [TANF]). It set a lifetime limit of five years of federally funded benefits. Funds were devoted to encouraging recipients to marry and avoid out-of-wedlock births. Scholars have traced the historical roots of this act and its rationale to Malthus's ideas and to the Poor Law reform of 1834.[19]

In its denigration of poor women's domestic dependent-care work, the 1996 Act also reprises Locke's welfare reform proposal more than three centuries earlier (see Chapter 2). AFDC was originally designed to enable white mothers to care for their children rather than work for wages, when the fathers were dead, disabled, or absent. This was consistent with Baxter's version of the work ethic, for Baxter recognized that women fulfill its demands in raising their children. When poor Black women gained access to AFDC in the 1960s and enrollments increased, Malthusian panic erupted. Critics drew on racist stereotypes to falsely portray recipients as lazy, dependent, and licentious, bearing additional children to draw higher benefits. (Never mind that benefits never came close to the cost of raising children, and that the number of children per case declined over time and was fewer than two in 1996.[20]) In fact, mothers were using AFDC primarily as a support when wage labor was unavailable or precluded by the need to personally care for dependent children. Most used AFDC sparingly and sought work when it was accessible and did not conflict with dependent-care responsibilities.[21] At its roots, opposition to AFDC hung on a gross undervaluation of the importance to poor children of being cared for by family members, at least when the children are Black.[22] Fifteen years after TANF had reduced means-tested cash benefits to a vestigial program for a small slice of very poor families, Newt Gingrich, the former Speaker of the House and longtime critic of welfare entitlement programs such as AFDC, declared that it wasn't enough to put impoverished mothers to work. Child labor laws should be abolished so that poor children could be put to work cleaning schools, replacing adult janitors, who should be fired.[23] Earlier, he had proposed to take away poor children from their mothers and house them in orphanages.[24] Taken together, his proposals are akin to Locke's workhouse for children, based on the cruel fantasy that poor children lack the work ethic and need to be subject to punitive incentives to acquire it.

The progressive work ethic, by contrast, holds that children will acquire the virtues needed for success when they are able to grow up with parents who love them and have adequate resources – financial, physical, emotional, and environmental – to tend to their developmental needs. Striking evidence for this view has been provided by Randall Akee and colleagues. Five years into a longitudinal study of poor children in North Carolina, a subset of their subjects' families began receiving $4,000 annual cash transfers representing their share of Eastern Band Cherokee Indian profits from a new tribal casino. Children in these families, but not the other families in the study, showed substantially reduced behavioral and emotional disorders, along with personality changes aligned with the work ethic. They showed increased conscientiousness (tendencies to be hardworking, responsible, and organized) and agreeableness (tendencies to be cooperative and unselfish). Children whose conscientiousness improved had higher educational attainment and rates of employment at age 25. It appears that better parenting brought about these improvements. The extra income enabled parents to better supervise their children and spend more time with them on enjoyable activities. Children had fewer arguments with their parents. Parents also had better relationships with each other and were less likely to seek mental health treatment.[25] "Free stuff," far from corrupting poor children, enables parents to better raise their children. Every parent knows this at some level when it comes to raising their own children. The conservative work ethic cannot explain how unearned income corrupts children when it comes from a state-run welfare program, but not when it comes from passive property ownership that may itself have been inherited.

The Priority of Desert over Capability. The preference for workfare over entitlements exemplifies a more general tendency in conservative welfare policy – the insistence that the disadvantaged show that they deserve benefits before receiving them, by submitting to external control. This is Bentham's "earn-first" principle for pauper management. As we learned from the British public works program during the Irish Famine, insistence on the earn-first principle has perverse effects when the benefits in question are needed to enable the behaviors that are deemed to make one deserving. In the United

States, programs for homeless people suffering from addiction or mental illness are dominated by a "housing readiness" approach, in which the homeless must show good behaviors under supervision, such as being clean, sober, and orderly, before they are deemed eligible for independent housing.[26] This reflects a Benthamite confidence that external control of the poor under the rigid rules of supervised congregate living is needed to produce good behavior.

The progressive work ethic, by contrast, urges us to consider how access to material goods may be a prerequisite to the ability to work and exercise other virtues. What if some homeless people are persistently angry, disorderly, or otherwise ill-behaved in part *because* they have no privacy or agency? What if having a stable home enables them to take better care of themselves, make better use of counseling services, and avoid criminal activity? "Housing first" approaches affirm the agency of the homeless by prioritizing housing them in ways that meet their stated needs – for example, for treatment off-site rather than where they live. Pathways to Housing, an organization dedicated to this approach, recruits the homeless as "consumers" to advise the organization on what they need, hires them to provide services such as peer counseling to the homeless, and includes them on its board of directors.[27] "Housing first" approaches have been found superior to "housing readiness" not only in reducing homelessness but in reducing resort to emergency health services and criminal activity.[28] This approach is aligned with the agency-enhancement orientation of Smith, Mill, and other advocates of the progressive work ethic.

Means-Tested Benefits Structured as a Poverty Trap. Social insurance benefits, to which most workers have access, are relatively generous compared to benefits that target the poor via means tests. Programs such as TANF, the Supplemental Nutrition Assistance Program (SNAP; formerly known as the Food Stamp Program), Medicaid, and Section 8 housing assistance limit eligibility to the extremely poor, as measured by income and sometimes asset tests. For example, SNAP eligibility is limited to families with income at or below 130 percent of the poverty line, with no more than $2,250 in liquid assets. Of all families receiving SNAP, 79 percent include at least one worker, indicating that they are paid less than a living wage.[29] The asset limitation ensures that poor families live in a state of permanent precarity, even if they are working. Even trivial accumulation pushes them

263 / Neoliberalism as the Return of the Conservative Work Ethic

off benefits without enough saved to weather the next storm. No wonder that the tight asset limits of SNAP and other benefits are associated with "churn" on and off the rolls.[30] In 2015, California set a household financial asset limit of $3,150 for Medi-Cal, the state's version of Medicaid. Consider a couple with one disabled partner who needs Medi-Cal for essential health care. They must liquidate their retirement savings, which may only be put into their house or one car. They can't save for their children's college – thus reinforcing the intergenerational transmission of poverty.[31] These limits function like the New Poor Law's workhouse test, combining suspicion of the dependent, the principle of less eligibility, and punishment. The result is similar to although less drastic than the Gregory Clause (see Chapter 4): the consignment of the needy to a state of permanent precarity.

Arbitrary Limits on Benefits. A hallmark of conservative welfare policy is the imposition of arbitrary limits on benefits that bear no relation to need. TANF imposed a five-year lifetime limit on individual receipt of benefits. It replaced AFDC's entitlement system with fixed nominal-dollar block grants to the states. The real value of the block grant declined 38.3 percent from 1997 to 2020, mostly due to inflation.[32] This impatience with the continuation of need, the desire to simply be done with it and make the plea for relief go away even if need persists, similarly characterized Britain's welfare reform and famine-relief policy.

Administrative Obstacles to Access. J. D. Vance, in his memoir of growing up poor in Appalachia, recalled his experience of attempting to apply for financial aid to attend Ohio State University. He and his grandmother, who was caring for him, found the application form incomprehensible. Vance eventually concluded that it would be easier for him to enlist in the Marine Corps for four years.[33] Financial aid eligibility is determined by a formula set by the federal government, which until recently was calculated on the basis of answers to more than a hundred questions on the application form, known as the Free Application for Federal Student Aid (FAFSA).[34] FAFSA discriminates in a fine-grained way between applicants with small differences in their levels of need. This complexity produces only the slightest gains in targeting need, at immense administrative costs for applicants and colleges. Even minor bureaucratic obstacles are known to deter poor people from the path to college. The FAFSA form thus defeats the ostensible purpose of government financial aid, to enable talented poor students to attend college.[35]

Yet FAFSA makes sense from the perspective of poor-law thinking. Like the workhouse test, FAFSA's complexity gives priority to deterring the poor from applying for aid. It also prioritizes screening out the purportedly undeserving from supporting the clearly needy. Let a million deserving students be denied an education, and a huge chunk of state resources be consumed by administrative costs, lest one student get more than they deserve. FAFSA is but one instance of the administrative burdens pervading the US welfare system, including SNAP food subsidies, Medicaid, and the Earned Income Tax Credit for low-income workers.[36]

In these ways, neoliberal welfare policies reproduce the priorities and techniques of British Poor Laws centuries ago. They thereby embody all of the attitudes toward the poor characteristic of the conservative work ethic – suspicion, blame, contempt, fear, callousness, impatience, resentment – along with policies that promote the precarity and suppress the agency of the poor.

Government Outsourcing and the Carceral State: The Return of Bentham

Bentham (Chapter 3) advanced two ideas in his version of the conservative work ethic: outsourcing provision of government services to private, for-profit firms, and subjecting the poor and disadvantaged to carceral institutions in which they are forced to labor for little or no pay. Both ideas play an important role in contemporary neoliberal policy.

Outsourcing Government Services to For-Profit Firms. Neoliberalism aims to replace state provision of goods with provision by private for-profit firms to the maximum feasible extent. This may involve a demand for complete withdrawal of the state from any provision. Even where the state is expected to play a role in provision – by funding the good or authorizing providers – neoliberalism favors outsourcing actual production of goods and services to private firms.

The case for this position does not hang on the possibility that competing private firms might offer more variety and freedom of choice to users. To be sure, this consideration has played a role in promoting vouchers for education rather than state-run schools. "A market permits each to satisfy his own taste."[37] However, neoliberals have advocated outsourcing and privatization even for monopoly provision, such as power and water utilities, city parking meters, and prisons. They appeal to public-choice theory, which justifies this position by claiming that state provision is less efficient than provision by private enterprise. Public-choice theorists claim that civil servants are just as self-interested as for-profit providers. But they lack incentives to provide goods of the highest quality at the lowest cost. Rather, they aim to maximize their agencies' budgets. The public would get a better deal if the state outsources provision to private firms.[38] Let competing firms bid for contracts to provide the goods in question, and let the state award the contract to the lowest bidder. The state may need to pay, but private enterprise is nearly always the more efficient provider, quicker to respond to changing conditions, and less wasteful of taxpayer dollars. Similar considerations are advanced for the superiority of private over publicly owned utilities, hospitals, and other facilities, although they may be paid for by user fees rather than exclusively through general tax revenues.

This argument reprises Bentham's case for outsourcing pauper management to a for-profit corporation. Government managers lack an incentive to make workhouses profitable, and so impose a great burden on taxpayers. Turn the workhouses over to private entrepreneurs, and they will make huge profits, returning a portion of the gains back to taxpayers (see Chapter 3). We have seen that Bentham's accounting was as wildly exaggerated as that of any con artist. Nevertheless there was some basis for his view that government officials were poorly motivated compared to entrepreneurs. England lacked a professional civil service in Bentham's day. In an undemocratic government run by aristocrats, government jobs existed not to serve the public, but to serve the aristocracy. Bentham complained that many offices were little more than sinecures set aside to provide for the aristocracy's lazy and untalented sons, who would thereby live off the taxpayers.[39]

But not all the rich had access to such sinecures. Until its repeal in 1828, the Test Act prohibited Dissenters, many of whom descended from the Puritans, from holding public office. Ambitious Dissenters, barred from competing for public office and imbued with the work ethic, poured their energies into business. Although they accounted for only 7 percent of the British population in Bentham's day, they were

41 percent of the leading entrepreneurs of the Industrial Revolution. Almost all of the pathbreaking industrialists of the day were Dissenters.[40] Philosophical radicals such as Bentham were allied with the industrious and frugal entrepreneurial class against the idle aristocrats and their useless sons, just as Locke's radical Whigs were. Their contempt for government workers relative to business owners, who had to keep on their toes in competitive markets, made some sense in historical context.

Since Bentham, Britain and many other states democratized and established professional civil services. Is Bentham's and modern public-choice theorists' argument for the superior efficiency of outsourcing state provision to for-profit businesses plausible, given the existence of professionalized bureaucracies? Consider the fact that controversies over this question greatly depend on the good or service being provided. No one expects municipalities to execute their own road construction, or school districts to manufacture the desks provided to students in public schools. Leading cases of controversy concern the provision of complex human services, such as education, social work, hospitals, prisons, and other detention facilities. Let us analyze the question solely in its own efficiency terms, setting aside momentous questions about such matters as the legitimacy of outsourcing public decisions, such as of criminal punishment, to private parties.[41]

The economic theory of the firm offers insight into this question.[42] Why do firms decide to employ their own workers to perform some tasks, and outsource others to outside firms? The boundary of the firm – the scope of tasks performed in-house – is the boundary where "government," or direct supervision of task performance, is more efficient than purchasing performance on the market.[43] In general, a firm will use markets for provision of a good or service as the more efficient option when it can completely specify the contract for the desired good or service, can easily judge whether all the terms of the contract have been met, when what matters is just a specific output and not the process by which it is produced, when outside providers know more about how to produce the good or service, and when it costs little to switch from one provider to another, because there are many competing providers and it is easy to switch midstream. A firm will choose to have its own workers produce a good or service when what is desired is too complex or open-ended to be fully specified in a contract, or too difficult to tell whether it was done well without direct supervision of the production process, when the production process matters as well as the final output, when the firm has expertise over the process, and when it is costly to switch from one outside provider to another.

Similar efficiency considerations apply to determining the boundary of the state – that is, the boundary between assigning a task to the civil service or outsourcing provision to a private, for-profit firm. It is clearly sensible for the state to procure the plumbing fixtures for its prisons from private manufacturers. It's easy to specify what is needed, and to tell whether the specifications were met. The state cares about the plumbing fixtures, not the manufacturing processes used to make them. Manufacturers know more than prison officials how to make them, there are plenty of competitors, and there is little cost in switching from one to another.

Operating a prison, by contrast, is a complex and open-ended human service with many desired outputs. Prisons need to secure safe conditions for prisoners and staff, prevent criminal activity within and deter inmates from returning to crime upon release, provide health care for prisoners including drug treatment and psychiatric services, run a library to secure prisoners' rights to do legal research on their own cases, manage visitation by lawyers, relatives, and friends, supply jobs for prisoners, and offer education and rehabilitative services, among many other tasks. It isn't easy to specify all that should be done along these many different dimensions of prison work, or to measure the quality of such services. The process of service delivery – *how* these things are managed – is constitutive of whether they are done well. There are not many competitors in the private prison industry. Contracts guaranteeing the number of beds that must be filled for long periods (demanded to cover the cost of constructing the prison) impose steep costs on switching providers. Even viewing the matter only from a narrow efficiency point of view, the theoretical case against outsourcing prison operations is strong.

When the service to be provided is complex and open-ended in these ways, outsourcing to a for-profit provider will predictably lead to cost-cutting at the expense of quality.[44] This prediction was confirmed by a US Office of the Inspector General (OIG) report on privatized federal prisons in 2016. Private prisons make profits primarily by cutting salaries, staff numbers, and staff training. This neoliberal redistribution of income from labor to capital comports with the conservative work ethic. The consequences are grave. The OIG report found that relative to state-run prisons, rates of assault by prisoners against other prisoners were 32 percent higher, and by prisoners against staff 260 percent higher. Rates of sexual assault against staff were 500 percent higher. Prisoners filed more grievances, lockdowns were more frequent, and prisoners were more often deemed guilty of serious disciplinary infractions.[45] These problems and much more pervade the private prison system.[46] The fact that the state cedes judgment over disciplinary infractions to private prisons, which render more guilty judgments, is particularly concerning due to the interaction of behavior records with eligibility for parole. It is highly questionable whether private entities should be entitled to exercise the essentially public function of determining the length of an indeterminate prison sentence. Concerns about the legitimacy of outsourcing such a function are only heightened given that the judges have an interest in a guilty judgment, as profits depend on maximizing the number of beds filled per day.

None of these reservations about outsourcing prison services to for-profit firms excuses the fact that state-run prisons are also horrific places for prisoners and guards alike. The profit motive in privatized punishment merely adds to the unconscionable harms and injustices of the American system of mass incarceration. Yet the very existence, extent, and harshness of this system is due in substantial measure to thinking that has its roots in the conservative work ethic, as elaborated by Bentham and others.[47]

An exploration of alternatives to the prison system is beyond the scope of this book. Here I note that how we envision the *labor* involved in deterring crime, vindicating victims, and rehabilitating people who have committed crimes is not incidental to envisioning alternatives. The labor required for all of these tasks involves the complex work of altering the way those involved in criminal activity relate to others, as well as how nonpenal social and economic institutions relate to them. Even if we focus just on institutions involved in law enforcement, it should be evident that many of the services required are complex, require expertise, have many dimensions of quality that are difficult to quantify, that are difficult for nonexperts to evaluate, that often critically depend on the quality of social relationships within which the service is delivered, tailored to the circumstances and background of the individual receiving services, and where the process of delivery matters and not just outputs.

Societies have invented a type of labor that provides such services. That is what professionals are for: people who are trained to high standards, typically including a journeyman experience under the supervision of senior practitioners, who care about doing their jobs well and getting recognized by their peers for outstanding work, who exercise judgment in a work context that affords them substantial autonomy, and who collectively develop standards for their profession. In organizational contexts where they are fully recognized and understand themselves as such, professionals comprise the largest class of unalienated workers in modern society.

Professional labor has always stood in tension with capitalist wage labor. When they get the chance, professionals prefer self-employment, partnerships, or employment in public or private non-profit organizations where they have a strong voice over the nature of the work they do, so as to retain the autonomy needed to exercise professional judgment. The capitalist firm, especially when driven by the neoliberal maxim to maximize profits by whatever means possible, aims to minimize labor costs by reducing labor to a commodity not just broadly but narrowly construed. In the narrow sense, this entails deskilling workers, mechanizing tasks to be performed by rote, and replacing nuanced expert judgment with uniform protocols. It entails reducing workers to interchangeable parts. Doing so disregards whatever values might be tied to developing long-term relationships between particular service providers and individual service recipients. It also neglects the nonquantifiable particularities of the service recipient. It entails stripping service providers of voice over the content and conditions of their work.

The relegation of health care, education, welfare services, and other professional work to for-profit corporations, the refusal to cultivate the professionalization of K-12 teachers, nurses, police officers and others, and the increasing emulation of for-profit corporate practices by nonprofit organizations all reflect the increasing power of the conservative work ethic over the organization of labor in modern society. Neoliberals defend the commodification and consequent deprofessionalization of labor in the name of lower cost. This has certainly not been the experience in American health care, which has the highest per capita costs in the world and outcomes far worse than peer countries.[48] It is doubtful whether the claim is true anywhere, even before quality reductions are considered. What is certain is that it entails far worse working conditions, and a redistribution of income from labor to capital, and from subordinate workers to executives.

The Criminalization of Poverty and the Corporate Exploitation of Carceral Labor. In Bentham's vision, the poor should be treated like criminals, forced to labor in prison for the private profit of capitalist entrepreneurs. Such a totalitarian idea might seem remote from purportedly enlightened twenty-first-century practices in liberal democracies. Yet both the criminalization of poverty, and the subjection of the criminalized poor to unpaid labor for corporate profit, exist in the United States today.

One major means of criminalizing poverty is through debt. (Other means exist, such as the criminalization of homelessness.[49]) The poor are often jailed because they cannot afford to pay court-ordered child support. Courts are supposed to adjust child support payments in line with the noncustodial parent's ability to pay. In practice, however, payments are set by Malthusian fantasies about how easy it is for poor men, especially poor Black men, to find employment that pays wages high enough to cover personal living expenses as well as child support.[50] The poor are often jailed because they can't make bail.[51] They are also jailed because they can't pay court fees or fines for minor infractions. Many jurisdictions have shifted the costs of the court and prison system from wealthy taxpayers to people who have committed infractions, in a system called "offender-funded justice." In some jurisdictions, this has fueled a systematic practice of targeting the poor for arbitrary infractions for the sole purpose of raising revenues to support the police, courts, and jails.[52] Police in such jurisdictions are so busy collecting their own and other municipal authorities' salaries through de facto armed robbery that they have little time to solve crimes. The greater share of a city's revenue collected through fees and fines, the lower the case closure rate for violent and property crimes.[53] This is but one of innumerable examples of how neoliberal policies make the better-off richer for doing their jobs less well. The poor are even routinely incarcerated for inability to pay debts to private businesses.[54] Debtors' prison is unconstitutional. While courts may imprison someone who willfully refuses to pay a fine or restitution, they must distinguish between such defendants and those who are too poor to be able to pay.[55] Yet courts routinely fail to inquire about defendants' abilities to pay before incarcerating them.[56]

Many jurisdictions have privatized probation for people convicted of misdemeanors who are unable to pay the fine and court fees upon conviction. Probation companies add crushing daily supervision fees on top of the misdemeanor fine and court fees. They extract the mounting payments in installments, threatening jail if offenders can't keep up. Accumulated debts with interest can amount to many times the original fine.[57]

Incarceration in prison or a local jail sets poor people up for exploitation in a forced labor system. New Deal laws once prohibited the use of prison labor except by state institutions. Businesses won the right to use prison labor in 1979. They won an exemption from minimum-wage laws for prison workers in 1995. This led to the employment of hundreds of thousands of inmates of federal and state prisons for mere pennies per hour. Many are forced to work in unsafe conditions without protective equipment, because workplace health and safety laws do not apply to prison workers.[58]

Private prison corporations have expanded into probation, parole, and alternative sentencing services. Such services sometimes involve halfway houses for convicts, who are required to work as part of their rehabilitation. As in Bentham's panoptic system for pauper management, workers only get to keep earnings in excess of the costs of their confinement and supervision by the prison corporation, plus any court fees and fines they owe.[59] In the United States, however, this practice descends not from the pauper workhouse but from the system of convict leasing, which was used to reimpose involuntary servitude on recently emancipated slaves. States would collect revenues by imposing fines on Black people for often arbitrary infractions, imprison them for inability to pay, and lease them to corporations where they would have to work until they paid off the fines.[60] Not surprisingly, modern American debtors' prisons, focused on the able-bodied and free of obligations to house anyone unable to work, yield immense profits for the capitalist and very little for the debt peon.

Drug addiction provides another path into involuntary servitude exploited by private corporations. Many jurisdictions divert individuals convicted of drug possession into halfway houses run by private corporations, rather than sending them to prison. The Cenikor Foundation, one such corporation with numerous facilities, purports to rehabilitate addicts by setting them to work without monetary pay. Shortly after his reelection, President Reagan visited Cenikor and praised its grounding in the work ethic:

I was glancing through your Cenikor booklet, and I liked the very first sentence I read. "In all the years that Cenikor has been in business, rehabilitating lives, we have found that nothing works as well as work itself." Work is therapy.[61]

Based on its practice of requiring its workers to work overtime without pay as part of its "treatment process," one might conclude that Cenikor believes that relentless unpaid labor cures addiction.[62] Courts nevertheless sentence addicts, who are overwhelmingly poor, to confinement in Cenikor's facilities as an alternative to prison. Those sentenced must obey innumerable arbitrary rules and submit to incessant criticism. But most of all, they work extremely long hours, sometimes up to 16 hours per day, which may include hard manual labor under questionable conditions, for the profit of Cenikor and the numerous corporations to whom Cenikor contracts out their labor.

The Center for Investigative Reporting has identified hundreds of other addiction-rehabilitation facilities that purport to cure addiction by means of unpaid labor. Major corporations, including Exxon, Shell, Walmart, and Tyson Foods have exploited their labor.[63] The Supreme Court ruled that such facilities must follow minimum wage, overtime, and maximum-hours regulations specified in the Fair Labor Standards Act (FLSA).[64] However, the ruling left a huge loophole in permitting deductions for room and board. Moreover, enforcement of the FLSA is negligible. In practice, forced labor without pay under the fraudulent claim that unpaid labor is therapeutic remains common in the United States. Bentham's conservative work-ethic vision of the transformative powers of forced labor on the poor and marginalized lives on.

Shareholder Capitalism: Neoliberal Business Ethics vs. Baxter and Locke

I have defined neoliberalism as an ideology that favors institutional arrangements that maximize the wealth and power of capital interests relative to labor. It is the contemporary version of the conservative work ethic, which had the same priorities. Neoliberalism comes with its own business ethic, known as shareholder capitalism – the principle that the duty of executives is to maximize profits. Shareholder capitalism might seem to be the twenty-first-century version of Baxter's commendation of "he ... who ... frugally getteth and saveth as much as he can."[65] And executives might claim to merit the immense growth of their compensation – of 940 percent between 1978 and 2018[66] – in virtue of how hard they work and how successfully they have maximized profits. Economist Gregory Mankiw has been happy to make the case for them.[67]

It may seem that we are a long way from the nineteenth century, when Whately deployed the conservative work ethic to defend the immense shares of the lazy, profligate, and greedy landlords, who used their control of Parliament to enclose vast expanses of land without even a pretense of right.[68] We may also seem to be at some distance from the eighteenth century, when Smith noted an inverse relation between income and hours worked.[69] For among workers in the US today, the higher-paid work longer hours.[70] One study of CEOs found that they worked 62.5 hours a week, including 9.7 hours per weekday and additional hours on the vast majority of weekend and vacation days.[71] Following Mankiw, might they not claim to deserve their immense pay in virtue of their outsized productive contributions to society?

We have already considered some grounds for doubting the claim that factor prices reward individuals in accordance with their specific productive contributions. Sanderson, Locke, Smith, Paine, and Mill all stressed the fact that the division of labor itself – a feature of overall social organization – enhances the productivity of each worker. This entails that those occupying higher positions in the division of labor owe their productivity not just to every subordinate worker within their firm, but to workers in the economy at large. Furthermore, the productivity of any factor is also due to the inheritance of past knowledge and technology to which no current worker can lay exclusive claim. As Ricardo, Fabian socialists, and American progressives stressed, "rents," – inframarginal factor returns – are pervasive. No individual can properly be said to deserve them in virtue of their marginal productive contribution. The distribution of rents is determined by institutional arrangements that no one deserves.[72]

Since 1965, the ratio of CEO compensation to the compensation of the typical worker has grown from 20-to-1 to 278-to-1. It is absurd to suppose that this massive growth is due to massively increased productivity of CEOs relative to all other workers. It can't be justified even by the neoliberal standard of shareholder wealth maximization, since CEO pay growth far exceeded the growth of equities.[73] Nor can CEO compensation be justified by profit growth at the level of the individual firm.[74] What, then, has enabled CEO compensation growth to far exceed both the growth of profits and of ordinary workers' pay?

Imagine each position or job classification in the division of labor as a rung in a ladder, arranged in order of compensation. The distance between each rung represents the pay gap between one position and another. The width of each rung represents the number of workers occupying that position. In the US since the early 1970s, the ladder has gotten much, much taller. Many of the middle rungs have been ripped out, so that the distance between rungs has increased. This has made it much more difficult for workers in the lower and middle rungs to climb up. Relative to the ladders of earlier decades, the bottom and middle rungs have barely moved up or even fallen, while the top 10 percent of rungs, even more the top 1 percent, and even more the top 0.1 percent and 0.01 percent, have shot up.

Some of this change in the ladder is due to the recommodification of labor in the fissured workplace.[75] Business executives have divided labor more finely. Such a fine-grained division of labor deskills workers and turns them into interchangeable parts. From 2005 to 2015, *all* the net growth in employment in the US was due to "alternative work arrangements" – temporary, part-time, or work by purported "independent contractors."[76] The fine-grained division of labor produces a workforce subject to part-time schedules on unpredictable hours. One study found that 38 percent of early career employees were informed of their work schedule no more than one week in advance, with a mean fluctuation of 10 weekly hours relative to the previous month for hourly workers. The vast majority of these fluctuations are determined at the employer's discretion.[77] Such workers are unable to plan ahead for further education, childcare, a second job, or spending time with friends and family. They suffer disturbed sleep, psychological distress, and unhappiness.[78] The outsourcing of jobs to temp agencies – even when the content of the jobs is identical to what formal employees do – bars workers from permanent employment at the firms where they work and hence from any promotion ladder that may exist there. Outsourcing, along with widespread misclassification of employees as independent contractors, empowers firms to shift training, equipment, health insurance, Social Security taxes, and other costs to workers, while avoiding obligations to pay minimum wages. Outsourced customer service representatives, for example, must pay for their own firm-specific training, are paid only pennies per call, must waste time being on call without pay, and don't get enough hours to cover their training or living expenses.[79]

Business executives are the main agents engaged in redividing labor in these and similar ways. Even if we suppose that executives are more productive as a result of stretching the ladder, pushing down the lowest rungs, and eliminating the middle rungs, this should not be viewed as a net individual contribution meriting reward. It is rather a redistribution to the top rungs of opportunities to contribute, at the expense of those below. A system that enables the hoarding of opportunities to contribute by a tiny group, at the expense of everyone else, can hardly be said to be promoting the overall welfare of society.

Smith argued that wage rates were the product of relative bargaining power between workers and employers.[80] He would analyze the activity of restructuring the ladder as a strategy of employers to minimize the bargaining power of ordinary workers by turning them into commodities in the narrow sense. It creates a precariat unable to hold out for better terms, and thereby redistributes income to the top rungs. The commodification of labor creates perfect competition in the labor market, which eliminates ordinary workers' producer surplus. Commodification thus enables top managers and capital owners to collect all the rents for themselves. This activity, in Ricardo's words, "is only one class profiting at the expense of another class."[81]

Let us consider shareholder capitalist ethics from the perspective of the original work ethic, as elaborated by Baxter, Locke, and their progressive successors. This ethic advances a distribution-constrained standard of what counts as activity that can justify inequality: it must promote the public good in ways that respect the needs of "every particular member" of society, in accordance with the institutions of a just society.[82] This standard implies an asymmetry between social arrangements that transfer income and wealth up as opposed to down the ladder. Social institutions must ensure that no one is left behind. In the more rigorous standard advanced by Condorcet and Rawls, the basic structure of society must ensure that everyone, especially the least advantaged, benefits from any inequality. Individuals are entitled to seek their self-interest, but only on condition that in doing so, they satisfy this standard.

Baxter and Locke agree that unequal industry – productive work – and frugality – saving for productive investment – are the only bases of justified inequality. Note that this desert-based standard is not the same as the social democratic standard of Condorcet and Rawls. The latter allows inequalities that redound to the advantage of everyone, especially those on the bottom rungs of the latter. In the domain of business ethics, however, the Baxter/Locke standard is more clearly action-guiding for executives.[83] Furthermore, it is liable to be instrumental to satisfying the Condorcet/Rawls standard for society at large. Baxter's and Locke's business ethics distinguishes economic activity that is truly productive – genuine work – from activity that isn't. The latter business strategies merely extract wealth from others, or shift risks and burdens onto the needy and vulnerable, or tread on others as mere "stepping stones of their own advancement."[84]

From this perspective, shareholder capitalism – the principle that the sole social responsibility of business is to maximize profits – gets matters backward. It tells executives to put the interests of shareholders first, and to pursue all legal methods of directing income to them. This encourages executives to pursue merely extractive activities that don't add real value. The law leaves open innumerable loopholes that enable this. It gives businesses the right to lobby for the creation of even more. Executives following the shareholder capitalist ethic may well ask: why go through the trouble of figuring out how to make money by actually benefiting others? Why not just skip that tedious step, and move directly to whatever legal means will channel money to oneself and shareholders?

Business schools appear to be good at teaching their students how to skip the tedium and go straight to collecting rents. One recent study examines how businesses in the US and Denmark change their strategies when they appoint a CEO with a business degree. Firms led by business-school-educated executives do not show higher sales, investment, or productivity growth than other firms. They are not better at exploiting new export opportunities. Instead, they cut wages and shift the firm's distribution of income from ordinary workers to shareholders and themselves.[85]

Baxter and Locke would insist rather that one may only justly reap profits as the *byproduct* of activity that benefits others, without exploiting the poor and desperate. Moreover, this ethical standard should apply at the margin and not just in aggregate. In other words, one should not be able to reap higher profits at the margin except by making others better off.

Alas, the US economy is riddled with business models that add no value, or even *subtract* value, in the neoliberal campaign to redistribute income and wealth to the top rungs. Baxter and Locke offer a guide to some of the worst business models. So far, I have focused on practices that force wage workers into poverty and precarity, in violation of Baxter's, Locke's, and Smith's insistence that workers be paid living wages. Many extractive business models work through other mechanisms.

Monopolization. Baxter and Locke criticize monopolies not only when they are the product of state charters, but also when they arise from private business strategies ("engrossing"). The virtual suspension of antitrust enforcement in the US has led to increasing concentration of industry in many sectors. One consequence of this is suppression of wages in the supply chains of monopsonistic firms such as Walmart. Such dominant players in an industry force many smaller suppliers to bid down their prices to win contracts. One study finds that such practices may have caused 10 percent of wage stagnation in businesses outside the financial sector since the 1970s.[86] Of course, workers are not the only victims of monopolies. Affordable Health Care insurance premiums are 50 percent higher in areas covered by monopolist insurers.[87] Gas company Chesapeake Energy appropriated $5 billion in royalties it owed to individuals who allowed it to pump natural gas from their properties, by hiking the transport fees on a local monopoly pipeline network charged by a separate company it created.[88] Deregulation enabled banks to monopolize warehouses for aluminum. By shuffling the metal from one warehouse to the next, they increased delivery times from six weeks to 16 months. These deliberate delays enabled them to collect higher rents for longer storage times, and increased the retail price of aluminum. Banks have engaged in other manipulations to raise prices on oil, wheat, and other commodities.[89] Amazon uses its control over online retail sales to undercut third-party businesses that sell on its platform.[90] The list of abuses is endless. Yet it's all fair game by the ideology of shareholder capitalism.

Financialization. Arthur J. Williams spent 15 years mastering a craft that yielded him nearly $10 million. He was a counterfeiter who meticulously reproduced all of the security features of the 1996 $100 bill, which was designed to be impossible to replicate. From the perspective of Baxter and Locke's work ethic, however *busy* Williams was, and however ingenious and aesthetically impressive his bills were, he wasn't *working*. From the perspective of neoliberal capitalism, however, Williams's only error was that he chose the wrong method for producing fake assets. He should have studied financial engineering and created new derivatives such as credit-default swaps, interest-rate swaps, collateralized debt obligations (CDOs), and synthetic CDOs (derivatives of CDOs). It should be obvious that such instruments cannot create real wealth. If I buy insurance on my house, I get security against the loss of an asset I own. If a hundred other people buy insurance on my house, they are merely gambling on a bet over what will happen to my house. If it burns down, even though a lot of money changes hands, the immediate real loss to society is the value of one house. All the other losses are matched by equal gains to others. However, when financial institutions offer insurance against thousands of bets on losses like this, they gratuitously create a risk of their own insolvency. The explosion of derivatives trading in the run-up to the 2008 financial crisis amounted to a gambling spree not on whether houses would burn down, but on whether their owners would default on their mortgages. The nominal value of these bets was many times the size of the home loans themselves. The failure of major financial institutions such as Lehman Brothers and AIG when their bets failed precipitated a collapse of credit and hence of production that brought the global economy to its knees in 2007–8, and a protracted recession in many countries.[91]

Locke worried that the concentration of money in London led to a banking system that promoted predatory loans, gambling, and profligacy, at the expense of serving the real economy.[92] Today, only 15 percent of funds generated in the financial sector serve nonfinancial businesses in the real economy.[93] The rest is dedicated to asset trading and other activities entirely within the financial sector. So much money is being made in finance that those raking in the profits, who have the ear of government officials and who staff its agencies in the revolving door of government appointees, do not wish to heed Keynes's argument that the profits of asset trading are "a mere transfer" of wealth from some to others.[94]

Yet it would be too generous to consider this speculative activity merely zero-sum. Finance pays such high salaries that it draws talent away from sectors that would actually add value to the real economy. That is, it draws talent away from real work.[95] Even worse, as noted above, reckless speculation in deregulated financial markets drives financial crises that cause recessions, the mass destruction of wealth, and protracted unemployment. In the run-up to the 2007–8 crisis, predatory subprime mortgage loans, especially targeting financially naive Black homeowners in racially segregated neighborhoods, stripped them of their homes.[96] Had the US followed Locke rather than Friedman, these disasters would have been avoided.

Excessive Intellectual Property Protections. Locke railed against absurdly long copyrights. Modern economic theory backs him up. In 1998, Congress extended the length of copyright on works for hire from 75 to 95 years. The entire rationale for copyright under the US constitution is to provide an incentive to produce creative works. Even if we generously assume constant sales over the entire period, the present discounted value of the 20-year extension offers a negligible incentive. No creator decides whether to create based on estimates of expected returns more than 75 years ahead. The real reason corporations such as Disney sought for the extension was pure rent-seeking: to extend copyright on already existing works, which need no incentive to exist.[97]

Vulture Private Equity as the New Enclosures. Locke criticized the lazy landlords for their failure to use their own property productively. His constraint on enclosures, that all with a stake in the land must consent, aimed to ensure that every stakeholder would gain from it, and that it would make no economic sense to enclose unless doing so would raise productivity enough to fully compensate all the stakeholders. The Parliamentary enclosures that followed his death reflected a different, conservative work ethic: to hand over property to the rich, just because they want it, even if they don't increase its productivity, but drive workers to ruin.

Neoliberalism has created new methods for pursuing the same end. But the results may be even worse. At least Parliamentary enclosures didn't shut down *all* production. Today, the laws governing leveraged buyouts permit private equity (PE) funds to make spectacular profits by driving the corporations they buy into bankruptcy, wiping out all other stakeholders.[98] For example, in 2004, a group of PE firms bought the profitable Mervyn's department store chain for $1.2 billion, putting down $400 million in equity and borrowing the rest.[99] As is standard in PE deals, the debt was put on Mervyn's books, not the PE firms' books. The owners divided Mervyn's into an operating company, which ran the stores, and a property company, which owned its 155 stores and carried the debt. It forced the operating company to sign 20-year leases on each store at above-market and steadily rising rents, to service the debt. After a year, the PE owners sold the property company, pocketing the proceeds. They awarded themselves dividends in 2005 and 2006 from the operating company's cash flows. To reduce costs, they drastically cut the workforce at each store, forcing the remaining employees to pick up the slack. They cut employees at its warehouses and turned its operations over to a third-party management company. They abrogated the bonus system for managers by forcing dishonest downgrades of their performance evaluations. They cut funding for employees' volunteer community service by 90 percent, a move that demoralized employees and undermined Mervyn's community ties. With so much cash flow going to high rents and dividend payments, Mervyn's was unable to improve its stores. With fewer janitorial and maintenance workers, customers complained about dirty stores. The third-party warehouse management company was less responsive to stores' needs than the in-house warehouse management system it replaced. When the financial crisis hit in 2008, vendors worried that Mervyn's stores would not be able to pay for its orders. Sun Capital, the main PE shareholder, failed to offer them the assurance they sought. Vendors responded by cutting back on deliveries for the critical back-to-school season. This pushed Mervyn's into bankruptcy. The PE owners had already profited immensely from the sale of the property company and extraction of dividends. So the liquidation of Mervyn's, which left vendors in the lurch for $102 million, and 18,000 employees without jobs, meant nothing to them.

Even when PE firms do not drive their acquired firms into bankruptcy, they still play a high-risk strategy. By burdening their acquisitions with high levels of debt and stripping them of assets, they raise the risk of failure while enabling higher leverage and hence higher returns on investment. No wonder that PE retail-chain acquisitions account for 10 of the 14 largest retail-chain bankruptcies between 2012 and 2019. These failures caused the loss of 1.3 million jobs.[100] Many PE business strategies generate profits by extracting wealth from the other stakeholders in the firm – workers, suppliers, creditors, customers, communities, and governments (through tax arbitrage). Because PE firms acquire companies with the intent to sell them again in about five years, they also rarely adopt strategies with long-horizon payoffs, such as research and development and cultivation of community loyalty.[101] As the Mervyn's case illustrates, many of their extractive strategies involve breaching trust (implicit contracts) with the other stakeholders in the firm.[102]

They aren't even above killing their customers for profit. Deaths in nursing homes increase when PE firms acquire them. This is the inevitable result of cutting staff, particularly nurses, and administering more antipsychotic drugs to deal with the patient distress caused by the lack of nurses. One study estimates that, from 2000 to 2012, PE ownership has increased nursing-home deaths by a thousand per year – and that was before the pandemic.[103] Families desperately looking for homes for their infirm relatives have no way to know, because nursing homes have gamed the quality ratings to hide reduced staffing levels and higher rates of antipsychotic medication.[104]

While PE firms exemplify shareholder capitalism more aggressively than other firms, this discussion should not be construed to let the latter off the hook. Notoriously, Purdue Pharma engaged in deceptive marketing of opioid painkillers to pump sales. This practice (in which many other businesses participated, including pharmacies, clinics, and consulting firms) caused an addiction epidemic leading to tens of thousands of deaths. Economists Anne Case and Angus Deaton compare its practices to the Opium Wars, when Britain became the world's biggest drug-pusher, inducing countless Chinese to become addicts.[105]

Baxter would not view the owners and executives of such firms as busy worker bees making honey for all the bees in the hive and thereby entitled to their fair share. They act more like parasitic mites, fattening themselves by eating the bees. While such highly profitable firms boast of higher productivity, Smith better describes their real motto: "All for ourselves, and nothing for other people, seems, in every age of the world, to have been the vile maxim of the masters of mankind."[106]

Exploitation of Tenants. Baxter condemned landlords who took advantage of vulnerable tenants to escalate rents above customary affordable rates and thereby force evictions. This practice is becoming more widespread across the US, leading to a mass eviction crisis.[107] Much of this crisis is located in mobile-home parks, a major source of affordable housing for more than twenty million people. The term "mobile" applied to manufactured homes is a misnomer. Many such homes can be safely moved only once, from the factory to the home park. Subsequent moves structurally damage the home. Even when they can be moved, the cost of moving is so high that it consumes years of equity in the house and may be unaffordable. Mobile homeowners are vulnerable because they must rent the land on which their home rests. If the rent is raised beyond what they can afford, or if the park is closed for a new development, they must either bear the costs of moving or abandon their home. They can't recover their investment by selling it. For unlike homes built on-site, manufactured homes depreciate like cars. Mobile park owners have long accommodated tenants in distress by offering forbearance, alternative schedules for repayment, or allowing them to work in maintaining the park in lieu of rents. PE firms have now acquired most mobile home parks. They increase profits by raising the rents, cutting utility maintenance, abolishing forbearance and accommodations, punishing late payments with draconian fees, imposing steep fines for matters such as failure to cut one's grass, and escalating evictions. By these means, PE firms have increased the operating income of mobile home parks by 87 percent between 2004 and 2018.[108] They generate huge profits by destroying the wealth of the poorest homeowners in the US.

This list is only the beginning of techniques of wealth extraction that flourish under neoliberal capitalism. Baxter and Locke offer a far from complete guide to some of the worst ones. In the twenty-first century, we must also contend with businesses that go beyond abuse of the firm's stakeholders. Among these are firms, such as those in the fossil fuel industry, that undermine global environmental sustainability, and media firms with business models that undermine democracy by destroying local news, promoting fake news over facts, and promoting content that heightens polarization, extremism, and distrust among citizens.[109]

Recall the metaphor of the ladder, restructured by neoliberalism to diminish the prospects of those at the bottom rungs and radically advance those on the extremely narrow top rungs. We might depict the proliferation of wealth-extracting business models as situating this ladder in a giant game of chutes and ladders. In this children's board game, players compete to get to the top of a series of ladders, but also face the prospect of sliding down chutes back to lower rungs. The game represents moves in terms of the conservative work ethic: good deeds enable one to climb up, naughty deeds cause one to slide down. In fact, moves in the game are determined by chance. One might read this as a critique of the ideological cant of the conservative work ethic. Yet by all appearances the game of chutes and ladders appears to accept the cant at face value.

Neoliberalism works like this. Suppose the game had extendable three-dimensional chutes and ladders, and gave opportunities to the game leaders to stretch the ladders higher, remove middle rungs, add longer chutes, attach stumbling blocks on rungs beneath them, and disguise chutes as higher rungs. Players sliding down chutes would power pulleys that would lift those on higher rungs even further above everyone else. Those at the top would resist any collective attempts to alter the architecture to limit how far players could fall or rise, or to equalize opportunities. They would claim that such changes interfere with the natural or most efficient order of things, or even God's laws. They thereby obfuscate the fact that, in excluding the other players from a hand in designing the game, they get to design its architecture and rules all by themselves. They would tell the others that everyone's place is determined by what they deserve. They would claim that the ladders must be stretched higher, and the chutes lower, to afford incentives to do good deeds and avoid bad deeds. They would object that removing stumbling blocks, shortening chutes, and eliminating chutes disguised as rungs interferes with the sacred natural liberties of those on higher and lower rungs alike. Those at the bottom have rights to *more* opportunities to trip and slide! Should anyone believe the top players' claims, once everyone sees how they have rigged the game?

10 CONCLUSION: WHAT SHOULD THE WORK ETHIC MEAN FOR US TODAY?

What Should Economists Make of the Work Ethic Today?

Much of this book is a history of classical economic thought. Since the classical era, economists have developed more sophisticated analytical and empirical tools than anything deployed by the classical economists. Might contemporary economics therefore rightly claim to have left behind the assumptions of the work ethic, which were so deeply embedded in classical economic thought?

Not quite yet. One function of history is to reveal the ways the past still lives in the present. Many default assumptions of contemporary economics reflect the legacies of the work ethic. Consider the default model of the capitalist firm in a competitive market. Firms aim to maximize profits. They are very efficient, constantly seeking to eliminate waste in the production process. They waste no time in responding to relevant information. This is why it is impossible to beat the market. They save in order to invest. (Indeed, most of the funds for investment in the real economy, as opposed to speculation in financial markets, come from firms' retention of their own profits.) The default assumptions about the firm make it the very model of a Puritan businessman – although one exclusively practicing the conservative work ethic. Workers, too, are assumed to have internalized the work ethic: their supply curve of labor is decidedly forward-bending, as Smith insisted. Some recent work in economics recognizes the role of competitive acquisition – what economist Thorstein Veblen called conspicuous consumption – in consumer behavior.[1] This reflects the persistence of Priestley's and Whately's conservative work-ethic view of life as a race for luxury.

In the first half of the twentieth century, neoclassical welfare economics also reflected several assumptions of the conservative work ethic. First, economic growth is good, regardless of how that growth is distributed. This is formalized in the Kaldor–Hicks criterion of efficiency, according to which a change counts as an improvement so long as the winners gain so much that they could *hypothetically* compensate the losers, even if the compensation never takes place.[2] Second, interpersonal comparisons of utility are impossible, or too controversial, so should be avoided.[3] This assumption disables arguments for redistribution on utilitarian grounds. We can't say that an extra hundred dollars to a poor person, which might be enough to prevent consignment to a de facto debtors' prison, adds more to total welfare than if it came to Jeff Bezos, who has a net worth of $117 billion, and who can't spend money as quickly as he makes it. Third, if someone is willing to pay for something, it must be adding to their welfare. (That is, market choices reveal personal preferences, which are assumed to track personal welfare.[4]) Relatedly, in the standard model of markets, if someone is making money in return for goods and services, they are assumed to be adding to social welfare. Fourth, and most importantly, it seemed to follow from these assumptions that, due to the efficiency of markets, states should try to implement policies through market means, rather than through direct regulations or public provision.

By the 1960s and 1970s, neoclassical economists were moving past these assumptions to explore such matters as interpersonal comparisons of utility, distributive justice, and social limits to growth.[5] Nevertheless, the earlier normative assumptions have shaped policy making even into the twenty-first century. The rise of neoliberalism in the late 1970s gave these assumptions even more influence, even among center-left political parties in Europe and North America.[6]

There is a case to be made for deploying neoliberal assumptions in policy making. Much government regulation in the postwar era was inefficient. When economic growth was high, the economy could easily absorb the costs. By the 1970s, stagflation hobbled the US economy. It made sense to seek ways to pursue policy objectives that did not drag down the economy. Consider the following widely touted neoliberal policy successes. (1) Until 1977, minute government regulations on which trucks could drive which goods at what price on which particular routes were escalating costs and wasting resources. They often forced trucks to drive back empty. Trucking deregulation improved efficiency and lowered costs by lifting barriers to entry, eliminating burdensome paperwork, and letting the market rather than the government decide whether a trucker was satisfying a demand for their services. (2) Environmental regulations in the 1970s imposed pollution abatement mandates on firms regardless of cost. This was very expensive. In 1990, the Environmental Protection Agency adopted an emissions permit-trading scheme for sulfur dioxide to reduce acid rain. Firms that could cheaply reduce their emissions could earn credits for dramatic reductions, which they could sell to firms that could not reduce their emissions so cheaply. This scheme helped to reduce emissions by 94 percent at far lower cost than across-the-board mandates, to the benefit of health and ecosystems. (3) A series of international trade liberalization agreements, culminating in the World Trade Organization, played a pivotal role in promoting strong economic growth, technological progress, and massive poverty reduction at an unprecedented scale in China and some other developing countries.

I do not disparage considerations of efficiency, economic growth, and the usefulness of markets. Market-oriented policies informed by neoliberal welfare assumptions have often delivered important benefits. I aim rather to expand the range of normative concerns in economics. A narrow focus on efficiency and aggregate growth in policy design neglects those left behind, as well as broader conceptions of fairness and distributive justice. This can be seen in the three neoliberal policy successes just noted. After deregulation, trucking declined from a secure working-class occupation into one of the most precarious jobs in the US.[7] Market-based pollution-abatement schemes permit pollution hotspots in some locales, often disproportionately populated by poor people of color.[8] Global trade agreements, while helping to dramatically reduce poverty in some developing countries, have seriously undermined the economic prospects of working-class people in rich countries.[9]

It is not difficult to integrate the distributive concerns just noted into an expanded version of market-friendly neoclassical welfare economics that would recommend ameliorative policies. However, beyond the distributive consequences of different policies lie a range of normative concerns that animated the classical economists' view of the world but are largely neglected today. Many of these concerns focus on the nature of work.

Consider the plight of long-haul truckers in the US today. Deregulation, along with union-busting, didn't just cut their income. Because they are paid by the mile rather than for their time, they must work excessive hours to meet their expenses. Long hours lead to severe fatigue and a high risk of accidents. Trucking companies subject them to comprehensive surveillance. Cameras film their eyes to ensure that they are looking at the road. They can be fired for momentarily glancing at their phone to change a podcast. Truckers also lack access to bathrooms.[10]

As the truckers' plight illustrates – and they are but one among a vast range of workers subject to degrading conditions – we have good reason to be concerned about how the organization of work, and the nature of work processes, profoundly affect workers' well-being. Neoclassical economics has little to say about such matters. When challenged on these issues, many dismiss these concerns by assuming that the right to quit is sufficient to address them, and that workers must somehow be sufficiently compensated with higher pay for whatever degradation they experience at work.[11]

For a long time, even Marxist economists neglected concerns about work. Communist countries, eager to promote economic development, adopted the most oppressive methods of deskilling, microdivision of labor, micromanagement of workers, and authoritarian control pioneered by capitalist firms. Marxist Harry Braverman revived the classical economists' concern with work processes in radical political-economy circles.[12] His work was enriched by his long personal experience as a metalsmithing worker who experienced his craft being deskilled, and as a worker in other industries, including white-collar work, experiencing similar degradation. Drawing on this experience, Braverman showed how skilled workers can design work processes with all of the productive advantages Smith found in the microdivision of labor, without divesting themselves of skills or agency, and without submitting to tedium or authoritarian control. He argued that the design of work processes was driven not simply by technical questions of productivity but by the capitalist's desire to extract maximum surplus value from workers. To put his point in neoclassical terms, the main driver behind the steady degradation of work and workers is to redistribute the rents generated in production from workers to capital

owners. Work is being degraded to serve neoliberal shareholder capitalism, at the sacrifice of human welfare, capabilities, autonomy, and
justice.

Neoliberalism is not only degrading work. As I argued in
Chapter 9, it is also degrading the autonomy and capabilities of people
in its design of welfare policies, its reliance on carceral institutions as
a means of addressing poverty, indebtedness, addiction, homelessness,
mental illness, and other social problems, its dismantling of democratic
state capacity through outsourcing, and its support for oppressive,
negative value-added business models.

Here I want to make the case for economists to expand their
range of normative tools so that they can better address these normative
concerns. In undertaking this task, they would be aided by recovering
insights from the classical tradition in economics. I would formulate the
key normative insight of classical political economists in the progressive
work-ethic tradition as follows: *by far the most important product of
our economic system is ourselves.* Hence, when confronting questions of
institutional design, our leading question should be: what do we make
of ourselves in organizing production, exchange, distribution, and provision of public goods in specific ways? This question devolves into at
least two more: (1) Do work and other institutional arrangements
enhance or degrade individuals' *capabilities and virtues?* And (2), how
do different ways of designing production and exchange, business
models, enterprise governance, the delivery of public goods, and social
welfare policies affect *how we relate to each other?* Do economic
arrangements encourage trust, sympathy, and cooperation, or do they
foment distrust, exploitation, domination, contempt, and antagonism
among individuals and social groups? As I argued in Chapter 9, these
questions are as relevant today as they were during the Industrial
Revolution. Their answers demand close empirical analysis of carefully
specified institutions. Markets, property laws, firm governance, and
regulatory regimes can be designed in a vast variety of ways. Different
designs lead to dramatic differences both in the outcomes prized in
neoclassical economics (efficiency, economic growth) and in distributive
justice, capabilities and virtues, and social relations. Given this variety,
abstract generalizations about markets, private property, and private
enterprise are not very helpful in normative inquiry, except perhaps to
rule out extremes involving the outright abolition of these institutions.

Some economists, often inspired by the classical tradition, have been developing tools to address these broader concerns. Amartya Sen, taking inspiration from Adam Smith, developed the capabilities approach to welfare measurement, which led to objective measures of human flourishing partially incorporated into the United Nations' Human Development Index.[13] His approach also offers a far better normatively grounded measure of freedom than prevails in libertarian and neoliberal circles.[14] Radical political economists such as Herbert Gintis and Samuel Bowles have evaluated economic institutions using the much richer welfare criteria of classical economics, especially as developed in the Marxist tradition. They have deployed these criteria in critical analyses of capitalism, and to support the democratic organization of the workplace.[15] Feminist economists have highlighted women's unpaid domestic labor as central to the reproduction of society, and the ways marriage and property law have subordinated women. They further develop the tradition of classical political economists such as Thompson and Mill, who worked in the framework of the progressive work ethic.[16] Serious attention to inequality has returned to economics, with a focus not only on the narrowly economic but also the malign *cultural* effects of inequality. Thomas Piketty, for example, has argued that inequality can get so extreme that inheriting or marrying into wealth dominates hard work as a basis for attaining social status.[17]

Economists can also draw inspiration from the remarkable boldness and creativity of the policy proposals of classical economists in the tradition of the progressive work ethic. The latter understood that property relations needed to change to meet the challenges of their times. Far from holding private property sacred, even the classical *liberal* political economists in the progressive work-ethic tradition proposed dramatic changes in property law to advance the welfare of ordinary people. Smith advocated the abolition of slavery, unpaid apprenticeships, chartered monopolies, private colonies, primogeniture and entails, and most joint-stock corporations. Paine advocated universal social insurance and stakeholder grants. J. S. Mill called for massive reforms of land tenure in the name of emancipating Irish peasants and English agricultural laborers, and advocated workers' cooperatives in the manufacturing sector. Mill was also a leader in considering how the government of firms could be redesigned on a democratic basis, with workers in charge. These classical liberal political economists were not as creative in considering market regulations. But they did not rule them out either.

Similar boldness and creativity is needed to meet the vast challenges of the twenty-first century, including global climate change, high and rising inequality, and democratic backsliding. Isabelle Ferreras, Julie Battilana, Dominique Méda and colleagues offer ambitious proposals to democratize the workplace and address climate change.[18] So does Thomas Piketty.[19] As he stresses, no one can pretend to know in advance that any bold proposal will work. The point of making such proposals is to expand our imaginations in democratic discussion so as to generate policies for experimentation.

What Should We Make of the Work Ethic Today?

In Chapter 1, I cited Weber, Keynes, and Graeber, three critics of the work ethic who hoped it would be superseded. Weber viewed the work ethic as a tool of worker exploitation by greedy capitalists. Keynes saw the advent of a society – which he thought would arrive about now – so prosperous that the economic problem of providing for needs would be solved. We could then repudiate greed as a vice and create a leisure society. There, everyone would enjoy life for its own sake, in the moment, rather than perpetually postponing enjoyment. The little socially necessary work that would need to be done could be shared around so that everyone could satisfy "the old Adam" with only three hours of daily labor.[20] Graeber called for the elimination of "bullshit jobs," which he defined as "paid employment so pointless, unnecessary, or pernicious that even the employee can't justify its existence."[21] He thought that doing so would enable us to enjoy freedom, which, like Keynes, he thought existed overwhelmingly outside the realm of paid work.

Graeber found that workers who saw themselves engaged in bullshit jobs were often in a white-collar, well-paid, relatively prestigious job. Yet they saw their work as pernicious (e.g., working for a corporate law firm) or pointless. When I polled my students on whether they had ever worked at a bullshit job, about 40 percent raised their hands, in line with Graeber's findings. My favorite example of a bullshit job comes from one of my students. He was hired to write business reports that no one read. Workers in these jobs report suffering the indignity of being consigned to uselessness. Indeed, the need to be useful to others is so powerful that prison administrators punish prisoners by depriving them of prison work – even though the work itself is often menial, such as cleaning toilets. Prisoners would rather perform useful drudgery than spend their days just watching TV.[22]

Graeber's critique of bullshit jobs for consigning people to uselessness fits better with the progressive work ethic than with Keynes's ideal of a leisure society. It also fits with other evidence on people's desire to work. Experiments with unconditional basic income regularly find very small effects on work hours, contrary to conservative predictions that giving poor people free stuff promotes sloth.[23] In 2001, Argentina adopted the Jefes de Hogar plan, a publicly funded employment program, to manage a deep recession. At its height it employed 13 percent of the labor force, mostly on community service projects. Job recipients listed income *last* among their reasons for seeking employment under the plan. Their leading reasons were to do something useful, work in a good environment, help the community, and learn valuable skills.[24] Their reasons are captured by Marx's ideal of unalienated labor.

Keynes looked forward to a leisure society because he supposed that only in leisure could people be truly free and pursue intrinsic goods for their own sake. He saw work as wholly instrumental. He deplored the reduction of life to a relentless seeking of means for ever-postponed ends in the frugal life of people chained to the work ethic – and to their offices and shop floors. Marx, who championed the cause of limits on the length of the working day, was no enemy of leisure as a domain of freedom. But he saw that work, too, could be a domain of freedom. Properly designed work can afford a rich domain for the intrinsically valuable free exercise of human skills in service to others. Work *would* be such a domain if workers controlled the content and conditions of their work. Self-governing workers would not appoint themselves to jobs they consider pointless or pernicious.

One might argue that Marx looked forward to a leisure society in which, ideally, the length of the working day is as low as possible:

> [T]he realm of freedom actually begins only where labour which is determined by necessity and mundane considerations ceases .... Freedom in this field can only consist in socialised man, the associated producers, rationally regulating their interchange with Nature, bringing it under their common control,

instead of being ruled by it as by the blind forces of Nature; and achieving this with the least expenditure of energy and under conditions most favourable to, and worthy of, their human nature. But it nonetheless still remains a realm of necessity. Beyond it begins that development of human energy which is an end in itself, the true realm of freedom, which, however, can blossom forth only with this realm of necessity as its basis. The shortening of the working-day is its basic prerequisite.[25]

In this passage, Marx claims that we are fully free only when we are not "determined by necessity." It is less evident that this entails that a free life is a life beyond work, understood as disciplined activity that involves the exercise of human excellences in ways that promote the flourishing of our fellow human beings. The astronauts in *Star Trek* enjoy life beyond physical necessity. Replicators produce all the material goods they require. Nevertheless, they are clearly all working. Their activity has an external and significant freely chosen goal: to explore new worlds. Their pursuit of this goal is systematic, highly organized, and disciplined. Its achievement requires a complex division of labor. It takes work to keep the starship *Enterprise* in good repair. Notwithstanding incredible medical technology, doctors still work to keep people alive and healthy. The astronauts on *Star Trek* rightly understand themselves as working most of the time. They draw a clear distinction between work and leisure. When they are at leisure, they play on the holodeck. (Of course, none of this activity involves wage labor or profit-seeking, as money does not exist in *Star Trek* society.) I think, had Marx lived to watch this show, he would have recognized the astronauts' disciplined activity as a realization of human freedom in *unalienated work beyond necessity*. And he would have thought that this work is a more worthy expression of human nature than spending *all* of one's time on the holodeck.[26]

Weber, Keynes, and Graeber were right to criticize what they saw as the work ethic. But what they criticized was the *conservative* work ethic. Lost from their view was the progressive work ethic, the course of which I have charted here. Why is knowing the history of the work ethic important? To avoid imprisonment in the past, it is helpful to recover its forgotten resources. From the start, the work ethic included both repressive and uplifting dimensions. These dimensions largely divorced during the Industrial Revolution, yielding the conservative and progressive work ethics, respectively. Classical liberalism was not one thing, but contained within it a long argument between these two versions of the work ethic. The socialist tradition, including Marx, continued to develop the progressive work ethic. Many of the ideas in this tradition failed, including utopian communes, the comprehensive replacement of markets by centralized planning, and the abolition of private property. Nevertheless, Marx laid the seeds for social democracy, which, as Bernstein rightly argued, is a successor tradition to liberalism. And social democracy in the postwar era was a highly successful rendition of the progressive work ethic.

Since the 1970s, neoliberal ideology has mounted a fierce assault on social democracy. Neoliberal institutions have eaten away at many of its achievements. Social democrats and their center-left allies, including US Democrats and UK Labour Party officials, failed to update their policies, political strategies, and vision to counteract neoliberalism. In many ways they were complicit in it. For the divorce of the conservative and progressive work ethics was never absolute. As we have seen with Locke and Mill, leading figures of the progressive work ethic sometimes appealed to ideas in the conservative work ethic when considering specific groups of workers. Even Marx and Bernstein saw European imperialism as an engine of progress.[27] Since the 1970s, the highly educated center-left has increasingly adopted a meritocratic ideology, promoting the "right to rise" – a fiction of equality of opportunity – as a substitute for substantive equality in an era of widening inequality of outcomes.[28] The rules of globalization have facilitated neoliberal financialization and constrained democracy, at the expense of the collective political power of workers. As Thomas Piketty and Sheri Berman have argued, social democracy, focused on the technocratic administration of policies designed for mid-twentieth-century society, has lost its emancipatory vision and thereby lost its way in the face of twenty-first-century challenges.[29]

I have written this book as a plea to recover and renew that vision. Its core ideas – that society should be organized to promote the welfare of *every particular member* of society, that doing so requires that all who are able do their part in the social division of labor, that finding the part one ought to take involves freely matching one's personal skills and interests with jobs that advance human welfare – lay at the core of the work ethic from its Puritan beginnings. The developers of the progressive work ethic from Locke, Smith, and Mill to Bernstein and beyond offered bold visions to uplift and emancipate workers, and to serve *everyone* in society. They rejected fixed rules of property, markets, and enterprise organization that were rooted in rigid conceptions of natural right or narrow normative visions of efficiency, economic growth, and maximizing wealth. Progressive classical liberals as well as their social democratic successors historicized these ideas, stressing how they needed to change to address altered circumstances and new challenges. This story is inextricable from the continuous expansion of democracy itself, understood as a mode of government and a way of life that gives voice to the perspectives of all, and responds to the concerns of all, on a basis of equality. Democracy in this sense is always a work in progress, and experimental in outlook. When well-designed, it enables the continuous improvement of institutions in response to public feedback on the consequences of policies for differently situated members of society.[30]

What resources could a revival of the progressive work ethic afford us today? Such a revival offers (1) a perspective for *critique*, (2) an agenda of unfinished business for workers, and (3) resources for meeting the challenges of the twenty-first century.

Critical Perspective. Consider first the critical perspective an updated progressive work ethic provides. The conservative work ethic has always reflected endless handwringing about an imagined lack of industry, frugality, and self-discipline among the poor and disadvantaged. The latter must not get free stuff, must only get what they have first earned, must be consigned to precarity, grueling labor, and subjection to their bosses, lest they slack off, indulge in vice, and withhold the socially necessary labor that upholds civilization and progress. Advocates of the progressive work ethic from Smith forward argued that this is nonsense. If workers aren't exercising the virtues of the work ethic, the fault lies with their poor pay; lack of opportunities to improve their condition through education, work, and saving; entrapment in de facto debt peonage that ensures that all the fruits of additional industry and frugality go to their creditors; lack of access to ownership and control of the means of production; exhaustion from onerous labor; lack of opportunities for leisure; and consignment to degraded, deskilled, and bullshit jobs that don't merit anyone's enthusiasm. Afford workers ample opportunities to improve their condition – both their material standard of living and their personal capabilities – through well-compensated, socially respected, meaningful work and enhanced autonomy at work – and there will not be a shortage of labor supply for any work that is worth doing.

Advocates of the progressive work ethic have always directed criticism upward, and not just to the *idle* rich. Their criticisms extend to those who busy themselves with lobbying for state favors, hoarding opportunities, rigging the rules of the economic game to enable predatory business models, evading their obligations to society, playing financial games that destabilize the economy and mire individuals and states in ever-accumulating debt, tyrannizing workers, and more generally extracting wealth without adding value. None of this activity can be excused by philanthropy. Philanthropy is no substitute for just institutions. In a just society, poverty and precarity would be abolished, not merely relieved. To the large extent to which philanthropy functions to satisfy the vanity and power of the rich,[31] it is merely an expression of covetousness. Here is *one* place where some degree of the old Puritan asceticism makes sense – in checking the greed and vanity of the very rich. It is useful more generally in criticizing the ethos of competitive acquisition that stigmatizes the less advantaged and prods the better-off to "win" by "tread[ing] on their brethren as stepping stones of their own advancement." As Mill stressed, the endless competitive accumulation of wealth is no proper end in itself. It poisons social relations when pursued as such.

This critique extends to the goals of the business enterprise. Social democracy recognizes that markets, private property, and private enterprises *can* be forces for great good. We can't flourish without them. Marx was wrong to suppose that markets make people selfish and greedy. To the contrary, the evidence suggests that people in *liberal* market societies uphold social norms of trust, cooperation, and public-spiritedness better than other societies.[32]

Markets play indispensable roles in a just society, but only if they are properly regulated. Private enterprise, too, often unleashes immense creative energies for projects that do help others, and that never would have been conceived or pursued under the weight of bureaucratic administration. But to accept profit maximization as the sole or ultimate goal of the firm encourages a vast array of destructive, corrupt, oppressive, and exploitative business plans. Laws and regulation are indispensable for limiting such plans. But these alone are insufficient. The government of firms needs to be reconfigured to empower stakeholders who would resist such plans. Workers already largely reject them. That's why they deplore the bullshit jobs to which so many are consigned. If they had a voice in governing the firm, they would reconfigure these plans, which don't add to and even subtract from social welfare.

The economy of esteem also needs to change, to reward firms and executives not merely for getting rich, but for promoting the welfare of stakeholders and the wider society. Baxter warned, against practices of mere wealth extraction, that it is "a prison and constant calamity to be tied to spend one's life in doing little good at all to others, though he should grow rich by it himself."[33] We would all be better off if norms of social esteem reflected this judgment, and thereby pressured business executives to internalize it. Of course, this is no substitute for laws and regulations against wealth-extracting business models. But it is sound ethics, and supplies some pressure against lobbying for and exploiting loopholes.

A Workers' Agenda. The progressive work ethic points to unfinished business for workers, especially in the United States. Despite its extraordinary wealth, the US stands alone among the rich democracies in its failure to guarantee universal health care. Leisure – time to live freely, apart from the demands of paid labor – has always been a central goal of the progressive work ethic. In the twentieth century, all of the rich democracies except the US mandated paid vacation and holidays. Where its peers typically guarantee workers some protections against arbitrary firing, the rule of at-will employment prevails in the US. Its labor force stands out among its peers in the percentage of low-paid workers, in poverty rates among individuals in households with at least one worker, and in low access to paid sick leave. Its proportion of workers covered by a collective bargaining contract is by far the lowest among its peers.[34]

Another domain of unfinished business for workers concerns the unpaid domestic labor of taking care of dependent family members and household needs. Baxter rightly recognized that this labor, mostly undertaken by women, is socially necessary. Anyone who raises children, takes care of infirm family members, and undertakes other unpaid domestic tasks fulfills the work ethic. Yet Baxter gave unwarranted preference to paid labor and male work roles in extolling the man who earns as much as he can. With important exceptions – Ricardian socialist William Thompson stands out[35] – classical political economists tended to neglect the centrality of care work to human welfare, and hence also neglected the economic roles of women.[36] Among rich countries, this neglect continues most strikingly in the US, where workers lack rights to paid family leave. Child allowances, common in social democratic countries, would not only dramatically reduce child poverty rates but accord some of the recognition due to dependent-care labor within the family. The US has also pursued a low-wage, low-skill strategy for dependent-care labor provided by the market. France offers free universal preschool to young children through a professional civil service. In the US, preschool is crushingly expensive, although preschool workers are mostly poorly paid and often have little training.

Such proposals would increase taxes, to be sure. Yet social democratic countries in Europe have enjoyed great improvements in ordinary workers' lives with such policies for decades, without appreciable costs other than high taxes. In many cases, particularly in health care, Americans pay vastly more and get worse health outcomes due to the ways neoliberal profit-maximizing firms dominate provision.[37]

Challenges of the Twenty-First Century. The progressive work ethic offers resources for meeting today's challenges. Democracy is in crisis across the world. Democratic backsliding and political polarization are exacerbated by plutocratic constraints on democracy and the capture of state institutions. Plutocrats also undermine democracy through their control of media and social media. Private equity is destroying local news. Major social media platforms algorithmically amplify propaganda and polarizing attacks for profit. This has fed populist backlash, which further undermines democracy by sowing division and distrust among citizens, and promoting a false promise of authoritarian restoration of past glories.

In fact, the glory days for ordinary working people in the postwar era were days of expanding democracy, not of authoritarianism. From the start, social democracy promoted such expansion, not just at the state level but at work. Social democrats pioneered codetermination, a system of joint management of firms by workers and representatives of capital. They promoted democratic labor unions. These models of workplace democracy, along with workers' cooperatives, need to be updated, strengthened, and expanded. This is not just a fulfillment of the progressive work ethic at work. It is part of the broad project of restoring democracy at the state level. When ordinary people have direct experience of how practicing democracy can improve their lives at work, they will be better informed and organized to revive democracy in their local, state, and national governments.

The globalization of neoliberalism has generated financial instability in many countries due to vast unregulated international financial flows. While international tariff reductions have enabled some developing countries to industrialize and massively reduce poverty, they have deprived many poorer countries of the tax revenues needed to fund national health care and education systems, which are required for equitable growth.[38] "Society," understood as comprising everyone involved in production, exchange, and cooperation, must be understood globally. To meet the challenges of the global economy, the progressive work ethic calls upon us to scale up our moral imaginations and institutions to consider what we need to do to ensure that every person on earth has the resources and opportunities to develop and exercise their talents, fully participate in social life, and engage with others on terms of trust, sympathy, and genuine cooperation.

Finally, humanity faces a protracted crisis of global climate change. Meeting it will require concerted cooperation on a global scale never before attempted. The dramatic changes in energy infrastructure, land use, production technologies, and consumption patterns necessary to mitigate and adapt to climate change will occupy us for at least the next century. For this reason, the prospect of a leisure society is well out of sight even if it were desirable. We need to roll up our sleeves and get working. The progressive work ethic can help us to think of how we can do so equitably, in ways that promote the development of everyone's capabilities as well as advance social relations of cooperation, trust, and sympathy through the expansion of democracy throughout our economic institutions.

ACKNOWLEDGMENTS

This book develops my Seeley Lectures, which I delivered at the University of Cambridge over the course of two weeks in May 2019, at the invitation of the History Department. I am very grateful to the University of Cambridge, my host Richard Bourke, and the many faculty, students, and audience members I engaged with during my visit, including John Dunn, Richard Saich, Daniel Coleman, Emma Stone Mackinnon, and other members of the Neoliberalism Reading Group. I also thank the London School of Economics, Ohio State University, McGill University, the London Philosophy Club, Wharton School of Business, the University of Amsterdam, King's College London, the Royal Institute of Philosophy/University College Dublin, the Berkeley Network for New Political Economy, Purdue University, University College Cork/Waterford Institute of Technology, the British Academy, Carolina Public Humanities, the Institute for New Economic Thinking South Asia Group, the PPE Society, University of Pennsylvania Philosophy, Oakland University, Minnesota State University Mankato, and Stanford University for inviting me to lecture on various aspects of the work ethic. I learned a great deal from lively discussions and written communications with faculty, students, and audience members at each of these institutions and thank everyone who participated.

I thank Dan Brudney, Jacob Levy, David Graeber, Johan Olsthoorn, Eric Schliesser, Rutger Claassen, Ingrid Robeyns, Lea Ypi, Alex Voorhoeve, David Edmonds, Justin D'Arms, Anthony Morgan, Amy Sepinwall, Hans Oberdiek, Irena Schneider, Samuel De Canio, Humeira Iqtidar, Roberto Fumagalli, Mark Pennington,

John Haldane, Tom Boland, Lisa Foran, Brad DeLong, Marion Fourcade, Sarah Dewitt Lucas, Jacqueline Mariña, William McBride, Ben Waterhouse, Sarah Stroud, Lloyd Kramer, Max Owre and the Maynard Adams Fellows at Carolina Public Humanities, Sattwick Dey Biswas, Geoffrey Sayre-McCord, Chetan Cetty, Cristina Bicchieri, Sam Freeman, Sukaina Hirji, Jennifer Morton, Dan Singer, Quayshawn Spencer, Kok-Chor Tan, Michael Weisberg, Daniel Wodak, Jesse Hamilton, Alexander Tolbert, Youngbin Yoon, Phyllis Rooney, Thomas Discenna, Joshua Preiss, Jacob Abolafia, David Hills, Wendy Salkin, and Allen Wood for comments in discussion. Holly Brewer, Luigino Bruni, Denise Celentano, Stephen Darwall, Henry Farrell, Axel Honneth, Eric MacGilvray, Paolo Santori, and Michael Schoenfeldt also gave me important insights into this project. I am especially grateful to the many scholars who very generously read the entire manuscript and provided vital comments on it, including Luis Flores, Miikka Jaarte, Lorenzo Manuali, Corey Robin, Paul Roemer, Peggy Somers, Robert Stern, Frank Thompson, Kevin Vallier, Tom Weisskopf, Leif Wenar, and two anonymous reviewers for Cambridge University Press. Above all, I thank Don Herzog for closely reading two manuscript drafts, sharing his astonishingly deep knowledge of historical texts in political economy relevant to this project, and his superb recommendations for revision, which enabled me to write a vastly improved book. I treasure Don's extraordinary generosity and enthusiastic support for my endeavors.

I dedicate this book to the memory of my parents, Evelyn and Olof Anderson, who passed away during the pandemic. I am forever grateful for their unconditional love, support, and inspiration.

MAJOR WORKS CITED

Frequently cited canonical works are cited as follows:

CD: Baxter, Richard. *A Christian Directory* (1664–65). London: Richard Edwards, 1825. In five volumes. Cited by volume, page number.

SER: Baxter, Richard. *The Saints' Everlasting Rest* (1650). Philadelphia: John Highlands, 1885.

PMI: Bentham, Jeremy. *Pauper Management Improved: Particularly by Means of an Application of the Panopticon Principle of Construction.* London: R. Baldwin, 1812.

SRP: Bentham, Jeremy. "Situation and Relief of the Poor," a letter to the Editor of the *Annals of Agriculture*, September 8, 1797, with "Observations on the Pauper Population Table" annexed, published as a preface to *PMI*.

ES: Bernstein, Eduard. *Evolutionary Socialism: A Criticism and Affirmation*, trans. Edith C. Harvey. New York: Huebsch, 1911.

BHB: Buonarroti, Philippe. *Buonarroti's History of Babeuf's Conspiracy for Equality*, trans. Bronterre (pseud.). London: H. Hetherington, 1836.

RRF: Burke, Edmund. *Reflections on the Revolution in France* (1790). In *Select Works of Edmund Burke: A New Imprint of the Payne Edition*, vol. 2. Indianapolis: Liberty Fund, 1999.

TDS: Burke, Edmund. "Thoughts and Details on Scarcity" (1795). In *Select Works of Edmund Burke: A New Imprint of the Payne Edition*, vol. 4. Indianapolis: Liberty Fund, 1999.

DNQ: Carlyle, Thomas. *Occasional Discourse on the N–r Question*, 2nd ed. London: Thomas Bosworth, 1853.

PHM: Condorcet, Jean-Antoine-Nicolas de Caritat, Marquis de. *Outlines of an Historical View of the Progress of the Human Mind*. London: J. Johnson, 1795.

HRC: Hone, William. "The Hypocrites' 'Reasons for Contentment' Examined." *Hone's Reformists' Register*. April 19, 1817: 389–403.

1T: Locke, John. *First Treatise of Government* (1690). In *The Works of John Locke in Nine Volumes*, 12th ed., vol. 4. London: Rivington, 1824. 212–337. Citations to paragraph number.

2T: Locke, John. *Second Treatise of Government* (1690). In *The Works of John Locke in Nine Volumes*, 12th ed., vol. 4. London: Rivington, 1824. 338–485. Citations to paragraph number.

CLI: Locke, John. "Some Considerations of the Consequences of the Lowering of Interest, and Raising the Value of Money, in a Letter Sent to a Member of Parliament" (1691). In *The Works of John Locke in Nine Volumes*, 12th ed., vol. 4. London: Rivington, 1824.

PL: Locke, John. "Proposed Poor Law Reform" (1697). In *The Life of John Locke*, ed. H. R. Fox Bourne, vol. 2. London: Henry King & Co., 1876. 377–91.

RoC: Locke, John. *The Reasonableness of Christianity* (1695). In *The Works of John Locke in Nine Volumes*, 12th ed., vol. 6. London: Rivington, 1824.

TCE: Locke, John. *Some Thoughts Concerning Education* (1693). In *The Works of John Locke in Nine Volumes*, 12th ed., vol. 8. London: Rivington, 1824.

PoP1: Malthus, Thomas Robert. *Principle of Population. An Essay on the Principle of Population, as It Affects the Future Improvement of Society. With Remarks on the Speculations of Mr. Godwin, M. Condorcet, and Other Writers*, 1st ed. London: J. Johnson, 1798. Page citations to PDF edition (not facsimile) from the Online Library of Liberty, generated September 2011, available at: https://oll.libertyfund.org/titles/311.

PoP6: Malthus, Thomas Robert. *Essay on the Principle of Population, or a View of Its Past and Present Effects on Human Happiness; with an Inquiry into Our Prospects Respecting the Future Removal or Mitigation of the Evils Which It Occasions*, 6th ed. London: John Murray, 1826. In two vols., cited as *PoP6.1*, *PoP6.2*. Page citations to PDF edition (not facsimile) from the Online Library of Liberty, generated September 2011. Vol. 1 available at: https://oll .libertyfund.org/title/312; vol. 2 available at: https://oll.libertyfund.org/title/1945.

MECW: Marx, Karl, and Engels, Friedrich. *Marx & Engels: Collected Works*. London and New York: Lawrence & Wishart and International Publishers, 1975. Citations to volume and page number.

CWM: Mill, John Stuart. *Collected Works of John Stuart Mill*, ed. J. M. Robson. Toronto: University of Toronto Press, 1963–91. Citations to volume and page number.

PLI: Nicholls, George. *Poor Laws – Ireland. Three Reports by George Nicholls, Esq., to Her Majesty's Principal Secretary of State for the Home Department*. London: W. Clowes and Sons, 1838.

AJ: Paine, Thomas. "Agrarian Justice" (1796). *The Writings of Thomas Paine, Vol. III (1791–1804)*, ed. Moncure Daniel Conway. New York: G. P. Putnam's Sons, 1894. 322–44.

RC: Paley, William. "Reasons for Contentment; Addressed to the Labouring Part of the British Public." Carlisle: F. Jollie, 1792.

LH: Priestley, Joseph. *Lectures on History, and General Policy: To Which is Prefixed, An Essay on a Course of Liberal Education for Civil and Active Life*, 3rd ed. Dublin: L. White and P. Byrne, 1791.

SEIP: Priestley, Joseph. *An Account of a Society for Encouraging the Industrious Poor*. Birmingham: Pearson and Rollason, 1787.

WC: Ricardo, David. *Works and Correspondence*, eds. Piero Sraffa and M. H. Dobb. Cambridge: University Press for the Royal Economic Society, 1951. Citations to volume and page number.

RCI3: Royal Commission for Inquiring into the Condition of the Poorer Classes of Ireland. *Third Report of the Commissioners for Inquiring into the Condition of the Poorer Classes in Ireland*. London: W. Clowes and Sons, 1836.

AP: Sanderson, Robert. "Ad Populum" (1627). *Sermons, by Robert Sanderson, Late Lord Bishop of Lincoln. With a Life of the Author by Isaac Walton and an Introductory Essay by R. Montgomery*, vol. 1. London: T. Arnold, 1841.

PLC: Senior, Nassau and Chadwick, Edwin. *Poor Law Commissioners' Report of 1834*. London: Printed for H.M. Stationery Office by Darling and Son, 1905.

ED: Smith, Adam. *An Inquiry into the Nature and Causes of the Wealth of Nations*, early draft, eds. R. L. Meek, D. D. Raphael, and P. G. Stein. In *The Glasgow Edition of the Works and Correspondence of Adam Smith*, eds. R. H. Campbell, D. D. Raphael, and A. S. Skinner, vol. 5. Oxford: Clarendon Press, 1978. Reprint Indianapolis: Liberty Fund, 1982. Page citations to non-facsimile PDF version generated September 2011.

LJA: Smith, Adam. *Lectures on Jurisprudence, Report of 1762–63*, eds. R. L. Meek, D. D. Raphael, and P. G. Stein. In *The Glasgow Edition of the Works and Correspondence of Adam Smith*, eds. R. H. Campbell, D. D. Raphael, and A. S. Skinner, vol. 5. Oxford: Clarendon Press, 1978. Reprint Indianapolis: Liberty Fund, 1982. Page citations to non-facsimile PDF version generated September 2011.

LJB: Smith, Adam. *Lectures on Jurisprudence, Report of 1766*, eds. R. L. Meek, D. D. Raphael, and P. G. Stein. In *The Glasgow Edition of the Works and Correspondence of Adam Smith*, eds. R. H. Campbell, D. D. Raphael, and A. S. Skinner, vol. 5. Oxford: Clarendon Press, 1978. Reprint Indianapolis: Liberty Fund, 1982. Page citations to non-facsimile PDF version generated September 2011.

TMS: Smith, Adam. *The Theory of Moral Sentiments* (1759), eds. D. D. Raphael and A. L. Macfie. In *The Glasgow Edition of the Works and Correspondence of Adam Smith*, eds. D. D. Raphael, A. L. Macfie, and A. S. Skinner, vol 1. Oxford:

Clarendon Press, 1976. Reprint Indianapolis: Liberty Fund, 1982. Citations to book, chapter, and paragraph number as tabulated in the Glasgow edition.

WN: Smith, Adam. *An Inquiry into the Nature and Causes of the Wealth of Nations* (1776). In *The Glasgow Edition of the Works and Correspondence of Adam Smith*, eds. R. H. Campbell, A. S. Skinner, and W. B. Todd, vols. 2a, 2b. Oxford: Clarendon Press, 1975. In two volumes. Reprint Indianapolis: Liberty Fund, 1981. Non-facsimile PDF generated September 2011. Citations to book, chapter (subchapters, where applicable), and paragraph number as tabulated in the Glasgow edition, regardless of volume.

LPE: Whately, Richard. *Introductory Lectures on Political Economy*, 2nd ed. London: B. Fellowes, 1832.

NOTES

Preface

1. Kimberly Kindy, Ted Mellnik, and Arelis Hernández, "The Trump Administration Approved Faster Line Speeds at Chicken Plants. Those Facilities Are More Likely to Have Covid-19 Cases," *Washington Post*, January 3, 2021.
2. As I have argued in Elizabeth Anderson, *Private Government: How Employers Rule Our Lives (And Why We Don't Talk about It)*, ed. Stephen Macedo, with discussants David Bromwich et al. (Princeton: Princeton University Press, 2017).
3. Lynn Rhinehart et al., "Misclassification, the ABC Test, and Employee Status," Economic Policy Institute, 2021, available at: www.epi.org/publication/misclassification-the-abc-test-and-employee-status-the-california-experience-and-its-relevance-to-current-policy-debates.
4. For a pivotal study in a now-burgeoning literature, see Martin Gilens and Benjamin Page, "Testing Theories of American Politics: Elites, Interest Groups, and Average Citizens," *Perspectives on Politics* 12, no.3 (2014): 564–81.
5. See, e.g., Thomas Piketty, *Capital in the Twenty-First Century*, trans. Arthur Goldhammer (Cambridge, MA: Belknap Press of Harvard University Press, 2014); Robert Kuttner, *Can Democracy Survive Global Capitalism?* (New York: W. W. Norton, 2018); John Kay, *Other People's Money: The Real Business of Finance* (Public Affairs, 2015); Quinn Slobodian, *Globalists: The End of Empire and the Birth of Neoliberalism* (Cambridge, MA: Harvard University Press, 2018).
6. Milton Friedman, *Capitalism and Freedom* (Chicago: University of Chicago Press, 1962); Friedrich A. Hayek, *The Constitution of Liberty* (Chicago: University of Chicago Press, 1960).
7. Bernard Harcourt, *The Illusion of Free Markets: Punishment and the Myth of Natural Order* (Cambridge, MA: Harvard University Press, 2011).
8. No one should be fooled by the turn of right-wing parties toward populist nationalism and against globalization that they have suddenly become pro-worker. Whatever their campaign slogans, when in power they serve plutocrats – just not all of them, but the ones in their corner. The Tory economic case for Brexit argued that it would free the UK from regulations protecting workers, so that it could adopt a more internationally competitive low-wage, low-welfare state economy. Kwasi Kwarteng et al., *Britannia Unchained: Global Lessons for Growth and*

Prosperity (London: Palgrave Macmillan, 2012). Viktor Orbán of Hungary passed a law empowering employers to impose 400 hours of overtime on their workers per year, and postpone compensation for three years. Palko Karasz and Patrick Kingsley, "What Is Hungary's 'Slave Law,' and Why Has It Provoked Opposition?" *New York Times*, December 22, 2018.

9. See, respectively, Robert Nozick, *Anarchy, State, and Utopia* (New York: Basic Books, 1974), 169; Richard Epstein, *Takings: Private Property and the Power of Eminent Domain* (Cambridge, MA: Harvard University Press, 1985); John Tomasi, *Free Market Fairness* (Princeton: Princeton University Press, 2012), 91–92; Friedrich A. Hayek, *The Road to Serfdom* (Chicago: University of Chicago Press, 1944).

10. William Faulkner, *Requiem for a Nun* (New York: Random House, 1951), 92.

11. Max Weber, *The Protestant Ethic and the Spirit of Capitalism*, trans. Talcott Parsons (Mineola, NY: Dover, 2003), 115, 116.

12. I discuss the centrality of self-employment in Anderson, *Private Government*, ch. 1.

1 The Dual Nature of the Protestant Work Ethic and the Birth of Utilitarianism

1. Catey Hill, "Would You Quit Your Job If You Won the Lottery? Many Say No," *MarketWatch*, May 27, 2016, available at: www.marketwatch.com/story/shocking-number-of-americans-keep-working-after-they-win-the-lottery-2016–05–24.

2. Isaac Kramnick, *Republicanism and Bourgeois Radicalism: Political Ideology in Late Eighteenth-Century England and America* (Ithaca, NY: Cornell University Press, 1990), 2.

3. Joan Williams and Heather Boushey, *The Three Faces of Work–Family Conflict* (Center for American Progress/Center for WorkLife Law, University of California, 2010), 53, available at: http://cdn.americanprogress.org/wp-content/uploads/issues/2010/01/pdf/threefaces.pdf.

4. Sylvia Hewlett and Carolyn Luce, "Extreme Jobs: The Dangerous Allure of the 70-Hour Workweek," *Harvard Business Review*, December 2006.

5. John Milton, *Paradise Lost* (1667), Book X, 1054–55, in *The Complete Poems* (New York: Penguin Books, 1998), 363. Thanks to Michael Schoenfeldt for pointing this out.

6. Weber, *Protestant Ethic*, 27, 113, 115.

7. John Maynard Keynes, "Economic Possibilities for Our Grandchildren" (1930), in *Revisiting Keynes: Economic Possibilities for Our Grandchildren*, eds. Lorenzo Pecchi and Gustavo Piga (Cambridge, MA: MIT Press, 2008), 24–25.

8. David Graeber, *Bullshit Jobs: A Theory* (New York: Simon & Schuster, 2018).

9. Both France under Macron and Germany under the Hartz reforms reduced unemployment by enabling the creation of precarious jobs with lower pay, unstable hours, and weaker employment protections.

10. Weber, *Protestant Ethic*, 17–18.

11. Weber observes that this is a characteristic of Calvinist denominations, in contrast to Lutheranism and other Protestant denominations focused on inner feelings of faith. Weber, *Protestant Ethic*, 63.

12. This terrifying doctrine postulates a deity who endows people with involuntary appetites and emotions such as lust and pride, and then condemns people to eternal damnation for sinfully yielding to them. To the secular, God's actions are appalling. From a Christian point of view, the identification of sin with involuntary thoughts, feelings, and behavior is a feature, not a bug. It demonstrates our depravity, and hence our dependence on God's grace for salvation. While training

to be a monk, Luther, in constant terror of damnation, spent hours every day confessing to endless faults, from farting to stumbling over his words in prayer. When every trivial involuntary imperfection is viewed as sin, each requiring an act of penance, the hopelessness of redemption through works becomes obvious. No wonder Luther viewed the doctrine of justification by faith alone as a huge relief, in allowing salvation for sinners unable to atone for every fault, and making belief in original sin irredeemable by one's own works not as a cause for despair, but a path to faith in God's grace. See Martin Luther, "The Heidelberg Disputation" (1518), Theses 17, 18, available at: https://bookofconcord.org/other-resources/sources-and-context/heidelberg-disputation, and Michael Massing, *Fatal Discord: Erasmus, Luther, and the Fight for the Western Mind* (New York: Harper, 2018), 125, 169–70, 187, 237–39.

13. Luther, "Heidelberg Disputation," Thesis 3. He explains Thesis 3 in Theses 7, 8, and 11.
14. Martin Luther, "The Bondage of the Will," in *Luther's Works*, vol. 33, eds. Philip Watson and Helmut Lehmann, trans. Philip Watson (St. Louis and Philadelphia: Concordia Publishing House and Fortress Press, 1972), 270.
15. Massing, *Fatal Discord*, 617, 628–58.
16. Massing, *Fatal Discord*, 706–7, 724–25, 761.
17. Luther, "Heidelberg Disputation," Thesis 26.
18. Martin Luther, "Commentary on Romans," in *Luther's Works*, vol. 35, ed. Hilton Oswald (St. Louis: Concordia Publishing House, 1973), 370–71.
19. Weber, *Protestant Ethic*, 41–43, 41n23.
20. Martin Luther, "Commentaries on 1 Corinthians 7," in *Luther's Works*, vol. 28, ed. Hilton Oswald (St. Louis: Concordia Publishing House, 1973), 39–40, 44–46.
21. Max Weber, *From Max Weber: Essays in Sociology*, eds. Hans Heinrich Gerth and C. Wright Mills (Oxford: Oxford University Press, 1946), 330–33.
22. Luther, "Heidelberg Disputation," Thesis 25.
23. In 1571, the Church of England incorporated Calvin's theology in Articles 9–18 of the 39 Articles of Religion. Article 13 follows Luther: works without faith "have the nature of sin."
24. Jean Calvin, *Institutes of the Christian Religion*, 7th American ed., trans. John Allen (Philadelphia: Presbyterian Board of Christian Education, 1936), vol. 2, 176 (bk. 3, ch. 21, sec. 5). Here I omit complexities in Luther's views. Richard Layton, "Martin Luther and John Calvin on Predestination," *Essays in History* 26 (1982): 5–18, argues that Luther did not ultimately disagree with Calvin on double predestination. Luther's successors deviated from Luther's doctrine in distinguishing single from double predestination, and God's foreknowledge from his willing of who would be damned.
25. *SER*, 186; cf. Article 11 of the 39 Articles.
26. *SER*, 225.
27. *SER*, 195, quoting 2 Pet. 10.
28. *SER*, 186.
29. *CD* II, 122.
30. *CD* V, 373.
31. Weber, *Protestant Ethic*, 112n107.
32. *SER*, v–vi.
33. See Jan de Vries, *The Industrious Revolution: Consumer Behavior and the Household Economy, 1650 to the Present* (New York: Cambridge University Press, 2008); Robert Allen and Jacob Weisdorf, "Was There an 'Industrious Revolution' before the Industrial Revolution? An Empirical Exercise for England,

c. 1300–1830," *Economic History Review* 64, no. 3 (2011): 715–29. De Vries, as befits an economist, credits the desire for consumer goods rather than the work ethic for workers' increased industriousness. However, he notes that the Reformed churches of England and the Netherlands abolished many holy days, thereby enabling a 20 percent increase in days worked per year (88). Allen and Weisdorf, while endorsing De Vries' consumerist thesis for urban workers, claim that agricultural workers increased their work effort simply to afford basic necessities, not to obtain new commodities. But see Gregory Clark and Ysbrand Van Der Werf, "Work in Progress? The Industrious Revolution," *Journal of Economic History* 58, no. 3 (1998): 830–43, casting doubt on the thesis that English workers increased their work effort before the Industrial Revolution.

34. Weber, *Protestant Ethic*, 63.
35. See Charles Taylor, *Sources of the Self* (Cambridge, MA: Harvard University Press, 1989), ch. 13, for further discussion of the theological underpinnings of nascent Puritan egalitarianism. Taylor stresses the Puritans' rejection of the idea that any time, place, person or specific activity (such as the Sabbath, a church, priest, or sacrament) brings us closer to God. This rejection opens the door to the sacralization of ordinary life.
36. William Perkins, *A Treatise of the Vocations, or, Callings of Men, with the Sorts and Kinds of Them, and the Right Use Thereof* (John Legat, Printer to University of Cambridge, 1603).
37. AP, 401.
38. AP, 403–4.
39. AP, 422–23.
40. AP, 404.
41. SER, 182.
42. CD II, ch. 5.
43. SER, 197, emphasis mine.
44. SER, 18.
45. CD I, 322; CD V, 478.
46. CD V, 373.
47. CD II, 88.
48. CD V, 367.
49. CD II, 72.
50. CD II, 583.
51. CD II, 122.
52. Weber, *Protestant Ethic*, 111.
53. CD V, 373.
54. CD II, 585.
55. CD II, 77.
56. E.g., CD I, 334.
57. AP, 400, 414.
58. CD III, 216.
59. Perkins, *Treatise of the Vocations*, 33.
60. CD III, 212–13.
61. CD III, 217.
62. CD III, 216.
63. CD III, 212.
64. John Angier, *An Helpe to Better Hearts for Better Times* (1647), 279.
65. AP, 407.

66. Taylor, *Sources of the Self*, 223–25, quotes numerous Puritan divines who stress the equality of callings. God loves any work, however menial, done in the right spirit, for the sake of serving others in fulfillment of God's commandment.
67. *CD* V, 209–10.
68. They were masterless in other ways, too – for example, literate, thinking for themselves, not dependent on priests to interpret the Bible for them. For discussion, see Don Herzog, *Happy Slaves* (Chicago: University of Chicago Press, 1989), ch. 2.
69. *AP*, 400.
70. *AP*, 410–11.
71. *CD* I, 333.
72. *CD* II, 579, quoting Gen. 3:19.
73. *CD* III, 187, 189–90.
74. *AP*, 417, 420–1.
75. *CD* III, 217.
76. *CD* V, 306–13.
77. *CD* V, 325.
78. *CD* V, 348.
79. *CD* V, 350, 351.
80. *CD* V, 356.
81. *CD* V, 357, 362.
82. *CD* V, 359.
83. *SER*, 194–95.
84. Richard Baxter, *Catholick Theologie* (London: printed by Robert White, for Nevill Simmons at the Princes Arms in St. Paul's Churchyard, 1675), I.ii, 51.
85. Bart Ehrman, *Jesus: Apocalyptic Prophet of the New Millennium* (Oxford: Oxford University Press, 1999), offers an accessible account of the consensus of Biblical scholars on this point.
86. Andrew Bradstock, *Radical Religion in Cromwell's England: A Concise History from the English Civil War to the End of the Commonwealth* (New York: I. B. Tauris, 2011).
87. *CD* II, 162; *CD* V, 356.
88. *CD* V, 479.
89. Peter Singer, *The Most Good You Can Do: How Effective Altruism Is Changing Ideas about Living Ethically* (New Haven: Yale University Press, 2015), vii.
90. Singer, *The Most Good*, 39–41.
91. Gertrude Himmelfarb, *The Idea of Poverty: England in the Early Industrial Age* (New York: Alfred A. Knopf, 1984), 35.
92. John Wesley, "The Use of Money – Luke 16:9" (Sermon 29), in *The Sermons of John Wesley: A Collection for the Christian Journey*, eds. Kenneth Collins and Jason Vickers (Nashville: Abingdon Press, 2013).
93. *CD* V, 373–74.
94. Baxter, unlike Locke, does not suggest that piling up a lot of gold avoids the no-waste requirement. Resources need to be put to timely use, lest they be wasted during the time they are left idle.
95. *CD* II, 72.
96. *CD* II, 162.
97. *CD* V, 490.
98. Baxter does not consider the possibility that business owners might reinvest their income to continuously grow their business as an end in itself. To seek endless accumulation of wealth as a *final* end is to commit the sin of covetousness. Wealth must be put to some use other than its accumulation in one's own hands. Puritans

do not appear to have entertained the possibility of endless economic growth, increasing *everyone's* material well-being. If they had – if, thereby, the poor would not always be with us – they would have had to confront an irresolvable contradiction among their commands to maximize earnings, waste nothing, and mortify the flesh.

99. *CD* V, 373; cf. *CD* I, 70; *CD* V, 374–75, 477–79.
100. *CD* V, 488; cf. Peter Singer, "Famine, Affluence, and Morality," *Philosophy & Public Affairs* 1, no. 3 (1972): 231.
101. Singer, *The Most Good*, 42–44.
102. *CD* II, 580.
103. *CD* V, 487.
104. Richard Cumberland, *De Legibus Naturæ Disquisitio Philosophica* (Londini: Typis E. Flesher, 1672) is commonly credited with inventing utilitarianism. Yet *A Christian Directory* was published in 1664–65. Cumberland may nevertheless be credited with a more systematic philosophical account of the theory.
105. *CD* V, 483.
106. *CD* V, 366–68.
107. This is the 14th of the 39 Articles of Religion. Classical utilitarianism, which defines the right act as the act that maximizes utility, agrees. J. S. Mill broke from orthodox utilitarianism in allowing for supererogation via his limitation of wrongdoing to acts that ought to be *punished* (CWM10, 246).

2 Locke and the Progressive Work Ethic

1. C. B. Macpherson, *The Political Theory of Possessive Individualism: Hobbes to Locke* (Oxford: Clarendon Press, 1962), ch. 5.
2. This reading takes Locke's famous theory of property in the *Second Treatise*, ch. 5, as its focal point. Although Macpherson was early to advance the account of how Locke justifies unlimited accumulation through wage labor, Robert Nozick supplied the first analytically rigorous libertarian reading of Locke. See *Anarchy, State, and Utopia*. Eric Mack offers a more textually sensitive libertarian interpretation of Locke that accepts some deviations from Nozick's orthodox reading, notably in allowing a limited right to charity. See *John Locke* (London: Bloomsbury Academic, 2013).
3. Richard Ashcraft, *Revolutionary Politics & Locke's Two Treatises of Government* (Princeton: Princeton University Press, 1986); Jacqueline Stevens, "The Reasonableness of John Locke's Majority: Property Rights, Consent, and Resistance in the Second Treatise," *Political Theory* 24, no.3 (1996): 423–63.
4. John Dunn, *The Political Thought of John Locke* (Cambridge: Cambridge University Press, 1969), offers a key reading of Locke as a follower of the work ethic. Kramnick's *Republicanism and Bourgeois Radicalism* offers an outstanding discussion of the role of the work ethic in late eighteenth-century liberalism. He considers Locke's influence in ch. 6.
5. Ashcraft, *Revolutionary Politics*, 145–53. Rates of enfranchisement peaked in the late seventeenth century and declined in the eighteenth century, not returning to their prior peak until the mid-nineteenth century. Richard Ashcraft, "The Radical Dimensions of Locke's Political Thought: A Dialogic Essay on Some Problems of Interpretation," *History of Political Thought* 13, no. 4 (1992): 749.
6. See Ashcraft, *Revolutionary Politics*, ch. 6, for a definitive account of the class conflict at issue in Locke's *Two Treatises*.
7. *2T*, §6.

8. 2T, §6.
9. 2T, §16.
10. 2T, §§6, 23. Locke's God-ownership argument does not contradict his claim that "every man has a property in his own person" (2T, §27). Locke distinguishes our *persons* from our *bodies*. To have property in our persons means that we are moral agents, accountable for our actions. But God has property in our bodies, in virtue of his creating us, and thereby lays down moral rules constraining our treatment of any body. See Don Herzog, *Without Foundations* (Ithaca, NY: Cornell University Press, 1985), 70–72; James Tully, *A Discourse on Property: John Locke and His Adversaries* (New York: Cambridge University Press, 1980), 105.
11. 2T, §8.
12. 2T, §6.
13. 2T, §5, emphasis mine.
14. The work ethic saturated moral and political discourse in seventeenth-century England, so much so that Locke takes its premises for granted. He was familiar with the work ethic not only from popular discourse, but as a scholar. Locke's library contained three books by Richard Baxter and three by Robert Sanderson. In his handwritten library catalog, Locke notes page references to four of these works, along with notes on Edmund Calamy's abridgment of Baxter's autobiography, showing that he had read them. John Harrison and Peter Laslett, *The Library of John Locke*, 2nd ed. (Oxford: Clarendon Press, 1971), 81, 99, 225.
15. 1T, §§21, 23, 33.
16. 1T, §45.
17. RoC, 9, quoting Rom. 4:4.
18. RoC, 8–9. Locke thus endorses Pelagianism, a doctrine condemned as heretical by the Council of Carthage in 418.
19. RoC, 13–14.
20. 2T, §6.
21. In RoC (139–40), Locke is less confident than he is in 2T about our ability to derive the foundations of morality or subordinate moral laws from reason alone. He does, however, cite Scripture in support of various work-ethic duties. We must avoid covetousness and lust, and practice asceticism. We must avoid pride, contempt for others, and self-exaltation – all offenses to our moral equality. We must not abuse our servants. We must give alms to the poor. We must love our neighbors and enemies alike, and express that love in compassion and service (RoC, 115–19). For "If any one will be first, let him be ... servant of all" (RoC, 117, quoting Mark 9:35).
22. Nozick, *Anarchy, State, and Utopia*, 175.
23. 2T, §32, emphasis mine.
24. 2T, §§26, 28.
25. 2T, §31.
26. 2T, §34.
27. See Nozick, *Anarchy, State, and Utopia*, 175–78; Mack, *Locke*, 61–74; Jeremy Waldron, *God, Locke, and Equality: Christian Foundations of John Locke's Political Thought* (New York: Cambridge University Press, 2002), 172–77.
28. 2T, §36.
29. 2T, §37.
30. 2T, §46.
31. 2T, §45.
32. 2T, §36.

33. *2T*, §41. Locke mistakenly supposes that indigenous Americans did not practice agriculture or trade. Indigenous Americans made their own judgments of Europeans: they had more possessions, but were covetous, ungenerous, and quarrelsome. They were shocked that Europeans did not care for their poor but left them to beg. David Graeber and David Wengrow, *The Dawn of Everything: A New History of Humanity* (New York: Farrar, Straus and Giroux, 2021), 38–39.
34. *2T*, §§40–44.
35. *2T*, §40.
36. *2T*, §43.
37. *2T*, §43.
38. Ashcraft, *Revolutionary Politics*, 272n181.
39. *2T*, §42.
40. As Ashcraft documents in *Revolutionary Politics*, ch. 3–6.
41. Waldron, *God, Locke, and Equality*, 176.
42. *2T*, §50.
43. Waldron, *God, Locke, and Equality*, 176.
44. CLI, 64.
45. *2T*, §§37, 46, 48.
46. *2T*, §48, 49.
47. Note that I am not claiming that Locke's remedy must be to equalize landholdings or to provide land to the poor. However, I shall argue that in the American colonial context, he came close to that view. For England, he proposed remedies other than land redistribution.
48. *2T*, §124.
49. *2T*, §125.
50. *2T*, §126.
51. *2T*, §33.
52. *2T*, §34.
53. *2T*, §38.
54. *2T*, §31; cf. §§39, 51.
55. *2T*, §124.
56. *2T*, §38.
57. *2T*, §45.
58. *2T*, §129, emphasis mine.
59. *2T*, §130.
60. *2T*, §89.
61. *2T*, §127.
62. *2T*, §131.
63. *2T*, §135.
64. *2T*, §57.
65. *1T*, §92.
66. *2T*, §138.
67. *2T*, §120.
68. Several Hands, "Agreement of the People" (1647), in *The English Levellers*, ed. Andrew Sharp (New York: Cambridge University Press, 1998), 92–101.
69. "Putney Debates," in *Puritanism and Liberty, Being the Army Debates (1647–9) from the Clarke Manuscripts with Supplementary Documents*, ed. A. S. P. Woodhouse (Chicago: University of Chicago Press, 1957), 1–124.
70. *2T*, §105.
71. *2T*, §§108–9.
72. *2T*, §110.

73. 2T, §§111–12, 162.
74. 2T, §111.
75. 2T, §§90–93.
76. 2T, §§215, 222.
77. 2T, §158.
78. 2T, §157.
79. Stevens, "Reasonableness of Locke's Majority," 433.
80. 2T, §143.
81. 2T, §§153–54.
82. Holly Brewer, "Slavery, Sovereignty, and 'Inheritable Blood': Reconsidering John Locke and the Origins of American Slavery," *American Historical Review* 122, no.4 (2017): 1067.
83. 2T, §150; cf. 2T, §149.
84. 2T, §§168, 220–33.
85. 2T, §132.
86. John Locke, "A Letter Concerning Toleration" (1689), in *The Works of John Locke in Nine Volumes*, 12th ed., vol. 5 (London: Rivington, 1824), 10–11.
87. 2T, §142.
88. 2T, §94, emphasis mine; cf. 2T, §§22, 87.
89. Ellen Wood, "Locke against Democracy: Consent, Representation and Suffrage in the Two Treatises," *History of Political Thought* 13, no. 4 (1992): 657–89, offers a characteristic example of this voluminous literature.
90. 2T, §138, emphasis mine.
91. 2T, §138.
92. 2T, §123.
93. Stevens, "Reasonableness of Locke's Majority," 434–35, argues that the Levellers advanced a similarly expansive definition of property, against the Grandees' complaint that the poor, having no property, lack any stake in the kingdom and hence should not have the vote. In a context where it was axiomatic that the state exists to protect the rights of property owners, an expansive conception of property is an argument for an expanded franchise. Soldiers in the Parliamentary army, having risked their lives for their country, ridiculed the claim that they had no stake in it.
94. 2T, §§128–30.
95. 2T, §§82, 85, 86.
96. As Waldron rightly insists for women, *God, Locke, and Equality*, ch. 2. Hence Carole Pateman's interpretation (*The Sexual Contract* [Stanford: Stanford University Press, 1988], 91–94), according to which husbands incorporate their wives into political society by disposing of their natural liberties in the social contract, contradicts Locke's account. However, Locke claims that where husband and wife disagree over matters for which marriage was instituted – mainly child-rearing – the husband "naturally" has the final authority, "as the abler and stronger" (2T, §82). He "grants" a "[f]oundation in nature" for laws and customs that subordinate wives to their husbands (1T, §47). These passages are hard to reconcile with Locke's insistence that consent alone legitimates authority relations. The trouble lies in his conceding any natural basis for authority, independent of consent, between rational adults. I think the best Locke can do is to note that the wife's consent to marriage is still necessary for the husband's authority over her, and that nothing in his theory forbids a different allocation of authority within marriage, either by positive law or prenuptial agreement. Still, what Waldron calls "an embarrassment for his general theory of equality" (p. 40) remains. Locke's allowance of a natural basis of authority threatens the strategy of 1T, to refute

Robert Filmer's grounding of absolute monarchy on the patriarchal premise of natural subjection to the authority of fathers and husbands. Filmer argued that the king was the father of his country and enjoyed absolute power over his subjects, as fathers and husbands have absolute power over their children and wives. (He also argued that the king enjoyed absolute authority over his subjects in virtue of his ownership of all the territory of his kingdom.) Robert Filmer, *Patriarcha: Or the Natural Power of Kings* (London: W. Davis, 1680). See Waldron's nuanced discussion of Locke's gender problem in *God, Locke, and Equality*, 28–43.

97. 2*T*, §§95–99.

98. Some scholars argue that the disenfranchised are made subject to the laws by Locke's doctrine of tacit consent (2*T*, §§117–21). However, Stevens, "Reasonableness of Locke's Majority," 441–43, argues that Locke ties tacit subjection to the state to ownership of land under its jurisdiction. Hence his argument is not addressing the poor but the rich, explaining why they cannot assert a right to internally secede from the state.

99. Ashcraft, *Revolutionary Politics*, 236.

100. 2*T*, §42.

101. CLI, 28, 29, 7, 55.

102. CLI, 20; cf. CLI, 53, 54, 71.

103. CLI, 41.

104. CLI, 20, 72.

105. CLI, 75.

106. John Locke, "Labour" (1693), in *Political Essays*, ed. Mark Goldie (Cambridge: Cambridge University Press, 1997), 327–28.

107. John Locke, "Venditio" (1695), available at: https://reconstructingeconomics.com/2014/06/06/venditio-by-john-locke.

108. Locke, "Venditio."

109. CLI, 5, 8.

110. Jeremy Bentham, "Defense of Usury" (1787), in *The Works of Jeremy Bentham*, vol. 3 (Edinburgh: William Tate, 1843), 1–29.

111. CLI, 64.

112. CLI, 64; cf. CLI, 8–9, 25.

113. CLI, 11.

114. Eric Mack, "In Defense of 'Unbridled' Freedom of Contract," *American Journal of Economics and Sociology* 40, no. 1 (1981): 8.

115. CLI, 12.

116. CLI, 62.

117. CLI, 29.

118. A figure of concern in CLI, 20.

119. 2*T*, §38.

120. John Locke, "Memorandum on Renewal of the Licensing Act" (1694), in *The Life of John Locke, with Extracts from His Correspondence, Journals, and Common-Place Books*, vol. 1, ed. Peter King (London: Henry Colburn and Richard Bentley, 1830), 379–80.

121. Locke, "Memorandum," §14.

122. Locke, "Memorandum," §11.

123. 1*T*, §41.

124. 1*T*, §42.

125. 1*T*, §43.

126. Charles Reid, "The Seventeenth-Century Revolution in the English Land Law," *Cleveland State Law Review* 43 (1995): 233–42.

127. *1T*, §92.
128. Under English law all private property since the Norman Conquest was enjoyed by grant from the Crown, with whatever incidents the Crown chose to attach to it, and all real estate ultimately belonged to the Crown. Locke's argument of 1T, §93, implies that even if one accepts William I's proprietorship of the entire realm, none of his successors inherited any of the feudal rights William had attached to the land. Locke rejects even the assumption that William I's conquest was legitimate in 2T, ch. 16.
129. *1T*, §93.
130. *1T*, §93.
131. Reid, "Revolution in English Land Law," 242.
132. *1T*, §88; cf. *1T*, §89.
133. *1T*, §89.
134. *1T*, §93; cf. *1T*, §91.
135. Brewer, "Slavery, Sovereignty, and Blood," 1045, 1065–67, 1070.
136. *2T*, §172.
137. By contrast, some libertarians accept slave contracts. See Nozick, *Anarchy, State, and Utopia*, 331; Walter Block, "Toward a Libertarian Theory of Inalienability: A Critique of Rothbard, Barnett, Smith, Kinsella, Gordon, and Epstein," *Journal of Libertarian Studies* 17, no. 2 (2003): 39–85; Larry Alexander, "Voluntary Enslavement," San Diego Legal Studies Paper No. 10–042 (2010), available at: http://ssrn.com/abstract=1694662.
138. *2T*, §23.
139. *2T*, §§182–83.
140. John Locke, "The Fundamental Constitutions of Carolina" (1669), in *The Works of John Locke in Nine Volumes*, 12th ed., vol. 9 (London: Rivington, 1824), 175–99.
141. Brewer, "Slavery, Sovereignty, and Blood," 1053–54. Additional details supplied by Brewer in personal correspondence, July 29, 2019.
142. Brewer, "Slavery, Sovereignty, and Blood," 1052.
143. David Armitage, "John Locke, Carolina, and the Two Treatises of Government," *Political Theory* 32, no. 5 (2004): 619.
144. Personal correspondence with Brewer, August 4, 2019.
145. Brewer, "Slavery, Sovereignty, and Blood," 1070–72.
146. The phrase is Alan Ryan's in "Locke and the Dictatorship of the Bourgeoisie," *Political Studies* 13, no. 2 (1965): 219–30, criticizing Macpherson's view.
147. Other scholars following Macpherson include Neal Wood, *John Locke and Agrarian Capitalism* (Berkeley: University of California Press, 1984); Wood, "Locke against Democracy."
148. *1T*, §93.
149. AP, 407.
150. Stevens, "Reasonableness of Locke's Majority," refutes Macpherson's arguments that the Levellers endorsed the disenfranchisement of wage laborers. She argues that Locke's arguments support a near-universal male franchise.
151. Locke, "Labour," 328.
152. *2T*, §28.
153. Macpherson, *Possessive Individualism*, 215–16, 218. Note, however, that the only thing in §28 that becomes my property is *cut* turfs, not the land from which the turfs have been cut.
154. *2T*, §86.
155. Evsey Domar, "The Causes of Slavery or Serfdom: A Hypothesis," *Journal of Economic History* 30, no. 1 (1970): 18–32.

156. There were other forms of customary tenure, where the customary rights were not written down. In addition, beneficial lessees held long-term leases nearly equivalent to copyholders. For simplicity, I shall use the term "copyholder" to refer to any peasant farmer with proprietary rights in the land short of freehold.
157. 2T, §37.
158. Wood, *Locke and Agrarian Capitalism*, 57–61.
159. Christopher Hill, *The World Turned Upside Down: Radical Ideas during the English Revolution* (New York: Penguin Books, 1991), 63, 119–23, 130.
160. 2T, §35.
161. Robert Allen, *Enclosure and the Yeoman: The Agricultural Development of the South Midlands, 1450–1850* (Oxford: Clarendon Press, 1992), 14, 54, 66–72.
162. It is worth quantifying this claim. The prime agricultural land of the South Midlands lay at the center of all waves of enclosure and controversies over it. There were three waves of enclosure in England: 1450–1524, 1575–1674, and 1750–1849. The first wave enclosed 7 percent of South Midlands land, the second, 18 percent, the third, 60 percent. Allen, *Enclosure and the Yeoman*, 29.
163. Wood, "Locke against Democracy," 680–82.
164. Reid, "Revolution in English Land Law," 250.
165. M. J. Daunton, *Progress and Poverty: An Economic and Social History of Britain 1700–1850* (Oxford: Oxford University Press, 1995), 109–10.
166. Reid, "Revolution in English Land Law," 260.
167. J. R. Wordie, "The Chronology of English Enclosure, 1500–1914," *Economic History Review* 36, no. 4 (1983): 483; Allen, *Enclosure and the Yeoman*, 28.
168. Reid, "Revolution in English Land Law," 259. Allen explains that this circuitous procedure was used to evade entails, so that landowners' heirs could not undo the agreement. Allen, *Enclosure and the Yeoman*, 27–28.
169. Daunton, *Progress and Poverty*, 72, 75, 102, 104. Allen estimates that in 1688, peasant proprietors held two-thirds of English land, half by freehold, half by copyhold. Allen, *Enclosure and the Yeoman*, 85.
170. Reid, "Revolution in English Land Law," 258. I further discuss the considerable bargaining power of the seventeenth-century yeomen, and their ability to blunt any negative impacts of enclosures, in Chapter 5.
171. 2T, §6.
172. 2T, §25.
173. 1T, §42.
174. Samuel Fleischacker, *A Short History of Distributive Justice* (Cambridge, MA: Harvard University Press, 2004), 25, 141n23.
175. PL, 382.
176. PL, 390.
177. 1T, §42.
178. PL, 382, 383.
179. Paul Slack, *Poverty and Policy in Tudor and Stuart England* (London: Longman, 1988), 27–31.
180. 1T, §93.
181. PL, 378.
182. PL, 378.
183. Steve Hindle, *On the Parish?: The Micro-Politics of Poor Relief in Rural England, c. 1550–1750* (New York: Oxford University Press, 2004), 13, 224–26.
184. PL, 380–81.
185. PL, 385–86, 390–91.
186. PL, 386.

187. Hindle, *On the Parish?*, ch. 3.
188. PL, 379–81.
189. PL, 380.
190. PL, 383–85.
191. PL, 384, 385.
192. Hindle, *On the Parish?*, 214, 194, 207–10.
193. Himmelfarb, *Idea of Poverty*, 25.
194. TCE, §129.
195. TCE, §§39, 63, 73, 74, 76, 108, 128, 130, 148–54.
196. TCE, §108.
197. PL, 383–84.
198. Hindle, *On the Parish?*, 186–87. Characteristically, national Poor Law reform followed rather than initiated parish experiments with modes of poor relief.

3 How Conservatives Hijacked the Work Ethic and Turned It against Workers

1. Gregory Clark, "Factory Discipline," *Journal of Economic History* 54, no.1 (1994): 128–63.
2. Robert Allen, "Engels' Pause: A Pessimist's Guide to the British Industrial Revolution," *Explorations in Economic History* 46, no. 4 (2009): 419–20.
3. As E. J. Hundert argues. "Market Society and Meaning in Locke's Political Philosophy," *Journal of the History of Philosophy* 15, no. 1 (1977): 39–40.
4. Christopher Hill, "The Bible in Seventeenth-Century English Politics," in *Tanner Lectures in Human Values*, vol. 14 (Salt Lake City: University of Utah Press, 1991), 105.
5. Weber, *Protestant Ethic*, 11–14.
6. There were also important thinkers on the side of the progressive work ethic who drew from or were influenced by Christian ideas through the late nineteenth and twentieth centuries. This includes Christian socialists such as R. H. Tawney, and British idealists T. H. Green, F. H. Bradley, and Bernard and Helen Bosanquet. We should also not forget a distinct Catholic tradition that could be described as a kind of progressive work ethic, although with different origins. Pope Leo XIII and Dorothy Day, a leader of the Catholic Worker Movement who founded the *Catholic Worker* newspaper, are pivotal figures in this tradition. I leave these actors aside, as my concern here is to trace the work ethic from its Puritan origins through its influence on the history of classical political economy.
7. *1T*, §92.
8. "Liberal tory" is an ideological designation, not a partisan one. Burke was a Whig.
9. *LH*, 355.
10. *LH*, 264.
11. *LH*, 249.
12. *LH*, 359.
13. *LH*, 357, 358.
14. CD II, 597, emphasis mine.
15. Joseph Priestley, *Letters to the Right Honourable Edmund Burke, Occasioned by His Reflections on the Revolution in France* (Birmingham: Thomas Pearson, 1791), 117.
16. *SEIP*, 5.
17. *SEIP*, 4. See also Joseph Priestley, *An Essay on the First Principles of Government, and on the Nature of Political, Civil, and Religious Liberty*, 2nd ed. (London: J. Johnson, 1771), 174.

18. *SEIP*, 4–5.
19. *SEIP*, 13.
20. *SEIP*, 14.
21. *SEIP*, 15.
22. *SEIP*, 12.
23. *SEIP*, 16–17.
24. *SEIP*, 15.
25. CLI, 60. In fact, Locke's argument is that *all* taxes ultimately fall on the landowner. Smith argued that not all taxes fall on the landowner, but taxes on rents do, assuming that the costs of improving the land are born by the landowner (*WN*, V.2.c.7–19).
26. *SEIP*, 6.
27. *CD* II, 587.
28. *CD* III, 189–90.
29. *CD* III, 187.
30. *PHM*, 10th epoch; AJ.
31. Nancy Fraser and Linda Gordon offer a more complex account of the idea of dependence and its development over centuries in "A Genealogy of Dependency: Tracing a Keyword of the U.S. Welfare State," *Signs* 19, no.2 (1994): 309–36.
32. William Hazlitt, *A Reply to the Essay on Population, by the Rev. T. R. Malthus* (London: Longman, Hurst, Rees, and Orme, 1807), 364.
33. Michel Foucault, *Discipline and Punish*, trans. Alan Sheridan (New York: Vintage Books, 1979), 205; Jeremy Bentham, *Panopticon, or The Inspection-House (1787), vol. 4 of The Works of Jeremy Bentham*, ed. John Bowring (Edinburgh: W. Tait, 1838), 40.
34. Himmelfarb, *Idea of Poverty*, 78. *Pauper Management Improved*, as published under that title in 1812, actually comprises SRP and *PMI* (entitled *Outline of a Work Entitled Pauper Management Improved*). As he was writing *PMI*, Bentham was also composing a longer manuscript entitled *Pauper Management Improved* which was never completed, and not published until 2010. See Jeremy Bentham, *Writings on the Poor Laws*, vol. 2, ed. Michael Quinn (Oxford: Clarendon Press, 2010), xvii–xix, for a discussion of the relationship of these two works.
35. SRP, 4–5.
36. Bentham denies that compelling the poor to work in panopticons amounts to punishment. He insists that it's more like the enforcement of truancy law (*PMI*, 147). However, Jacob Abolafia, *The Prison before the Panopticon: Incarceration and the History of Political Philosophy* (Cambridge, MA: Harvard University Press, in press), ch. 6, persuasively argues that Bentham is unable to clearly distinguish punitive from purportedly nonpunitive uses of the panopticon.
37. Hindle, *On the Parish?*, 187.
38. Bentham's critique of state management was partly grounded in personal experience. He had wasted years on fruitless negotiations with Treasury and Home Office officials on his plan to win a government contract to operate a for-profit panopticon prison. He contrasted his initiative and elaborate planning to the confusion, lethargy, and uncooperativeness of government officials. L. J. Hume, *Bentham and Bureaucracy* (New York: Cambridge University Press, 1981), 138.
39. SRP, 8; *PMI*, 9–10.
40. SRP, 29.
41. Bentham's aesthetic of geometrical symmetry neglects huge variations in population density across England.

42. *PMI*, 7, 41, 146; *SRP*, 35–39.
43. *PMI*, 218–19.
44. *PMI*, 5.
45. *PMI*, 62.
46. *PMI*, 54–55, 126.
47. *PMI*, 94–95.
48. *PMI*, 66.
49. *PMI*, 81–82.
50. *PMI*, 62–63.
51. *PMI*, 171.
52. *PMI*, 87–88.
53. *WN*, V.2.k.3.
54. *PMI*, 28–29, 42–44.
55. *PMI*, 52, 56–57.
56. *PMI*, 54–56.
57. Isaac Kramnick stresses that Bentham was joined by many other bourgeois radicals at the time in proposing such plans. "Though these radicals preached independence, freedom, and autonomy in polity and market, they preached order, routine, and subordination in factory, school, poorhouse, and prison." Kramnick, *Republicanism and Bourgeois Radicalism*, 97.
58. *PMI*, 39, emphasis in original.
59. *PMI*, 16.
60. *PMI*, 70.
61. *PMI*, 34.
62. *PMI*, 97.
63. *PMI*, 57.
64. *PMI*, 121–22.
65. *PMI*, 146.
66. Weber, *Protestant Ethic*, 70.
67. *PMI*, 101.
68. John Wesley, "On Dress" (1778) (Sermon 88), in *The Works of the Rev. John Wesley, A.M.*, vol. 7 (London: J. Mason, 1837), 15.
69. *PMI*, 267–71.
70. *PMI*, 135.
71. Weber, *Protestant Ethic*, 58. "Now, he had not run far from his own door, but his wife and children, perceiving it, began to cry after him to return; but the man put his fingers in his ears, and ran on, crying, Life! life! eternal life! [Luke 14:26] So he looked not behind him, but fled towards the middle of the plain. [Gen. 19:17]" Paul Bunyan, *The Pilgrim's Progress* (1678) (Project Gutenberg, 1994), 18.
72. *PMI*, 128; *SRP*, 25–26.
73. *SRP*, 16.
74. *PMI*, 234.
75. Jeremy Bentham, *Writings on the Poor Laws*, vol. 1, ed. Michael Quinn (Oxford: Clarendon, 2001), 191. What of the fact that under his plan, indigent children are separated from their parents from infancy, whereas rich children are not sent to boarding school until they are eight years old? And that indigent children may only work, whereas rich children enjoy play at boarding school? Bentham replies that pleasures never previously experienced will never be missed. Hence indigent children will not suffer from these deprivations. "No home, no hardship." Ibid., 213.
76. *PMI*, 159.
77. *SRP*, 32.

78. The demographics of the workhouse population during the Victorian era show how hopeless was the prospect of operating them profitably. Because entering the workhouse entailed a complete loss of freedom and dignity, very few able-bodied male inmates were found in periodic workhouse headcounts. Only the absolutely desperate would enter. The vast majority were the elderly, disabled, sick, insane, widows, orphans, and other children – people who could not support themselves with their own labor. Derek Fraser, *The Evolution of the British Welfare State: A History of Social Policy since the Industrial Revolution*, 4th ed. (New York: Palgrave Macmillan, 2009), 68.

79. *WN*, V.2.k.74.

80. Bentham, *Writings on the Poor Laws*, vol. 1, 278.

81. Hume, *Bentham and Bureaucracy*, 134–35.

82. Vinita Damodaran, "Famine in Bengal: A Comparison of the 1770 Famine in Bengal and the 1897 Famine in Chotanagpur," *Medieval History Journal* 10, no. 1–2 (2007): 149–54.

83. As I have argued in *Value in Ethics and Economics* (Cambridge, MA: Harvard University Press, 1993), ch. 4.

84. Jeremy Bentham, *The Rationale of Reward* (London: R. Heward, 1830), 206.

85. Thanks to Don Herzog for alerting me to this delicious passage in his *Poisoning the Minds of the Lower Orders* (Princeton: Princeton University Press, 1998), 236, quoting Jeremy Bentham, "Jeremy Bentham to Greek Legislators" (1823), in *Securities against Misrule and Other Constitutional Writings for Tripoli and Greece*, ed. Philip Schofield (Oxford: Clarendon Press, 1990), 194. Herzog cites numerous other egalitarian passages from Bentham.

86. *PMI*, 152.

87. *PMI*, 162. He also laments the gifts people give to beggars, pointing to the disutility to workers of seeing beggars enjoy any luxury as a reason to force beggars into slavery (*PMI*, 142). If the purpose of the utilitarian calculus is to replace inegalitarian prejudice with impartial reasoning, then allowing resentment against those less advantaged than oneself to count as disutility is self-defeating. Bentham's system is more generally vulnerable to letting in the back door precisely the arbitrary and tyrannical moral judgments he wanted to exclude, insofar as it allows moral feelings such as resentment and anger, based on nonutilitarian judgments, to count in the hedonic calculus. See Jeremy Bentham, *The Principles of Morals and Legislation* (New York: Hafner Press, 1948), ch. 2.

88. *PoP1*, 10.

89. William Godwin, *An Enquiry Concerning Political Justice, and Its Influence on General Virtue and Happiness* (London: G. G. J. and J. Robinson, 1793).

90. *PoP1*, 26.

91. *PoP1*, 27.

92. *PoP1*, 31.

93. Gregory Clark, *A Farewell to Alms: A Brief Economic History of the World* (Princeton: Princeton University Press, 2007). Clark credits natural selection of individuals disposed to practice the work ethic for the West's emergence from the Malthusian trap. But see Robert Allen, "A Review of Gregory Clark's *A Farewell to Alms: A Brief Economic History of the World*," *Journal of Economic Literature* 46, no. 4 (2008): 946–73, for a skeptical view.

94. *PoP6.2*, 142.

95. *PoP1*, 24, 36.

96. *PoP6.2*, 7, 18.

97. *PoP1*, 29, 45; *PoP6.2*, 37–38.

98. *PoP6.2*, 194.
99. This was an old complaint about "indoor relief" offered to the destitute in work-houses. Daniel Defoe, better known as the author of *Robinson Crusoe*, opposed workhouses on this ground a century earlier. See *Giving Alms No Charity, and Employing the Poor a Grievance to the Nation* (London: Printed and sold by the booksellers of London and Westminster, 1704). Bentham, imagining that for-profit workhouses run by private entrepreneurs would be extremely efficient, did not answer the charge that they would force independent workers into them.
100. *PoP1*, 27; *PoP6.2*, 31, 39, 40, 42. Malthus's reasoning relies on the wages-fund theory, according to which the amount of money available to support the working classes is fixed by the size of the capital stock. On this view, poor relief simply redistributes this amount from the deserving to the undeserving poor.
101. *PoP6.2*, 153.
102. *PoP6.2*, 134.
103. *PoP1*, 30; *PoP6.2*, 39.
104. *PoP1*, 32.
105. *PoP6.2*, 48n28, 138–39.
106. *PoP1*, 30; *PoP6.2*, 38.
107. *PoP6.2*, 50, 89–90.
108. *PoP6.2*, 117, emphasis mine.
109. *PoP6.2*, 118–19.
110. *PoP6.2*, 107.
111. *PoP6.2*, 119.
112. *PoP6.2*, 38.
113. *PoP6.2*, 39.
114. *PoP6.2*, 140.
115. *PoP6.2*, 141.
116. *PoP1*, 94.
117. *PoP1*, 95.
118. *PoP1*, 97–100; *PoP6.2*, 107.
119. *PoP6.2*, 151.
120. *PoP6.2*, 154.
121. 2*T*, §142.
122. *PoP1*, 78, 79.
123. *PoP6.2*, 57.
124. *PoP1*, 45.
125. *PoP6.2*, 38.
126. *PoP6.2*, 176.
127. Charles Tilly, *Popular Contention in Great Britain, 1758–1834* (London: Routledge, 2005), 197, 201.
128. RC, 3–4.
129. RC, 5.
130. RC, 8–9.
131. RC, 10.
132. RC, 12.
133. RC, 14.
134. RC, 16.
135. RC, 15.
136. RC, 11.
137. RC, 12.
138. RC, 16.

139. RC, 15.
140. CD II, 162.
141. Fred Block and Margaret Somers, *The Power of Market Fundamentalism: Karl Polanyi's Critique* (Cambridge, MA: Harvard University Press, 2014), 143.
142. HRC, 393–94.
143. RC, 14.
144. HRC, 401–2.
145. Hazlitt, *Reply to Malthus*, 365.
146. HRC, 397–98.
147. RC, 5, 6.
148. Tilly, *Popular Contention in Great Britain*, 204–5.
149. Compare RC, 17–19, with *TMS*, III.3.31.
150. *TMS*, I.3.2.2.
151. *TMS*, I.3.2.1.
152. RC, 13.
153. Peter Mandler, "Tories and Paupers: Christian Political Economy and the Making of the New Poor Law," *The Historical Journal* 33, no.1 (1990): 84.
154. Mandler, "Tories and Paupers," 83–84.
155. *RRF*, 142.
156. *RRF*, 170.
157. TDS, 67.
158. *RRF*, 170–71.
159. TDS, 61.
160. TDS, 62.
161. Paul Slack, *The English Poor Law, 1531–1782* (Basingstoke: Macmillan, 1995), 35.
162. Margaret Somers, "Citizenship and the Place of the Public Sphere: Law, Community, and Political Culture in the Transition to Democracy," *American Sociological Review* 58, no.5 (1993): 603–4.
163. TDS, 64.
164. TDS, 65.
165. TDS, 69.
166. TDS, 68–69.
167. TDS, 81.
168. TDS, 70.
169. TDS, 67, 76.
170. TDS, 72.
171. PoP6.2, 139.
172. Bruce Scott, *Capitalism: Its Origins and Evolution as a System of Governance* (New York: Springer, 2011).
173. Harcourt, *The Illusion of Free Markets*.
174. William Blackstone, *Commentaries on the Laws of England*, vol. 1, 1st ed. (Oxford: Clarendon Press, 1765), 413–14.
175. TDS, 64.
176. Margaret Somers argues that national wage regulations had different effects in the arable and pastoral/rural industrial regions due to regional differences in the power of landlords and in the political solidarity and associational capacities of workers. In arable districts, landlords controlled the appointment of justices of the peace (JPs), and agricultural laborers were atomized and disempowered. JPs therefore set maximum wage rates. In pastoral/rural industrial districts, landlords were weak and workers had greater solidarity due to the prevalence of partible inheritance. Younger sons would

stay in the community given the prospect of inheritance, enabling stronger associational practices and worker participation in selecting local JPs and constables, who were drawn from the workers' ranks. Hence, local officials set minimum-wage rates. Somers, "Citizenship and the Place of the Public Sphere," 599–606.

177. E. Merrick Dodd, "From Maximum Wages to Minimum Wages: Six Centuries of Regulation of Employment Contracts," *Columbia Law Review* 43, no. 5 (1943): 648–49.
178. Corey Robin offers an excellent discussion of this point, taking Burke as an exemplar, in *The Reactionary Mind: Conservatism from Edmund Burke to Sarah Palin* (New York: Oxford University Press, 2011), ch. 1.
179. Mandler, "Tories and Paupers," 103.
180. Mandler, "Tories and Paupers," 84–86.
181. Mandler, "Tories and Paupers," 87.
182. *LPE*, 101.
183. *LPE*, 106–7.
184. *LPE*, 122–24.
185. *LPE*, 139.
186. *LPE*, 147.
187. Bernard Mandeville, *The Fable of the Bees or Private Vices, Publick Benefits* (Indianapolis: Liberty Fund, 1988). Vol. 1 first published in 1714, vol. 2 in 1729.
188. *LPE*, 46.
189. *LPE*, 149, 162.
190. *LPE*, 56.
191. *LPE*, 149–50.
192. *LPE*, 193.
193. *RCI*3, 7.

4 Welfare Reform, Famine, and the Ideology of the Conservative Work Ethic

1. Block and Somers, *Market Fundamentalism*, 135–36; Mark Blaug, "The Myth of the Old Poor Law and the Making of the New," *Journal of Economic History* 23, no. 2 (1963): 162.
2. Fred Block and Margaret Somers, "In the Shadow of Speenhamland: Social Policy and the Old Poor Law," *Politics & Society* 31, no. 2 (2003): 309–10.
3. Gregory Clark and Marianne Page, "Welfare Reform, 1834: Did the New Poor Law in England Produce Significant Economic Gains?" *Cliometrica* 13, no. 2 (2019): 222.
4. Thomas Paine, *Rights of Man. Part the Second. Combining Principle and Practice*, 8th ed. (London: J. S. Jordan, 1792), is a classic late eighteenth-century source of this critique.
5. Peter Lindert, "Poor Relief before the Welfare State: Britain versus the Continent, 1780–1880," *European Review of Economic History* 2, no. 2 (1998): 114.
6. Mark Blaug, "The Poor Law Report Reexamined," *Journal of Economic History* 24, no. 2 (1964): 229–31.
7. Blaug, "Myth of the Old Poor Law," 177.
8. *PLC*, 49.
9. *PLC*, 59.
10. *PLC*, 43; cf. *SEIP*, 5.
11. *PLC*, 44, 51, 63–64.
12. *PLC*, 227.
13. *PLC*, 262.

14. Hindle, *On the Parish?*, 2–14, 92–95, 171–81, 445–49.
15. Himmelfarb, *Idea of Poverty*, 159–66.
16. *PLC*, 264–68.
17. *PLC*, 276.
18. Himmelfarb, *Idea of Poverty*, 175–76.
19. Mandler, "Tories and Paupers."
20. Mandler, "Tories and Paupers," 101. Fraser, *The Evolution of the British Welfare State*, 68, argues that the overriding goal of deterring able-bodied men from applying for aid led to workhouses largely populated by people who couldn't work, for whom therefore deterrence was irrelevant. They were subject to gratuitous deprivation and humiliation in order to deter a different population.
21. Gulielmi IV Regis, CAP. LXXVI, Articles 15, 23, 52, available at: www .workhouses.org.uk/poorlaws/1834act.shtml.
22. Clark and Page, "Welfare Reform, 1834," 222; Blaug, "Myth of the Old Poor Law," 157.
23. Norman Longmate, *The Workhouse* (New York: St. Martin's Press, 1974), 94–95.
24. *Digest of the Evidence Taken before the Select Committee of the House of Commons on Andover Union* (London: J. Murray, 1846), 180–91.
25. Blaug, "Poor Law Report Reexamined," 231, 233, 242.
26. Block and Somers, "Shadow of Speenhamland," 294–97.
27. Allen, *Enclosure and the Yeoman*, 269, 288–90, 301.
28. Blaug, "Myth of the Old Poor Law," 151, 170; Block and Somers, *Market Fundamentalism*, 134, 136–41.
29. Block and Somers, *Market Fundamentalism*, 138–39.
30. Blaug, "Myth of the Old Poor Law," 154.
31. Clark and Page, "Welfare Reform, 1834."
32. Himmelfarb, *Idea of Poverty*, 167.
33. John-Paul McGauran and John Offer, "Christian Political Economics, Richard Whately and Irish Poor Law Theory," *Journal of Social Policy* 44, no. 1 (2015): 50–51; Christine Kinealy, *This Great Calamity: The Irish Famine, 1845–52* (Dublin: Gill & Macmillan, 1994), 17.
34. Kinealy, *This Great Calamity*, 15.
35. *RCI3*, 4–6.
36. *RCI3*, 8, 17–21.
37. *RCI3*, 25.
38. *RCI3*, 31–33.
39. *RCI3*, 23–24.
40. *PLI*, 12, 23–24, 49.
41. *PLI*, 14, 43.
42. *PoP6.2*, 185–86.
43. *PLI*, 15–16.
44. *PoP6.2*, 54–55, 157–59.
45. *PLI*, 38.
46. Kinealy, *This Great Calamity*, 168, 297, 343.
47. Slack, *Poverty and Policy in Tudor and Stuart England*, 50, 52, 145–46.
48. Kinealy, *This Great Calamity*, 43.
49. Cecil Woodham-Smith, *The Great Hunger* (London: Hamish Hamilton, 1962), 75–76. Banning exports would not have prevented famine, as Ireland was forced to become a net food importer at the height of the crisis. It would have bankrupted the commercial farmers, causing a deeper economic disaster. Although, as

Woodham-Smith notes, food exports stimulated great resentment of British rule, Russell was not wrong to resist calls for an export ban.

50. Kinealy, *This Great Calamity*, 53.

51. Kinealy, *This Great Calamity*, 99.

52. Cormac Ó Gráda, *Ireland before and after the Famine: Explorations in Economic History, 1800–1925*, 2nd ed. (New York: Manchester University Press, 1993), 103.

53. Kinealy, *This Great Calamity*, 91–95.

54. Kinealy, *This Great Calamity*, 87.

55. Kinealy, *This Great Calamity*, 30.

56. Ó Gráda, *Ireland before and after the Famine*, 18–21.

57. Kinealy, *This Great Calamity*, 4.

58. Nassau Senior, *Journals, Conversations, and Essays Relating to Ireland*, 2nd ed. (London: Longmans, Green, and Co., 1868), 215–17.

59. Kinealy, *This Great Calamity*, 137–52.

60. Richard Whately, *Substance of a Speech Delivered in the House of Lords, on Friday, the 26th of March, 1847, on the Motion for a Committee on Irish Poor Laws* (London: B. Fellowes, 1847), vi.

61. Whately, *Substance of a Speech*, 16, 17, 20.

62. G. Poulett Scrope, *Reply to the Speech of the Archbishop of Dublin, Delivered in the House of Lords, on Friday, March 26th, 1847* (London: James Ridgway, Piccadilly, 1847), 2, 4, 5.

63. Scrope, *Reply to . . . the Archbishop of Dublin*, 14.

64. Ó Gráda, *Ireland before and after the Famine*, 129.

65. Kinealy, *This Great Calamity*, 195, 246, 252.

66. Edward O'Boyle, "Classical Economics and the Great Irish Famine: A Study in Limits," *Forum for Social Economics* 35, no. 2 (2006): 21–53.

67. Ó Gráda, *Ireland before and after the Famine*, 128, quoting Alexis de Tocqueville, *Correspondence & Conversations of Alexis de Tocqueville with Nassau William Senior from 1834 to 1859*, ed. M. C. M. Simpson (London: H. S. King & Co., 1872), 52.

68. Woodham-Smith, *The Great Hunger*, 373.

69. For an explanation of how this can be so, see Elizabeth Anderson and Richard Pildes, "Expressive Theories of Law: A General Restatement," *University of Pennsylvania Law Review* 148, no. 5 (2000): 1503–75; Margaret Gilbert, "Modeling Collective Belief," *Synthese* 73 (1987): 185–204; Margaret Gilbert, *Sociality and Responsibility* (Lanham, MD: Rowman and Littlefield, 2000).

70. See Bernardo Zacka, *When the State Meets the Street: Public Service and Moral Agency* (Cambridge, MA: Belknap Press of Harvard University Press, 2017) for a nuanced study of the variety of attitudes and emotions individual street-level bureaucrats have toward the rules they are expected to enforce, and toward the people they are expected to serve.

71. I thank Leif Wenar for critical comments that helped me to clarify my position on this issue, and for informing me about Chadwick's career.

72. *MECW* 35, part VIII.

73. *TDS*, 64.

74. *RCI* 3, 5.

75. The seminal study of this theory is Lee Ross, "The Intuitive Psychologist and His Shortcomings: Distortions in the Attribution Process," *in Advances in Experimental Social Psychology*, vol. 10, ed. Roger Berkowitz (New York: Academic Press, 1977), 173–220.

76. Steve Clarke, "Appealing to the Fundamental Attribution Error: Was It All a Big Mistake?" in *Conspiracy Theories: The Philosophical Debate*, ed. David Coady (London: Routledge, 2006), summarizes evidence that this attribution error is primarily found in the West. Thomas Pettigrew, "The Ultimate Attribution Error: Extending Allport's Cognitive Analysis of Prejudice," *Personality and Social Psychology Bulletin* 5, no. 4 (1979): 466, cites evidence that observers are liable to reverse attributions for high-status individuals, attributing their negative traits to circumstance and their positive features to their internal dispositions.

77. I thank Manuali Lorenzo for this suggestion.

78. Ó Gráda, *Ireland before and after the Famine*, 132.

79. O'Boyle, "Classical Economics and the Great Irish Famine," 40.

80. *PoP*6.2, 149–51.

81. William Thompson, *Labor Rewarded. The Claims of Labor and Capital Conciliated: Or, How to Secure to Labor the Whole Product of Its Exertions, by One of the Idle Classes* (London: Hunt and Clarke, 1827), 102.

82. Finn Dwyer, "Landlords & Mass Evictions," in *Irish History Podcast: The Great Famine XXXII* (2019), 27:08–30:50, available at: https://irishhistorypodcast.ie /landlords-mass-evictions-exploiting-the-great-hunger.

5 The Progressive Work Ethic (1): Smith, Ricardo, and Ricardian Socialists

1. Allen, "Engels' Pause."
2. Kinealy, *This Great Calamity*, 249.
3. *WN*, V.1.f.50.
4. *TDS*, 62.
5. *WN*, I.8. As noted by Emma Rothschild, *Economic Sentiments: Adam Smith, Condorcet, and the Enlightenment* (Cambridge, MA: Harvard University Press, 2001), 64. I have corrected her count.
6. *TMS*, 3.3.2.
7. *TMS*, 3.3.2–7.
8. *TMS*, 7.2.1.49.
9. *LJA*, 56–57, 66, 105, 117, 363.
10. *TMS*, 2.2.2.1.
11. *TMS*, 1.3.3.1.
12. *TMS*, 1.3.3.2.
13. *TMS*, I.3.3.4.
14. *TMS*, 1.3.2.1.
15. *TMS*, 1.3.2.1.
16. *TMS*, 1.3.2.2.
17. Smith's view of class biases in attribution is more sophisticated than the fundamental attribution error. It's that we tend to attribute socially disapproved conduct to vice and socially approved conduct to external factors if the target is a social inferior, and tend to make the reverse attribution if the target is a social superior. Smith's claims have empirical support. See Pettigrew, "Ultimate Attribution Error," 466.
18. *WN*, I.8.45.
19. *WN*, I.8.44.
20. *WN*, I.8.48.
21. *WN*, I.10.2.14.
22. *WN*, II.3.28.
23. *TMS*, 1.3.2.5.

24. *TMS*, 5.2.9.
25. *WN*, I.11.p.8.
26. *WN*, I.11.p.10; *WN*, I.10.c.27.
27. *WN*, II.3.36.
28. *WN*, V.1.g.10.
29. *LJA*, 297–98; cf. *LJB*, 419.
30. *ED*, 474.
31. *WN*, I.6.8; *WN*, I.6.24.
32. *LJB*, 419–21; *WN*, I.1.4; *WN*, I.10.c.24; *WN*, IV.9.33–35.
33. *WN*, I.10.c.17–26.
34. Carl Menger, "Die Social-Theorien der Classischen National-Oekonomie und die Moderne Wirthschaftspolitik," in *Kleinere Schriften Zur Methode und Geschichte der Volkswirtschaftslehre* (London: London School of Economics, 1891), 223. Quoted in translation in Rothschild, *Economic Sentiments*, 65.
35. Samuel Fleischacker, *On Adam Smith's* Wealth of Nations: *A Philosophical Companion* (Princeton: Princeton University Press, 2004), 195–96.
36. *TMS*, 7.2.3.16.
37. *TMS*, 6.3.1.
38. *TMS*, 6.1.11.
39. *TMS*, 4.2.6.
40. *TMS*, 4.2.8; cf. *TMS*, 6.3.13, 7.2.3.16.
41. Quoted in Daniel Baugh, "Poverty, Protestantism, and Political Economy: English Attitudes Toward the Poor, 1660–1800," in *England's Rise to Greatness, 1660–1763*, ed. Stephen Baxter (Berkeley: University of California Press, 1983), 103n74. Young also suggests that the unemployed poor be used as cannon fodder to prevent their weighing down the industrious. Fleischacker, *Distributive Justice*, 85.
42. *WN*, II.3.36.
43. *WN*, I.11.d.1.
44. *WN*, I.1.10.
45. *WN*, IV.9.47.
46. *WN*, I.1.8.
47. *LJB*, 460.
48. *WN*, V.1.g.12, 15.
49. *WN*, III.4.
50. *WN*, III.4.5–6.
51. *WN*, III.4.10.
52. *WN*, III.4.10.
53. *WN*, III.4.3.
54. *WN*, III.4.4.
55. Allen, *Enclosure and the Yeoman*, 67–71, 206–10, 235, 240–41.
56. Allen, *Enclosure and the Yeoman*, 95–104, 240–52.
57. Allen, *Enclosure and the Yeoman*, 19, 200–10, 248.
58. Somers, "Citizenship and the Public Sphere," 601–2, distinguishes inheritance patterns in arable and pastoral regions of England. In the feudal era, manorial lords dominated arable regions and enforced primogeniture. Villagers in the relatively poor pastoral regions enjoyed substantial independence from the lords, and practiced partible inheritance.
59. *LJA*, 79.
60. *LJA*, 92; cf. *WN*, III.2.6.
61. *LJA*, 82–84.
62. *LJA*, 93.

63. *WN*, III.2.20.
64. *WN*, III.2.7.
65. *WN*, III.2.8–13.
66. *LJA*, 93; cf. *WN*, III.4.19.
67. *WN*, III.2.10.
68. *LJA*, 179.
69. *WN*, I.2.2.
70. As I argue in greater detail in *Private Government*, 1–4, 17–22.
71. *WN*, V.1.e.18–27.
72. *WN*, I.9.20.
73. *WN*, III.8; *LJA*, 172–85.
74. *LJA*, 178–80; *WN*, IV.7.b.54–55.
75. *LJA*, 178.
76. Fleischacker, *On Adam Smith's* Wealth of Nations, 247.
77. *LJA*, 176, 180.
78. *WN*, I.10.6.8.
79. *WN*, I.10.c.12.
80. *WN*, I.10.c.22. Margaret Somers, "The 'Misteries' of Property: Relationality, Rural-Industrialization, and Community in Chartist Narratives of Political Rights," in *Early Modern Conceptions of Property*, eds. John Brewer and Susan Staves (London: Routledge, 2014), 62–92, argues that Smith underestimated the value of apprenticeship to workers, particularly in rural-industrial textile manufacturing. This industry was not governed by guilds but by associated families in pastoral villages. Apprenticeship comprised a kind of property in social capital that supported the labor movement in its demands for political rights as well as higher wages.
81. *WN*, I.10.c.4.
82. *WN*, IV.8.45.
83. *WN*, IV.8.49.
84. *WN*, IV.8.4.
85. *WN*, IV.8.30.
86. *WN*, IV.7.b.2–3.
87. *WN*, IV.7.a.15–16; *WN*, IV.7.b.7; cf. *WN*, IV.7.b.57.
88. *WN*, IV.7.b.44.
89. *WN*, IV.7.c.29.
90. *WN*, I.8.35.
91. *WN*, I.8.36.
92. Baugh, "Poverty, Protestantism, Political Economy," 76–78.
93. *WN*, IV.7.c.61.
94. *WN*, IV.7.b.11; *WN*, IV.7.c.103–4.
95. *WN*, I.8.26.
96. *WN*, IV.7.c.101.
97. Rothschild, *Economic Sentiments*, 108.
98. *WN*, 1.1.
99. *WN*, V.1.f.50.
100. *WN*, I.10.c.24–25. This passage reflects Smith's ignorance of how far the condition of the typical farm laborer had already fallen in his day. The eighteenth-century consolidation of farms into large estates enabled a more fine-grained division of agricultural labor. This process deskilled most workers, who were reduced to single tasks, such as ploughing or harvesting, and thus could be employed part-time as precarious day laborers at lower wages than servants on annual contracts. Allen

criticizes the division of eighteenth-century English agricultural labor in the same terms that Smith criticizes the division of manufacturing labor. Allen, *Enclosure and the Yeoman*, 219–20, 289–90.

101. *WN*, V.1.f.51.
102. *WN*, V.1.f.54.
103. *WN*, V.1.f.61.
104. Cf. Paley's recommendations in "Reasons for Contentment," 3–4.
105. Rothschild, *Economic Sentiments*, 97–98.
106. *WN*, II.2.90.
107. *WN*, II.2.91.
108. *WN*, II.2.94.
109. Bentham, "Defense of Usury."
110. *WN*, II.4.15.
111. *WN*, I.10.2.61.
112. Rothschild, *Economic Sentiments*, ch. 2.
113. Dugald Stewart, *Account of the Life and Writings of Adam Smith, LL.D from the Transactions of the Royal Society of Edinburgh* (Edinburgh: S.N., 1794).
114. TDS, 53.
115. Rothschild, *Economic Sentiments*, 64.
116. Rothschild, *Economic Sentiments*, 61.
117. *WN*, I.10.c.45–59.
118. *WN*, I.10.c.56.
119. *WN*, I.10.c.59.
120. Kinealy, *This Great Calamity*, 180.
121. *WN*, IV.5.b.
122. *WN*, IV.5.b.5.
123. *WN*, IV.5.b.5; cf. *WN*, IV.5.b.21.
124. *WN*, IV.5.b.43.
125. *WN*, IV.5.b.3–25.
126. *WN*, IV.5.b.36.
127. *WN*, IV.5.b.31–34, 38.
128. Baugh, "Poverty, Protestantism, Political Economy," 87.
129. *WN*, IV.5.b.38.
130. *WN*, IV.5.b.39.
131. *TMS*, 6.2.2.17.
132. See, e.g., James Otteson, "Adam Smith and the Right," in *Adam Smith: His Life, Thought, and Legacy*, ed. Ryan Hanley (Princeton: Princeton University Press, 2016), 494–511.
133. *TMS*, 6.2.2.18.
134. Fraser, *Evolution of the British Welfare State*, 67. This estimate is for the Victorian era, after the passage of the New Poor Law, and applies only to Great Britain (not Ireland).
135. Baugh, "Poverty, Protestantism, Political Economy," 85–92.
136. *WN*, V.f.61.
137. WC9, 238–39.
138. By contrast, utilitarian philosopher Hastings Rashdall declared, "probably no one will hesitate [to agree that] ... the lower Well-being ... of countless Chinamen or negroes must be sacrificed that a higher life may be possible for a much smaller number of white men." *The Theory of Good and Evil*, 2nd ed. (Oxford: Oxford University Press, 1924), 237–38. Rashdall (1858–1924) was a theologian and Anglican priest.

139. WC1, 425.
140. WC5, 273–74, 276–77, 283.
141. WC5, 28–29, 112, 284–88.
142. WC5, 33, 44–45, 47, 82, 109–10, 292, 296, 307, 323.
143. WC5, 1, 6, 68–69.
144. WC1, 5.
145. Humphrey Southall and the Great Britain Historical GIS Project, "A Vision of Britain Through Time (1801–2001)," Census Reports, 1811 Census, available at: https://web .archive.org/web/20161016063943/http://www.visionofbritain.org.uk/census/ SRC_P/2/GB1811PRE.
146. Robert Allen, "Class Structure and Inequality during the Industrial Revolution: Lessons from England's Social Tables, 1688–1867," *Economic History Review* 72, no. 1 (2019): 105, table 3. The 1759 statistics are drawn from "social tables" focused on occupation and social class, which were precursors to the modern census in counting households or families rather than individuals.
147. Allen, "Class Structure and Inequality," 105, table 3; 108, table 6. In Ricardo's simplified class model, farmers are assumed to be pure capitalists who have nothing but a capital stock. Ricardo's model ignores yeomen who owned their land (by then a very small group in England), and the fact that some of the income of capitalists should be considered wages for their managerial labor. Allen's factor-income estimate divides capitalists' income between profits (returns on capital ownership) and wages.
148. See the discussion of Ricardo's theory in Mark Blaug, *Economic Theory in Retrospect*, 4th ed. (Cambridge: Cambridge University Press, 1985), 88–94.
149. WC1, 37.
150. WC1, 93–95.
151. WC1, 67–70, 261 n*.
152. WC1, 71.
153. WC1, 83.
154. WC1, 101–2.
155. WC4, 21; cf. WC1, 335.
156. WC1, 76 n*.
157. WC1, 398–99, 400.
158. WN, V.2.e.10.
159. James Mill, *Elements of Political Economy* (London: Baldwin, Cradock, and Joy, 1821), 198.
160. In England, this process was more gradual. Recall that Smith argued that the rise of commercial society in England led the lords to gradually cede their authority to the national government. The 1660 Tenures Abolition Act ended the feudal obligations of landlords without abolishing their nonpecuniary feudal privileges, and hence was very partial compared to the declaration of August 4.
161. Thomas Piketty, *Capital and Ideology*, trans. Arthur Goldhammer (Cambridge, MA: Harvard University Press, 2020), 99–109.
162. Mill, *Elements of Political Economy*, 200–203.
163. WC1, 203–4.
164. WC1, 122.
165. WC1, 106.
166. WC1, 109.
167. WC5, 69, 45.
168. WC4, 21.

169. Ricardo allows that technological improvements in agriculture, and opening markets to foreign trade in food, could stave off the falling rate of profit and hence the arrival of the stationary state (WC4, 22–23).

170. WC1, 406–7.

171. In fact, in an era where labor's share of national income was stagnant even as population was growing, the profits of capital were rapidly overtaking the share taken by rents. Allen, "Class Structure and Inequality," 108, table 6. Ricardo cannot be faulted for not knowing this, as national income accounting was yet to be invented. It is a formidable task even for economic historians today to reconstruct quantitative estimates of past economic conditions.

172. Some of this reflects the fact that enclosed farms did not have to pay tithes, as tithe owners were compensated for this loss with an allotment when the land was enclosed. The landlords took the entire gain from the release from tithes, rather than splitting it with the farmers, in accordance with Ricardo's model. Allen, Enclosure and the Yeoman, 178–80.

173. Allen, Enclosure and the Yeoman, 179–87, 199–200. Allen argues, however, that it took generations for rents to converge on Ricardo's predictions, because accounting methods at the time were too primitive for anyone to calculate a farm's surplus, and because it took time to erode norms under which landlords, concerned about their reputations, were less aggressive in raising rents.

174. WC1, 35.

175. WC1, 389–90.

176. WC5, 49.

177. WC5, 68–69.

178. As I shall explain below, Ricardian socialists confuse Ricardo's labor theory of value (which holds that the long-run equilibrium price of a commodity is roughly proportionate to its cost of production in terms of the labor hours needed to produce it) with Locke's labor theory of value (which attributes virtually all gains in wealth to the exertions of workers).

179. Piercy Ravenstone, A Few Doubts as to the Correctness of Some Opinions Generally Entertained on the Subjects of Population and Political Economy (London: Printed for J. Andrews, 1821), 207.

180. Thomas Hodgskin, Labour Defended against the Claims of Capital: Or, the Unproductiveness of Capital Proved with Reference to the Present Combinations amongst Journeymen, 2nd ed. (London: Printed for Knight and Lacey, 1825), 24.

181. Hodgskin, Labour Defended, 8–16.

182. Hodgskin, Labour Defended, 27.

183. John Francis Bray, Labour's Wrongs and Labour's Remedy: Or, the Age of Might and the Age of Right (Leeds: D. Green, 1839), 49.

184. Thomas Hodgskin, The Natural and Artificial Right of Property Contrasted: A Series of Letters Addressed without Permission to H. Brougham ... (Now the Lord Chancellor) (London: B. Steil, 1832), 24–36, 44–54, 68, 80, 102. He also accepts the right to charge interest, without considering how this would reintroduce the same class differentiation and exploitation he complained about in Labour Defended. Ibid., 101.

185. Bray, Labour's Wrongs, 57.

186. Bray, Labour's Wrongs, 23–24, 33, 41–43, 50, 109–10, 154–62, 172–73.

187. Bray, Labour's Wrongs, 123–26, 165–68; Thompson, Labor Rewarded, 108–14.

188. Owen was a friend of Ricardo's. However, Ricardo thought his communal plan "inconsistent with the principles of political economy" and "calculated to produce infinite mischief" (WC5, 30).

189. Thompson, *Labor Rewarded*, 16–24, 37.
190. Esther Lowenthal, *The Ricardian Socialists* (New York: Columbia University, 1911), 82–83.
191. *WC*1, 20–21. Ricardo advances this idea only as a rough empirical estimate of the cost of production, not as a scientific law. As others have noted, his discussion of the labor theory of value admits so many exceptions that they swallow the rule. Profits (interest) are a separate cost of production in addition to wages. The theory doesn't apply to goods exchanged in foreign trade, due to the relative immobility of labor and capital. And it fails to explain the relative prices of goods produced with different ratios of fixed and variable capital (*WC*1, 30–42, 134–35).
192. Hayek, *Constitution of Liberty*, ch. 6; Friedrich A. Hayek, "The Use of Knowledge in Society," *American Economic Review* 35 (1945): 519–30. These works offer a penetrating account of why prices that serve this allocative function do not reward people according to desert.
193. Bray, *Labour's Wrongs*, 169; Hodgskin, *Labour Defended*, 101.
194. Lowenthal, *Ricardian Socialists*, 296–97.
195. Bray, *Labour's Wrongs*, 84; Thompson, *Labor Rewarded*, 4.
196. Bray, *Labour's Wrongs*, 42–43; Thompson, *Labor Rewarded*, 4.
197. Thompson, *Labor Rewarded*, 9.

6 The Progressive Work Ethic (2): J. S. Mill

1. *WN*, 1.1.3.
2. *WN*, V.1.f.50.
3. *WN*, V.1.f.51.
4. *SEIP*, 12; *LPE*, 139, 145–47; Kramnick, *Republicanism and Bourgeois Radicalism*, 7–17. Kramnick traces the "race" idea to Locke and Smith, who endorsed the motive of bettering one's standard of living. He is doubly mistaken. First, as Bunyan's pilgrim shows, the idea of life as a race is in the Bible (see, e.g., 1 Cor. 9:24–27; Gal. 5:7; 2 Tim. 4:7; Heb. 12:1). Second, neither Locke nor Smith endorse the idea that people should view life as a race for luxury. As a thinker closer to Puritan asceticism, Locke, while endorsing "comfort" and "convenience," viewed the luxury trades as drags on the economy. Smith is more ambivalent. He regards the restless ambition to better one's condition, aroused by viewing what the rich have, as a useful spur to industry. But the idea that all that climbing will deliver happiness is a "deception," and the desire for ostentatious luxury is a childish vanity (*TMS*, 4.1.8–10; *WN*, 3.4.10). Moreover, the theme of *competitive* consumption, so prominent in Priestley, is muted in Smith. He acknowledges that people see themselves as aiming to beat their competitors in a "race for wealth, for honours, and preferments," (*TMS*, 2.2.2.1). But he never endorses the value judgments that ground this view of life.
5. *LPE*, 147.
6. *CWM*3, 754–55.
7. *CWM*10, 210.
8. *CWM*10, 211.
9. *CWM*2, 367.
10. *CWM*3, 768.
11. *CWM*21, 293.
12. *CWM*10, 232.
13. *CWM*1, 128.
14. *CWM*3, 756.

15. *CWM*3, 755.
16. 2*T*, §89; 1*T*, §92.
17. *CWM*3, 768.
18. *CWM*2, 215, 218.
19. *CWM*2, 208.
20. *CWM*2, 225.
21. *CWM*2, 230.
22. *CWM*2, 230.
23. *CWM*2, 227; cf. 2*T*, §37.
24. 2*T*, §38.
25. *CWM*6, 184. Compare Bray, *Labour's Wrongs*, 84 (the independently wealthy are "mere drones of society—the utterly unproductive, and worthless"), with Thompson, *Labor Rewarded*, 4 (workers should "refuse any portion of their honey to mere drones").
26. *CWM*2, 248.
27. *CWM*2, 216, 218.
28. 1*T*, §93; cf. 1*T*, §91.
29. *CWM*2, 221.
30. *CWM*2, 225–26.
31. *CWM*3, 889.
32. *CWM*2, 228–29; *CWM*3, 892.
33. *CWM*3, 892.
34. *CWM*3, 892–93.
35. *CWM*3, 887.
36. *CWM*3, 811–12.
37. Blaug, *Economic Theory in Retrospect*, 82–83, observes that Ricardo's conclusion depends on the fact that his model supposes that land is exclusively dedicated to the production of corn. As soon as land has alternative uses, rent serves an allocative function and enters into the cost of production. Mill was the first political economist to note this. But the core of his argument still stands, since all rents above the best alternative use of land can still be taxed away.
38. Or at least it *can*, provided financial intermediaries use it to that end, rather than to fleece naive borrowers or tempt naive investors to buy worthless bonds bearing high interest rates.
39. *CWM*3, 820.
40. *CWM*29, 416–31.
41. 2*T*, §43.
42. *CWM*2, 229–30.
43. *CWM*2, 319.
44. *CWM*2, 313–19.
45. *CWM*2, 422.
46. *CWM*2, 227.
47. *LJA*, 297–98; *LJB*, 419.
48. *CWM*2, 207.
49. *CWM*2, 326.
50. *CWM*2, 278, 281–82.
51. *CWM*2, 252, 256–76, 283–95.
52. *CWM*2, 299, 326.
53. *CWM*2, 280–81.
54. *CWM*2, 326.
55. *CWM*2, 330.

56. CWM2, 328, 422.
57. Paul Bew, *Ireland: The Politics of Enmity, 1789–2006* (Oxford: Oxford University Press, 2007), 568.
58. Timothy Guinnane and Ronald Miller, "The Limits to Land Reform: The Land Acts in Ireland, 1870–1909," *Economic Development and Cultural Change* 45, no. 3 (1997): 591–612.
59. CWM3, 951–52.
60. CWM3, 952–53.
61. CWM3, 956–58.
62. WN, I.1.7.
63. CWM2, 127.
64. CWM2, 116–17.
65. CWM3, 933.
66. CWM3, 934.
67. Mill's pessimism on this point follows from the wages-fund theory. On this theory, the funds available to pay wages are fixed by the size of the stock of circulating capital in the previous period. Hence, holding the labor supply fixed, wages can grow only in concert with the growth of profits. Unions cannot force a change in labor's share of income. Mill recanted the wages-fund theory in 1869. He argued that the capitalist can choose to increase the funds available to hire workers by reducing his own income. By combining, workers can therefore force capitalists to do what they could have chosen to do all along. John Stuart Mill, "Thornton on Labour and Its Claims" (1869), in *Collected Works of John Stuart Mill*, vol. 5, ed. J. M. Robson (Toronto: University of Toronto Press, 1986), 643–46. For discussion, see Kevin Vallier, "Production, Distribution, and J. S. Mill," *Utilitas* 22, no. 2 (2010): 103–26.
68. CWM3, 932.
69. CWM3, 933.
70. CWM3, 772.
71. CWM3, 768.
72. CWM3, 758.
73. CWM3, 760.
74. CWM3, 759–61.
75. CWM3, 763–64.
76. CWM3, 768.
77. On this point, Mill is more optimistic about cooperatives in CWM3 than in CWM6, 190–91.
78. CWM3, 793.
79. CWM2, 337–38, 344.
80. Blaug, *Economic Theory in Retrospect*, 68, notes that Malthus failed to take note of the British population boom in the first two editions of *Principle of Population*, even though the second edition appeared years after the 1801 census. Of course, even the boom was less than the maximum possible rate of growth.
81. CWM2, 345–46.
82. CWM2, 352.
83. CWM3, 960–61. See also CWM6, 203, where Mill endorses the Puritan principle that no able-bodied person who does not work is entitled to be supported at public expense.
84. CWM2, 358.
85. CWM2, 360.

86. CWM24, 1006. The public works program enacted during the Famine paid by the task. That incentive structure would certainly have secured sufficient labor effort had the starving Irish workers been physically capable of it. Did Mill suppose that the Irish were so lazy that they preferred starvation to task work? On that supposition, peasant proprietorship would also not motivate them to work hard. Nor could Mill consistently argue that paying by the task is inherently coercive. He thought it was the most just form of labor compensation because it rewarded work in proportion to industry (CWM3, 784). Henry Farrell argues that Mill's grounds for opposing Scrope's temporary job guarantee utterly neglected the immediate needs of the starving Irish for food. "Millian Liberalism and the Irish Famine," *Crooked Timber*, January 28, 2016, available at: https://crookedtimber.org/2016/01/28/millian-liberalism-and-the-irish-famine. I agree. Smith wisely distinguished short-term emergency measures from long-term policy in his discussion of famine policy (see Chapter 5). English debates over famine-relief policy largely regarded the emergency as an occasion to force a dramatic long-term reorganization of Irish agriculture, neglecting the urgent needs of millions of Irish (see Chapter 4).
87. CWM24, 923–26.
88. Hazlitt, *Reply to Malthus*, 151.
89. PoP6.1, 169–72; PoP6.2, 142, 194.
90. Hazlitt, *Reply to Malthus*, 296.
91. CWM3, 709.
92. CWM3, 960.
93. CWM3, 961.
94. Mill's reasoning on this point is dubious. To be sure, population restraints limit the supply of labor, and thereby tend to raise wages. But they also reduce the demand for the products of labor, and hence the demand for labor. This will tend to lower wages.
95. Mill also supported the right of working-class men to vote, a right they obtained in 1918. Women got the vote in 1928.
96. CWM2, 372–75.
97. CWM2, 376–77.
98. CWM21, 92.
99. CWM2, 232–33.
100. CWM18, 299.
101. CWM3, 953–54.
102. CWM21, 151.
103. DNQ, 7.
104. DNQ, 11.
105. DNQ, 28, 42.
106. CWM21, 89, 92, 87.
107. CWM21, 91–92.
108. CWM21, 91.
109. CWM18, 224.
110. CWM2, 353.
111. CWM2, 353; cf. CWM2, 247.
112. CWM19, 393–94.
113. CWM19, 419.
114. CWM21, 93.
115. CWM21, 93.

116. Bart Schultz, "Mill and Sidgwick, Imperialism and Racism," *Utilitas* 19, no. 1 (2007): 104–30, offers a thoughtful literature review on the question of Mill's racism. Schultz concludes that Mill was a cultural if not a biological racist.

117. CWM18, 122.

118. CWM18, 122.

119. CWM19, 394.

120. CWM19, 395.

121. In Britain, Olaudah Equiano, *The Interesting Narrative and Other Writings*, ed. Vincent Carretta (New York: Penguin Books, 2003), originally published in 1745, was a literary sensation and pivotal work for the abolitionist movement, which successfully lobbied for the Slavery Abolition Act in 1833, ending slavery in the British Empire outside India.

122. *TMS*, 5.2.9.

123. CWM18, 224; cf. CWM19, 394–95.

124. CWM19, 567.

125. CWM19, 418–19.

126. CWM19, 401.

127. CWM19, 577.

128. CWM21, 264, 283–86.

129. CWM21, 278–80, 288–89, 294–96.

130. CWM19; CWM30.

131. Alan Ryan, "Introduction," in *J. S. Mill's Encounter with India*, eds. Martin Moir, Douglas Peers, and Lynn Zastoupil (Toronto: University of Toronto Press, 1999), provides an excellent brief account of the history of the Company and Mill's career in it.

132. CWM19, 567–68.

133. CWM19, 569.

134. CWM19, 571.

135. On China, see CWM18, 273.

136. Piketty, *Capital and Ideology*, 380–81.

137. Mill complains that China's ban on opium imports violates the liberty of consumers (CWM18, 293). He fails to explain why his principle of liberty should apply to the Chinese, given what he took to be their "semibarbarian" unreadiness for freedom. Nor does he explain how turning them into drug addicts would improve their work ethic or prepare them for life in a free society by training them to regulate their affairs by reason rather than impulse.

138. CWM21, 117.

139. Oona Hathaway and Scott Shapiro, *The Internationalists: How a Radical Plan to Outlaw War Remade the World* (Simon & Schuster, 2017), ch. 2.

140. *WN*, I.8.26.

141. Damodaran, "Famine in Bengal."

142. Damodaran, "Famine in Bengal," 144.

143. Edmund Burke, *Mr. Burke's Speech, on the Motion Made for Papers Relative to the Directions for Charging the Nabob of Arcot's Private Debts to Europeans, on the Revenues of the Carnatic. February 28th, 1785* (London: Printed for J. Dodsley, 1785), 50–57.

144. Seymour Drescher, *The Mighty Experiment: Free Labor versus Slavery in British Emancipation* (Oxford: Oxford University Press, 2002), 47–53.

145. *TMS*, 6.2.2.17.

7 The Progressive Work Ethic (3): Marx

1. *MECW*1, 3–9.
2. In Chapter 7, I argue that Marx's conception of the motivation to work in unalienated labor is Luther's. Nevertheless his celebration of continuous economic progress in service to humanity, especially in *The Communist Manifesto*, has a distinctively Calvinist bent, in contrast to Luther's static, traditionalist economic vision.
3. Daniel Brudney, *Marx's Attempt to Leave Philosophy* (Cambridge, MA: Harvard University Press, 1998), ch. 4; Jan Kandiyali, "The Importance of Others: Marx on Unalienated Production," *Ethics* 130 (2020): 555–87; Allen Wood, *Karl Marx* (London: Routledge, 2004), ch. 2.
4. *CWM*10, 210.
5. *CWM*18, ch. 3.
6. *CWM*10, 232.
7. *CWM*3, 768.
8. *MECW*3, 228.
9. *MECW*3, 276.
10. *MECW*6, 506.
11. *MECW*24, 87.
12. Ludwig Feuerbach, *The Essence of Christianity*, trans. Marian Evans (George Eliot) (London: J. Chapman, 1854).
13. *MECW*3, 227–28; Kandiyali, "Importance of Others," 563–70.
14. *CWM*18, ch. 3.
15. Here I draw from Frederick Neuhouser's excellent account in *Foundations of Hegel's Social Theory: Actualizing Freedom* (Cambridge, MA: Harvard University Press, 2000).
16. Louis Althusser rejects this view. He argues that there is a sharp "epistemic" break between the "humanist" Marx before 1845, and the purportedly "scientific" Marx after that point. Marx "ceaselessly struggled against ideological interpretations of an idealist, humanist type that threatened Marxist theory." *For Marx*, trans. Ben Brewster (New York: Pantheon Books, 1969), 11. Granted, after 1844, Marx drops the Hegelian language of alienation and species-being. And he proclaims a break from his earlier humanism to a scientific approach in *The German Ideology* (1846) (*MECW*5). My interest in this book is not Marx's epistemology but his normative concerns. These concerns are continuous throughout Marx's life. How else could Marx have proclaimed in the "Critique of the Gotha Program" (1875) that in communist society, labor will be "life's prime want," a domain for "the all-round development of the individual" (*MECW*24, 87)? I document below how Marx repeatedly echoes in *Capital*, vol. 1 (1867) (*MECW*35) the normative concerns he articulated in the *1844 Manuscripts* (*MECW*3).
17. *MECW*3, 237; *MECW*35, 360n2.
18. *MECW*3, 272.
19. *MECW*35, 374, quoting *CWM*3, 756.
20. *MECW*35, 435.
21. *MECW*3, 272.
22. *MECW*35, 367; cf. *MECW*3, 320.
23. *MECW*35, 334, 426.
24. *MECW*3, 245, 274–75, 279.
25. *MECW*35, 428–29, 465–71.
26. *MECW*35, 354–55, 368, 406–20.

27. *MECW*3, 274–75.
28. *MECW*3, 238–40, 245.
29. *MECW*3, 259–63, 250.
30. *MECW*3, 311.
31. *MECW*35, 337, 363, 426–27.
32. *MECW*3, 275–77.
33. *MECW*3, 286.
34. *MECW*35, 342.
35. *MECW*35, 355.
36. *MECW*35, 363.
37. Jonathan Sperber, *Karl Marx: A Nineteenth-Century Life* (New York: W. W. Norton/Liverlight, 2013), 116–19, 135, 331, 356–57.
38. *MECW*3, 313.
39. See, e.g., Thomas Johnson, *A Plea for Free-Mens Liberties: Or the Monopoly of the Eastland Merchants* (London: n.p., 1646).
40. *MECW*6, 489.
41. *MECW*3, 273.
42. *MECW*35, 489–90.
43. *MECW*6, 499.
44. *MECW*24, 85.
45. *MECW*6, 501–2.
46. *MECW*22, 332.
47. *MECW*24, 321.
48. Rosa Luxemburg, *The Mass Strike: The Political Party and the Trade Unions. And, The Junius Pamphlet* (New York: Harper & Row, 1971).
49. François-Noël Babeuf, "Babeuf's Defense from the Trial at the Vendome, February–May, 1797," in *Socialist Thought: A Documentary History*, eds. Albert Fried and Ronald Sanders, (New York: Columbia University Press, 1964), 67–68.
50. *BHB*, 164.
51. *BHB*, 160–61.
52. *BHB*, 180.
53. *BHB*, 163.
54. *BHB*, 203–8.
55. *BHB*, 206.
56. *BHB*, 210.
57. Babeuf, "Babeuf's Defense," 67.
58. Babeuf, "Babeuf's Defense," 65.
59. Babeuf, "Babeuf's Defense," 66.
60. Kurt Vonnegut, *Short Stories by Kurt Vonnegut: Harrison Bergeron, EPICAC, 2BR02B, Welcome to the Monkey House, Miss Temptation, Report on the Barnhouse Effect* (Memphis, TN: Books LLC, 2010).
61. *BHB*, 11, 324.
62. *BHB*, 323–24.
63. *BHB*, 318.
64. Piketty, *Capital in the Twenty-First Century*, 238–42.
65. *BHB*, 321–22, 222.
66. *BHB*, 167.
67. Sperber, *Marx*, 203–11.
68. *MECW*6, 505.
69. *MECW*6, 514.
70. *MECW*24, 87.

71. *BHB*, 154, 220.
72. *MECW*35, 426–27.
73. *MECW*6, 487–89.
74. Sperber, *Marx*, 538.
75. *MECW*5, 292.
76. *MECW*5, 47. Terrell Carver, "Communism for Critical Critics? *The German Ideology* and the Problem of Technology," *History of Political Thought* 9, no. 1 (1988): 129–38, argues that this passage is a send-up of the utopian socialists, who romanticized the preindustrial occupations listed. As a scientific socialist, Marx insists that advanced technology is required to realize communist society. Yet Marx never gave up on the idea that communism would abolish the division of labor, a goal he preserved in the "Critique of the Gotha Program" (1875) (*MECW*24, 87).
77. *MECW*24, 323–25.
78. *MECW*24, 87.
79. *MECW*24, 87–88.
80. Marx's vision of the motivation to work is strikingly similar to Luther's idea that Christians of faith serve others in their calling out of brotherly love. Marx shares many other qualities with Luther. Both combined spectacular scholarly erudition with belligerent polemics. Both frequently aimed their polemics at thinkers whose views they themselves had previously held. Both indulged in rash political talk with catastrophic consequences.
81. *MECW*24, 95.
82. This is how I read the implications of Lea Ypi, "Democratic Dictatorship: Political Legitimacy in Marxist Perspective," *European Journal of Philosophy* 28 (2020): 277–91. The strength of Ypi's interpretation of the transitional regime is that only in a model in which workers collaboratively and autonomously work out how to emancipate themselves through discussion of the coordination problems they face together could the state as a coercive apparatus plausibly "die away." It certainly couldn't do so if society is run like an army. The bottom-up model of transition that Marx extolls in *The Civil War in France* broadly fits Ypi's view.
83. *MECW*6, 504.
84. *MECW*6, 505.
85. William Sewell, *Work and Revolution in France: The Language of Labor from the Old Regime to 1848* (Cambridge: Cambridge University Press, 1980), 201–5.
86. *MECW*22, 332.
87. *MECW*22, 335.
88. *MECW*24, 321.
89. *MECW*27, 279.
90. This is the key argument of Hayek, "Use of Knowledge." The key contribution of markets to solving the allocative problem is informational. Incentives are secondary.
91. Sperber, *Marx*, 506–15, 535–36.

8 Social Democracy as the Culmination of the Progressive Work Ethic

1. Sperber, *Marx*, 529.
2. Hayek, *Road to Serfdom*.
3. Here I concur with Sperber, *Marx*.
4. Abby Phillip, "Ben Carson: Obamacare is 'Slavery'," *ABC News*, October 11, 2013, available at: https://abcnews.go.com/blogs/politics/2013/10/ben-carson-obamacare -is-slavery.
5. *PHM*, 328–30.

6. *PHM*, 331–33.
7. John Avery, *Progress, Poverty, and Population: Re-Reading Condorcet, Godwin, and Malthus* (New York: Routledge, 2013), 11–12.
8. *PHM*, 328–29.
9. AJ, 325.
10. *BHB*, 318–24.
11. AJ, 329.
12. AJ, 332.
13. AJ, 337.
14. AJ, 332.
15. AJ, 337.
16. *PHM*, 318. Two centuries later, John Rawls advanced a comparable conception of justice. "All social values – liberty and opportunity, income and wealth, and the social bases of self-respect – are to be distributed equally unless an unequal distribution … is to everyone's advantage." John Rawls, *A Theory of Justice*, rev. ed. (Cambridge, MA: Harvard University Press, 1999), 54.
17. AJ, 340.
18. Alexander Hicks, *Social Democracy and Welfare Capitalism: A Century of Income Security Politics* (Ithaca, NY: Cornell University Press, 1999).
19. George Steinmetz, *Regulating the Social: The Welfare State and Local Politics in Imperial Germany* (Princeton: Princeton University Press, 1993), 50, 123–25.
20. Pope Leo XIII, *Rerum Novarum*, Papal Encyclical (1891), available at: www.papalencyclicals.net/Leo13/l13rerum.htm.
21. Gøsta Esping-Anderson, *The Three Worlds of Welfare Capitalism* (Princeton: Princeton University Press, 1990), 33, 44–45, 49–50.
22. James W. Russell, *Double Standard: Social Policy in Europe and the United States*, 2nd ed. (Lanham, MD.: Rowman & Littlefield Publishers, 2011), 120–21.
23. Craig Calhoun, *The Roots of Radicalism: Tradition, the Public Sphere, and Early Nineteenth-Century Social Movements* (Chicago: University of Chicago Press, 2012).
24. Sperber, *Marx*, 211, 357–60.
25. In German, *Die Voraussetzungen des Sozialismus und die Aufgaben der Sozialdemokratie* (Stuttgart: J. H. W. Dietz, 1899). English translation of the 1902 German edition published in 1911.
26. *ES*, xiv.
27. *ES*, xxii–xxiii.
28. *ES*, 21–22. This was why Ricardo argued that the use of machinery and other fixed capital requires a "considerable" modification of the rule that the relative value of commodities is determined by the relative number of labor hours required to produce them (*WC1*, 30–39). Marx devoted the third volume of *Capital* to solving this problem. Blaug, *Economic Theory in Retrospect*, 234, argues that his entire effort presupposes what he needs to prove – namely, that "each worker generates a constant surplus no matter where he is employed." As rates of surplus value are neither observable nor able to be inferred from behavior, there is no basis for this assumption.
29. *ES*, 32–35.
30. Bernstein hastens to add that the labor theory of value does not supply a sound normative standard of distributive justice (*ES*, 39). Here he follows Marx (*MECW*24, 84–87).
31. *ES*, ch. 2.
32. *ES*, 103–7.

33. *ES*, 100–1, 108.
34. *ES*, 115–19.
35. *ES*, 128–31.
36. *ES*, 131–35, 161.
37. *MECW*24, 89.
38. *ES*, 141–42.
39. *ES*, 149.
40. *ES*, 152.
41. *ES*, 140, 141.
42. *ES*, 151.
43. *ES*, 181–86.
44. *ES*, 191.
45. *ES*, 197.
46. *ES*, 186.
47. Sperber, *Marx*, 92, 201.
48. *ES*, 48–49.
49. *ES*, xxii.
50. Sheri Berman, *The Primacy of Politics: Social Democracy and the Making of Europe's Twentieth Century* (New York: Cambridge University Press, 2006), 111–12.
51. Berman, *Primacy of Politics*, 110.
52. T. H. Marshall, "Citizenship and Social Class," in *Citizenship and Social Class and Other Essays* (Cambridge: Cambridge University Press, 1950), 10–11.
53. William Beveridge, *Social Insurance and Allied Services* (London: HMSO, 1942); Marshall, "Citizenship and Social Class," 48.
54. *CWM*3, 768.
55. Berman, *Primacy of Politics*, 176.
56. *WC*1, 37.
57. John Bates Clark, *The Distribution of Wealth: A Theory of Wages, Interest and Profits* (New York: Macmillan, 1899).
58. *MECW*24, 84–85.
59. Sidney Webb, "The Rate of Interest and the Laws of Distribution," *Quarterly Journal of Economics* 2, no. 2 (1888): 188–208. American progressives made the same argument. See the excellent discussion of this issue in Barbara H. Fried, *The Progressive Assault on Laissez Faire: Robert Hale and the First Law and Economics Movement* (Cambridge, MA: Harvard University Press, 1998), ch. 4.
60. See John Rawls, *Justice as Fairness: A Restatement*, ed. Erin Kelly (Cambridge, MA: Harvard University Press, 2001), 61–64. Rawls's theory of distributive justice is in the progressive work ethic/social democratic tradition. However, most of what he said about the organization of work and the division of labor – a central concern of this tradition – was only in passing. Samuel Freeman, "Property-Owning Democracy and the Difference Principle," *Analyse & Kritik* 35, no. 1 (2013): 9–36, offers a helpful discussion of these passages.
61. *PHM*, 318.
62. Jon Elster, *The Cement of Society* (Cambridge: Cambridge University Press, 1989), provides an excellent account of Scandinavian sectoral bargaining.
63. Steve Lohr, "Making Cars the Volvo Way," *New York Times*, June 23, 1987, D1.
64. *WN*, IV.9.47.
65. *CWM*21, 91.
66. Kathleen Thelen, "The American Precariat: U.S. Capitalism in Comparative Perspective," *Perspectives on Politics* 17, no. 1 (2019): 15, fig. 7.
67. Marshall, "Citizenship and Social Class," 47.

68. Marshall, "Citizenship and Social Class," 56–58.
69. Marshall, "Citizenship and Social Class," 66–68.
70. Daniel Markovits, *The Meritocracy Trap: How America's Foundational Myth Feeds Inequality, Dismantles the Middle Class, and Devours the Elite* (London: Penguin Press, 2019).
71. As I have argued in Elizabeth Anderson, "Fair Opportunity in Education: A Democratic Equality Perspective," *Ethics* 117 (2007): 595–622.
72. Beveridge, *Social Insurance and Allied Services*.
73. Esping-Anderson, *The Three Worlds of Welfare Capitalism*, 46–48, 50–52.
74. Robert Goodin, "Work and Welfare: Towards a Post-Productivist Welfare Regime," *British Journal of Political Science* 31, no. 1 (2001): 13–39.
75. Henrik Kleven, "How Can Scandinavians Tax So Much?" *Journal of Economic Perspectives* 28, no. 4 (2014): 77–98.
76. Karl Moene and Michael Wallerstein provide a sober analysis of the decline of social democracy in Sweden due to globalizing pressures in "How Social Democracy Worked: Labor-Market Institutions," *Politics & Society* 23, no. 2 (1995): 185–211. Scaling up social democracy beyond the nation-state thus becomes a critical challenge. Given its nationalist foundations, social democracy from the start has been troubled by issues of global justice. Germany's SPD Reichstag members voted overwhelmingly to enter the First World War. Thomas Piketty offers some ambitious ideas for scaling up social democracy (or what he calls "participatory socialism") to a global scale through a system of international federations in *Capital and Ideology*, ch. 17.
77. See Deborah Malamud, "'Who They Are – Or Were': Middle-Class Welfare in the Early New Deal," *University of Pennsylvania Law Review* 151, no. 6 (2003): 2019–75, showing how New Deal special-relief policies were designed for middle-class workers to spare them the stigma of being welfare recipients by hiding that fact. This is an excellent case study of how the welfare state constitutes sharp class distinctions that were previously softer. That current US welfare policies for the middle class continue to be hidden although they are much more generous than transfers to the poor helps to explain middle-class hostility to government social welfare programs. On this point, see Suzanne Mettler, *The Government–Citizen Disconnect* (New York: Russell Sage Foundation, 2018).

9 Hijacked Again: Neoliberalism as the Return of the Conservative Work Ethic

1. Milton Friedman, "The Social Responsibility of Business Is to Increase Its Profits," *New York Times Magazine*, September 13, 1970.
2. David Weil, *The Fissured Workplace: Why Work Became So Bad for So Many and What Can Be Done to Improve It* (Cambridge, MA: Harvard University Press, 2014). See also Peter Capelli, *The New Deal at Work* (Boston: Harvard Business Review Press, 1999); Lawrence Katz and Alan Krueger, "The Rise and Nature of Alternative Work Arrangements in the United States, 1995–2015," *ILR Review* 72, no. 2 (2019): 382–416.
3. Gerald Davis, *The Vanishing American Corporation: Navigating the Hazards of a New Economy* (Oakland, CA: Berrett-Koehler Publishers, 2016), 136, emphasis in original.
4. Economic Policy Institute, *The Productivity–Pay Gap* (2022), available at: www.epi.org/productivity-pay-gap.
5. N. Gregory Mankiw, "Defending the One Percent," *Journal of Economic Perspectives* 27, no. 3 (2013): 21–34, available at: http://pubs.aeaweb.org/doi/pdfplus/10.1257/jep.27.3.21.

6. Piketty, *Capital and Ideology*, ch. 14, documents the virtually universal shift of center-left parties to the better educated across the rich democracies.

7. Michael Sandel, *The Tyranny of Merit: What's Become of the Common Good?* (New York: Farrar, Straus and Giroux, 2020), ch. 3.

8. "Massachusetts Body of Liberties" (1641), in *Colonial Origins of the American Constitution: A Documentary History*, ed. Donald Lutz (Indianapolis: Liberty Fund, 1998), Article 91.

9. George Fitzhugh, *Cannibals All! Or, Slaves without Masters* (Richmond, VA: A. Morris, 1857); James Henry Hammond, "Speech in the Senate, 35th Congress, Session 1," *Congressional Globe*, March 4, 1858, appendix, 68–71.

10. John Patrick Daly, *When Slavery Was Called Freedom: Evangelicalism, Proslavery, and the Causes of the Civil War* (Lexington: University Press of Kentucky, 2002).

11. See, e.g., William Graham Sumner, *What Social Classes Owe to Each Other* (New York: Harper and Brothers, 1911), a work influenced by his English teacher Herbert Spencer, *Social Statics* (London: John Chapman, 1851).

12. See, e.g., *Black Reconstruction in America: An Essay Toward a History of the Part Which Black Folk Played in the Attempt to Reconstruct Democracy in America, 1860–1880*, ed. Henry Louis Gates (Cary, NC: Oxford University Press, 2007); Martin Luther King Jr., *"All Labor Has Dignity,"* ed. Michael Honey (Boston: Beacon Press, 2011); Cornel West, *Toward a Socialist Theory of Racism* (New York: Institute for Democratic Socialism, 1989).

13. Chris Jennings, *Paradise Now: The Story of American Utopianism* (New York: Random House, 2016).

14. Eric Foner, *Free Soil, Free Labor, Free Men: The Ideology of the Republican Party before the Civil War*, with new introduction (New York: Oxford University Press, 1995).

15. Anderson, *Private Government*, ch. 1.

16. See, for one of many examples, William Harper, "Slavery in Light of Social Ethics," in *Cotton is King, and Pro-Slavery Arguments*, ed. E. N. Elliott (Augusta, GA: Pritchard, Abbott, & Loomis, 1860), 551–52, 596.

17. Martin Gilens, *Why Americans Hate Welfare: Race, Media, and the Politics of Antipoverty Policy* (Chicago: University of Chicago Press, 1999). See also Donald Kinder and Lynn Sanders, *Divided by Color* (Chicago: University of Chicago Press, 1996), which shows how opposition to state-provided benefits is not grounded in individualism or libertarianism, but in racial resentment of Blacks, who are stereotyped as lazily depending on the fruits of white industry.

18. Center on Budget and Policy Priorities, *Policy Basics: Federal Tax Expenditures* (Washington, DC, 2020), available at: www.cbpp.org/research/federal-tax/policy-basics-federal-tax-expenditures.

19. Margaret Somers and Fred Block, "From Poverty to Perversity: Ideas, Markets, and Institutions over 200 Years of Welfare Debate," *American Sociological Review* 70, no. 2 (2005): 260–87; Joseph Persky, "Retrospectives: Classical Family Values: Ending the Poor Laws as They Knew Them," *Journal of Economic Perspectives* 11, no. 1 (1997): 179–89; William Kern, "Current Welfare Reform: A Return to the Principles of 1834," *Journal of Economic Issues* 32, no. 2 (1998): 427–32.

20. US Department of Health & Human Services, *Aid to Families with Dependent Children the Baseline: Family and Household Characteristics* (Washington, DC, 1998), 1, available at: https://aspe.hhs.gov/basic-report/aid-families-dependent-children-baseline.

21. I summarize some of this research in Elizabeth Anderson, "Welfare, Work Requirements, and Dependent Care," *Journal of Applied Philosophy* 21 (2004): 249–51.

22. Glenn Loury, "Comment on Michalopoulos and Berlin's 'Financial Work Incentives for Low-Wage Workers,'" in *The New World of Welfare*, eds. Rebecca Blank and Ron Haskins (Washington, DC: Brookings Institution Press, 2001), 286.

23. Maggie Haberman, "Newt: Fire the Janitors, Hire Kids to Clean Schools," *Politico*, November 18, 2011, available at: www.politico.com/story/2011/11/newt-fire-the-janitors-hire-kids-to-clean-schools-068729.

24. John MacDonald, "Reforms of Welfare Debated," *Hartford Courant*, December 8, 1994.

25. Randall Akee et al., "How Does Household Income Affect Child Personality and Behaviors?" *American Economic Review* 108.3 (2018): 775–827. The authors cite a substantial supporting literature with cognate findings.

26. Deborah K. Padgett, Benjamin F. Henwood, and Sam J. Tsemberis, *Housing First: Ending Homelessness, Transforming Systems, and Changing Lives* (Oxford: Oxford University Press, 2016), 7–8.

27. Padgett, Henwood, and Tsemberis, *Housing First*, 6.

28. Julia Woodhall-Melni and James Dunn, "A Systematic Review of Outcomes Associated with Participation in Housing First Programs," *Housing Studies* 31, no. 3 (2016): 293–94.

29. Tracy Loveless, *About a Third of Families Who Received Supplemental Nutrition Assistance Program Benefits Had Two or More People Working* (Washington, DC: US Census Bureau, 2020), available at: www.census.gov/library/stories/2020/07/most-families-that-received-snap-benefits-in-2018-had-at-least-one-person-working.html. In 2018, at the peak of a boom, 12 percent of US families received SNAP.

30. Leah Hamilton et al., "Guarding Public Coffers or Trapping the Poor? The Role of Public Assistance Asset Limits in Program Efficacy and Family Economic Well-Being," *Poverty & Public Policy* 11, no. 1–2 (2019): 12–30.

31. Andrea Campbell, "How Medicaid Forces Families Like Mine to Stay Poor," *Vox*, July 28, 2015, available at: www.vox.com/2014/12/9/7319477/medicaid-disability.

32. Gene Falk and Patrick Landers, *The Temporary Assistance for Needy Families (TANF) Block Grant: Responses to Frequently Asked Questions*, RL32760 (Washington, DC: Congressional Research Service, 2021), 2, available at: https://crsreports.congress.gov/product/pdf/RL/RL32760.

33. J. D. Vance, *Hillbilly Elegy: A Memoir of a Family and Culture in Crisis* (New York: Harper, 2016), 154–57. This was not his only reason. However, his defeat by the form contributed to his sense of unreadiness for college.

34. Congress passed a simplification of FAFSA at the end of 2020, cutting it down to 36 questions for 2022 and beyond.

35. Susan Dynarski and Judith Scott-Clayton, "Complexity and Targeting in Federal Student Aid: A Quantitative Analysis," *Tax Policy and the Economy* 22, no.1 (2008): 109–50.

36. Pamela Herd and Donald Moynihan, *Administrative Burden: Policymaking by Other Means* (New York: Russell Sage Foundation, 2019).

37. Friedman, *Capitalism and Freedom*, 94.

38. William A. Niskanen, "The Peculiar Economics of Bureaucracy," *The American Economic Review* 58, no. 2 (1968): 293–305.

39. Hume, *Bentham and Bureaucracy*, 195.
40. Kramnick, *Republicanism and Bourgeois Radicalism*, 47–49.
41. On the momentous questions, see Chiara Cordelli, *The Privatized State* (Princeton: Princeton University Press, 2020); Alon Harel, "Private Gain, Public Loss," *Aeon*, June 22, 2020, available at: https://aeon.co/essays/privatisation-is-bad-economics-and-worse-politics; Simon Chesterman and Angelina Fischer, eds., *Private Security, Public Order: The Outsourcing of Public Services and Its Limits* (Oxford: Oxford University Press, 2009).
42. John Donahue, *The Privatization Decision* (New York: Basic Books, 1989), shows how the theory of the firm applies to the privatization of government services.
43. R. H. Coase, "The Nature of the Firm," *Economica* 4, no. 16 (1937): 386–405.
44. Oliver Hart, Andrei Shleifer, and Robert Vishny, "The Proper Scope of Government: Theory and an Application to Prisons," *Quarterly Journal of Economics* 112, no. 4 (1997): 1127–61.
45. US Office of the Inspector General, *Review of the Federal Bureau of Prisons' Monitoring of Contract Prisons* (Washington, DC, 2016), 11, 14, 64–65, available at: https://oig.justice.gov/reports/2016/e1606.pdf.
46. A compilation of research on the practices of private prisons may be found at the Prison Policy Initiative, available at: www.prisonpolicy.org/research/privatization.
47. Foucault's account of the transformation of punishment from violent spectacle to panoptic discipline should be understood as informed by the conservative work ethic as elaborated by Bentham and others. Foucault, *Discipline and Punish*. See also Harcourt, *The Illusion of Free Markets*, who ties the rise of capitalism to an expansive punishment regime.
48. Anne Case and Angus Deaton, *Deaths of Despair and the Future of Capitalism* (Princeton: Princeton University Press, 2020).
49. Don Mitchell, "The Annihilation of Space by Law: The Roots and Implications of Anti-Homeless Laws in the United States," *Antipode* 29 (1997): 303–35; Justin Olson, Scott MacDonald, and Sara Rankin, "Washington's War on the Visibly Poor: A Survey of Criminalizing Ordinances & Their Enforcement," Seattle University School of Law Research Paper No. 15–19, Published by the SU Homeless Rights Advocacy Project (2015), available at: http://ssrn.com/abstract=2602318.
50. Tonya Brito, "Fathers Behind Bars: Rethinking Child Support Policy Toward Low-Income Noncustodial Fathers and Their Families," *Iowa Journal of Gender, Race & Justice* 15 (2012): 617–73.
51. Alysia Santo, "When Freedom Isn't Free," *Washington Monthly*, March/April/May 2015, available at: https://washingtonmonthly.com/2015/02/22/when-freedom-isnt-free.
52. Radley Balko, "How Municipalities in St. Louis County, Mo., Profit from Poverty," *Washington Post*, September 3, 2014; Sarah Childress, "Has the Justice Department Found a New Town that Preys on Its Poor?" *Frontline*, April 27, 2015, available at: www.pbs.org/wgbh/pages/frontline/criminal-justice/has-the-justice-department-found-a-new-town-that-preys-on-its-poor; Neil Sobol, "Charging the Poor: Criminal Justice Debt & Modern-Day Debtors' Prisons," *Maryland Law Review* 75 (2016): 486–540.
53. Rebecca Goldstein, Michael Sances, and Hye Young You, "Exploitative Revenues, Law Enforcement, and the Quality of Government Service," *Urban Affairs Review* 56, no. 1 (2018).
54. Eli Hager, "Debtors' Prisons, Then and Now," *The Marshall Project*, February 24, 2015, available at: www.themarshallproject.org/2015/02/24/debtors-prisons-then-and-now-faq#.NMDB59iCr.

55. *Beardon v. Georgia*, 461 US 660 (1983).
56. ACLU of Ohio, *The Outskirts of Hope: How Ohio's Debtors' Prisons Are Ruining Lives and Costing Communities* (Cleveland, OH, 2013), available at: www .acluohio.org/en/publications/outskirts-hope-how-ohios-debtors-prisons-are-ruining-lives-and-costing-communities; Sobol, "Charging the Poor."
57. Jessica Pishko, "Locked up for Being Poor: How Private Debt Collectors Contribute to a Cycle of Jail, Unemployment, and Poverty," *The Atlantic*, February 25, 2015; Sarah Stillman, "Get Out of Jail, Inc.," *The New Yorker*, June 23, 2014.
58. Heather Ann Thompson, "The Prison Industrial Complex: A Growth Industry in a Shrinking Economy," *New Labor Forum* 21, no. 3 (2012): 40–43.
59. Stillman, "Get Out of Jail, Inc."
60. Douglas A. Blackmon, *Slavery by Another Name: The Re-Enslavement of Black Americans from the Civil War to World War II* (New York: Doubleday, 2008).
61. Shoshana Walter et al., "American Rehab Chapter 5: Reagan with the Snap," *Reveal* (Podcast), July 25, 2020, available at: https://revealnews.org/episodes/ american-rehab-chapter-5-reagan-with-the-snap.
62. Shoshana Walter et al., "American Rehab Chapter 7: The Work Cure," *Reveal* (Podcast), August 1, 2020, available at: https://revealnews.org/episodes/american-rehab-chapter-seven-the-work-cure.
63. Shoshana Walter, "At Hundreds of Rehabs, Recovery Means Work without Pay," *Reveal* (Podcast), July 7, 2020, available at: https://revealnews.org/article/at-hundreds-of-rehabs-recovery-means-work-without-pay.
64. *Tony and Susan Alamo Foundation v. Secretary of Labor*, 471 US 290 (1985).
65. CD V, 373.
66. Lawrence Mishel and Julia Wolfe, "CEO Compensation Has Grown 940% since 1978," Economic Policy Institute, 2019, available at: www.epi.org/publication/ ceo-compensation-2018.
67. Mankiw, "Defending the One Percent."
68. CWM29, 420.
69. LJA, 297–98.
70. Markovits, *Meritocracy Trap*, ch. 4, provides extensive documentation for this generalization in the US. See also Alexander Bick, Nicola Fuchs-Schündeln, and David Lagakos, "How Do Hours Worked Vary with Income? Cross-Country Evidence and Implications," *American Economic Review* 108, no. 1 (2018): 170–99, who find that Smith's observation nevertheless holds within-country for all but the richest countries, and that it also holds across countries: the poorer the country, the longer the typical adult works.
71. Michael Porter and Nitin Nohria, "How CEOs Manage Time," *Harvard Business Review*, July–August 2018, available at: https://hbr.org/2018/07/how-ceos-manage-time#what-do-ceos-actually-do.
72. John Roemer, "What is Socialism Today? Conceptions of a Cooperative Economy," *International Economic Review* 62 (2021): 6, argues that in an economy that satisfies the classic Arrow-Debreu conditions of perfect competition, "workers and investors receive *precisely their contributions* to production, whereas the firm owners receive the entire surplus." This is a generalization of Ricardo's theory of rents. His point is that even under such ideal conditions, this distribution of rents is unfair. He shows that this distribution cannot be rationalized by the fiction that rents are compensation for entrepreneurial labor. We agree that the distribution of rents is a critical issue for justice. I would add that in the real world, the scale of wage theft alone is sufficient to undermine the claim that

workers receive their marginal products. Wage theft exceeds total losses from robbery, burglary, and auto theft. In the ten biggest states, employers steal almost a quarter of the earnings of minimum-wage workers. David Cooper and Teresa Kroeger, "Employers Steal Billions from Workers' Paychecks Each Year," Economic Policy Institute, 2017, 6, available at: www.epi.org/publication/employ ers-steal-billions-from-workers-paychecks-each-year.

73. Mishel and Wolfe, "CEO Compensation."

74. Michael B. Dorff, *Indispensable and Other Myths: Why the CEO Pay Experiment Failed and How to Fix It* (Berkeley: University of California Press, 2014).

75. Lawrence Mishel and Josh Bivens, "Identifying the Policy Levers Generating Wage Suppression and Wage Inequality," Economic Policy Institute, 2021, available at: https://epi.org/215903, attribute most of the US gap between productivity and pay growth to the following deliberate policy choices by firms and government: austerity macroeconomics; globalization; eroded collective bargaining; weaker labor laws and enforcement; worse labor contracts (e.g., noncompete clauses, mandatory arbitration); and changes in corporate and labor market structure, from the fissured workplace to deregulation and labor monopsony. I focus on the fissured workplace because it raises normative issues concerning the division of labor, such as deskilling, that go beyond income distribution, and that were deep concerns of classical economists in the progressive work-ethic tradition. See chapter 10 for further discussion.

76. Katz and Krueger, "The Rise of Alternative Work Arrangements."

77. Susan Lambert, Peter Fugiel, and Julia Henly, *Precarious Work Schedules among Early-Career Employees in the U.S.: A National Snapshot* (Chicago: EINet, 2014), 6, 11, 13, available at: https://ssa.uchicago.edu/sites/default/files/uploads/lambert .fugiel.henly_precarious_work_schedules.august2014_0.pdf.

78. Daniel Schneider and Kristen Harknett, "Consequences of Routine Work-Schedule Instability for Worker Health and Well-Being," *American Sociological Review* 84, no. 1 (2019): 82–114.

79. Ken Armstrong, Justin Elliott, and Ariana Tobin, "Meet the Customer Service Reps for Disney and Airbnb Who Have to Pay to Talk to You," *ProPublica*, October 2, 2020, available at: www.propublica.org/article/meet-the-customer-service-reps-for-disney-and-airbnb-who-have-to-pay-to-talk-to-you.

80. *WN*, I.10.

81. *WCI*, 76 n*.

82. *1T*, §92.

83. The Condorcet/Rawls standard applies to the overall structure of opportunities in society and not directly to any particular firm's decisions. A given firm may compete so successfully on the market that others are driven out of business. Its activities certainly don't redound to the advantage of its less well-off competitors! Nevertheless, a well-regulated economy will afford the losers in competition alternative opportunities, including unemployment insurance and retraining. Properly regulated markets function to efficiently allocate resources and promote innovation overall, even if not every business decision taken in isolation redounds to the advantage of the less well-off.

84. *CD* V, 350, 51. Ricardian socialist John Gray echoed Baxter's thought two centuries later: "God could never have intended his creatures to be the mere stumbling-blocks of each other." John Gray, *The Social System: A Treatise on the Principle of Exchange* (Edinburgh: William Tait, 1831), 339.

85. Daron Acemoglu, Alex He, and Daniel le Maire, "Eclipse of Rent-Sharing: The Effects of Managers' Business Education on Wages and the Labor Share in the US and Denmark," NBER Working Paper 29874 (2022), available at: www.nber.org

/papers/w29874. The authors also find that these effects are caused by business-school education and not due to prior dispositions of the students who seek a business degree.

86. Nathan Wilmers, "Wage Stagnation and Buyer Power: How Buyer–Supplier Relations Affect U.S. Workers' Wages, 1978 to 2014," *American Sociological Review* 83, no. 2 (2018): 213–42. See also José Azar, Ioana Marinescu, and Marshall Steinbaum, "Labor Market Concentration," *Journal of Human Resources* 57, no. 6 (2022): 1167–99 (finding that an increase of labor market concentration from the 25th to the 75th percentile "is associated with a 15–25% decline in posted wages.")

87. Jessica Van Parys, "ACA Marketplace Premiums Grew More Rapidly in Areas with Monopoly Insurers than in Areas with More Competition," *Health Affairs* 37, no. 8 (2018): 1243–51.

88. Abrahm Lustgarten, "Chesapeake Energy's $5 Billion Shuffle," *ProPublica*, March 13, 2014, available at: www.propublica.org/article/chesapeake-energys -5-billion-shuffle.

89. David Kocieniewski, "A Shuffle of Aluminum, but to Banks, Pure Gold," *New York Times*, July 20, 2013.

90. Lina Khan, "Amazon's Antitrust Paradox," *Yale Law Journal* 126 (2016–17): 710–805.

91. Michael Lewis, *The Big Short: Inside the Doomsday Machine* (New York: W. W. Norton, 2010), provides a popular and accessible account of the financial engineering that led to this disaster. For more details, see National Commission on the Causes of the Financial and Economic Crisis in the United States, *The Financial Crisis Inquiry Report* (Washington, DC: US Government Printing Office, 2011), available at: www.govinfo.gov/content/pkg/GPO-FCIC/pdf/GPO-FCIC.pdf.

92. CLI, 8–9, 25, 29, 64.

93. Mariana Mazzucato, *The Value of Everything: Making and Taking in the Global Economy* (New York: PublicAffairs, 2018), 136.

94. Mazzucato, *Value of Everything*, 118. See also Kay, *Other People's Money*, 2. ("If a closed circle of people continuously exchange bits of paper with each other, the total value of these bits of paper will not change much, if at all. If some members of that closed circle make extraordinary profits, these profits can only be made at the expense of other members of the same circle.")

95. Before the 2007–8 financial crisis, Princeton University alone sent 43 percent of its graduates to work in the financial sector. Brett Tomlinson, "Finance Jobs Top '07 Work Plans," *Princeton Alumni Weekly*, September 26, 2007, available at: https:// paw.princeton.edu/article/finance-jobs-top-07-work-plans.

96. Jacob Rugh and Douglas Massey, "Racial Segregation and the American Foreclosure Crisis," *American Sociological Review* 75, no. 5 (2010): 629–51.

97. Hal Varian, "Copying and Copyright," *Journal of Economic Perspectives* 19, no. 2 (2005): 127.

98. For a general account of how owners can profit from bankruptcy, see George Akerlof and Paul Romer, "Looting: The Economic Underworld of Bankruptcy for Profit," *Brookings Papers on Economic Activity* 1993, no. 2 (1993): 1–73. One documented method is to purchase the debt of a distressed firm for pennies on the dollar, insure the debt for multiples of its face value through CDOs, and then sue the firm over a technical default and refuse to settle even though it is solvent, thereby driving it into bankruptcy. William Cohan, "What Hedge Funds Consider a Win Is a Disaster for Everyone Else," *New York Times*, May 12, 2019.

99. Eileen Appelbaum and Rosemary Batt, *Private Equity at Work: When Wall Street Manages Main Street* (New York: Russell Sage Foundation, 2014), 86–89.
100. Jim Baker, Maggie Corser, and Eli Vitulli, "Pirate Equity: How Wall Street Firms Are Pillaging American Retail," United4Respect, 2019, 3, available at: https://united4respect.org/wp-content/uploads/2019/07/Pirate-Equity-How-Wall-Street-Firms-are-Pillaging-American-Retail-July-2019.pdf.
101. Appelbaum and Batt, *Private Equity at Work*, ch. 3.
102. See Andrei Shleifer and Lawrence Summers, "Breach of Trust in Hostile Takeovers," in *Corporate Takeovers: Causes and Consequences*, ed. Alan Auerbach (Chicago: University of Chicago Press, 1988), 33–68, for a general account of how this works.
103. Atul Gupta et al., "Does Private Equity Investment in Healthcare Benefit Patients? Evidence from Nursing Homes," NBER Working Paper w28474 (2021).
104. Jessica Silver-Greenberg and Robert Gebeloff, "Maggots, Rape, and Yet Five Stars: How U.S. Ratings of Nursing Homes Mislead the Public," *New York Times*, March 13, 2021.
105. Case and Deaton, *Deaths of Despair*, ch. 9.
106. WN, III.4.10.
107. Matthew Desmond, *Evicted: Poverty and Profit in the American City* (New York: Crown, 2016).
108. Sara Silverstein, "Investors Are Pouring Billions into US Mobile Home Communities – but Residents Are Feeling Trapped by Rising Rents," *Business Insider*, February 15, 2020, available at: www.insider.com/mobile-home-community-owners-private-equity-investment-2020-2; Peter Whoriskey, "A Billion-Dollar Empire Made of Mobile Homes," *Washington Post*, February 14, 2019.
109. Margaret Sullivan, *Ghosting the News: Local Journalism and the Crisis of American Democracy* (New York: Columbia Global Reports, 2020); Brent Kitchens, Steven Johnson, and Peter Gray, "Understanding Echo Chambers and Filter Bubbles: The Impact of Social Media on Diversification and Partisan Shifts in News Consumption," *MIS Quarterly* 44, no. 4 (2020): 1619–49.

10 Conclusion: What Should the Work Ethic Mean for Us Today?

1. Thorstein Veblen, *The Theory of the Leisure Class* (New York: Macmillan, 1899); Robert Frank, *Luxury Fever: Why Money Fails to Satisfy in an Era of Excess* (Princeton: Princeton University Press, 2000).
2. J. R. Hicks, "The Foundations of Welfare Economics," *Economic Journal* 49, no. 196 (1939): 696–712; Nicholas Kaldor, "Welfare Propositions of Economics and Interpersonal Comparisons of Utility," *Economic Journal* 49 (1939): 549–52.
3. Lionel Robbins, *An Essay on the Nature and Significance of Economic Science*, 2nd ed. (London: Macmillan, 1948), 136–41. Interpersonal comparisons are not needed for general equilibrium or game theory. But Robbins advanced the view that they should not be used for normative purposes.
4. Amartya Sen, "Behavior and the Concept of Preference," *Economica* 41 (1973): 241–59, offers a classic critique of this assumption.
5. Fred Hirsch, *Social Limits to Growth* (Cambridge, MA: Harvard University Press, 1976) is one of the most thoughtful contributions to welfare economics in this era.
6. Elizabeth Popp Berman, *Thinking Like an Economist: How Efficiency Replaced Equality in U.S. Public Policy* (Princeton: Princeton University Press, 2022);

Stephanie L. Mudge, *Leftism Reinvented: Western Parties from Socialism to Neoliberalism* (Cambridge, MA: Harvard University Press, 2018).

7. Brett Murphy, "Rigged: Forced into Debt. Worked Past Exhaustion. Left with Nothing," *USA Today*, June 16, 2017.

8. Studies have not found hotspots arising from the acid rain program. See, e.g., Jason Corburn, "Emissions Trading and Environmental Justice: Distributive Fairness and the USA's Acid Rain Programme," *Environmental Conservation* 28, no. 4 (2002): 323–32. However, California's cap-and-trade program for greenhouse gases appears to have created co-pollutant hotspots, including for sulfur dioxide, in poor communities of color. See, e.g., Lara Cushing et al., "Carbon Trading, Co-Pollutants, and Environmental Equity: Evidence from California's Cap-and-Trade Program (2011–2015)," *PLOS Medicine* 15, no. 7 (2018): e1002604.

9. See, e.g., David Autor, David Dorn, and Gordon Hanson, "The China Syndrome: Local Labor Market Effects of Import Competition in the United States," *American Economic Review* 103, no. 6 (2013): 2121–68; Branko Milanovic, *Global Inequality: A New Approach for the Age of Globalization* (Cambridge, MA: Belknap Press of Harvard University Press, 2016), ch. 2.

10. Robin Kaiser-Schatzlein, "How Life as a Trucker Devolved into a Dystopian Nightmare," *New York Times*, March 15, 2022.

11. See Tyler Cowan's comments on my argument in Anderson, *Private Government*, ch. 6, and my reply to him in ch. 7.

12. Harry Braverman, *Labor and Monopoly Capital: The Degradation of Work in the Twentieth Century*, foreword by Paul M. Sweezy, introduction by John Bellamy Foster (New York: Monthly Review Press, 1998). Braverman ties the Marxist neglect of concerns about work to communist adoption of capitalist management principles on pp. 7–11.

13. Amartya Sen, *Commodities and Capabilities* (Amsterdam: North-Holland, 1985).

14. Amartya Sen, *Rationality and Freedom* (Cambridge, MA: Harvard University Press, 2002).

15. For one example in a large literature, see Samuel Bowles and Herbert Gintis, *Democracy and Capitalism* (New York: Basic Books, 1987).

16. See, e.g., Nancy Folbre, *Greed, Lust, & Gender: A History of Economic Ideas* (New York: Oxford University Press, 2009).

17. Piketty, *Capital in the Twenty-First Century*, 238–42.

18. Isabelle Ferreras et al., *Democratize Work: The Case for Reorganizing the Economy* (Chicago: The University of Chicago Press, 2022).

19. Piketty, *Capital and Ideology*.

20. Keynes, "Economic Possibilities for Our Grandchildren," 23.

21. Graeber, *Bullshit Jobs*, 3.

22. Graeber, *Bullshit Jobs*, 82.

23. Abhijit Banerjee et al., "Debunking the Stereotype of the Lazy Welfare Recipient: Evidence from Cash Transfer Programs Worldwide," *World Bank Research Observer* 32, no. 2 (2017): 155–84.

24. Stephanie Kelton, *The Deficit Myth: Modern Monetary Theory and the Birth of the People's Economy* (New York: PublicAffairs, 2020), 3, 327n37.

25. MECW37, 807. Thanks to Miikka Jaarte for making this argument and calling my attention to this passage.

26. Hence, I disagree with Thomas Hurka and John Tasioulas, "Games and the Good," *Proceedings of the Aristotelian Society* 106, no. 1 (2006): 217–35, who argue that playing games, which are defined in terms of goals that are "intrinsically trivial," satisfies modern conceptions of value such as Marx's.

27. *ES*, 172–79.
28. Sandel, *Tyranny of Merit*, ch. 3.
29. Piketty, *Capital and Ideology*, ch. 14–16; Berman, *Primacy of Politics*, ch. 9.
30. Elizabeth Anderson, "The Epistemology of Democracy," *Episteme* 3, no. 1–2 (2006): 8–22.
31. Anand Giridharadas, *Winners Take All: The Elite Charade of Changing the World* (New York: Knopf, 2018).
32. Samuel Bowles, *The Moral Economy: Why Good Incentives Are No Substitute for Good Citizens* (New Haven: Yale University Press, 2016), ch. 5. Bowles defines the liberalism in liberal market societies in terms of respecting equality of political rights, tolerating diversity, enforcing nondiscrimination rules, and observing the rule of law.
33. *CD* II, 584.
34. Thelen, "American Precariat."
35. William Thompson, *Appeal of One Half of the Human Race, Women, against the Pretensions of the Other Half, Men to Retain Them in Political and Thence in Civil and Domestic Slavery (1825)*, ed. Dolores Dooley (Cork: Cork University Press, 1996). Lamentably but characteristically for his era, Thompson failed to credit his collaborator, Anna Doyle Wheeler, for this work.
36. See Katrine Marçal, *Who Cooked Adam Smith's Dinner?: A Story about Women and Economics*, trans. Saskia Vogel (London: Portobello Books, 2015).
37. Case and Deaton, *Deaths of Despair*, part II.
38. Piketty, *Capital and Ideology*, 1028.

INDEX

abolition, 65–66, 192–94, 289–90

absolutism, 40, 41, 43–44, 48–50

accumulation, of wealth, xvii, 17–18, 20, 21–22, 35–36, 51–52, 53–54, 65–66, 128–29, 170, 171–73, 295, *see also* competitive acquisition

Agreement of the People, 38, 40–43

agricultural workers, 91, 100–1, 107, 110, 147–48, 170, 182, 192, 289–90

agriculture, 27–28, 56, 91, 95, 107, 182, 238, *see also* collectivized farming

alienation, 206–12

altruism, effective, 16–19

anarchists, 21–22, 235

Andover Union workhouse, scandal over administration of, 106, 189

Anglican Church, 5–6, 15, 24, 65–66

antitrust doctrine, weakening of, x–xi, 254–55

apprenticeship, 60, 61, 143–44, 147, 148, 155–56, 210, 289–90

appropriation, 28, 29, 30–31, 34–35

  consent and, 32–33, 54–55

  just, 27–28, 29, 31–32

aristocratic paternalism, 91–99

Arminianism, 13–14, 17

artisans. *See* craftsmen

asceticism, xvii, 17, 64–65, 88, 128–29, 271–72, 295

autonomy, 128–29, 181–82, 186–87, 206–7, 219–20, 242–43, 248–49, 250, 288

Babeuf, François-Noël, 213–24, 227, 229, 232

  distributive justice and, 246

Bakunin, Mikhail, 224

banking system, 254–55, 277, 278, *see also* financialization

bankruptcy laws, x–xi, 254–55

bargaining power, 275, *see also* collective bargaining

Baxter, Richard, 6–7, 13–14, 15, 17, 26, 45–46, 60, 67, 69, 88, 97, 98, 251–52, 258–59, 260–61, 275, 277–78, 281

  business ethics and, 34, 46, 276–77, 281–82

  Christian Directory, 8–9, 10, 11, 12–13, 15–16, 17–18, 19, 65

  condemnation of exploitation of poor, 13

  dignity of labor and, 71

  dual nature of work ethic and, 15–16

  good works and, 26–27

idle rich and, 71, 85
justified inequality and, 275, 276–77
progressive work ethic and
shareholder capitalism and, 272–73
slavery and, 10–11, 12–13, 51
unpaid domestic labor and, 71,
296–97
utilitarianism and, 18–19, 169–70
begging, 1, 2, 59, 60, 62, 111
Bengal famine, East India Company and,
146–47, 201–2
Bentham, Jeremy, xiv, xv, 63, 73–81,
102, 105, 109, 123–24, 127–28,
179–80, 264, 272
government outsourcing and, 199,
258–59, 264–72
interest rates and, 46, 149
panopticon and, 73–75, 76–77, 78–79,
80–81, 271
Pauper Management Improved,
73–74, 75–79, 80–81
the poor and, 63–99
Puritanism and, 66, 73–74, 76–77, 91
Smith and, 75–76, 79
utilitarianism and, 73–74, 76–77, 78,
79, 80–81, 105
utopian fanaticism and, 125,
128–29
Bernstein, Eduard, xiv, 127, 213,
225–26, 235–37, 238, 240, 244–45,
293–94
Evolutionary Socialism, 225–26, 236
Marx/Marxism and, 236–37, 243–44
social democracy and, 234–42,
243–44, 292–93
"workers" cooperatives and, 238, 240
Beveridge, William, 252
Bible, 1, 4–5, 14–15, 65
Bismarck, Otto von, 232, 234, 252
Blacks
Black activists, 258
civil and political rights of, 259
stereotypes of, 259, 260–61
subjection of, 257–58
Blum, Léon, 250

bourgeoisie, 62, 73–81, 123, 167,
210–11
Bray, John Francis, 163, 164, 165–67,
174, 244
bullshit jobs, 290–91, 295–96
Bunyan, Paul, *Pilgrim's Progress*, 77–78
Buonarroti, Philippe, 214, 215
Burke, Edmund, xv, 63, 87, 91–99,
115–16, 127–28
aristocracy and, 91–99
commodification of labor and, 247–48
free markets and, 93–95
in Rockinghamite faction of Whigs, 93
Reflections on the Revolution in
France (1790), 93
Smith and, 130, 146, 154
Speenhamland system and, 92–95
"Thoughts and Details on Scarcity"
(1795), 113, 150–51
business ethics, 276, 277
business executives, xi, 255–56,
272–75, 276

calling, 5, 8, 11–12, 15–16, 67, 88–89,
168–69
Calvin, John, 5–6
Calvinism, 3–7, 13–14, 17, 204–5
capitalism, xvii, 2, 9, 53, 212, 237, *see
also* laissez-faire capitalism
alienation and, 206–12
anarchist, 163–64
critical analyses of, 289
democracy and, 236
Marx's critique of, 206–12
Puritanism and, 254
shareholder capitalism, xii–xiii, 255,
258–59, 272–83
stakeholder capitalism, 255
work and, 203, 206–12
capitalist class, xiii, 20, 63–65, 122, 172
carceral state, 264–72, *see also* prisons
care work, 296–97
Carlyle, Thomas, 193–94, 195–96
Catholic Church, xvii–xviii, 1, 233
Chadwick, Edwin, 102, 104–5, 119–20

charity, 11, 25–26, 45–46, 69, 94, 120–21, *see also* poverty relief
  Christian, 16–19
  discouraged by conservative work ethic, 126
  duty of, 18, 19, 57–58, 67, 83
  effective altruism and, 16–17
  Locke and, 67, 68, 69
  Malthus and, 83, 86
  natural law and, 57
  punishment of, 126
  right to, 57, 58
  vs. workhouses, 111
Charles I, 15, 38–39, 48–50
Charles II, 24, 38–39, 49–51, 176–77
Chartism, 170–71, 186, 234
chastity, xiv, 67–68, 81–87, 122, 179–80
child care, 60, 71, 259–61, 296–97
child labor, 75–76, 78, 102, 182, 235, 260–61
child poverty, 75–76, 78, 102, 260–61, 296–97
children, 57, 60, 61, 260–61
  apprenticeship and, 60, 61
  child development, 187–88
  deprived of care, 121–22
  education of, 191–92
  poverty and, 57, 60, 61, 84–85, 259–61
  in workhouses, 75–76, 77–78, 102
China, 200–1, 213, 215–16, 285–86
Church of England. *See* Anglican Church
citizenship, 243, 244–45, 250–51
civil servants, 264–65, 266, 267
class conflict, xv–xvi, 123–24, 162, 167, 230–31, 232, 243, 244–46
class differences, 63–64, 128–29, 166–67, 179–80, 238–39, 240–41, 243, 250–53
  Malthus and, 85–86, 96–97, 128–29
  social democracy and, 244–45, 253
  work ethic and, 64–65, 243
classes, 161, 162, 185–86, 209, *see also* class conflict; class differences; specific classes

classical economic thought, xvii, 284, 286–88, 289–90
classical liberalism, xiii, 127–28, 226, 227–34, 256–57, 292–93
codetermination, 187, 240–41, 243, 249, 297
collective bargaining, 243, 248–49, 296
colonialism, 199, 200–1, *see also* imperialism
colonies, 49–50, 140–41, 145–47
commercial society, rise of, 138–40, 142–43
Commission for Inquiring into the Condition of the Poorer Classes of Ireland, 109–10
commodification of labor, xi–xiii, 248, 256, 269–70, 274–75
commodity, meaning of, 248
commons, 34–36, 54–55
communes, 165, 238, 292–93
communism, x, 178–79, 204, 213–24, 227, 237, 287–88
  institutional structure of, 213, 214, 215, 221–23
  institutions eliminated by, 213
  luck egalitarianism and, 216, 217
  totalitarianism and, 213, 214–16, 224, 225–26
competitive acquisition, 128–29, 170, 172–73, 182, 245, 247, 258–59, 284–85, 295
Condorcet, Nicolas de Caritat Marquis de, 63, 71–72, 96, 127, 226–34, 247, 275, 276
conservative, use of the term, xv
conservative relief policies, poverty-promoting features of, 120–22, 123
conservative work ethic, xi–xii, xiv–xv, xvi, 14, 24–25, 62, 63–99, 172–73, 233, 254–59, 292–93
  aggregative utilitarianism and, 169–70
  attitudes toward working poor and, 130
  Bentham and, 264, 272
  child care and, 261

class and, xv–xvi, 120, 123–24, 132,
    179–80
consumption and, 170, 172–73, 182
contradiction inherent in, 123,
    170–71, 179–80
definition of, ix–x
English welfare reform and, 100–8
harshness toward workers and, 120
hijacking of work ethic by, xiv–xv
ideas of moral desert and, 129,
    133–35, 136–37
ideology and, xvi, 100–26
imperialism and, 257–58, 259
Industrial Revolution and, 292–93
inegalitarian and antidemocratic
    sentiment fueled by, 253
Irish famine policy and, 108–19
Malthus and, 190–91, 257–58
Mill and, 192, 195–96, 202, 293
neoclassical welfare economics
    and, 285
neoliberalism and, xii, 253, 254–83
nonutilitarian normative attitudes
    of, 85
poverty policies and, 67–68, 69–70,
    71, 101, 120–22, 123
progress and, 169–70
secularization and, 66–67
shareholder capitalism and, xii–xiii
taxation and, 120, 121–22
United States and, 250, 254–55,
    257–58
Weber and, 292–93
welfare reform and, 100–8
Whately and, 108–9, 257–58,
    259–64, 273
conspicuous consumption, 15–16,
    17–18, 66, 170, 172–73, 182,
    284–85
Constitution (English), 38–44, 90
contract(s), xi–xii, xiii–xiv, 51–53,
    149–50, 192–93, see also social
    contract
    freedom of, xiii–xiv, 22, 46, 183–84
    regulation of, 37–38, 45, 48, 183–84

copyholders, 54, 55–56, 63–64, 108–9
Corn Laws, 107, 110, 152, 173–81
cottier system of renting land, 174–75,
    177–78, 180, 181
craftsmen, 64, 210–11
    factory system and, 63–64, 234
    Marx's romanticized view of,
        210–11
    radical artisans, 210, 221–22, 235
    replaced by factory system and wage
        workers, 63–64, 170

decommodification of labor, 247–49,
    250–53
democracy, 243, 293–94, 297–98, see
    also social democracy
    backsliding of, x, 290, 297
    capitalism and, 236
    constraining of, xi, 293
    distributive justice and, 247
    in the workplace, 297–98
deregulation, xii–xiii, 254–55, 277,
    285–86, 287
desert, 216, 217, 232, 245–46, 247,
    261–62
Diggers, 31, 42, 43, 54
dignity of labor, 71, 242–43
disability insurance, 230, 231, 243
discipline, xvii, xviii, 6–7, 13–14, 64–65,
    88, 122, 129–30, 136–37, 291–92
    ascetic, 8, 9, 14, 88–89, 114, 137, 180,
        249, 271–72, see also asceticism
    in the workplace, 65, 125, 170–71,
        178, 179, 188, 189, 209, 218–19,
        248–49
distributive justice, 164, 245–46, 247,
    285, 286–87, 288
    democratic perspective on, 245–47
    desert and, 245–46, 247
    Equals and, 219–20
    Ricardian socialists and, 162, 164,
        165, 245–46
division of labor, 15–16, 168–69,
    172, 181–87, 208, 211, 235,
    249, 273

division of labor (cont.)
  European progress attributed to,
    168–69
  Mill and, 172, 182, 184–85, 273
  Smith and, 147–48, 184–85, 273
  women and, 184
drudgery, xvii, 9, 61, 62, 73, 128–29,
    137, 154–55, 169, 170, 173, 182,
    191–92, 208, 248–49
Du Bois, W. E. B., 258
duty to work, ix–x, 11–12, 23–24, 26,
    59, 68

East India Company, 146–47
economic growth, x, 285–86
education, 61, 147–48, 191–92, 248–50
  expansion of access to, 251–52, 257
  inequality of, 228, 251–52
  publicly funded, 233–34, 243, 248–49,
    250–51
  radicalizing effects of, 248
  rights to, 243, 250
  schooling provided by factory
    owners, 182
  social stratification and, 251–52
  universal, 147–48, 228, 242–43
  of workers, 186, 192
efficiency, criterion of, 285, 286
egalitarianism, 11, 14–15
  luck egalitarianism, 216, 217
enclosure(s), 13, 30–31, 34–35, 55–56,
    63–64, 139, 161
  Locke and, 32–33, 53, 54–55, 56, 279
  Mill and, 177, 192
  Parliamentary, 55–56, 89–90, 91,
    273, 279
  vulture private equity as new, 279–81
Engels, Friedrich, 214, 222, 223, 224,
    236, 237
  Communist Manifesto, 204, 221–22
  "dictatorship of the proletariat"
    and, 221
  freedom and, 219–20, 223–24
  institutional structure of communism
    and, 213

Engels's Pause, 64–65, 170, 234–35,
    254, 256
England. See also United Kingdom
  classical liberalism in, xiii
  land tenure, 173–81
  Poor Law and, 81–82
English Civil War, 15, 38, 40–43,
    48–49
Enlightenment, 96, 153–54, 227
entails, 140–42, 176–77, 289–90
equality, x, 43–44, 242–43
  attempts to create strict, 229
  of citizenship, as basis for shared
    normative perspective, 244–45
  distributive justice and, 247
  Equals' radical principle of, 216,
    217–18
  under the law, 42, 43
  of status, 250–51
Equals, 214, 217, 229
  distributive justice and, 219–20
  Marx and, 218–20
  material equality and, 216, 217–18
  military-style central planning
    and, 223
  Paine and, 229, 230–31
estate taxes, 71–73, 230
evictions, 13, 55–56
  as death sentence, 126
  Irish famine policy, 112–13, 115–16,
    117–18
  in United States, 281–82
executive compensation, 255–56,
    272–75

Fabian socialists, 246, 247, 273
Factory Acts, 182, 183
factory system, 63–64, 122, 170, 182,
    234, 235
faith, 3–7, 13–14
famine, 100–26, 151, 189–90
  Bengal, 146–47, 201–2
  British policy toward, 100
  Irish, 100, 111–12, 129, 151, 177–78,
    189–90

Mill and, 177–78
  state intervention to prevent, 94, 95
feudalism, 48–50, 54, 137–38, 142–45,
  147, 159
finance, 254–55, 277–79, 293
financial aid, 263–64
firm, the, 266–67, 269, 284–85, 288,
  295–96
forced labor, 188–89, 259, 270–72, *see
  also* slavery
France, 87, 89–90, 100–1, 214, 233–34,
  250, 252, 296–97, *see also* French
  Revolution
franchise
  expansion of, xiii, 24, 90,
    155–56
  propertyless men and, 43–44
  restricted, xiii, 20, 21–22, 38–39, 43
  universal male, 38, 170–71
  women and, 43–44
Franklin, Benjamin, secularization of
  work ethic and, 65–66
freedom, 206, 223–24, 242–43, 289
freedom of contract, xiii–xiv, 22, 46,
  183–84
free labor, xvii–xviii, 140–41,
  142–45, 258
free markets, xiii, 93–95, 122, 123–24,
  129, 135–48, 155–56, 182, 256–57
French Revolution, 81, 87, 91–92,
  100–1, 124, 140–41, 150, 153–54,
  159, 214–15, 218, 221–22, 226–27
Friedman, Milton, 255, 278–79
frugality, xiv, xviii, 8–9, 64–65, 67–68,
  122, 129–30, 136–37, 174, 179–80,
  276, *see also* asceticism

Germany, xvii–xviii, 225–26, 234,
  235–36, 241–42, 252
Gilbert's Act (1782), 93, 104
government outsourcing, x, 264–72
grace, 5–7, 13–14, 26–27
Great Famine. *See* Irish famine
Gregory Clause, 117, 262–63
guild system, 210, 234

Hansson, Per Albin, 244–45, 247
Hayek, Friedrich, *Road to Serfdom*
  (1944), 225–26
Hazlitt, William, 72, 89, 189–90
health care, x, 232, 243, 250–51,
  269–70, 296, 298
Hegel, G. W. F., 96, 206–7, 219–20
historical progress, 96, 97–98, 206, 236
history, xvii, 96, 97–98, 168, 206, *see
  also* historical progress
Hodgskin, Thomas, 163–64, 166–67,
  176–77, 248
Hone, William, 89–90
Hooker, Richard, 25–26
House of Commons, 38, 40, 106
House of Lords, 38, 43
human capabilities, 171–73, 181–82,
  204, 208–9, 242–43, 249–50,
  288, 291
human flourishing, 203–4, 248–49,
  250, 289

ideologies, xvi, 125
  critique of, 119–20
  epistemic functioning of, xvi, 123–24
  historical origins of, xvi
idleness, 8, 12, 44–45, 47, 51–62, 65,
  69–70, 111
idle poor, 24–25, 52–62, 65, 69–70
idle rich, 24–25, 26, 30–32, 34, 42,
  44–45, 47, 51–52, 65, 71, 85,
  88–89, 101, 243, 245, 247, 295, *see
  also* leisure class
imperialism, 98, 187–202, 254, 257–58,
  259, 293
indentured servitude, 51, 52–54
independence, 72, 186–87
  cult of, 68–73
independent contractors, xi, 256, 274–75
India, 200–1
individualism, 66–67, 71, 231, 258–59
individuality, 205–6, 210, 214–15
Industrial Revolution, 57, 63–64, 65,
  101, 122, 168, 170, 211–12,
  234–35, 265–66, 288, 292–93

Industrial Revolution (cont.)
  commodification of labor and, 248
  labor productivity and, 189–90
industry, xiv, 67–68, 122, 128–30,
    136–37, 174, 179–80, 191–92
  idleness and, 44–45, 47, 51–62
  micro-division of labor in, 182
inequality, 228, 230–31, 250–53, 290
  decommodification of labor and,
    250–53
  justified, 9, 230–31, 275,
    276–77
  malign cultural effect of, 289
  private property and, 217–18
  social democracy and, 250–53
inheritance, 48–49, 120, 141–42, 143,
    173–81, 254–55
intellectual property, x–xi, 47, 48,
    254–55, 279
interest, 46, 47, 176–77, 245–46, 247–48
International Working Men's
    Association, 210, 224, 235–36
Ireland, 99, 108, 181
  agricultural system in, 111–12, 118
  birth rates in, 118
  cottier system of renting land in,
    174–75, 177–78, 180, 181
  division of labor in, 108–9
  inheritance in, 173–81
  land reform in, 177–79
  land tenure in, 173–81
  poverty relief in, 111–12, 177–78, see
    also Irish famine policy
  unemployment in, 109
  workhouses in, 111–12, 124–25
Irish famine, 112–19, 129, 151, 177–78,
    see also Irish famine policy
Irish famine policy, 100, 112–20, 181
  British government and, 120–21,
    124–25, 153, 177–78, 181,
    261–62, 263
  evictions, 112–13, 115–16, 117–18
  exacerbation of famine and, 112–13,
    118, 189–90
  Gregory Clause, 117

public works, 112–14
  punishment of charity and, 126
  temporary soup kitchens, 112–13, 115
  workhouses and, 112–13, 115–18
Irish landlords, 112–13, 115–16, 117,
    177–78, 181
Irish peasantry, 99, 289–90
  conversion into wage laborers,
    111–12, 117, 118, 177–78
Irish poor law, 100, 108–12, 119–20

Jacobins, 214, 218, 229
Jesus, 14–15
justice, 22, 25–26, 31–32, 186–87, see
    also distributive justice

Kaldor, Nicholas, 285
Kant, Immanuel, 96
Keynes, John Maynard, 2, 247–48, 278,
    290, 291, 292–93
King, Martin Luther, Jr., 258
Knatchbull's Act, 62, 93. See also
    Workhouse Test Act (1723).

labor, 21, 47, 107, 157, 163, 207, 208,
    221, 252–53
  alienated, 206–12
  commodification of, xi–xiii,
    94, 126, 245–46, 248, 256, 269–70,
    274–75
  decommodification of, 247–48,
    250–53
  dignity of, 11, 71
  as expression of individuality,
    205–6, 208
  forced, 188–89, 259, 270–72, see also
    slavery
  labor supply, 123, 170–71, 191,
    284–85
  professional, 269–70
  property rights and, 47
  unalienated, 203–6, 207, 219–20,
    223, 235
  unfree, 140–41, 142–45
  unpaid domestic, 71, 289, 296–97

laboring poor, 103, 130, 228, *see also* working poor
labor theory of property, 174–75, 180, 230
labor theory of value, 29–31, 70, 162, 165–66, 231–32, 236–37
labor unions. *See unions*
laissez-faire capitalism, 46, 112–13, 114, 127–28, 148, 150, 151–55, 182, 183–84, 241, 257–58
land, 47, 54, 122, 174, 177, *see also* enclosure(s); property rights; labor value of property
landlords, xiii, 13, 24, 30, 44–45, 56, 64, 65, 91, 95, 110, 125, 147–48, 172, 243, 254, 273, 279, 281–82 *see also* landowners
  authority of, xiii, 95, 105, 107, 108, 110
  Irish, 111–13, 115–16, 117, 125, 177–78, 181
landowners, 24, 29–31, 38–39, 44–45, 47, 49–50, 63–64, 156–58, 161
land reform, 177–79, 181
Land Tenure Reform Association, 176–77
land tenure system, 173–81, 289–90
leisure, 1, 169–70, 249–50, 290, 291–92
  vs. luxury, 182–83
  Mill and, 183–84, 249–50
  progressive work ethic and, 66, 137, 296
  Puritan attitudes toward, 73–74
  Smith and, 137, 249–50
  work and, 2
  workers and, 66, 182, 186, 192, 242–43
Lenin, Vladimir, 213, 221, 227
"less eligibility," principle of, 104, 111, 120–21, 188
Leveller movement, 23–24, 38–39, 40–43, 48, 52–53, 54–55, 87, 90, 170–71, 210
liberalism, 57, 127–28, 239, 240

liberal Toryism, 91, 105, 108, 110, 118. *See also* Tories
libertarianism, xiii, 21–26, 27–29, 31–32, 33, 36–37, 40, 45–46, 127–28, 152–53, 256–57
liberty, 247, *See also* freedom
Locke, John, xiv, 26, 32–33, 39–40, 43–44, 45–46, 50–51, 53, 57, 67, 138, 169–70, 187–88, 209, 236–37, 293–94
  on begging, 59, 60
  business ethics and, 276–77
  charity and, 67, 68, 69
  class analysis and, 39–40, 179–80
  constitutional remedies of, 40–44, 52–53, 170–71
  on contracts, 37–38, 45, 48, 51–53
  on copyright, 47, 48, 279
  distributive justice and, 164, 247
  on enclosures, 32–33, 53, 54–55, 279
  franchise and, 23–24, 43–44
  Fundamental Constitution of Carolina, the, 53–54
  head of Board of Trade under King William III, 41, 49, 51
  idleness and, 24–25, 26, 31–32, 42, 44–45, 47, 51–62, 65, 71, 85, 279
  on indentured servitude, 51, 52–54
  on inheritance, 48–49, 52–53, 141, 175–76
  justified inequality and, 275, 276–77
  labor-mixing provision and, 27, 29
  labor theory of value and, 29–31, 70
  Leveller movement and, 23–24, 40–43, 48, 52–53, 54–55
  libertarian reading of, 20–25, 27–29, 33, 36–37, 40, 45–46
  Mill and, 173–81, 190–91
  on monarchy, 39–40, 43–44, 49
  on monopolies, 52–53, 277
  moral theory of, 25–26, 27
  natural law and, 57
  need for state and, 34–38
  on children, 60, 61, 187–88, 260–61

Locke, John (cont.)
poverty and, 57–59, 60, 62, 64–65, 68,
187–88, 260–61
property regimes and, 24–25, 34–36,
47, 48, 49–50, 51–53, 54, 55,
163–64, 172
pro-worker orientation of, 24–25, 44,
49–50, 52–53, 54, 57, 60, 63
Reasonableness of Christianity (1695),
26–27
rejection of libertarian historical
entitlement theory, 31–32
scarcity and, 34–37
Second Treatise, 26–27, 32–33, 42, 43,
55, 59–60, 65
secularization of work ethic and, 65
on slavery, 49, 50–53, 54
Smith and, 149
social contract and, 36–38, 43–44, 229
Some Thoughts Concerning Education
(1693), 61
spoilage proviso and, 27, 30–31, 33
sufficiency proviso and, 27–29, 30,
32–33, 34–35, 49–50, 54–55,
58–59, 174
Two Treatises, 23–24, 41
on wage labor, 53–54, 143
Whig party and, 23–24, 38–39, 110,
265–66
work ethic and, xv, 20–62, 63–64, 65,
190–91, 203–4, 258–59, 275,
277–78
London Corresponding Society, 87, 89
Luther, Martin, 3–6, 15
Lutheranism, 3–7
Luxemburg, Rosa, 213
luxury, 8–9, 17–18, 69, 88, 170,
182, 245
vs. leisure, 182–83
luxury consumption, 8–9, 17–18, 66,
88, 170, 245

Macpherson, C. B., 20, 52, 53–54
Malthus, Thomas Robert, xiv, xv, 63, 66,
81–87, 89, 91, 94, 105, 111, 118,
129, 146, 160–61, 179–80, 190–91,
199, 256–59
charity and, 83, 86
chastity and, 67–68, 83–84
class and, 85–87, 96–97,
128–29
influence of, 102, 108–9, 123–24,
156–58, 189–91, 257–58, 259–64
Mill and, 188, 189, 190–91
Poor Law and, 81–83, 84, 189
population theory of, 82–83, 96,
155–58, 172–73, 188, 189, 190
poverty relief and, 67–68, 72, 81–83,
84, 89, 102, 189
Ricardo and, 155–56, 158–59, 160
theory of rent and, 155–56, 157–58
utilitarianism and, 84, 85
welfare policy and, 259–64
Mao Zedong, 213, 215–16, 218
Maréchal, Sylvain, 214
Marshall, T. H., 243, 250–51
Marx, Karl, 63, 96, 122, 127–28, 163,
203, 204, 206–12, 213–24, 226,
235, 236–37, 238–39, 249, 291–92,
293, 295
Capital, 207, 226, 235
Civil War in France, 222
"Comments on James Mill, Élémens
d'Économie Politique
(1844)," 205–6
commitment to autonomy of
revolutionary workers, 223–24
Communist Manifesto, 204, 210–11,
221–22
Critique of the Gotha Program,
204, 218
"dictatorship of the proletariat"
and, 221
distributive justice and, 246, 247
Economic and Philosophical
Manuscripts of 1844, 204
Equals and, 218–20
freedom and, 219–20,
223–24, 291
human flourishing and, 203–4

ideal of unalienated labor and,
203–6, 235
institutional structure of communism
and, 213
labor theory of value and, 165–66,
236–37
launches democratic path for
"workers" emancipation, 224
Mill (John Stuart) and, 127–28, 204,
210–12, 224, 226
progressive work ethic and, xiv,
127–28, 203–24, 226, 244, 292–93
radical artisans and, 221–22, 235
social democracy and, 226, 292–93
stress on work as central meaningful
activity, 204–6
totalitarianism and, 225–26
on work as expression of individuality,
205–6
Marxism, 213, 214, 225–27, 234,
243–44, 287–88, 289
mercantilist policies, 143, 145–47
meritocracy, 251–52, 256–57, 293
Methodism, 17, 77
micro-division of labor, 147–48, 168–69,
182, 186–87, 248, 256, 287–88
Mill, James, 155, 159, 176–77, 178–79,
204, 205–6, 208, 246
Mill, John Stuart, xv, 63, 127–28, 155,
167, 168–202, 204, 212, 225–26,
238, 239, 249, 293
abolition and, 192–93
classical liberalism and, xiii,
127–28
colonialism and, 199, 200–1
competitive conspicuous consumption
and, 172, 257, 295
cottier system and, 174–75, 177–78,
180, 181
on despotism, 195–96, 197–98
division of labor and, 172, 182,
184–85, 273
domestic imperialism and, 187–92
foreign imperialism and, 192–202
Irish famine policy and, 177–78, 181

laissez-faire economics and, 182,
183–84
land reform and, 177, 178–79, 181
laws of inheritance and, 174–76
leisure and, 183–84, 249–50
Locke and, 173–81, 190–91
Malthus and, 188, 189, 190–91
Marx and, 204, 210–12, 224, 226
New Poor Law of 1834 and, 188–89,
190–91, 192
non-white peoples and, 195–98, 202
as officer of British East India
Company, 198–99, 202
Petition of the East India Company,
198–99
poverty policy and, 188–89, 190–91
on primogeniture, 176–77
progressive work ethic and, xiv, 173,
187–88, 190–91, 193–95, 236–37,
289–90, 293–94
promotion of leisure, 182–83
property rights and, 172, 186–87
rejection of hierarchy, 172,
185–86, 198
Ricardian socialists and, 173,
176–77
slavery and, 192–94, 195–98, 200–1
Smith and, 173, 184–85
support for forced labor, 188–89
sympathy and, 172
unions and, 184–85
utilitarianism and, 173–74
women's rights and, 183, 191–92,
198, 289
workers' cooperatives and, 184–85,
186–87, 238, 244
Milton, John, 2
minimum wage, 94–95, 150–51,
256, 272
monarchy, 39–40, 41, 43–44, 49–50
money, 28–29, 30, 32–33, 35–36, 53,
148–49
monopolies, xi, xiii, 45, 46, 47, 48, 254,
264–65, 277, see also antitrust
doctrine

natural law, 21–22, 25–34, 35–36, 49, 57, 108
natural liberties, 43–44, 149
natural rights, 21–22, 23–24, 36–37, 163–64
neoclassical economics, xvii–xviii, 245–46, 272–73, 287, 288
neoliberalism, xii, 22, 253, 254–83, 285
  consequences of, xi,
  definition of, xii–xiii, 272–73
  origins of, xiv, xvi
  policymaking and, 285–86
  Poor Laws and, 264
  Protestant work ethic and, xiv
  racism and, xvii–xviii
  rise of, x, 254–59, 285
  social democracy and, xiii–xiv, 254–55, 293
  in United States, xvii–xviii, 258–64
  welfare policy and, 259–64, 288
New Poor Law of 1834, 100, 105, 107, 109, 115–16, 119–20, 124–25, 188–89, 190–91, 192, 258–64
Nicholls, George, 111–12, 115
Noetics, 95, 96, 98, 99, 105, 109, 122, 243
Nozick, Robert, 25–26, 27

Old Poor Law. See Poor Law
original sin, doctrine of, 26–27, 97, 98
outdoor relief, 102–3, 109, 111–12, 115–16
outsourcing, x, 256, 258–59, 264–72, 274–75, 288
Owen, Robert, 165
Owenites, 172–73

Paine, Thomas, 63, 127, 226–34
  Babeuf and, 227, 229, 232
  Equals and, 229, 230–31
  labor theory of value and, 231–32
  Poor Law regime and, 230
  progressive work ethic and, xiv, 289–90
  Rights of Man, 87
  social insurance and, 71–72, 289–90

Paley, William, 63, 66, 67–68, 87–90, 91
Parliament (UK), 38–39, 56, 181, 183, 198–99
peasant proprietors, 180–81, 186, 192
peasantry, 55–56, 99, 289–90, see also peasant proprietors
  conversion into wage laborers, 111–12, 117, 118, 122, 177–78
  Irish, 99, 108–9, 111–12, 117, 118, 125, 177–78
  social democrats and, 240–41
Peel, Robert, 95, 113
Perkins, William, 8, 9–10
personal responsibility, 81–87
philanthropy, 295, see also charity
Piketty, Thomas, 217, 289, 290, 293
Pitt, William, 94–95, 150–51
Pol Pot, 213, 215–16, 218
poor, the, 57, 58, 63–99, 120, 135, see also idle poor; poverty relief
  able-bodied, 58, 59, 60, 62, 102–3, 104–5, 116–18
  criminalization of, 270–72
  distinction between "deserving" and "undeserving," 9, 11, 58–59, 83, 103, 121, 124, 261–62, 264
  duty of charity to, 18, 19
  Malthus and, 81–87, 89
  right to poverty relief and, 188
Poor Law, 58, 67–68, 70, 71–72, 74, 81–82, 93, 95, 100, 101, 105, 107, 153, 160, 188, 189, 228, 230, 258–59, 264, see also New Poor Law of 1834; poor law reforms
  Locke and, 58–59, 60, 62, 64–65
  Malthus and, 81–83, 84, 102, 189
  neoliberal welfare policy and, 264
Poor Law Commissioners' Report of 1834, 106, 107, 118–20, 129, 188
poor law reforms, 57–58, 102–3, 104–5, 106, 108, 111–12, 115, 187–88, 189, 190–91, 259–60
population theory, 82–83, 96, 155–58, 172–73, 188, 189, 190

positive rights, 23–24, 34–38, 57
poverty, 67–68, 170–71, 179–80,
    233–34, 285–86, *see also* poor, the;
    Poor Law; poverty relief
  children and, 57, 60, 61, 84–85,
    259–61, 296–97
  criminalization of, 270–72
  stigmatization of, 83
  vice and, 122, 123–24, 129, 133–35,
    136–37, 228
  workers and, 242–43, 245,
    247, 296
poverty relief, 63–99, 100–1, 103,
    115–16, 120–22, 123, 150–51, 153,
    188, 229
  abolishment of, 72, 105
  conservative relief policies,
    120–22, 123
  for-profit outsourcing of, 120–22
  humiliating forms of, 120–21, 123–24
  Locke and, 58–59
  Malthus and, 81–83, 123–24, 189
  Mill and, 188, 190–91
  right to, 58–59, 116, 188
  in Speenhamland, Berkshire (English
    county), 102
  workhouses and, 104–5, 109,
    111–12, 188
  work requirements and, 104–5,
    120–22
precarity, 121–22, 126, 170–71, 179–80,
    228, 242–43, 245–46, 247–48, 275
Priestley, Joseph, 63, 66, 67–73, 91,
    92–93, 123, 127–29, 179–80, 230,
    231, 256–57
  competitive acquisition and, 97–98,
    170, 257, 258–59, 284–85
  idea of life as competitive race, 167
  individualism and, 71, 72,
    231
  mandated savings and, 69–70, 72
  Poor Law and, 70, 71
  secularization of work ethic and, 69,
    70, 72–73
  shareholder capitalism and, 258–59

primogeniture, 49, 52–53, 140–42,
    175–77, 289–90
prisons, xi, 267–68, 269, 270–72
private equity, vulture, 279–81
private property, 229, 240–41, 288
  abolition of, 217, 292–93
  classical liberalism and, xiii
  distribution of, 178–79
  inequality and, 217–18
  labor theory of, 174–75, 180
  Locke's theory of, 44, 173–81
  Marx and, 208, 212, 213
  Mill's Lockean theory of, 173–81
  property laws, 89–90, 120, 288, 289
  redistribution of, 43, 89–90
  regulation of, xiii–xiv, 34, 37–38, 45
  workers and, 182, 192
productivity, x–xi, 21, 27, 47, 51–52,
    56, 107, 186, 189–90, 249, 256, 273
professionals, 210, 269
profits, 156–58
  maximization of, xi–xii, 255–56,
    272–73, 295–96, 297
  as unearned income, 245–46
  wages and, 156–58, 163
progress, 236
  conservative view of, 169–70,
    171–72
  Eurocentric view of, 168–69
  historical, 96, 97–98, 236
  human history as, 206
  imperialism seen as engine of, 293
  Mill's conception of, 172–73
  Smith's account of, 137–40, 142
  theory of historical progress, 96,
    97–98
progressive, use of the term, xv–xvi
progressive work ethic, xiv, 13, 14,
    127–67, 172–73, 181–82, 236–37,
    239, 242–43, 289, 293–96
  common roots of economic liberalism
    and social democracy in, 240
  definition of, ix–x
  Industrial Revolution and, 292–93
  leisure and, 137, 296

progressive work ethic (cont.)
Locke and, xiv, 20–62, 187–88, 236–37, 293–94
Marx and, xiv, 203–24, 226, 244, 292–93
Mill and, xiv, 168–202, 236–37, 289–90, 293–94
Paine and, xiv, 289–90
Puritan work ethic and, xiv–xv
Ricardian socialists and, xiv, 167, 236–37
secularization and, 66
Smith and, xiv, 154–55, 182, 236–37, 289–90, 293–95
social democracy and, x, xiv, 225–53, 292–93
social insurance and, 71–72
virtues of, 128–29
vision for workers offered by, xvii
vision of duties to fellow human beings, xiv–xv
"workers" agenda afforded by, 294, 296–97
property. See private property; property rights
property rights, xiii–xiv, 20, 22, 43, 57, 89–90, 163–64, 227, 229, 240–41
of copyholders, 54, 55–56
feudal, 45, 48–50, 54
natural, 163–64
state and, 21–22, 58–59
in state of nature, 53–54
Protestant work ethic, 2
Baxter and, 6–7
dual nature of, 1–19
influence of, 20–25
as revaluation of values, 1–3
pro-worker work ethic. See progressive work ethic
Puritanism, xvii–xviii, 3–4, 6–7, 9–10, 17, 88–89, see also Puritan work ethic
calling and, 8, 11–12, 168–69
exaltation of workers and, 11–12
idle rich and, 85

moral egalitarianism and, 10–11
sanctification of work and, 11, 14
utilitarianism and, 16, 169–70
Puritan work ethic, xiv–xv, 8–16, 63–64, 65, 88–89, 203–4, 257–58, 265–66
Putney debates, 43–44

racism, xvii–xviii, 118, 257–64, 286
Rawls, John, 275, 276
Reformation, 2, 3–4, 15
Reign of Terror, 218, 221, 223–24, 228
rent(s), 13, 156–58, 161
distribution of, 245–46, 273
economic function of, 176–77
Fabian socialists and, 273
in Ireland, 181
landlords and, 156–58, 176–77, 178, 230
Malthus's theory of, 155–56, 157–58
Ricardo and, 176–77, 178, 246, 273
as unearned income, 245–46
Ricardian socialists, xiv, 63, 72, 127, 155, 161–67, 173, 178, 236–37, 245–46, 258, 296–97
Ricardo, David, 100–1, 155–56, 158–61, 173, 175, 245–46
on classes, 161, 162
labor theory of value and, 165–66
Malthus and, 155–59, 160
rents and, 176–77, 246, 273
theory of inverse relation of profits and wages, 163
workers' rights and, 155–56
Robespierre, Maximilien, 218, 221, 223–24, 229
Russell, John, 111–13, 124–25

salvation, 2, 4–5, 6–7, 8, 10–11, 13–15, 17, 26–27, 42, 66–67, 77–78, 204–5
Sanderson, Robert, 8, 11, 12–13, 67, 85, 88–89, 172, 203, 236–37, 273
Scandinavia, xiii, 247–48, 252
Scrope, G. Poulett, 116, 118, 188–89

self-employment, xii–xiii, xvii–xviii, 122,
147–48, 186, 210, 258
Senior, Nassau, 63, 98, 102, 104–5,
118–20, 124–25, 129, 188
servants, 53, 91, 92, 94–95, 107
settler colonialism, xvii–xviii, 258–59
Shaftesbury (Anthony Ashley Cooper,
first Earl of Shaftesbury), 24, 50–51
shareholder capitalism, 255, 258–59,
272–73, 275, 276, 277, 281
sin, 8, 14, 26–27, 97, 98
Singer, Peter, 16–17, 18
slavery, xvii–xviii, 10–11, 12–13, 45,
53–54, 257–58. *See also* abolition
advocates of, 259
Locke on, 50–51, 52–54, 192–93
Mill and, 192–94, 195–98, 200–1
slaveholders, 124, 254
slave trade, 50
Smith on, 143–44, 197, 289–90
in United States, 192–93, 257–58
Smith, Adam, xv, 63, 75–76, 79, 90, 96,
98, 107, 127, 130–35, 146, 154,
178–79, 180, 186–87, 210, 225–26,
281, 289
on bargaining power, 275
biases in sentiment and, 130–31, 132
critique of conservative work ethic,
130–35
"Digression Concerning the Corn
Trade and Corn Laws," 151–52
division of labor and, 184–85,
273
East India Company and, 79, 201–2
free markets and, 142–43, 150, 151,
152–55
human progress and, 90, 137–41, 142,
154–55
"laboring poor" and, 103
laissez-faire and, 148, 150, 151,
152–55
on leisure, 137, 249–50
libertarian reading of, 147,
152–53
Locke and, 149

Malthus and, 146
Marx and, 208, 209, 226
micro-division of labor and, 168–69,
182, 186–87, 287–88
Mill and, 173, 184–85
poverty relief and, 150–51
pragmatism vs. dogmatism,
148–55
progressive work ethic and, xiv, 182,
236–37, 289–90, 293–95
pro-worker economic policies and,
130–35, 149–51, 182
reforms proposed by, 140–48
slavery and, 154–55, 197,
289–90
supply curve of labor and,
284–85
Theory of Moral Sentiments, 130–31,
132, 135–36
tradeoff of prosperity against human
capabilities, 182, 184
on virtues, 135–37
wage labor and, 143, 273, 275
Wealth of Nations, 137–41, 150,
152–53, 154
social contract, 21–22, 36–37, 43–44,
173–74, 229
social democracy, xiii–xiv, xvii–xviii,
127–28, 186–87, 213, 225–27,
243–44, 249, 253, 292–93
classical liberal tradition and,
227–34
codetermination and, 240, 297–98
decommodification of labor and,
247–48, 250–53
market economies and, 252–53,
295–96
neoliberalism and, xiii–xiv,
254–55, 293
origins of, 226, 234–42
persistence of class inequality and,
250–53
pre-Marxist origins of, 226–34
progressive work ethic and, x, xiv,
225–53, 292–93

Social Democratic Party (SAP) (Sweden), 225, 243–45
Social Democratic Party (SPD) (Germany), 225–26, 234, 235–36, 241–42
social democratic political parties, xiv, 225–26, 240–41, 243–44, 257, 293
Social Democratic Workers' Party of Germany, 235–36
social insurance, x, xi–xii, 64, 70, 71–72, 84, 226–27, 232, 243, 247–48, 252, 262–63, 289–90, see also means-testing
  origins of, 227–34
  socialist parties and, 233
  universal, 233–34
  in United States, 227, 233–34
socialist tradition, xvii–xviii, 127–28, 232, 240, 292–93, see also Ricardian socialists
Soviet Union, 213, 221
Speenhamland system, 92–95, 102, 106, 107, 189–90
Spencer, Herbert, 96
spoilage proviso, 21, 27, 30–31, 33, 34
stakeholder grants, 230, 231–32, 233–34, 289–90
Stalin, Joseph, 213, 215–16, 218
state of nature, 21, 22, 29, 33, 34, 35–37, 53–54, 173–75
stationary state, 156–58, 160–61, 172–73, 182
sufficiency proviso, 21, 27–29
  enclosure and, 32–33
  failure of, 34–36, 37–38, 54–55, 58, 174, 229
  Locke and, 30, 32–33, 34, 49–50, 54–55, 58–59, 174
suffrage, 191–92, 214, 222
Sweden, 225, 242, 243–45
sympathy, 172, 181–82, 186–87, 204, 288, 298

Tarnow, Fritz, 242
taxes/taxation, xiii–xiv, 20, 22, 37–38, 47, 48–49, 57, 70, 71, 74, 246, 257, 297, 298
  capital income and, 120, 254–55
  conservative work ethic and, 120, 121–22
  cutting, x
  distributive justice and, 246
  estate, 71–73, 230
  income, 120, 247, 254–55
  inheritance, 254–55
  labor and, 120, 252–53
  landowners and, 47
  local, 121–22
  poverty relief and, 111
  progressive, 254–55
  redistributive, xiii–xiv
  regressive, 120
  rents and, 159–60, 176–77
  social insurance and, 71–73
  tax deductions, 259
  tax farmers, 79
  war, 101
  wealth, 231, 247
  welfare policy and, 252–53
Tenures Abolition Act, 48–49, 55
Test Act, 265–66
Thatcher, Margaret, 254–55
Thompson, William, 126, 164, 165, 166–67, 172–73, 232, 244, 246, 289, 296–97
Tocqueville, Alexis de, 118–19
Tories, 24, 31–32, 43–44, 91, 175
totalitarianism, xiii–xiv, 213, 214–16, 224, 225–27
trade agreements, x, 254–55, 257, 285–86
trade unions. See unions
Trevelyan, Charles, 112–13, 119–20, 129, 151

unemployment, 59, 62, 100–1, 109
unemployment insurance, 106, 107, 243, 256

unions, xi–xii, xiii–xiv, 64, 181–87, 192,
    234–35, 240, 243, 247–48, 254–55,
    257, 258
  assault on, x–xi, 255–56, 287
  Mill and, 184–85
  social democracy and, 297–98
United Kingdom, 108, 250–51, 254–55
United States, xvii–xviii, 250, 254–55,
    257–58
  abolitionism in, 65–66
  Black activists in, 258
  changes in business model in, 255–56
  conservative work ethic in, 250,
    254–55, 257–58
  ideal of self-employment in, xvii–xviii
  individualism in, 258–59
  means-tested welfare programs in, 259
  neoliberalism in, xvii–xviii, 258–64
  progressive movements in, 65–66,
    254–55
  progressive work ethic in, 257–58
  Puritanism in, 65–66
  racism in, 258–59
  shareholder capitalism in, 277
  slavery in, 65–66, 192–93, 257–58
  social democracy in, 254–55
  social insurance in, 227, 233–34
  welfare policy in, 257–64
utilitarianism, 7, 16–17, 37, 66, 155, 285
  aggregative view of, 169–70
  ascetic theology and, 17
  Baxter and, 169–70
  Bentham and, 73–74, 76–77, 78, 79,
    80–81, 105
  birth of, 1–19
  classical, 169–70
  duty of universal benevolence and,
    18–19
  Locke and, 169–70
  Malthus and, 84, 85
  Mill and, 173–74
  natural rights and, 173–74
  Puritanism and, 16, 169–70
  social contract and, 173–74
  theological derivation of, 19

utility, interpersonal comparisons of, 285
utopianism, 122, 125, 126, 258, 292–93

Veblen, Thorstein, 284–85
virtue(s), xiv, 87–90, 122, 123–24, 129,
    133–35, 136–37, 181–82, 186–87,
    215, 223–24, 288, 294–95

wage labor, 53–54, 63–64, 94–95,
    108–9, 111, 117, 118, 121, 122,
    123, 143, 170, 171–72, 177–78, 180
wages, 21, 156–58
  ceiling on, 94–95
  grain prices and, 100–1
  growth of, 234–35
  labor supply and, 191
  low, 182, 245, 248, 296
  minimum wage, 94–95, 150–51,
    256, 272
  profits and, 156–58, 163
  stagnating, x–xi, 64–65, 254, 256
  subsistence, 160–61
  unions and, 184–85
  wage rates, 275
wages-fund theory, 188
wealth
  accumulation of, xvii, 17–18, 20,
    21–22, 35–36, 51–52, 53–54, 170,
    295, see also competitive acquisition
  distribution of, 173
  dynastic, 176
  inequality of, 228
  redistribution of, 20, 21, 22
  virtue and, 122, 123–24, 129, 133–35,
    136–37
  wealth extraction, 281–82, 283, 296
Weber, Max, xvii, 2, 3–4, 5, 7, 9–10,
    65–66, 77–78, 290, 292–93
Weimar Republic, 241–42
welfare policy, xi–xii, 20, 57, 112–13,
    187–92, 257, 259–64, 288, 289
  arbitrary limits and, 263
  bureaucratic requirements and,
    123–24, 263–64
  Poor Laws and, 264

welfare policy (cont.)
  racism and, xvii–xviii, 257–64
  taxation and, 252–53
  in United States, 257–64
welfare reform, 100–8, 119–21, 257,
  260–61. *See also* specific legislation
welfare state, x–xi, xiv, 82, 243,
  252–53, 258
Wesley, John, 17, 77
Whately, Richard, 63, 66, 91–99, 102,
  105, 115–16, 125, 128–29, 146,
  166, 179–80, 195–96, 256–57,
  258–64
  commodification of labor and, 247–48
  competitive acquisition and, 170,
    284–85
  conservative work ethic and, 108–9,
    257–58, 259–64, 273
  doctrine of original sin and,
    97, 98
  imperialism and, 98
  Irish famine policy and, 115–16, 118
  land appropriation and, 122
  landlords and, 95, 273
  poverty and, 67–68, 123
  theory of historical progress and,
    97–98
  welfare policy and, 187–92, 259–64
Whig government, 112–19
Whig party, 23–24, 31–32, 38–39,
  43–44, 93, 110, 111–12, 114, 125,
  265–66
William III, King, 41, 49–50, 51
women
  childbearing and, 188
  child care and, 260–61
  division of labor and, 184
  economic roles of, 296–97
  franchise and, 43–44
  freedom of contract and, 183
  limits on labor of, 235
  in Locke's political philosophy,
    43–44
  subordination of, 21–22, 289
  as teachers, 12

  unpaid domestic labor of, 71, 289,
    296–97
work, 211–12, *see also* labor
  as ascetic discipline, 271–72
  as expression of individuality, 205–6,
    208, 210
  Baxter's definition of, 211–12
  calling to, 5, 8, 11
  degradation of, 286–88
  ideal, 203, 204, 205–6
  legitimate, 12–13
  Marx's romanticized view of artisanal,
    210–11
  Puritan attitudes toward, 2, 73–74, *see
    also* Puritan work ethic
  sacralization of, 3–4, 7, 11
workers, 224, *See also* labor; specific
    kinds of workers
  agency of, 128–29, 181–87
  autonomy and, 242–43, 248–49
  capitalists and, 63–65, 172
  deskilling of, 274–75
  dignity of, 11, 13, 242–43
  education of, 147–48, 186, 192
  emancipation of, 127–28, 138–40,
    147–48, 224
  entitled to fruits of labor, 128–29, 192
  free markets for, 135–48
  harshness of conservative work ethic
    toward, 120
  leisure and, 182, 192, 242–43
  precarity and, 228, 242–43, 245–46,
    247–48
  property ownership and, 192
  self-employed, 147–48
  self-governing, 291, 295–96
  subordination of, 21–22, 53
workers' compensation, 232
workers' cooperatives, 64, 184–85,
  186–87, 192, 238, 240, 244–45,
  258, 297–98
workers' organizations, 120. *See also*
  unions
work ethic, xv, xviii, 63, 68–73, 93,
  168–69, 186–87, 217, 258–59,

260–61, 275, 277–78, 281, 290–91, 292–93, *see also* conservative work ethic; progressive work ethic; Protestant work ethic; Puritan work ethic; *specific theorists and approaches*
as contested ideal, 2
developments in the late eighteenth century, 63–68
European progress attributed to, 97–98, 168, 194–96
hijacking of, xiv–xv, xvii, 63–99, 127, 256–57
workfare, 259–61
workhouses, 62, 74, 102, 104, 105, 121–22, 124–25, 153, 189–90, 192, *see also* workhouse test
abuses in, 189
as both test and punishment, 123–24
child labor in, 75, 260–61
Gilbert's Act and, 93
incarceration in, 189
in Ireland, 111–13, 115–16, 117–18, 124–25
poverty relief and, 109, 111–12, 188

privately run, 74–79, 80–81, 265
scandal over administration of, 106
workhouse test, 104, 116–18, 262–63, 264
Workhouse Test Act (Knatchbull's Act), 62, 93, 104
working classes, 81, 82, 87–88, 89, 90, 91, 125, 289–90
"civilization" of, 125
in rich countries, 285–86
rising radicalism among, 81, 100–1, 124, 170–71, 237–38
working day, length of, 182, 183–84, 234–35, 250
working poor, 130–31, 187–92, 227, 296
workplace
democratization of, 289, 290, 297–98
fissured, 256
workplace conditions, 235, *see also* working conditions
works, 3–7, 26–27, *see also* charity
Woytinsky, Wladimir, 241–42

yeoman class, 52–53, 55, 56, 63–64, 139, 141–42, 143, 181
Young, Arthur, 136–37, 140

THE SEELEY LECTURES

The John Robert Seeley Lectures have been established by the University of Cambridge as a biennial lecture series in social and political studies, sponsored jointly by the Faculty of History and Cambridge University Press. The Seeley Lectures provide a unique forum for distinguished scholars of international reputation to address, in an accessible manner, topics of broad interest in social and political studies. Subsequent to their public delivery in Cambridge, the University Press publishes suitably modified versions of each set of lectures. Professor James Tully delivered the inaugural series of Seeley Lectures in 1994 on the theme of *Constitutionalism in an Age of Diversity*.

A full list of titles in the series can be found at: www.cambridge.org/seeley-lectures